THE PEOPLES OF IRAN

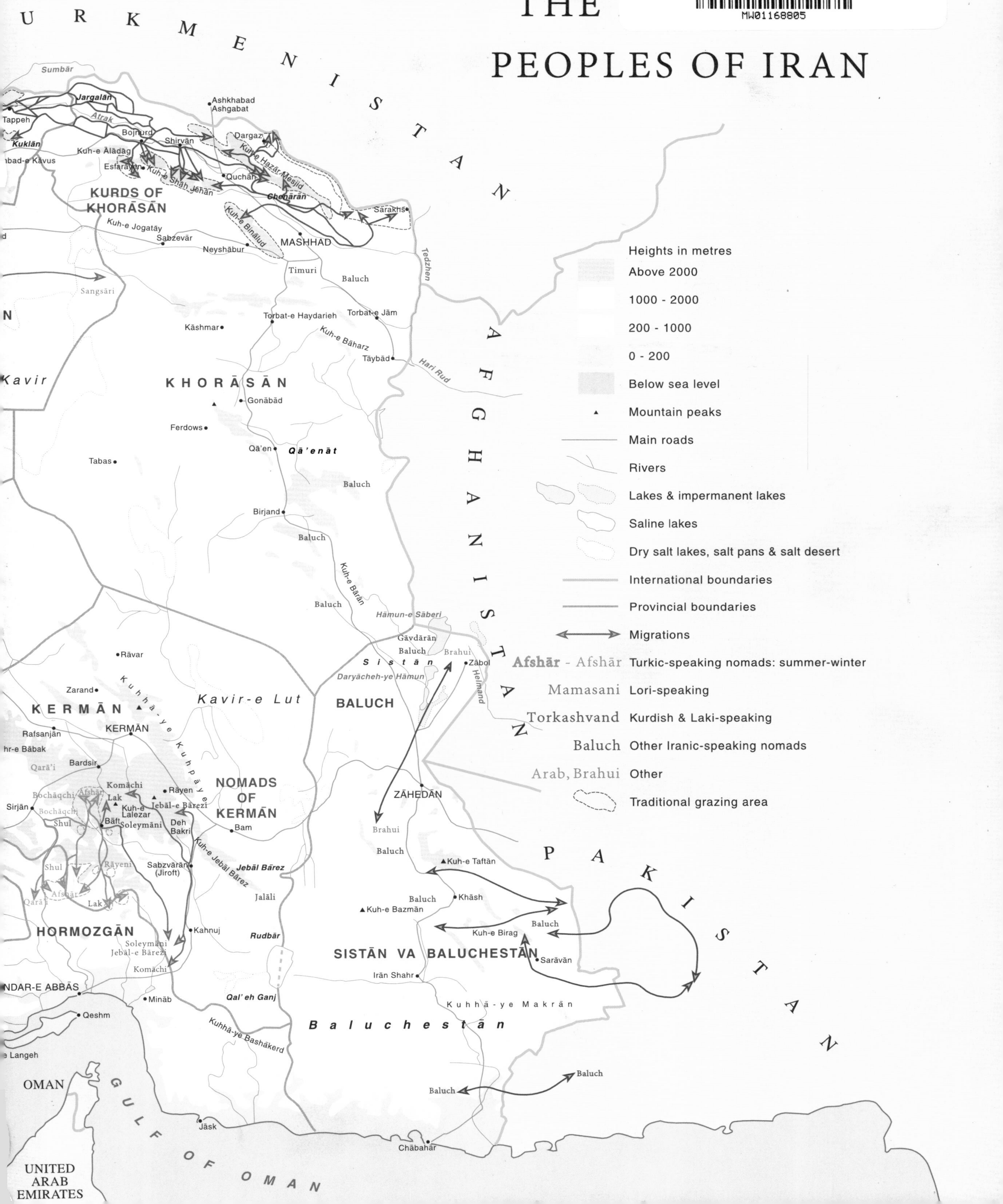

Heights in metres

Above 2000

1000 - 2000

200 - 1000

0 - 200

Below sea level

Mountain peaks

Main roads

Rivers

Lakes & impermanent lakes

Saline lakes

Dry salt lakes, salt pans & salt desert

International boundaries

Provincial boundaries

Migrations

Afshār - Afshār Turkic-speaking nomads: summer-winter

Mamasani Lori-speaking

Torkashvand Kurdish & Laki-speaking

Baluch Other Iranic-speaking nomads

Arab, Brahui Other

Traditional grazing area

URKMENISTAN

Sumbār

Jargalān

Ashkhabad
Ashgabat

Tappeh

Atrak

Bojnurd

Shirvān

Dargaz

Kuklān

Kuh-e Ālādāg

Kuh-e Hazār Masjid

bad-e Kāvus

Esfarāyen

Kuh-e Shāh Jehān

Quchān

Chenārān

KURDS OF KHORĀSĀN

Sarakhs

Kuh-e Binālud

Kuh-e Jogatāy

Sabzevār

MASHHAD

Neyshābur

Tedzhen

Timuri

Baluch

Sangsāri

N

Torbat-e Haydarieh

Torbat-e Jām

Kāshmar

Kuh-e Bāharz

Tāybād

Hari Rud

Kavir

KHORĀSĀN

Gonābād

AFGHANISTAN

Ferdows

Qā'en

Qā'enāt

Tabas

Baluch

Birjand

Baluch

Kuh-e Bārān

Baluch

Hāmun-e Sāberi

Gāvdārān

Baluch

Brahui

Sistān

Zābol

Daryācheh-ye Hāmun

Helmand

Rāvar

Kuhhā-ye Kuhpāye

Zarand

Kavir-e Lut

BALUCH

KERMĀN

KERMĀN

Rafsanjān

hr-e Bābak

Qarā'i

Bardsir

Komāchi

NOMADS OF KERMĀN

Bochāqchi

Afshār

Lak

Rāyen

Sirjān

Bochāqchi

Kuh-e Lalezar

Jebāl-e Bārezi

ZĀHEDĀN

Shul

Bāft

Soleymāni

Deh Bakri

Bam

Brahui

Baluch

Shul

Rāyeni

Sabzvārān (Jiroft)

Kuh-e Jebāl Bārez

Jebāl Bārez

Kuh-e Taftān

PAKISTAN

Qarā'i

Afshār

Lak

Jalāli

Baluch

Khāsh

Kuh-e Bazmān

Baluch

HORMOZGĀN

Kahnuj

Rudbār

Kuh-e Birag

Soleymāni

Jebāl-e Bārezi

Komāchi

SISTĀN VA BALUCHESTĀN

Sarāvān

Irān Shahr

NDAR-E ABBĀS

Mināb

Qal'eh Ganj

Kuhhā-ye Makrān

Qeshm

Baluchestān

Kuhhā-ye Bashākerd

Langeh

OMAN

GULF OF OMAN

Baluch

Baluch

Jāsk

Chābahār

UNITED ARAB EMIRATES

THE NOMADIC PEOPLES OF IRAN

THE NOMADIC PEOPLES OF IRAN

EDITED BY RICHARD TAPPER AND JON THOMPSON
PHOTOGRAPHS BY NASROLLAH KASRAIAN

The Nomadic Peoples of Iran
Published in the United Kingdom by—
Azimuth Editions
Unit 2A The Print Works,
Colville Road,
London, W3 8BL

Distributed by—Thames & Hudson

ISBN—1-898592-24-1

Design—Anikst Associates

Cartography—Catherine Lawrence

Printed by—PJ Print, London

ON THE USE OF THE TERMS PERSIA, PERSIAN, IRAN AND IRANIAN.
Throughout the nineteenth century the terms Persia and Persian for the country and its people were widely used by politicians, writers and academics in the English-speaking world, and to a degree still are. In the second half of the twentieth century, since the reign of Rezā Shah, the terms Iran and Iranian have become increasingly used, particularly in the scholarly world where there is an awareness that over half the population have languages other than Persian as their mother tongue. Roger Stevens in *The Land of the Great Sophy* sums up the matter and provides the guidelines for this book: 'Iran is the official name of the country and Iranians is what the inhabitants like to be called. Therefore, defying long-standing tradition and ingrained and instinctive English habit I propose generally though not invariably to refer to the country as Iran and the people as Iranian'. The main exception is where works by authors who use the terms Persia and Persian in their writing are being discussed. Here the pattern of their language and usage is generally retained.

SPELLING, TERMINOLOGY AND TRANSLITERATION
While some attempt at consistency of spelling has been made, it has not been entirely rigorous. Most spellings are rendered from the viewpoint of a Persian speaker. The observant reader will, however, note that the spelling of certain terms and names differs between chapters. While consistency of spelling has been the aim, variations remain; some because they are favoured by individual authors, others because they are conditioned by the rules of spelling required by the particular language, for example *tayfeh* and *tayfa*. We believe that there is unlikely to be confusion as to which word is intended. Likewise, some words already current in English are too well established to be altered for the sake of consistency, for example Lur and Kurd as opposed to Lor and Kord; both spellings are therefore retained. Place names on the map (though not invariably in the text) follow the transliterations used for English language maps currently produced in Iran.

Diacritical marks have been kept to a minimum, however the distinction in Persian between the long ā (as in fāther) and short a (as in back) is important and should be useful to readers wishing to get some idea of how words and place names are to be pronounced.

No attempt has been made to alter the transliterations of local languages and dialects provided by individual authors except when they were initially written in a language which has later been translated into English.

ACCURACY OF INFORMATION
Information on the place, the date, and the name of the tribal group or clan in each photograph is given wherever this is available from the photographer. Sometimes the information is lacking. In some instances the raw information is accurate but the accompanying assumptions are not. For example the Bahme'i who resemble the Bakhtiāri were assumed to belong to that tribe whereas they do not, although they are Lurs. Occasionally the information given has been self-evidently wrong and has been corrected. In a few cases there is room for doubt—some queries remain as to the correct identification of some of the nomads of Alvand Kuh. Here the identifications are as given in the photographer's notes.

PHOTOGRAPHY
All photographs are by Nasrollah Kasraian except for the following: Marcel Bazin 294, 295; David Brooks 54, 82, 92, 93, 94, 95, 100 (below), 102,106; Jean Pierre Digard 77, 80, 81; Nancy Lindisfarne-Tapper 275 (below), 276; Georg Stöber 307, 309; Richard Tapper 264, 274, 275 (top).

Frontispiece
Women milking goats at their winter quarters west of Farrāshband in 1986. These nomads live among the Shesh Boluki but do not appear to be connected to them.

CONTENTS

Crossing the Monar pass, the most difficult part of the Bakhtiāri spring migration. Bābādi clan, May, 1984.

PREFACE

Jon Thompson

This book has a curious history, and it is only thanks to the patient efforts and extraordinary generosity of friends that it has come to fruition. The idea for it was born when Nasrollah Kasraian came to see me with a collection of photographs of the many nomadic groups still to be found in Iran today. The particular interest of his photographs was that after the fall of the Pahlavi dynasty in 1979, post-revolutionary Iran was difficult of access for European and American anthropologists, ethnographers and geographers and there were conflicting reports as to how the various nomadic groups had been faring.

For example in the case of the Qashqa'i, the dismal failure of Naser Khan's leadership when he returned to Iran in 1979 after twenty-five years of exile imposed by the Shah, the collapse of the Qashqa'i insurgency, the effective crushing of the Qashqa'i leadership so vividly described in the last chapter of Lois Beck's *The Qashqa'i of Iran*, the effects of the nationalisation of grazing lands, and the infiltration of the tribe by revolutionary guards, all seemed to signal the beginning of the end for the Qashqa'i as an independent confederation of nomadic tribes. Even before this, it had become evident that pastoral nomadism was losing ground in the competition for increasingly scarce resources, and indeed some nomadic groups had already ceased to exist.

On the other hand there were reports that some nomads who had been compulsorily settled under the Shah's regime had returned to former patterns of migration during the period of confusion in the early days of the Islamic Republic and the war with Iraq. If this were so, the disappearance of the nomadic way of life might not be proceeding as fast as the pre-1979 trends had indicated.

Kasraian's offering of pictures seemed an ideal opportunity for a review of the state of nomadism in Iran in the late twentieth century. I put the idea to Richard Tapper, now Professor of Anthropology at the School of Oriental and African Studies, London. He was clearly enthusiastic and encouraged me to speak to Jean-Pierre Digard of CNRS, Paris. He too was supportive of the idea and between us we put together a list of specialists who might be willing to contribute their knowledge.

The subsequent passage of the book has hardly been smooth. Unexpected events have caused major and deeply frustrating delays for which I must bear my share of criticism. The problems surrounding the obtaining of texts from authors in five different countries and their subsequent translation and editing were minor compared to the difficulties which then arose in terms of raising finance necessary for getting the book to press.

The problem was one of perception. My idea was to put together a book in the form of a written review accompanied by a visual record of the various nomadic groups in Iran at the close of the twentieth century. The photographs were to to be supported by a series of texts contributed by people who had lived, worked and studied in Iran. The willing cooperation of those who were asked to contribute seemed in some measure to be related to the idea of having a book which was both academically based and illustrated with images which were themselves a form of documentation. This support may have been born out of frustration with a familiar type of academic publication with only a few black and white illustrations, a very small print run and a disconcertingly high price. But the very thing that the contributors found attractive caused misgivings in the world of publishing. Such a book seemed to have no proper place either in the catalogue or on the bookshelf. There is in certain quarters an undoubted tendency to dismiss books with numerous coloured illustrations as 'not serious'. This, however, was clearly not a 'coffee-table' book, but if not 'coffee-table', then what was it? At this stage, Inge Mortensen's plentifully illustrated monograph

Nomads of Luristan had not appeared, and a book along the lines I was proposing seemed just too improbable to be worth supporting.

Mention of Mortensen's monograph brings into focus some of the key factors which had convinced me in the first place that a book of this kind was needed. With some notable exceptions, few ethnographers and anthropologists have studied the art of photography. Today visual images have an enormously important role in the study of peoples and societies; yet photographs are a very imperfect mirror of reality. The world they reveal is inevitably coloured by the filter of the photographer's own subjectivity—he directs the gaze of his camera in conformity with his particular view of the world. In a thoughtful and challenging study of photography, anthropology, and the power of imagery, Margaret Blackman proposes that, 'always the image has as much to say about its maker as its subject' (Banta & Hinsley 1986: 11).

All too often the ethnographer in the field is concerned to record specific pieces of information. Photographs of such things as utensils, clothing and other artefacts reveal a narrowly focussed interest in which a sense of context is too often missing. Alternatively the pictures may be so badly composed, out of focus or poorly lit as to be unpublishable. A professional photographer, on the other hand, put in the same situation, is tempted to seek out the poetic and the beautiful, and is often unable to refrain from manipulating his subject in pursuit of some chosen effect. I spent hours looking through the results of one professional photographer's field trip among nomads in Iran which included groups of people at night illuminated by the light of the fire, splendid landscapes and sensitive portraits. He clearly possessed a fine artistic sensibility, but his images were almost entirely devoid of information. As one gifted photographer taught me, the art of photography lies in what you exclude; in this respect our professional had truly excelled.

Kasraian, a lawyer by training, and now well known in his own country as a photographer, succeeds in avoiding either of these two extremes. A number of his photographs have been published in France and Germany, but otherwise he has had relatively little exposure to the fashionable norms of today's photographic market. He is largely self-taught and his view of the world is direct, uncomplicated, even naïve; he makes no attempt to present an idealised or romanticised view of the nomadic world. Apart from the occasional portrait he avoids arranging and composing his subjects; he presents what he sees without affectation or interpretation, and overall he remains remarkably unencumbered by any of the self-conscious mannerisms of western photography today.

Nevertheless Kasraian's images reveal both his difficulties and his interests. He is clearly interested in the techniques of daily life and his images record the hardship and struggle associated with it. At the same time he avoids the curiously fashionable obsession with poverty, squalor and physical suffering which are not difficult to find among nomads living on the borderline of subsistence. Sometimes we see the unwillingness or uncertainty of his subjects, occasionally their fear. Many look directly at the camera, not always comfortable with his presence. I have been inclined to omit images where there is a sense that the photographer is intruding, but on reflection the way the subject looks at the camera is information in itself, and on this thorny point I have at times changed my mind.

The key issue, as I see it, is inherent in the language. We speak of 'taking' a photograph, and faced by a camera, many people intuitively sense that the photographer is taking something which in essence is for his own use. Even though a promise may be made to send prints—a promise often broken—the feeling remains that there is a predatory aspect to his work. This is especially the case when pictures are taken without a person's permission or knowledge. The situation becomes abundantly clear to anyone foolish enough to use a polaroid camera in the field. As soon as the subjects discover that they can get hold of the image and keep it for themselves, and furthermore they can control the image they present, all resistance vanishes and the clamour to be photographed is unending.

In spite of reservations about the nature of photography and the role of the photographer in the field, Kasraian's images are unique documents recorded at a critical moment in history, and they should provide abundant material for study in the future. It is remarkable how one can continue to learn from a photograph as one's knowledge increases. Only the other day I glanced at an image I had taken from an old Russian article and used in a publication sixteen years ago. I was astonished to realise in the light of new knowledge that the photograph was in fact a 'set-up' which purported to show a situation that did not in reality exist.

Kasraian's application to the task of searching out the people he wanted to photograph, often in the remotest and most inaccessible places, has been extraordinary, and I am sincerely grateful to him for all his efforts. He travelled the length and breadth of the country, wore out three cars in the process, was arrested several times, had film confiscated, and almost lost his life in a terrifying flood. He even made a special trip at my request to photograph the little-known Gurani tent screens *in situ* (p. 29). These screens, made of canes wrapped with coloured wool, and clearly distinct from the well-known reed screens of the Kazakh and Kirghiz, had been appearing in the Istanbul bazaar from time to time. Although they had been documented long ago (Jéquier, 1914), the only colour picture I knew was a photograph of a tent set up at a regional fair published in 1977 in Jay and Sumi Gluck's valuable work, *A Survey of Persian Handicraft*.

Those who know of my personal interest in weaving and textiles have urged me to include specific examples of the weavings of the various tribes, but there has never been any intention to do this. Quite the contrary; enduring falsehoods in the field of nomadic weaving derive from the fact that when nomads settle, their weavings—mostly unsigned and undated—tend to enter the market place. Being easily transportable they often turn up far from their source, which may not have been accurately known in the first place, and in the course of their travels they are inclined to acquire an accretion of false, inaccurate or fanciful information which somehow adds to their mystique and general desirability. It is worth noting that a number of the weavings illustrated in Mortensen's *Nomads of Luristan* were bought in local bazaars. With today's knowledge we can be confident that not all of them were made by the Lurs of Luristan (as opposed to the Bakhtiāri)

In this book several photographs actually show weavings both being produced and being used in daily life of the people that made them. In the future these photographs may provide some of the best evidence we have for the precise source and function of specific objects. A photograph that gives me particular satisfaction is the one of a woman cooking on p. 217. She actually has her hand inside her salt bag, a type of object that frequently appears in the market place. Though correctly described as salt bags by dealers, I have heard it said that such objects could not have been used for that purpose because they never have traces of salt in them!

Though a number of Kasraian's older photographs in this volume have already been published both in Iran and Europe, it was a matter of considerable disappointment that a substantial number of those given for publication appeared subsequently in his album *Nomads of Iran*. However, in spite of the sense that they have thereby lost some of their freshness I have felt it worthwhile continuing with the project because there is a wealth of background information available in the supporting texts which provides a key for the reader to learn so much more from the photographs than would be possible without them. The texts also raise a host of important questions—for example how people define their own identity and the relationship between poverty and anti-social behaviour—that have an importance far beyond the specific circumstances to which this book refers.

Of all those who have worked so hard in support of this book during the long period in which it has taken shape I wish to thank particularly all the authors for their forbearance, Caroline Beamish and Paul Bergne for their work on translation, Parviz Tanavoli for the initial contact, Malcolm Ward for hours of careful editorial work, Cary Wolinsky for much helpful advice on the images, Barbara Wolinsky for all her work in the early stages on the design and the dummy which went largely unrewarded and Mikhail Anikst for his remarkable tolerance. I also wish to express my deeply felt gratitude to George Hecksher for his support at a difficult stage in this project, without whose great generosity and patient encouragement this book would never have been completed.

Special mention must be made of David Brooks. While working in Iran in 1966 he suffered a serious car accident which resulted in denervation of the left side of his diaphragm. Twenty years later his right lung was removed for a malignancy and as a result he developed intermittent respiratory insufficiency, an extremely distressing condition which obliged him to live his life attached to a ventilator. In spite of his many difficulties, he gave his wholehearted and generous support to this project and set to work to write what turned out to be his last work. A reluctant author at the best of times, it is a particular sadness to all those who knew him that he died before he could see the publication of this book which is dedicated to his memory.

Darrashurlu women milking goats. One holds the animal to be milked while another spins as she watches the flock. Mehrgerd, north of Semirom, summer 1985.

INTRODUCTION: THE NOMADS OF IRAN

Richard Tapper

IMAGES

The nomads of Iran present a variety of striking images to the outside world: a pastoral idyll of tented camps surrounded by green meadows and carpets of flowers; trains of camels and donkeys winding through spectacular mountain gorges; and colourfully dressed women whose skills produce some of the finest carpets in the world. These images, contrasting with both the squalor of village life and the hurly-burly of modern metropolitan existence, appeal not just to outsiders, be they foreign observers or Iranian villagers and city-folk, they form part of the nomads' own presentation of themselves and their way of life as well.

Foreign travellers over the centuries have seen in these images echoes—however superficial—of the biblical patriarchs, leading the uninformed to assume that nomadic life has remained unchanged for millenia. But the images and their resonances go much deeper for settled Iranians, whose historical memory records the destruction wrought by the Mongol nomad hordes, the tribal turmoil of the eighteenth century, and, for many still alive in the 1990s, the depredations of nomad warriors in the early decades of the twentieth century.

For Iranians, images of pastoral nomads contain several paradoxes, reflected today in debates about their future. Historically, mounted warriors from the nomadic tribes provided a valuable source of military manpower for the state, yet posed a potential threat to state security—even if today their famed horsemanship and marksmanship are no match for the military hardware deployed by the modern state. The nomadic tribes represent a reservoir of traditional virtues: independence of spirit, bravery, hardiness, hard work, honour, generosity and hospitality, based on a simple pastoral existence; yet that existence is harsh and dangerous and the nomads are by national standards poor, illiterate and ill-provided with health, welfare and other modern facilities. Nomad women are visibly tougher and freer than their settled sisters, yet their life consists of back-breaking work fetching huge loads of fuel and water and long hours at the loom. Further, while many in government recognise the value of the nomads' contribution to the national economy in exploiting otherwise unusable range lands and supplying the country with meat, wool and dairy produce, others choose to focus on their primitive pastoral technology, the overgrazing of the pastures and the damage caused by nomad flocks to village crops. Debates tend to polarise between those who see nomads as backward primitives, an anachronism in the modern world, whose only future is settlement and integration into the modern industrial economy, and those who see them as 'noble savages', repositories of lost values and skills, including the intelligence and the ability to adapt their nomadism to the modern world.

Many of these paradoxes are perhaps evident in the photographs presented in this book. The accompanying texts are intended to go some way towards resolving them, as well as contributing to the growing literature about nomad life, which now includes not only the specialised accounts of anthropologists and other academic researchers, both Iranians and foreigners, but also writings by people of nomad extraction themselves.

ORIGINS AND HISTORY OF IRANIAN NOMADS[1]

Present conformations of nomadic peoples in Iran date in the main from the time of the invasions of the Islamic Arabs from the west in the seventh century AD, and the Turks and Mongols from central Asia between the tenth and fifteenth centuries. Pastoralism as a way of life in Iran is, however, considerably older, though its origins remain unclear and are still debated by archaeologists and Iranologists.

Numerous observers have noted how the geography and ecology of Iran, like most Middle Eastern countries, favour pastoral nomadism. The terrain and climate make large areas uncultivable under pre-industrial conditions, and suitable only for seasonal grazing. Since only a small proportion of such pasture can be used by village-based livestock, vast ranges of steppe, semi-desert and mountain are left to be exploited by nomads—mobile, tent-dwelling pastoralists. However, this is not a complete explanation of the origins and distribution of nomadism, which has experienced repeated extreme expansions and contractions in response to economic and political developments. At times in the past, nomad flocks grazed vast areas of present-day irrigated lands, while remote valleys used only for grazing today were once richly cultivated.

Extensive semi-nomadic pastoralism may have been practised in the Zāgros mountains since the seventh millennium BC, but definite evidence of nomads—mobile tent-dwellers—is slight until the first half of the second millennium BC. Early incursions of nomads from the north who made their presence felt in Iran included Scythians and others during the first millennium BC. For a thousand years before the coming of Islam, Iranian rulers occupied seasonal capitals, surrounded by the camps and flocks of pastoralists, and would appear to have had important contingents of nomad warriors in their armies.

One influential theory[2] proposes that nomadism developed in the Iran–Anatolia–Mesopotamia region out of a settled society which practised a mixture of rain-fed agriculture and pastoralism. It argues, in brief, that the introduction of intensive canal irrigation and the specialised cultivation of wheat brought an increase in population, and subsequently the pastoral and cultivating schedules fell out of step. Some of the pastoralists, especially those owning larger numbers of animals, became marginalised from the settlements, and sought more distant pastures in the steppes and mountains. They began to migrate seasonally and became nomadic, but remained linked with the settled society through the market. The world of canal and city demanded pastoral produce, and gave wheat in exchange.

Pastoral nomadism, in Iran as elsewhere, has always been associated with agriculture and settled society, and in complex ways. Nomads are mobile and militarily adaptable, and in many cases when a city-based central government has been weak they have provided the power base for a conqueror to sweep into the city to take control and found a new dynasty. At the same time, the pastoral economy is particularly vulnerable to climatic fluctuations, and nomads have been prone to raiding villages and the trade routes between the cities. In peaceful times, however, with a strong centre, nomads and settlers have pursued mutually beneficial economic exchanges, while the cities provided the basis for economic strength and cultural superiority.[3]

The development of nomadism out of settled society, and the cycle of alternation between strong and weak central state control, are processes that have been replicated many times in Iranian history, as the delicate balance between nomad and settled has shifted back and forth.

The Arab-Islamic invasions of the seventh century found a largely settled population, including the ancestors of groups later prominent as nomads: the Kurds and Lurs of the Zāgros (Fārs, Isfahān, Khuzestān) and the Baluch of Kermān and the east. The Arabs too settled, in cities around the country, though a few of them took up a nomadic life, mainly in the south and east. Nomads are recorded as serving in the armies, and also at times as highway robbers endangering the trade routes, but they were not a major political component of the state until the Turco-Mongol invasions.

Oghuz Turkish nomad groups from Central Asia, led by the Saljuqs, began moving into Iran in the early eleventh century. For the next nine hundred years the rulers of Iran were of nomad background or brought to power by the support of nomad tribes. The Saljuqs themselves were settled in orientation, and did little to disrupt the settled Iranian society whose administration they took over. The Turkish nomads pushed the Baluch south out of Khorāsān but on the whole moved into otherwise unoccupied range lands in Syria, Anatolia, Āzarbāijān, Gorgān and Marv, intruding little on native pastoral areas such as the Zāgros. When disorder was recorded among the nomads, it was less likely to concern competition over pasture land than tribal resistance to the rulers' desire to tax and control.

Very different was the effect of the Mongol onslaught in the thirteenth century. The invaders were militarily organised and despised agriculture and settlement; they destroyed irrigation and crops, and massacred villagers and townspeople. The Mongols, and the fresh wave of Turks they

A Bakhtiāri woman carrying a bundle of dry shrubs for use as fencing and firewood. Nomad women are visibly tougher and freer than their settled sisters, yet their life consists of back-breaking work fetching huge loads of fuel and water and long hours at the loom. At a summer camp in the foot hills of Zardeh Kuh, 1985.

brought with them, swept through Iran westwards; many remained in Āzarbāijān. In other areas such as Lorestān and Khorāsān, under the Ilkhanids (1256–1336) and Tamerlane (1370–1405) there was a massive expansion of nomadism and pastoralism at the expense of settled agriculture. Tamerlane himself travelled surrounded by nomadic families and flocks. Nomadism was further reasserted in the 15th century under the Qaraqoyunlu and Aqqoyunlu nomad dynasties in Eastern Anatolia, Armenia and Āzarbāijān, and later in the centre and south of Iran.

By this time, Turkic elements formed approximately a quarter of the population of Iran, as they have remained, more or less, ever since. The major cleavages in Iranian society were established: between 'Turk' and 'Tajik', and between nomad and settled. Overall unity however proved elusive, and was not to come until the rise of the Safavids, the most successful of many Sufi orders that entered the political arena since the Mongol invasions. In the late 15th century, the Safavid sheykhs, espousing an extreme form of Shi'ism, recruited followers from various nomad tribes, mainly Turks from Anatolia, who became known as the Qizilbash or red-heads. With their support, Isma'il Safavi swept to power in Iran, becoming Shah in 1501.

For 250 years the Safavid Shahs ruled an empire that at its greatest extent included much of the southern Caucasus and present-day Iraq and Afghanistan. At first the realm was dominated by the Qizilbash chiefs, who were appointed as provincial governors or heads of government departments as well as military leaders and chiefs of their own tribes. Following the pattern which had prevailed among major tribal groups from the Mongol invasions onwards, conquest by nomadic military forces led to at least partial settlement of the leaders and many of their followers. The chiefs' domains comprised not only pasture lands and nomads but cultivation and peasants, trade and city-based households. Many chiefs, and their nomad followers, were shifted around the country to different appointments and associated territories. Under Isma'il's successors increasing rivalry and disorder among the chiefs led to their suppression, particularly by Shah 'Abbās the Great (1587–1629) who, in order to counter the Qizilbash tribes, formed a standing army of slave and non-tribal origins. By the mid-17th century, irregular tribal troops were no longer a political threat, and the nomad groups from which they came were relegated to outlying pasture lands, though their economic contribution to settled society continued to be important.

The Safavid dynasty weakened in the late 17th century, and unrest grew, starting in distant areas of the empire, particularly among non-Persian and non-Turkish tribal elements. In 1722 the capital Isfahān fell to rebel Afghan tribes (not nomads), and Russian and Ottoman forces invaded in the north-west. For the rest of the 18th century, under a succession of competing rulers from the Ghaljai, Afshār, Zand, Bakhtiāri and Qājār tribes, Iran saw a general resurgence of tribalism and nomadism. Settled people abandoned both towns and villages to go into exile or join the nomads. Again, there were considerable shifts of nomadic population: Nāder Shah Afshār in particular moved thousands of families from the west to his home province of Khorāsān. Under his successors, notably Karim Khan Zand, many of these returned westwards, not all to their original homelands.

In the 1790s Aqa Muhammad Qājār established the final dynasty of nomad tribal origins in Iran. Qājār rule was both ensured and constrained by Anglo-Russian imperial rivalry during the 19th century, and once again the pendulum swung away from nomadic dominance towards settled control of society. The nomadic tribes in the 19th century numbered 2–3 million, or one quarter to one half of the total population of 6–8 million, but they were increasingly marginalised. However, the rulers themselves retained nomadic habits for many decades: they continued to move seasonally to highland summer camps, whether to Ujān in Āzarbāijān or to Damāvand near their new capital Tehran. Irregular cavalry from the nomad tribes continued to provide the backbone of the national army and were used both in limited campaigns on the now constricted frontiers and to help extract revenue from both the settled and the nomadic population. Only occasionally did the later Qājār authorities resort to either relocation (so common in the early reigns) or enforced settlement, in response to frontier problems. Central control, security and tax collection broke down in some areas after 1900, with the Constitutional Revolution and occupation of much of the country by Russian, Turkish and British troops. Security for settled society declined, and raids by nomads forced many villagers once more to join them or take refuge in the cities.[4]

The Pahlavi regime (1925–1979) took a radically different line. Rezā Shah attempted to create a culturally integrated, Persian-speaking nation-state in a country where only half the population (some say less) had Persian as their mother tongue, and where most of the nomadic tribes belonged to the rich variety of cultural and linguistic minorities. He saw nomadic tribes as a threat to the national integration of the state and as a cultural anachronism in the modern world. In a successful military campaign of pacification in the 1920s he undermined the tribal structures, subduing most of the chiefs (many of whom were killed) and disarming their followers. In the 1930s he thought to remove the tribal problem for good by abolishing nomadism through comprehensive enforced settlement. Migration routes were blocked and tents destroyed, yet little or no provision was made to help nomads settle and start farming. The result was an economic and social disaster: no increase in agricultural production, huge losses of livestock and the impoverishment, misery and resentment of the former nomads.

After Rezā Shah's abdication in 1941, there was a return to nomadic pastoralism; but the attack on the nomadic tribes and other minorities was resumed in the 1950s–70s. There were tribal revolts after the 1940s, but none, in the age of aircraft and tanks, could seriously threaten the government. Mohammad Rezā Pahlavi pursued a modified version of his father's policies towards the nomad tribes: pastoralism was to continue, but on new terms, with a long-term development policy of planned settlement of nomads, mainly through neglect. Tribal leaders were removed, pastures were nationalised, commercial stock-breeders were allowed to invade—and overgraze—tribal range lands, while traditional pastoralism was neglected and massive agro-industrial schemes were launched in tribal territories. The government wilfully ignored the contribution pastoral nomads had made to the national economy, notably in exploiting otherwise inaccessible range lands and supplying meat for the increasingly voracious domestic market.[5]

By the mid-1970s, following the oil boom, the livestock economy generally had been undermined by subsidised imports of meat and dairy products. Though this was partly offset by the fact that grain prices were also subsidised, large numbers of former nomads were impoverished and settled, many joining the mass migration to the cities.[6] At the same time, the tribes were considered to have ceased to exist as a political element in society, while the pastoral nomads were marginalised to the extent that they could be regarded as colourful, folkloric relics from the past, a tourist attraction. As Beck reports, the government facilitated the access of foreign researchers to tribal areas, and urban Iranians were officially encouraged to drive out to the mountains and spend a day as uninvited guests of the nomads, whose banditry and unrest had so recently been a source of government anxiety.[7]

The Pahlavi regime's defeat of the nomads and other minorities was celebrated in the Festival of Popular Traditions held in October 1977 in Isfahān, in which nomadic cultures were taken out of their social and especially political contexts and displayed in public as museum pieces—a 'culture bazaar', as one Iranian anthropologist has described it.[8] A major role in this was played out in the famous Meydan-e Shah in central Isfahān by groups of tribesmen, and some of tribeswomen, who performed for public entertainment dances normally confined to specific social and cultural contexts such as wedding celebrations. For this occasion, the dancers introduced inappropriate new movements, and the women wore make-up. In the electric revolutionary atmosphere of the time, all this was intensely inflammatory for the Isfahānis present, many of whom were of tribal origins; several men attempted to mount the platform where the women were dancing, and police had to intervene to quell the resulting disturbance.

There was apparently a growing focus on tribal values among urban revolutionary elements. Sometimes this was explicit, as when some Tehran youth identified with the Bakhtiāri as portrayed in the classic (1924) film *Grass*: their struggle against the elements symbolised the contemporary struggle against the oppressive regime.[9] However, nomads themselves played little part in the events surrounding the Islamic Revolution of 1978–9, which was largely an urban phenomenon, although settled tribespeople did participate in events in the cities, and in some parts of the countryside such as Kurdistān.[10]

The Islamic Republic has seen a revival in the fortunes of the nomadic tribes. Ayatollah Khomeyni declared them to be one of two sectors of the population (the other being the mullahs) particularly oppressed by the previous regime. He termed them Treasures of the Revolution (*zakhāyer-e enqelāb*), and the fourth Armed Force; officially they are considered to have had a vital historical role in protecting the independence and territorial integrity of the country. Special efforts have been made to foster their social, economic and cultural life and to make sure that they have the same facilities as the rest of the population, as will be described below.

WHO ARE THE NOMADS?

In summer 1987 the first ever comprehensive and reliable census of pastoral nomads in Iran was carried out. The total number of nomads, in a population of about 55 million, was nearly 1.2 million, which is perhaps surprisingly close to the figure of 2–3 million nomads usually estimated for much of the 19th century, though the proportion of nomads in the population has drastically declined since then.

For the purpose of the census, nomads (*'ashāyer-e kuchandeh*, 'migrating tribes') were defined by a combination of three criteria:

1. tribal (*qabileh'i*) social organisation, "in which individuals feel themselves and their families (*khānavādeh*) to belong to a larger social group, usually based on kinship, and usually called a tayfeh";
2. reliance for livelihood mainly on animal husbandry (*dāmdāri*);
3. a pastoral (*shabāni*) or nomadic (*kuch*) way of life, moving anything from a few to 500 kilometres between natural, seasonal pastures.[11]

This official definition of nomads is clear; it was precise enough for the purposes of the 1987 Census, the organisers of which were well aware of past problems of counting the nomads: what constitutes the 'mobile population', what time of the year to count them, and the omission of pastoral nomads who happened to be in houses at the time of the census.[12] Nevertheless, strictly applied, it excludes non-tribal nomads and non-pastoral nomads, as well as settled tribespeople. In practice, application of the criteria, whether by government officials or by 'nomads' themselves, has been flexible: it depends on what is at stake, what is being demanded of nomads, or offered to them, in terms of taxation, government budgets, services and facilities.

Seen in a wider perspective, however, such a definition is idiosyncratic, particularly in the way it combines nomadism, pastoralism and tribalism—three distinct elements which in other parts of

Some scholars find pastoralism to be the dominant criterion of nomadism; others specify a mix of pastoralism with mobility. For present purposes, the seasonal movements of people and their flocks are enough for us to continue calling those involved 'nomads'. Qashqa'i, Amala on migration, 1988.

the world are not the same thing at all. Each of these elements constitutes a dimension of variation largely independent of the others.

Thus, pastoralism is usually considered to be a specialised, family-based, way of life dedicated to the raising of livestock. As an economy, it is distinct from cultivation, craft-work, trading and hunting. Pastoralism is neither a subsidiary adjunct to cultivating activities, nor is it industrial ranching or the feedlot-farming of livestock—though it may evolve or be developed into one of these.

Definitions of 'nomadism', the second element, vary widely. Elsewhere, nomadism commonly signifies various kinds of patterned mobility of families and communities, as distinct analytically from settlement and settled existence. It shades into village-based transhumance,[13] vagrancy, and various forms of labour migration. Some scholars attempt to restrict the notion of 'pure nomads' to those with no fixed dwellings, or to those with no fixed movements, or to those who are in constant movement, between fixed dwellings perhaps, or on fixed routes. Such restrictions can lead to the claim that none of the nomads of Iran are 'pure', that at most they practise 'semi-nomadism', or transhumance, to the extent that they have fixed migratory routes, or fixed dwellings at some point in their migratory cycle. Other scholars find pastoralism to be the dominant criterion of nomadism (from the Greek *nomas* = herder); yet others specify a mix of pastoralism and mobility; individual groups exhibit various combinations of the two elements.[14] For present purposes, seasonal movements of people and their flocks are enough for us to continue calling those involved 'nomads'.

There is less consensus on the definition of tribalism, the third element. Many accept the sense inherent in the Iranian formulation above: a tribe is a group of families (in a wide sense) feeling primary moral loyalties to each other because of shared kinship links. Others focus more on the political aspect, in which a tribe unites under a leader to defend a common territory; if there is a notion of kinship, typically in the form of descent from a common ancestor, this may be seen as an ideology, rather than the basis of unity, and it may well be created or manipulated by a leader. In the most general terms, a tribe can be said to be a social and political group whose members have primary loyalties to each other and to their leader (if any) rather than to the nation and state. This distinguishes tribes analytically from the peasantry in a pre-modern state and from the citizenry in a modern bureaucratic system.

Around the world, these three elements rarely coincide. In Iran, however, in the past, as in the recent census definition, there was in fact considerable coincidence between nomads, pastoralists and tribes. But even in Iran, pastoralists are not always nomadic: some communities practise transhumance, raising livestock from settled bases, with specialised herders accompanying the animals. Nomads are not always pastoralists: some make a living from hunting, specialised craft work (gypsies), or trading.

Pastoral nomads are not always tribal in the above sense: some live in small, family-based communities (which anthropologists in other contexts would term 'bands'), with no systematic relations linking different communities and no formal leadership; the Komāchi of Kermān would be an Iranian example.[15]

Tribespeople are often neither nomadic nor pastoral, but settled farmers. Government officials living in towns or cities may claim tribal identity. Pastoral nomadic tribespeople have long experienced settlement and urbanisation without necessarily losing their tribal loyalties.

Nomads, pastoralists, and tribes typically live in ecologically and politically marginal areas or situations—mountains, deserts, steppes, frontiers—though not necessarily. Some, like the Sangsāri of the Alborz, live or migrate close to major cities.

In the majority of cases in Iran, where there was a coincidence between nomad, pastoralists and tribes, outsiders have come to assume these elements to be synonymous, and to coincide further with 'national minorities'. In the past, as we have seen, some nomads were culturally, linguistically and politically related to the rulers of the country. Under the Safavid, Afshār, and Qājār dynasties in Iran, Turkish nomads could claim such an ethno-linguistic identity with the ruling elite.[16] But under the Pahlavis the languages and cultures of minorities, notably Turks, Kurds, Lurs, Baluches, Turkmens, Arabs, including almost all the tribal and pastoral nomadic peoples, were systematically suppressed. Many nomads (Kurds, Baluches, Turkmens, some Arabs) are Sunni Muslims, some Kurdish nomads belong to an extremist Shi'a sect, the Ahl-e Haqq, and many of the Sangsāri are Baha'i; these minority religious identities further complicated relations with the Shi'a central authorities, particularly after the Islamic Revolution.

As a result, urban Iranian officials and intellectuals, at least in the 1950s to 1970s, tended to assume that nomad tribes belonged to cultural and linguistic, if not religious minorities, and regarded tribes, nomads and pastoralists as one and the same thing. 'Proper' tribes, it was thought, must be pastoral nomads.[17] In Persian, until very recently, the terms *ilāt* (Perso-Arabic plural of the Turkish *il*, 'people', 'tribe') and *'ashāyer* (plural of the Arabic *'ashireh*, 'tribe', 'clan') were used more or less interchangeably, often indeed as a pair, as in '*ilāt va 'ashāyer*', meaning 'nomadic tribes'. Other terms have in the past been used synonymously with them: *qabāyel*, *tavāyef*, and the obsolete *oymaqat*, *ulusat*. All these too are plural forms, of the singulars *qabileh* (Arabic), *tāyfeh* (Arabic), *oymaq* (Turko-Mongol), *ulus* (Turkish).[18]

As plurals, *ilāt* and *'ashāyer* are shifting, ambiguous terms. What is implied by these terms—pastoralists, nomads, tribes—to the average Iranian today, compared with fifty or a hundred years ago? How indeed should the terms be translated into English? It is not just a question of definition, but also of thorny political and ideological issues—the notion of 'tribe' perhaps smacks more of anachronism, of powerful chiefs, of difficult times in Iranian history, than do either 'nomad' or 'pastoralist'; but terms which can mean *all* of these, carry *all* their connotations. It seems that the prime reference of the terms has been political, to 'tribes', so that there is sometimes, where necessary, the added precision of *dāmdār* (pastoralist), *kuchandeh* or *kuch-neshin* (nomadic, migrating), or *chādor-neshin* (tent-dwelling). But increasingly the terms have become differentiated, *ilāt* being reserved for 'tribes', and *'ashāyer* for 'nomads'.[19]

Thus, around 1990, the name of the government department (*sāzmān-e omur-e ʿashāyer-e Iran*) that was concerned with providing services to nomads, and indeed had helped to organise the census, was translated into English as 'Iran's Tribal Affairs Organisation.' In 1992 the translation was changed to 'Organisation for the Nomadic Peoples of Iran', at least for the purposes of an international conference convened by the department, and the title of the conference (*ʿashāyer va touse'eh*) was translated as 'Nomadism and Development'. Nomadism implied pastoralism, and clearly—and usefully—steered conference discussion in the direction of 'the future of nomadic pastoralism', a topical issue in development studies; one cannot conceive of a similarly useful conference being convened to discuss the development or future of 'tribes'. Significantly, the conference brochures avoided any use of the term 'tribe' in the English text, or of *ilāt* in the Persian, where only *ʿashāyer* was used.[20]

This shift was a decision by a few individuals concerned perhaps with the international image of Iran. The English notion of 'the tribes', and the Persian-Turkish plural term *ilāt*, have been eased out, and replaced by the Arabic *ʿashāyer* in its new sense of 'pastoral nomads' and *qabileh* (as in the census definition) as an analytical term for 'tribe', with social, and no longer political connotations.

But the singular *il* continues to be used for specific tribal groups, and rather more subtle redefinitions and refinements have been produced within official circles. In publications associated with and following the census, *il* is defined in more detail:

"An *il* is composed of several *tāyfeh* united on the basis of kinship, or social, political or other ties; usually located in a defined geographic area, known as the tribal territory (*qalamrou*). *Tāyfeh* of an *il* usually have distant kinship links with each other by blood (*nasabi*) or marriage (*sababi*); but some have no kinship links but form an *il* through social or political necessity (*zarurat*). The speech, customs and manners and way of life of the different *tāyfeh* of an *il* are by and large the same.

"The most well-defined and important pastoral nomad (*ʿashāyeri*) social level is the *tāyfeh*, a community (*jamāʿat*) usually united by near and distant kinship, linked through a number of generations, by blood or marriage, to a common origin (*mabnā*); a pastoral nomad (*ʿashāyeri*) individual is usually identified primarily by his *tāyfeh* name.

"Independent *tāyfeh* are those which have no *il* membership."

Below this level (the definition continues) the various subdivisions in the tribal structure are peculiar to each tribal group. At the minimal level, however, there is invariably a small group of households linked by close blood relationship or affinity. Other forms of group, formed for example for migratory or herding purposes, are not counted in the census.[21]

Despite the qualifications, this definition is quite precise and comprehensive. However, although it includes the political notions of territory and unity, there is no mention anywhere of the element of leadership, once the *sine qua non* connotation of 'tribe'. Apart from this omission, the definition has two major differences from its predecessors: on the one hand, it is both more explicit and more flexible than any previous one; on the other, for the first time individuals whose own background is that of ordinary nomadic tribespeople have had a hand in the definition.

PASTORAL ECOLOGY AND ECONOMICS

Pastoral nomads continue to play a vital role in the Iranian economy on regional, national and international levels, despite recent encroachments on tribal territories as a result of the nationalisation of the range lands in the 1960s and 1970s, the expansion of village-based cultivation, and incursions from the flocks and herds of commercial stock-breeders. According to the 1987 census, pastoral nomads had 17 million sheep and goats and 500,000 other livestock, around a third of the country's total, and they contributed a rather larger proportion of marketed produce.

James Morier wrote of Iranian pastoral nomads in the early 19th century:

"An Iliyat of middling fortune possesses about a hundred sheep, three or four camels, three or four mares, ten asses, &c., which may yield him a revenue of forty to fifty tumans. A man who possesses a thousand sheep, thirty camels, twenty mares, &c., is reckoned a rich man. Each sheep may be valued at two piastres [rials?], a camel at ten, a mare at eight, an ass at three. Such a property would yield a revenue of four hundred tumans. This is to be derived from the wool and milk of the sheep, the wool and hire of the camels, the colts from the mares and asses ... The encampments of the Iliyats are generally of about twenty to thirty tents together, which they pitch mostly without any great attention to regularity ... The tents are close to each other, but the different encampments may be a mile or two asunder, according to the convenience of grass and water ... excepting their clothes, copper utensils, pack-saddles and ornamental luxuries, they supply all their own necessities ... Their mode of calculating property is by sheep ... A shepherd has the care of three hundred sheep, and is paid in kind, both in wool and lambs."[22]

This account of pastoral economics is particularly important both in stressing the cash values attributed to the animals—the nomads' 'capital'—as well as to their 'revenue', and in hinting at the degree to which they depended economically on selling their produce, and hiring their animals, to members of settled society. What evidence exists in earlier sources strongly indicates that this emphasis on production and exchange had been a feature of pastoral nomadism in Iran for a very long time, and though the monetary values (and a few other items) need adjusting, Morier's description of nomadic life is more or less valid for late twentieth-century Iran. Within the general parameters he suggests, however, there are very wide variations in the ecological circumstances of the nomads and in the economic activities they pursue.

The earliest modern detailed account of a group of Iranian nomads, Fredrik Barth's study of the Basseri (Bāseri), a tribe of some 3,000 households belonging to the Khamseh confederacy in Fārs, has now become a classic in social anthropology, and the Persian translation has been widely read in Iran.[23]

Barth's book, based on fieldwork in 1958, offers, in summary, an account of the Bāseri tribe at two levels. First, it is a study of the ecological and economic processes generating the forms of social life among Bāseri pastoral nomads. Bāseri households, based on nuclear families and averaging 5.7 members, own their own flocks. The average household flock is nearly 100 head of sheep, while the minimum viable flock—given the productivity of the flocks, sales of lambs, skins and produce to the market, and expected levels of household consumption—is 60 head. When a father finds a bride for his son, he soon provides him with a separate tent and his share of the flock as anticipatory inheritance, enabling the new couple to set up a separate household. Groups of roughly five households, not necessarily close paternal relatives, co-operate to herd joint flocks of 400 animals. The basic nomadic community is the 'camp', 10 to 40 households that move and camp together on migration between winter and summer quarters. The camp has a leader (*riz safid*, white beard) with limited personal authority over his followers.

Secondly, Barth shows how higher levels of organisation than the camp are dependent on processes involving the Bāseri chief and factors outside the tribe: the government, settled society, and other nomadic groups. The Bāseri *il*, as administered by the chief, divides into *tira* (sections), which comprise one or more *oulād*. The *oulād* is a patrilineal descent group, usually 50 to 100 households, with grazing rights in specific pasturages in winter and summer quarters; to have access to grazing, a nomad must be able to claim membership of an *oulād*. Most *oulād* comprise two or more camps, but these are not defined patrilineal descent segments of the *oulād* and their membership is irregular and liable to change. The *tira* are weakly developed as groups, and the chief deals directly and arbitrarily with *oulād* headmen (*katkhodā*) and often with camp leaders. To be effective as a leader and patron, the chief must have power and resources which set him, his family and his entourage apart from ordinary nomads, and on a level with regional and national elites. Barth's account of political structure and leadership is qualified to an extent by the fact that at the time of his study the chiefship had recently been abolished, and a new system integrating the Bāseri into the state administrative structure using army officers had yet to take full effect.

Barth details the external economic relations and demographic processes affecting the nomads; and discusses the political relations between different tribal and ethno-linguistic groups in Fārs province: the Persian-speaking Bāseri are linked with the Il-e 'Arab and the Turkish-speaking tribes Inānlu (Ainālu), Nafar and Bahārlu in the Khamseh ('Five') confederacy, who are collectively known as 'Arabs' and are traditional rivals of the Qashqa'i 'Turks'. All of them have market and other relations with the settled peasantry who are mostly Persian speakers.

The economic, social, religious and political organisation of the Bāseri, as described by Barth, have been widely assumed to typify Iranian pastoral nomads, and many recent scholars have extrapolated from the Bāseri in both space and time. Anthropologists have constructed the Bāseri into a 'type' of pastoral nomadism,[24] and historians have used the Bāseri as a guiding 'text' for their reconstructions of pre-modern, especially mediaeval, nomadic societies in Iran, Turkey and elsewhere, particularly in terms of pastoral economics and nomadic social and political organisation.[25]

According to the 1987 census, pastoral nomads had 17 million sheep and goats and 500,000 other livestock, around a third of the country's total, and they contributed a rather larger proportion of marketed produce. By and large the nomads are specialised livestock producers, who trade with both cultivators (especially of grain or dates, the pastoralists' staple foods) and a variety of craftsmen. They mostly keep sheep and goats as their main source of livelihood, though in widely differing proportions; according to the census, goats are less than 10% in Āzarbāijān, but more than 80% in Kermān, Sistān and Baluchestān. Amala on migration to their summer camp near Kāzerun, 1987.

Unfortunately, the Bāseri example is inappropriate for such extrapolation onto other 'nomadic tribes', whether mediaeval or contemporary, for various reasons, which should be obvious to readers of other chapters in this book:

First, comparison with other contemporary nomadic societies, whether in Iran or elsewhere, shows the Bāseri, in virtually all the features outlined in the summary above, to constitute just one pattern among many. This is not surprising, given the very specific natural, economic, political and historical circumstances of the Bāseri, most of which are ignored by those who extrapolate from the text, and which are quite different from those of other tribal and nomadic societies.[26]

Secondly, the Bāseri case is not merely specific but actually rather unusual, as is suggested both by Barth's own limited comparison with the neighbouring Qashqa'i Turks and Khamseh Arabs and by other sources on the social, economic and political organisation of nomadic tribal groups elsewhere or at other times.[27]

Thirdly, Barth's observations derive mainly from his residence in the camp of the Bāseri chief's personal entourage, the Darbār, which must throw doubt on their representativeness even of 'ordinary' Bāseri nomadic society. Moreover, he was able to stay there for only the 3 months of the spring migration.[28]

None the less, substantial advances in the reconstruction of nomadic and tribal societies in the Islamic world could be achieved by more carefully contextualised readings of Barth's study, and by contrasting it with other modern ethnographies.

Classifications and comparisons of the different pastoral nomadic groups of Iran have been attempted along a number of dimensions. One is that of patterns of nomadic movement, where the following major categories may be distinguished:

First, long-range, vertical (between mountain and plain) migrations are practised by the major nomadic groups in the Zāgros, such as the Bāseri, the Bakhtiāri (see chapters by Brooks and Digard), the Qashqa'i (see Amir-Moez), the Lur (see Bradshaw), minor groups such as the Torkashvand (see Ehlers), groups elsewhere like the Shahsevan of the north-west (see Tapper) and some of the nomads of Kermān (see Stöber).[29]

Short-range vertical transhumance is conducted by many village-based pastoralists, for example the Tālesh (see Bazin), many of the Kurds of Āzarbāijān (see Yalçın-Heckmann) and Khorāsān (see Papoli-Yazdi), and the Boyer Ahmadi (see Friedl and Loeffler).

Long range, horizontal nomadism (with little change of altitude) is practised by the Sangsāri of the Alborz, and some others, while short-range horizontal nomadism characterises the Yomut Turkmen[30] and a variety of groups near Zanjān and Qazvin, as well as the Gāwdārān of Sistān (see Stöber).

Finally, a few groups conduct a form of horizontal nomadism based on oasis settlements, such as the multi-resource economy of the Baluch.[31]

This type of classification is of limited value. Each major category includes extremes; for example, long-range vertical nomadism is found in both the densely populated high rainfall areas of the north-west, and the arid, sparsely populated south and east. Moreover, there are significant variations in nomadic practices within each named nomadic group. It is clearly impossible to argue a simple ecological explanation, that the highly varied environments in which they live give rise to specific ecological and economic adaptations.

At a more subtle level, however, ecology and economics do affect the way nomads move within their environment, and to an extent also their forms of social organisation. These factors influence the size, character and composition of social groups, and the nature of relations between them, as well as other forms of association and differentiation.

Nomads in Iran live and organise in fluid and flexible camps, though their movement schedules are usually quite regular. We find several kinds of variation. For example, because of the differing nature of their range-lands, the Shahsevan in summer scatter in small herding camps which congregate into larger settlements in the winter, while the opposite is true of the Qashqa'i and the Bāseri. Similarly, because of the heat of their winter quarters in Fars, Qashqa'i leave on the spring migration for the mountains by Nowruz (21 March); the Kermān nomads of the plateau delay until after this date; while the Shahsevan of Moghān often do not leave until well into May. Further, on the crowded Zāgros migration routes, where thousands of nomads, often from many different tribes, must cross narrow passes and defiles in a matter of weeks if not days, strict organisation of the schedule is essential; while in other areas much greater flexibility is possible. In recent decades, with trucks, tractors and trailers increasingly being used for transporting flocks, or homes, or both, very different scheduling patterns for these 'migrations' have taken effect.

Another dimension of variation among nomads in Iran is that of economic production and trade. Many nomadic groups have long conducted their own cultivation, as well as other non-pastoral activities—hunting, collecting, raiding, trade, weaving. By and large, however, the nomads are specialised livestock producers, who trade with both cultivators (especially of grain or dates, the pastoralists' staple foods) and a variety of craftsmen. They mostly keep sheep and goats as their main source of livelihood, though in widely differing proportions; according to the census, goats are less than 10% in Āzarbāijān, but more than 80% in Kermān, Sistān and Baluchestān. A few (not just those described by Stöber) specialise in cattle.

In all cases, animals are raised for market production: nomads sell milk and a range of milk products, wool and carpets, hides, hair and guts, and livestock on the hoof. Here too there are wide variations: among sheep-herders, for example, the Bāseri sell their young male lambs, while the Shahsevan keep the lambs for a year or more as yearling or older wethers before selling them (see also the chapters by Ehlers, Stöber, and Amir-Moez). Shahsevan have been selling milk and milk products commercially since the 1950s, while many Zāgros nomads are said, even now, to regard such sales of 'white' products as shameful (Digard p. 63). Clearly, to understand pastoral economics it is vital to consider the 'terms of trade': the relative values of agricultural

The camels, donkeys, horses, mules traditionally kept for personal, household and commercial, transport are increasingly being replaced by jeeps, trucks and tractor-drawn trailers. Kurds of West Āzarbāijan, west of Māku, spring 1986.

and pastoral produce, which are largely determined—and in many cases have been for centuries—by prices on international markets.

Nomads keep animals for other purposes than production. The camels, donkeys, horses, mules traditionally kept for commercial, household and personal transport are increasingly being replaced by jeeps, trucks and tractor-drawn trailers. Dogs are as important as ever for guarding home and herd: in most groups there is just the one breed, though among the Bakhtiāri (see Brooks and Digard) herd and house dogs are kept separate. A few wealthy chiefs used to keep imported hunting dogs.[32]

There is also variation in the size and organisation of nomadic households. The 1987 census counted a total of 182,782 nomadic households, with a national average of 6.4 persons per household. In practice, average household sizes range from 5–6 persons for Baluch and other nomadic groups in the east and south (like the Bāseri), to around 8 for Kurds, Shahsevan and Qaradāghis in the north-west. This discrepancy reflects different marriage and inheritance customs as much as any differences in fertility and mortality. Some groups, like the Bāseri, or the Komāchi in Kermān, practise anticipatory inheritance, where a man receives a share of his father's flock at or soon after marriage. Among others, such as the Shahsevan, division of the father's property is delayed until after his death, and even then married sons often stay within the same joint household and property for some years.

Among the Qashqa'i and some Lur groups, individual households attempt to be self-sufficient for all herding practices. Most pastoralists, however, form associations of households in order to pool herding labour and manage their grazing resources jointly. Hired shepherds (*chobān*) usually play a vital economic role, but there is considerable variation in the amount and manner of their payment, and in their position in nomadic society.[33] The size and composition of herds relate to grazing practices, with seasonal variations depending on the timing of lambing and of market sales, and on the constraints of the terrain: again there is variation between, for example, the Bāseri, whose herds reach 400 head of ewes and lambs; the Shahsevan or the Komāchi whose maximum herd size is 300 head, with older lambs kept separately from the ewes; and the Hasanwand Lurs described by Black-Michaud, where the optimum flock of ewes is reckoned at 130 head. The Shahsevan and the Komāchi are alike again in that they time the lambing in their flocks for late autumn (November–December), where in other groups the lambing season is spring.

The jobs of domestic husbandry—lambing, milking, shearing, marketing—are normally matters for individual households, though co-operation may be arranged. Gender roles and responsibilities vary widely: whether women or men do jobs like milking, pitching and striking tents, weaving and other household production; the degree to which women and girls are involved in herding; the extent of women's ownership of animals, tents and other property; the degree of segregation and veiling of women; how far women are involved in decision-making, and whether women form 'sub-societies'.[34]

A final dimension of economic and ecological variation concerns the pastures, and the social groups which form to exploit them. Of central importance to pastoral nomads is the nature of their rights to land for grazing, farming or the accumulation of wealth; whether these rights are individualised or communal at some level; what size of groups own or exploit and defend them; how far these groups vary from season to season; and how permanent and how exclusive the rights are. Many nomads in Iran have not only the classic range of summer pastures (*yaylaq*, *sardsir*, *sarhad*) and winter pastures (*qeshlaq*, *garmsir*), but also defined autumn and spring grazing areas, as well as 'schedules' comprising rights of passage and grazing on the migration routes (*il-rāh*, *elyolu*). There was wide variation between systems like that of the Bāseri, with extensive communal territories, and those like the Shahsevan, with near-individuated grazing rights which could be bought and sold or rented. Never formally recognised by the government, these traditional systems were abolished in the 1960s and 1970s by the nationalisation of the nomadic grazing grounds, which have increasingly been taken over, legally or otherwise, by the flocks of city-based commercial stock-breeders.

Among most if not all nomads in Iran, as elsewhere, the basic nomadic group (the camp, in the Bāseri case) is an egalitarian pastoral community of some twenty to fifty families. In many cases (though not usually that of the Bāseri camp) shared or joint grazing rights form one of the common interests of this basic pastoral community. It is usually led by a 'grey-beard' and linked by common patrilineal descent or other ties of kinship and affinity. Members, who camp and move together or nearby and make certain joint economic decisions, form a congregation for certain religious ceremonies, and maintain a strong degree of social integrity through shared customs and knowledge. Other local-level social groups among the nomads tend to form according to one of the above economic or socio-cultural principles: to herd joint flocks or manage joint pastures, to move and camp together on migration, to form a religious congregation. In practice, actual social groups often combine several such functions. Standard ethnographic accounts of nomadic societies in Iran since Barth's studies of the Bāseri have analysed elements of nomadic social structure in such terms.

Differences between pastoral nomadic societies in patterns of camp and community structure and inter-community relations often reflect their varying economic and ecological situations as pastoralists and as nomads. These include patterns of interaction with their social and political environment, with settled villagers, the wider society, and with the agents of the state. As has been stressed above, nomads are not isolated from or independent of settled society, but regularly interact with it through 'trade or raid', the exchange of both information and personnel, and longer-term processes of settlement or nomadisation.

Nomads and pastoralists are thus part of regional, national and wider economic systems, and whether there is harmony or antagonism in these relations depends on a further multiplicity of factors and processes: geographical situation, competition for resources, political struggle or accommodation, perceptions of ethnic difference or identity, and so on. In the common Iranian case of pastoral nomadic tribespeople, relations with village peasant cultivators, urban craftsmen and government agents are historically complex, dynamic and deeply rooted.

In sum, later studies of Iranian nomads—such as the chapters in this volume—and comparisons with Barth's classic study have shown that the organisation of the Bāseri pastoral camp community is highly specific: many configurations found among the Bāseri are not repeated elsewhere. However, Barth's two-level analysis, in which the political organisation of the tribe is distinct from the ecology and economy of pastoral nomad camps, is valid and useful generally; the processes operating at each level are quite different. Following Barth's insight, though relevant historical sources are only suggestive, it seems likely that basic nomadic communities have always been the product of the ecological conditions of nomadic pastoralism and internal demographic and cultural factors. His analysis of tribes and confederations documents what has long been recognised, that these larger political groupings are artefacts of external political and cultural relations, notably with neighbouring groups and with central authorities.

TRIBES

As we have seen, the notion of 'tribes' (*ilāt va 'ashāyer*) as the political and social dimension of pastoral nomadism is so strongly entrenched in academic and administrative thinking about Iranian society that the category of 'the tribes' has been conventionally synonymous with 'the nomads'. Further, 'tribes' were strongly associated with powerful leaders, who at points in the past rivalled—and on occasion overthrew and replaced—the rulers of the state. However, as discussed earlier, since the Islamic Revolution official definitions of 'tribes' have played down this political aspect, omit all reference to chiefs, and focus instead on the social dimension. Tribes in Iran, or at least the major components, the *tāyfeh*, are now defined as groups of kin—almost as extended families.

To be sure, the redefinition of the terminology recognises changing political realities—the chiefs no longer exist; but it is also an attempt to fix current reality in a way that facilitates government control. This is also evident in the implication in the official definition that there is, and always has been, a more or less uniform pattern of political and social structure among the nomadic tribes, which is far from the case. Even the upper level of the structure—*il* divided into *tāyfeh*—is idealised. It is not an exact representation of any one tribal group, but somehow the average of all of them, a model of uniformity, and it is a fiction for the purposes of administration, in a grand tradition of many centuries during which governments have defined, created and classified 'the tribes'.

The notion of tribe as the social dimension of pastoral nomadism is shared by numerous historians and other writers on the Middle East, who assume in addition that tribes comprise what anthropologists used to call 'segmentary lineages', where members claim descent from a common ancestor (the founder of the lineage, which often bears his, or her,name) and form a series of nesting sub-groups (segments) descended from more recent ancestors. Patricia Crone, for example, writes that it is likely that "tribe in the specific sense of the word is an overwhelmingly or exclusively pastoral phenomenon (or so at least if we add the criterion of segmentary organisation)." The tribe, moreover, "is that descent group within which control of pasture land is vested", which shares the obligation to pay blood-money for an injured member, and which has a chief and forms

left and right
Women of the Chahārdah Cherik subtribe looking after the flocks while on migration. Their name means Fourteen Guerrillas and they joined the Qashqa'i confederation in the 1860s. They have their summer quarters at Dozkord north of Ardekān and winter south of Qir. Spring 1988.

a community. She finds nomads to be "pitiful creatures", doomed to "tribalism" by their environment, marginal, and hence inclined to avoid states; and she finds it "surprising" that certain nomadic people became conquerors on a gigantic scale.[35]

Other historians, however, take a diametrically opposed view of the nature of tribes and tribe-state relations in earlier Islamic societies. For Rudi Lindner, clans and tribes are essentially political groups gathered around a leader, concerned about shared interests as much as blood ties. Though he underplays the role of kinship ideologies in recruiting and uniting tribal groups, Lindner is correct in observing (from the Bāseri model) that in the Middle East all tribal political groups, whether large confederacies or even quite small tribes, are historically of mixed origins, sometimes recognised, sometimes forgotten.[36]

But as we have seen, there is no necessary connection of tribe with nomadism or pastoralism; nor are tribes necessarily formed on the basis of shared descent or central leadership. In the Middle East, where nomads numbered tens of millions until very recently, it is true that historically most nomads were organised politically as tribes under chiefs, and that many tribes (defined in political terms) had a pastoral economic base and led a nomadic way of life. However, Crone's insistence that tribes in the Middle East and Central Asia are necessarily pastoralists organised in descent groups excludes most major groups in Anatolia, Iran and Afghanistan. In Anatolia the Ottomans were not originally a descent group, while few of the Pashtuns of Afghanistan were pastoralists. In other Middle Eastern countries too, important tribal groups were settled cultivators with little or no leaning to pastoralism or nomadism. Well-known groups in Iran, such as the Qashqa'i, Bakhtiāri, Kurds, Baluch, Turkmen or Shahsevan, were at least partly settled agriculturalists, and complex and heterogeneous in composition.

By conventional definitions many of these were not 'tribes' at all, but 'chiefdoms', or even 'proto-states'; often such groups were the creation of the central state, but at times they were a threat to the state, or were feared as such. In most other contexts around the world, the English term 'tribe' is applied specifically to social groups quite unlike the best known so-called 'tribes' of Iran, groups that not only are not pastoral nomads, but have neither chiefs nor large-scale political organisation.

These camels, probably hybrids between the Bactrian and Arab camel, belong to a Turkic group, the Laraki, who own the only camels to be found in Bakhtiāri territory since the Bakhtiāri neither own nor use camels. The Laraki winter in Fārs and because the route to their summer quarters involves crossing difficult terrain, they migrate independently of the Bakhtiāri using a less precipitous route via Izeh and Ardal. Here they are getting ready to move on after an overnight stop near Shalamzār, April 1984.

Social groups that have been labelled 'tribes' do indeed vary considerably in their predominant mode of organisation: and hence definitions of 'tribe' vary.[37] They may be organised and led centrally in a hierarchical political structure, sometimes up to the level of a major tribal confederacy and powerful paramount chiefs. Other tribes are organised diffusely in egalitarian groups, perhaps united by an ideology of unilineal descent. Commonly 'tribes' are organised by some combination of these two principles (the political one of allegiance to chiefs, or the cultural one of descent ideology), but neither of the two is necessary or universal in groups referred to as 'tribes'. Indeed, as we shall see, some pastoral nomadic tribes in Iran (as elsewhere) have neither chiefs nor descent groups, forming for the purpose of economic co-operation and on the grounds of neighbourhood. There are cases too of nomads in Iran who have neither formed tribes nor followed chiefs.

We should perhaps remember that, according to popular sociology, football supporters' clubs, street gangs, and the organised crime syndicates of the inner cities of the industrial world form 'tribes', and behave 'tribally', by which is usually meant that they organise with lines of loyalty and authority which ignore the community bounds and local frameworks sanctioned by the state.

There is nothing in either pastoralism as a production system or nomadism as a mobile way of living that necessarily leads to organisation in 'tribes', whether these are defined politically in terms of chiefship and territory or culturally in terms of common descent, and any coincidence between pastoral nomads and tribes is not so much a causal relation as a function of relations of both with the central state. Both tribespeople, by virtue of their personal allegiance to each other or to chiefs, and nomads, with their shifting residence, are classically unpopular with any settled state administration intent on registering and taxing the population it claims to control. In some cases, indeed, mobility can be a deliberate policy for escaping such control and exploitation.[38] Sedentary rulers have

A Sanjābi family east of Kermānshāh. The Sanjābi Kurds were politically influential in times past. Now many are settled and their influence has declined. Spring 1989.

thus tended to classify the nomads and tribespeople together and indeed to administer them similarly.

From the rulers' perspective, even the most autonomous inhabitants of the territory over which they claim sovereignty are assumed to have similar or comparable patterns of organisation, including leaders who may be treated as their representatives; if they do not have these leaders or patterns, they may be encouraged to produce them.[39] In some cases, governments have created tribes where none existed previously in order to administer rural groups and minorities—whether nomadic or settled—the chiefs being appointed from among local notables or even complete outsiders. One of the best known examples in Iran is the foundation of the Khamseh confederacy (including the Bāseri) under the chiefship of the Shirāz merchant family of Qavām al-Molk in 1861–2; but there are many twentieth-century examples on a smaller scale. In Iran there is perhaps a longer history than elsewhere of such government practices, whose latest manifestation is the recent official redefinition of 'tribe' for census and administrative purposes, referred to earlier.

The names of such government-created 'tribes' may appear in the records but exist only on paper. Again, tribal names found in official sources imply a uniformity of socio-political structure which, in so far as it exists, may be entirely due to administrative action, and may disguise fundamental disparities of culture and society. The political history, geography, and cultural orientations of the various tribes are so different that, *a priori*, there is a very wide and rich variation in nomadic society and culture in Iran.

In the previous section, attention was drawn to certain major differences among the nomads of Iran, notably in their ecological and economic situations as mobile pastoralists. They have been classified in a variety of other ways, for different purposes. Official classifications, for example, have used three types of criteria, alone or in combination: ethnic, provincial, political

opposite left above and below
Tents of the Bāseri, one of the five tribes of the former Khamseh confederacy.
North of Shirāz, 1992.

above
A tent belonging to a Kurdish Gurāni family. The tent wall is made of canes individually wrapped with coloured wools. The wrapped canes are bound together on a primitive loom to form a screen with a large-scale pattern. Near Sar-e Pol-e Zahāb. Summer 1989.

left
Camomile, a medicinal herb, being dried on the tent cloth. The method of joining tent cloth panels together with wooden pins is clearly seen here. The tent is that of the Mamasani, the 'unknown Lurs' who occupy territory in Fārs, near Nurābād, surrounded by Qashqa'is. Winter 1986.

Groups of Arabic-speaking nomads live as herders in the agricultural region of western Khuzestān close to the Iraqi border. They live all the year round in black tents and practise short-range horizontal nomadism, moving with their herds between plots of cultivated land. South of Shush, 1985

Various official or historical documents, and some contemporary accounts taking the perspective of the state, list nomad tribes by 'ethnic' affiliation, that is, by language, supposed origins or both. Examples are Lambton's and Towfiq's Encyclopædia articles, and earlier documents such as the *Tohfeh-shāhi*.[40] The major categories, typically, are: (a) Iranians such as Lur and Lak, Kurd, Baluch and Brahui, held to be native to the country; (b) immigrant Turks; and (c) Arabs. Tribal groups are listed under one of these headings, together with numbers of families, names of chiefs and assessments of revenue and military levies. Some scholars would maintain that such an ethnohistorical classification has sociological correlates. In an interesting recent article, Barfield, for example, has revived the idea that 'indigenous Middle East tribes', such as Arabs, Kurds and Pashtuns (and presumably Lurs and Baluch), have egalitarian lineage structures and are resistant to domination, features which differentiate them from the more ephemeral but powerful centralised confederations and dynastic states associated with the Turco-Mongol nomadic tradition originating in Central Asia.[41]

Other sources classify the nomad tribes by province, listing the dominant named groups present in each, and estimates of their numbers. Examples include Lambton's key article again, and several local histories, as well as those publications of the 1987 Census concerned with the practical issue of the provision of services for the nomads.

The census's main classification, however, has been according to political and administrative units. Having defined *il* and *tāyfeh*, the census identified 96 *il*, of which 17 constitute the following 'major' *il* (in order of size): Bakhtiāri, Qashqa'i, Mamivand (Lurs), Boyer Ahmad Soflā (Lurs), Ilsevan (Shahsevan), Khamseh, Qaradāgh (Arasbārān), Mamasani (Lurs), Bahme'i (Lurs), Boyer Ahmad 'Olyā, Tayyebi, Jabāl-e Bārezi, Zelqeh, Jalāli, Baluch, Afshār, Kord. In addition, 547 independent *tāyfeh* belong to no *il*.[42]

A further mode of classification of the nomad tribes focuses on socio-political structures and relations to the state.[43] Tribal political structures, as we have seen, have nothing much to do with either pastoralism or nomadism *per se*. As Barth showed for the Khamseh, the powerful chiefs and tribal groups in Iran were, in large part, moulded if not created by the state and by government policies. Tribes in Iran have formed and derived their character from their relation to particular states at particular times, and there has been much theorising as to the complex processes involved.[44]

The best-known groups, for obvious reasons, are the large centralised confederacies, once led by powerful chiefly dynasties. Earlier examples included various Qizilbash groups and others which founded dynasties or challenged the rulers; examples from the twentieth century are the Bakhtiāri, Qashqa'i and Khamseh. None of these major groups were exclusively or even mainly pastoral nomads, and their chiefs were not merely leaders of nomads, but had two or more legitimate sources of personal wealth and power: not only flocks and herds, but agricultural land and commonly city-based trading houses. In addition, chiefs received income through tax collection, and often subsidies from the Iranian state and sometimes others, including (in the Bakhtiāri case early in the twentieth century) royalties from oil exploration. Such chiefs sometimes depended on recognition by the rulers, sometimes were strong enough to challenge them. They commanded well-armed irregular cavalry, drawn from their extensive entourage of kinsmen and personal followers as well as from the families of subordinate chiefs, none of whom participated directly in the hard work of the pastoral economy. These forces might be mobilised as levies by a strong government to fight its campaigns, but could, and sometimes did, bring the chiefs to power in government. Even where government had created these major confederacies and appointed their leaders as part of a 'tribal policy', they continued to constitute a 'tribal problem' for the central state.

Less powerful and numerous, and usually of concern to the state only at a regional level, were a range of locally centralised chiefdoms including different Kurdish groups in Western Iran and Khorāsān, Boyer Ahmadi and other Lurs in the west, Shahsevan and Qaradāghi in Āzarbāijān, Baluch in the southeast, and, on occasion, component elements of the major confederations.

Other tribal groups in Iran had no centralised political structure. They were diffusely organised and had no prominent leadership—like 'jellyfish', as Malcolm Yapp put it—and followed a strategy of 'divide that ye be not ruled', in Ernest Gellner's felicitous phrase.[45] The best example is the Yomut Turkmen of Gorgān, who were able to resist government control longer than many groups by virtue of their diffuse organisation, as well having the advantage being located on a frontier

Sangsāri of the Alborz live and migrate quite close to Tehran and practise mainly long range, horizontal nomadism, that is with little change of altitude. They, like the Tālesh and the Komāchi and others in Kermān, are one of the smaller groups which has managed to avoid the attention of both government and historians and a result their existence and numbers were more or less unknown until recently. Many of the Sangsāri adhere to the Baha'i faith which has made for difficult relations with the Shi'a central authorities, particularly since the Islamic Revolution.

across which they could escape. Numerous smaller groups, such as the Tālesh (see Bazin) the Sangsāri, and the Komāchi and others in Kermān, usually managed to avoid the attention of government—and historians—altogether. As a result their existence and numbers were more or less unknown at least until recently.[46]

The nomad census recorded the names of a number of 'tribes', including at least one 'major *il*' (the Zelqeh), whose existence before was obscure. Some of these probably fall into the previous category of diffusely organised groups, who successfully avoided attention until now. Others, such as Il-e Kerend, may be recent local agglomerations of tribal fragments, constituted as 'tribes' by administrative action or fiat.[47] Yet other cases may result from spontaneous political union of local nomads.

Clearly, no simple model of 'the tribes' or 'nomads of Iran' will be adequate, unless perhaps for very specific and drastic administrative or political purposes. Many recent academic and official studies of the tribes, however, have based their analyses on the apparent assumption of a uniformity of structure.[48] Typical formal schemes tend to include the following common elements:

(a) A regular segmentary structure of nesting territorial/political units, with groups at each level distinguished by terminology (for example, *il*, divided into *tāyfeh*, each divided into *tireh*, and their equivalents); the structure is usually depicted graphically as a star or tree.

(b) A matching segmentary framework of nesting descent groups, with a genealogical charter of pedigrees of descent from a common ancestor; again, a tree is the common model.

(c) A matching hierarchical structure of political leadership roles (*ilkhāni*, *khān*, *kalāntar*, *kadkhodā*, *rish-sefid* and so forth), accompanied by pyramid-shaped diagrams.

(d) A matching pyramid model of class structure, for example: chiefly families, independent commoners, employees, dependants and servants.

Careful reading of Barth's account of the Bāseri shows them to diverge at many points from this model of 'tribal structure', none the less his account has been frequently mis-read, by both Iranian and outside academics, as confirming the elements of the model.[49] Indeed, all the major Zāgros confederacies (Bakhtiāri, Qashqa'i, Khamseh), despite radical differences between them, are sometimes represented as the archetypes of 'tribal structure' and of pastoral economies and societies in Iran, while other tribal groups are held to be more or less imperfect approximations to them, with fewer levels of organisation, less centralisation, less powerful chiefs and so forth.

However, the idea that there is—or was—a uniform or archetypal 'tribal structure' of Iran, a fixed pattern of hierarchical political and social organisation among nomads, is wishful thinking on the part of tidy-minded government officials and academics.

Even if certain nomadic societies have similar social and political structures on paper, this says

Two Lur tents pitched near Varāmin belonging to the Hadāvand sub-tribe, which has its summer on the slopes of Mount Damāvand. The Lur tent is characterised by having its canopy supported by two separate ridge-poles. 1990.

right
A Lur family from the same encampment. Though milking is always women's work, men and boys will help to catch and hold the animals. Hadāvand sub-tribe, near Varāmin, 1990.

nothing about the functions of groups at any level, the power and role of a particular leader, or the political behaviour of particular individuals. Indigenous terms for political and descent groups, according to which nomads and tribespeople identify themselves and act, are not as systematically related or consistent as standard hierarchical models of tribal structures suggest. The terms they use tend to denote facets or functions, rather than levels in a hierarchy of groups. Ethnographers often report that individual nomads could not specify whether a given named group of people was a *tāyfeh* or a *tireh* or an *il*; this is not evidence of confusion or imprecision on the part of informants, but rather of the contextual nature of the terms. Many such terms are used interchangeably or apparently inconsistently, partly because—like the English terms 'section', 'department', 'division', 'family', 'group', 'lineage', 'tribe', 'clan', 'community'—they are ambiguous, partly because different terms are appropriate descriptions of the same 'group' in different contexts of action. The same Shahsevan social group may be called a *tireh* in the political context of tribal sections, a *göbak* as a descent group, or a *jamahat* as a ritual and moral community.[50] The same term may have different connotations in different tribal cultures, signifying, for example: community, grazing-group, tribal section, followers of a leader, descent group. Further, *il*, now officially used (see above) for major tribal groups throughout Iran, in the Turkmen language and culture means 'peace', 'obedience'.

Much the same is true of the terminology of leadership positions. Terms such as *khān*, *beg*, *katkhodā*, *rish-safid/aq-saqal*, which may be neatly listed in a hierarchical, quasi-military, model of tribal political structure, in practical usage in different tribal contexts may rather differentiate between leaders who are self-promoted, government appointees, or popularly elected or approved.

As for the assumption that nomads conceive their tribal identity in terms of a nesting set of descent groups, this is true in only a very limited sense. The Bakhtiāri, and one or two other groups, are reported to have a unifying tribal genealogy, but other major groups, with histories and traditions of heterogeneous origins, make no pretence at such unity, and invoke frameworks of common descent only at low levels of organisation.[51] Commonly, indeed, pedigrees and descent claims are only invoked where, as in the case of the Bāseri *oulād*, they bring rights of access to an important resource such as pasture land. At the level of the local community, such as the Bāseri camp, common descent is often no more important than other kinds of inter-personal ties as a basis for day-to-day relationships and loyalties. Local-level groupings tend to be of very mixed

composition, like the major confederacies themselves; most commonly, it is ties between women that structure the composition of the smallest groups of households.

Formal segmentary and hierarchical models of nomadic tribal society, as they are reproduced in academic and official analyses, appear to create rather than depict or discover structures. They are convenient as administrative blueprints, models for use by central government or by tribal chiefs. But they seldom represent tribal structure as it is seen and lived by ordinary nomads, whose stories of the origins of different tribal sections and the connections between them often differ radically from the official, chiefly version.[52] And they certainly do not explain the political behaviour of nomadic individuals: the networks of personal ties of loyalty and friendship, modes of negotiation and accommodation, the formation and maintenance of alliances and rivalries, and the emergence of leaders, including women (whether as wives or mothers of male leaders, or in their own right). These informal processes occur at all levels of nomadic society. At the level of tribe and confederacy they tend to be obscured if not suppressed by processes emanating from the state, following the official hierarchical political model. At the local level, on the other hand, these processes reflect real economic and social forces in nomadic society.

Tribal organisation in the old sense no longer exists in Iran. The centralised chiefdoms and confederacies, condemned as socially unjust and politically unnecessary and incompatible with a modern state structure, have finally been abolished, and the state, through the ONPI, has taken over the political and economic functions of the former tribal leaders. Government has redefined *'ashāyer*, *il* and *tāyfeh* to include no reference to tribal political organisation or chiefship, but specifically to imply both pastoral nomadism and the moral ties of kinship, or shared economic interest. It has in effect recognised the basic social and economic reality of nomad 'tribes'.

IDENTITY AND CULTURE

In foregoing sections, we have seen how pastoral nomads live in camps and local communities which reflect the economic and social exigencies of their daily lives. We have also discussed how they unite in wider and more inclusive patterns of organisation—for example on the basis of shared descent or allegiance to a leader—in defence of a common resource such as pasture land, or to mount a military offensive. Outside pressures—such as the state—may generate political unity and leaders in the form of tribes and chiefs, but the state itself creates tribes and chiefs as part of its formal structures of power and authority for the purpose of maintaining order and extracting taxes and military levies.

Tribes, then, are political, not ethnic or cultural groups. Nonetheless, nomads do feel wider cultural loyalties and a sense of identity with groupings larger than local communities on various bases, such as supposed common origins, shared cultural practices, and moral community.

The present nomadic population of Iran is very mixed in origins. The obvious ethnic and cultural complexity (as between Kurds, Lurs, Turks, Baluch, Arabs, etc.) is only part of the story. Every named ethnic population and tribal group is itself heterogeneous, as a result of both forced migration of whole populations, especially under rulers such as Shah 'Abbās Safavi, Nāder Afshār, Aqa Mohammad Qājār and others, and voluntary migration and exile of individuals and small groups. Heterogeneous origins may be evident in continuing ethno-linguistic diversity, for example in the relatively recently formed Khamseh tribal confederacy; or in memories of former diversity preserved by the now more or less culturally homogeneous components of a tribal group such as the Bāseri, the Shahsevan, the Qashqa'i or the Bakhtiāri; or it may be evident only in historical sources, present populations having, through generations of co-residence and intermarriage, assimilated to what seems now a single identity.

Trying to trace histories of tribal groups is a somewhat fruitless task, of little present-day relevance. Historical data on tribes often consist merely of records of the movements of names of groups and their chiefs, names which are little indication of either origins or present identity, despite appearances. As Basile Nikitine warned many years ago:

"The notions of ethnic unity and political organisation are no longer the same when one enters the field of Asian ethnology. At any one moment one can discern some units which now unite in the form of a vague confederation, and now, just as easily, split apart. Even names offer no consistency nor certainty ... [a tribal name] may be the name of the chief during a period of prosperity, which will in time give place to another. If we add the constant fission and fusion of groups through time, we soon see the difficulties faced by the researcher."[53]

The name of a particular chief (and his tribe) may indicate his paternal origin, but not that of his followers, who may be distant relatives but are more likely a flotsam and jetsam of varied origins, linked to each other and the leader, perhaps, by marriage, so that, after a generation or two of stability, shared customs and understandings may emerge, and one can begin to talk of ethnic-cultural homogeneity. In many cases, the fact that people have been in such close association will argue for what Lancaster terms 'must-have-been' kinship relations between them, but historically, most tribes began as organisations for the promotion of warfare and looting, and genealogies depicting supposed common descent appeared only later.[54]

At the same time, more important than kinship ideology *per se*, the defence of shared grazing rights is clearly a basis on which political groups, with or without leaders, can form. Such groups, and rivalries and factions between them, all run counter to any shared ideology and inhibit wider unity in the face of an outside threat.

Nomadic communities form at two main levels, commonly coinciding with groups formed on other principles. The basic nomadic local communities of 20 to 50 families, such as the Bāseri 'camps', have been mentioned earlier. In the major tribal systems of western Iran, these basic communities commonly join to form larger communities of one to several hundred families, groups in this case of some continuity, independent of leadership, with a strong degree of cultural identity and notions of common origins, maintained by endogamy and other cultural practices.[55] These communities, more 'imagined' than experienced, for which the English term 'clan' might be appropriate, may also constitute politically defined 'tribes', with jealously guarded territories and in many cases hereditary chiefs. Terms used by nomads themselves for the larger communities are hard to identify, particularly when they thus coincide with political and often state-sanctioned groups. Perhaps the most common are *tāyfeh* and *tireh*, both terms implying a group that is itself part or section of a yet larger grouping, such as an *il*: a tribal cluster, confederacy or chiefdom.

How do nomads define their own identities? Do people classified by administrators, historians, anthropologists or other outsiders as 'nomads' or 'tribes', actually identify themselves as such, or by some other category? The answers, as in other questions of identity, depend on context: indeed, on who is asking the question, in what situation, and for what purpose. What are the elements of their identity?

First, for many nomads, the most conscious element of their identity has always been their religion; whether in the case of those adhering to the majority Shiʿa faith of Iran, or the Sunni or Ahl-e Haqq minorities. Barth's account of the Bāseri supports a conventional Middle Eastern stereotype of nomads as lax Muslims, uninterested in the religion of the mullahs; but there are other, contrary stereotypes, such as that derived from Ibn Khaldun, according to which nomads have a simple, desert religion that brings them close to God, and makes them liable to respond quickly to the call to reform. More recent accounts of nomads, such as the Shahsevan and the Komāchi, show them to be sincere, committed Muslims.[56]

In the traditional context of political relations with the state, with non-tribal peasants or with members of other tribes, nomads would often identify themselves generically as 'tribespeople' (*ilāti*, *ʿashāyer*), or specifically by the name of a tribal group to which they belonged, depending on the situation. In this context, markers of identity were commonly martial symbols such as firearms and stories of past exploits. In the larger tribal groups, as we have seen, members of the chiefly classes supplied the warriors and did little herding work; they would be more likely than ordinary nomads or hired shepherds to maintain this tribal identity.

In economic and social contexts, where ordinary nomads share the distinctive experiences and problems of tent-dwellers, camp-dwellers, migrants and stock-keepers, as opposed to settled cultivators, traders, city-dwellers, a number of relevant identities (in different languages) are available. The tents themselves, the hearths around which families gather, tend to carry important symbolic meanings associated with this kind of identity, as do the herding skills and practices and aspects of the migration (see pp. 94, 207 and 265).

The richest area of symbolic potential for distinctive markers of identity is that of culture and ethnicity: language, history and tradition, religion, custom, and material culture. Cultural differences among the nomads of Iran have been much discussed, and the more visual and tangible aspects such as dwellings, textiles (pp. 203 ff & 225 ff), clothing, food and domestic paraphernalia have been displayed in museums and described in the more popular ethnographic literature. Material items such as tents and clothing are sometimes used as cultural markers by the nomads themselves, but linguistic differences appear to embody more important elements of cultural identity. Recently there has been a boom in publication of the poetry and other oral literature of nomads.

But there is one area of culture that holds for nomads (as for other people) deeply rooted, and usually unarticulated, meanings: the realm of ceremonies and rituals, in particular those associated with marriage. In basic outline, weddings and other ceremonies (described in some detail in many chapters, and depicted in some of the photographs) are very similar among the different nomad groups; but their richness, and much of the implicit importance for the participants, lies in the details which distinguish the customs and symbolism of each group, often of each clan and sometimes each local community. Nomadic identity seems to be encapsulated in the forms of music and dance practised at weddings—hence, in part, the reaction to the dance displays in the 1977 Isfahān Festival referred to earlier.

These various identities are not exclusive, but are alternatives, and individuals can and do claim more than one, shifting between them according to circumstances. Much daily interaction between individuals can be interpreted as the continuing negotiation of identities.

What determines nomads' changing self-perceptions? Following Barth, much hinges on relations between neighbouring groups, which can be manipulated by local or outside leaders. Where groups of different backgrounds are allied (for presumably practical reasons) they can adopt a common identity as pastoral nomads, playing down their ethnic-cultural differences, which may over time disappear. This ethnic convergence is more likely perhaps in the case of small groups or minorities adapting to majority or dominant groups, as has frequently occurred in Iranian tribal history, for example between Kurdish and Turkish groups at a local level. In other cases, there is a long history of ethnic rivalry, for example between Qashqa'i 'Turks', Bakhtiāri 'Lurs', and Khamseh 'Arabs'. This 'ethnic' rivalry often focuses on cultural differences such as wedding customs; it may also affect each group's perceptions of their religious identity, for example (between two Shiʿa groups) of their comparative piety.[57]

Much also depends on how far nomads share cultural, linguistic and religious traditions with the

left
A Qashqa'i girl with the fruiting branch of a date palm. Girls wear a smaller version of their mothers' dress and gradually acquire the different parts of their distinctive head-dress as they grow up. Amala tribe, autumn 1987.

rulers of the state, and on the changing political and economic realities of privilege and discrimination, in terms of social status, and, these days, access to jobs and contracts and government funding. Before the Pahlavis, the rulers were of tribal origins, and tribal identities carried some status in society. The Pahlavis attempted to abolish the tribes, and encouraged an urban contempt for rural and tribal peoples as dirty and ignorant savages, beneath attention. Those who were once proud to be 'tribespeople', led by chiefs and a threat to the state, either attempted to merge into the rural landscape as ordinary citizens, or became 'pastoral nomads', which at least carried the connotation of harmless, specialised, even valued producers.

This identity and that of Shi'a Muslims have become more respectable in the Islamic Republic, but dominant religious and nationalist values mean that the state is ambivalent in its attitude towards distinctive tribal (even in the redefined sense) and minority identities and cultural practices, such as those involving music and dancing and women's dress. Significant perhaps are recent reports (see Friedl, for example) of the 'privatisation' of weddings and much of the rest of daily life among the nomads; no longer are ceremonies and daily life based on community participation and values, rather they are focused on the individuals concerned, and have become private, exclusive and idiosyncratic affairs.[58]

NOMADS AND THE FUTURE

In 1860 Keith Abbott, British consul-general at Tabriz, commenting on government measures to curb the Shahsevan nomads of Moghān, of whom the Russians were complaining, made the following observations:

"I think it impolitic in the Persian Government to seek to render it's [sic] great nomad Tribes a stationary people. Persia is differently circumstanced to most other countries and the nature of it's climate, it's natural features and the general habits of the people require that it should possess a population which can adapt itself to variations of mountain and plain and draw from that condition of life resources which are in a great measure denied the fixed inhabitants. It is on these great pastoral communities that the population of the cities and plains nearly depend for their supplies of animal food—for the flocks—for the butter, cheese and other preparations from Milk which are so largely consumed in Persia and for many coarse but useful articles of woollen and other manufacture for which the produce of the fields and cities is exchanged. The Tribes are a further advantage to the country in consequence of their wealth in camels which afford a cheap means of conveyance for merchandise to the most distant parts; but these advantages are in great measure lost to the country when the tribes are compelled to renounce their nomadic condition to become cultivators of the soil—and the State in authorising these changes lessens it's resources in a military point of view—for whereas the Young men of the nomad Tribe are to a great extent available for military service, the duties and labour of the community being chiefly performed by the females, the labour of cultivating the soil must fall principally on the males—and no doubt also the hardiest races in Persia and the most valuable for military duties are the men of the wandering Tribes."[59]

These observations on the nature of nomadic pastoralism in Iran are remarkably modern in tone, and would have held good until quite recently as an assessment of the value of the nomad tribes and of the arguments against a policy of enforced settlement. Many of the arguments are still valid, and sectors of the modern administration are well aware of them.

Since the 1970s, Iran has seen widespread economic and social development and massive population growth. There have been improvements in communications, education, and other services, but also expansion of cultivation at the expense of pasture lands. Pastoralism continues to be a valuable mode of exploiting the national range lands, producing meat and other important commodities for the market, and nomadism is a rational mode of pastoralism under certain conditions, though it requires the support of a government willing to provide infrastructural and marketing facilities as well as controls, for example on overgrazing.

At the beginning of the Islamic Revolution of 1978–9, some educated young people of nomadic background mobilised forces within their own tribes against the chiefs, especially among the Bakhtiāri and the Qashqa'i. Young nomads with Islamic leanings associated themselves with the Islamic revolutionaries in the cities and argued for some kind of planning and organisation for nomadic peoples, and for representation at the highest levels in the new regime. These enthusiastic young men initiated major development plans in some nomadic areas, under the auspices of the Campaign for Reconstruction (*jehād-e sāzandegi*), though these plans were postponed after the onset of war with Iraq in 1980.

Before the Revolution there was an Organisation for Mobile Pastoralists (*sāzmān-e dāmdārān-e motaharrek*), but its brief is evident from the fact that it was part of the Ministry of Housing and Urban Development. After the Revolution this organisation was reformed and transferred to the Ministry of Agriculture, then in 1983 to the Campaign for Reconstruction (*jehād-e sāzandegi*, later a Ministry). Renamed the Organisation for the Nomadic Peoples of Iran (ONPI, see above), it was from 1986 to 1992 directed by an economist of Bakhtiāri origins, with the status of Deputy Minister, who also sat on the High Council of Nomads (*shurā-ye 'āli-ye 'ashāyer*), of which the Prime Minister, and later the President, was the head.

At the provincial level, where it is staffed partly by members of the tribes, ONPI provides infrastructural services and organises local and regional representation of the nomads. Other services for nomads, such as health, education, security and the control of pasture-lands, are organised through other Ministries, though the basic groundwork is done by ONPI. ONPI also conducts research, which it publishes in books and reports, and in the interesting quarterly journal *Zakhāyer-e enqelāb* (*Treasures of the Revolution*), started in 1987.[60]

Nomads initially had no great expectations of any improvement resulting from the Revolution. In practice, life has improved in several respects, largely thanks to the work of the Reconstruction Ministry and ONPI. In many nomad areas there are now roads, water and power supply, schools, bath-houses, veterinary services, health-care, shops, and co-operatives for selling pastoral produce and buying basic supplies. Nomads have greater control over their land, and are allowed both to farm and to build on it, which they were not before. The fact that the provision of services, and relations with government, are now in the hands of educated young men from their own tribes appears to have made a considerable difference to nomad attitudes to government.

Although in several quarters old ideas persist about the backwardness of the nomads and the need to settle them, the general improvement in their status means that many of the new generation in Iran, including people of nomad origins, value the nomads' way of life and their political and economic contribution to the country. ONPI, taking the perspective of the nomads and not that of the state, promotes an image of the nomads which is the opposite of that purveyed by the Pahlavi regime. Indeed, the murky histories of many nomad tribes as raiders, as threats to state security, and as agents of imperial powers, have been transformed into a glorious past as freedom-fighters against the oppressive Shahs and as frontier guards, not least in the recent war with Iraq.

Nomad settlement is no longer directly enforced, though government encourages it with some vigour. Meanwhile the growth in population means a continuing, indeed increasing, flow of spontaneous settlement. Wealthier nomads who have land, as well as the poorest who have nothing, are the most likely to settle, the former as farmers, the latter as migrant workers in the cities. The remaining nomad camps have as neighbours the herdsmen of wealthy village-based ex-nomads; but many large extended nomad families have diversified, with some members farming, others in trade or transport, and others continuing to migrate with the animals. The new roads have eased the seasonal migrations, which are increasingly conducted by truck and trailer—few transport camels are left.

Many former chiefs, deposed officially in the 1950s and 1960s, retained their role as patrons until the 1970s, and several returned to power briefly after the Revolution. But they and their families are now gone, many of them abroad, a few remaining only as private citizens, with some wealth but little or no influence. Authority in the tribes is now in the hands of elected councils of young enthusiasts loyal to the regime. Privileges that used to go to chiefly families now go to families of martyrs, mullahs and government officials. In a final reversal of Pahlavi policy, armed tribal militias are now charged with security in the nomad areas, and once again young nomads proudly carry arms along with their tribal clothes.

A major problem for the nomads continues to be access to pasture. Under the Pahlavis, the pastures were nationalised and traditional systems of grazing rights were abolished. Access is now regulated by a system of permits, which has not yet proved satisfactory. Schemes are under consideration for assuring pastoralists access to particular pastures on a basis regular enough to motivate them to conservation. Other, older, problems continue to be reported: the invasion and seizure of tribal territories by both village cultivators and city-based, non-nomadic commercial stock-raisers, and the consequent overgrazing and need for supplemental fodder supplies; extortion by some government representatives; escalating prices, for example for transport; and continuing usury from money-lending merchants. Generally, however, the nomads, at least in the major tribes, with their ability to produce at least some of their own food, appear to enjoy a rather better standard of living than many middle-class city dwellers.[61]

In September 1992, ONPI convened an international conference on Nomadism and Development at Shahr-e Kord near Isfahān, with co-sponsorship from FAO and other international bodies. In the discussions, many government officials expressed views on the future of the nomads that were positive, enlightened and ambitious, compared with those of other modern states with nomadic populations. There was heated debate between modernists (from ONPI and the Reconstruction Ministry) who wish to encourage and facilitate either nomadic pastoralism (and economic diversification) or guided settlement, according to the nomads' wishes; and traditionalists (mainly from the Plan and Budget Organisation and the Ministry of Agriculture) for whom settlement is the only 'solution' to what they see as the 'problem' of nomadism. But modernists and traditionalists were agreed on the undesirability of forced settlement because it would lead to further urban migration which the overcrowded cities cannot absorb. The modernists were building a high level of nomad participation (by men at least) into both the planning and the implementation of their development policies.

Also significant at the conference was evidence of shifts in the political culture of the Islamic regime: the earlier ban on music and dancing was relaxed, and nomadic women were conceded the right to dress in styles not conforming closely to urban 'Islamic' conventions. Once more, nomadic pastoral cultural practices and products are being promoted for their inherent interest and value as part of a rich national tradition, but this time there is greater respect for their living role in both past, present and future society. It remains to be seen how far these changes will affect the nomads and their perceptions of themselves. Preliminary indications are that, just as 'pastoral nomadism' has become a more respectable concept in government and society at large, so also 'settlement' has become increasingly acceptable to nomads who once would have rejected it as threatening the very foundations of their identity.[62]

This essay began by identifying paradoxes in the images of nomads in Iran. Nomads themselves today have ambivalent images of themselves and their past. On the one hand they are nostalgic for what they see as a golden age of abundance, when tribal values of independence and martial valour were respected (see Bradshaw, Friedl and Loeffler, all on the Lur),[63] and complain of the present degradation of the environment, the growth of population, the disappearance of the game, the expansion of cultivation, the intrusion of ineffective development projects, and so forth; but they also recall difficult times of climatic disaster and oppression by both chiefs and governments.

Nomads in Iran are not, and never have been, backward relics of primitive society. They have for centuries been very much part of wider economic and political systems, and have made informed and rational, if sometimes heavily constrained, choices about their involvement in the world. Today they are no different from other citizens in wanting to be part of the modern world, not least by acquiring some of its material trappings such as radios, televisions, refrigerators, cars and trucks—all of which could be found in nomad camps even in the 1960s.

But such material changes do not automatically bring radical changes in social forms and cultural practices at the camp level. Family structures, gender relations, and even herding patterns and practices, are to some extent adaptations to pastoral and nomadic conditions which continue to prevail, and they are likely to change slowly among those pursuing the nomadic way of life.

Despite the improved social status which nomads are now accorded, the overall process in the twentieth century—with the radical expansion of the world economic-political system, the revolution in communications and the military power available to the state—has been a decisive and irreversible turn to the ascendancy of settled society. The long-term future of pastoral nomadism in Iran, as elsewhere, must remain in doubt.[64]

A Shahsevan camp high on mount Savalan near Qotur Su where there are hot mineral springs. Spring 1984.

MOUNTAIN NOMADISM IN IRAN

Eckart Ehlers

The forms of animal husbandry and pastoralism practised in Iran are a response to the specific environmental conditions prevailing in the country's mountainous regions. These mountains more or less surround a central arid area, which includes the deserts of the Dasht-e Kavir and the Dasht-e Lut. To the north are the Alborz and Khorāsān ranges, with Damāvand, the highest elevation in the country (18,602 feet/5,670 metres); in the east the volcanoes of the Kuh-e Bazmān (11,450 feet/3,490 metres) and Kuh-e Taftān (over 13,000 feet/4,000 metres); in the south the Makrān ranges along the Gulf coast; and in the west the Zāgros with Zardeh Kuh (over 14,800 feet/4,500 metres).

The mountains provide two types of habitat for pastoralism, one in the high sub-alpine regions and the other in the foothills. The high sub-alpine meadows and grasslands are snow-covered in winter and spring and conditions are harsh. Grazing is restricted to late spring, summer and early autumn, and there is little agriculture and permanent settlement. The forelands, foothills and intramontane basins are mostly semi-arid steppes and steppe-like grasslands. Here the grazing is best in winter and the agricultural potential is limited by scarcity of suitable arable land and scanty rainfall.

It is the great achievement of the nomads in the mountain belt that crosses Turkey, Iran and Afghanistan to have successfully combined the use of these high and low habitats into an economically fully viable form of animal husbandry, so that in former times mobile pastoralism was a flourishing mature economic system that coexisted with the agricultural and urban economies.

There is not much usable land in Iran. The total land area is 636,296 square miles (1,648,000 square km), and only 15 per cent is considered actually or potentially useful for agriculture. Another 15 per cent is usable for forestry and pasture (Figure 1). The type of land for these latter uses is so vulnerable that even slight misuse of it has devastating consequences. Loss of vegetation can lead to wind erosion, gullying and desertification. Figure 1 attempts to give a general picture of the current pattern of land use in Iran.

LAND DISTRIBUTION IN IRAN (APPROXIMATE)

Figure 1

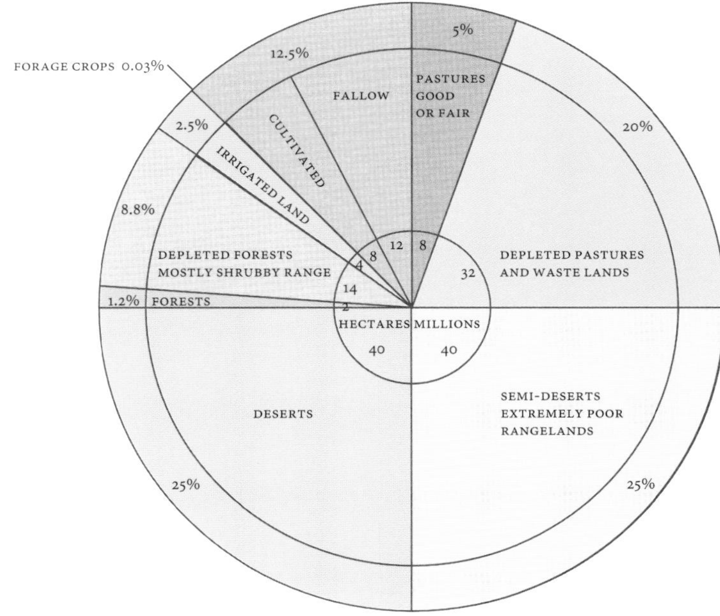

Iran's population is growing rapidly, and approximately half of it continues to live on the land as peasant farmers or nomads. Around 1900 the population was only about 10 million; by 1950 this had increased to about 17.5 million; and by 2000 it was approximately 70 million.

At the 1986 census there was a non-settled population of 215,000, which is less than 0.5 per cent of the general population. A more detailed survey by the Organisation for the Nomadic Peoples of Iran, part of the Ministry of Rural Construction, gave a figure for 1986/87 of over 180,000 families in tribal lands. Of this figure more than 100,000 nomadic families were living in the west, and there were sometimes remarkably large differences between the numbers in the summer pastures (*yaylaq* in Turkish, *sarhad* in Persian) and the winter pastures (*qeshlaq* in Turkish, *garmsir* in Persian). Large-sized groups of nomads were still living in the provinces of Esfahān, Fārs, Kordestān, Lorestān, Kermānshāh and Ilām. There were about 20,000 families living in the southern parts of Kermān, again with considerable differences between the sizes of the summer and winter populations, for example, 5,830 families in yaylaq compared to only 3,621 in qeshlaq in the shahrestan of Bāft, and 5,562 and 3,321 in the Kahnuj administrative division. Approximately 20,000 nomads were living in Baluchestān/Zahedān.

The present-day mountain nomads follow an unvarying yearly cycle that they have developed to combine the use of summer and winter pastures, and so maximise the size of their flocks. The following is their yearly schedule:

March to beginning May:	Migration from winter to summer pastures.
May to August/September:	Stay in summer pastures.
End August to November:	Migration from summer to winter pastures.
November to mid-March:	Stay in winter pastures.

Within this general pattern there is an almost infinite variety of adaptations and survival strategies.

Archeological and anthropological evidence suggests that forms of mobile and nomad-like pastoralism existed in Iran's mountain belt in pre- and early historic times. Zagarell (1975, 1982) has analysed early cultures in the Zāgros and concludes that the forms of migratory transhumance

MODEL OF THE RURAL ECONOMY IN 2ND AND 3RD MILLENNIUM BC (AFTER PULLAR 1977)

Figure 2

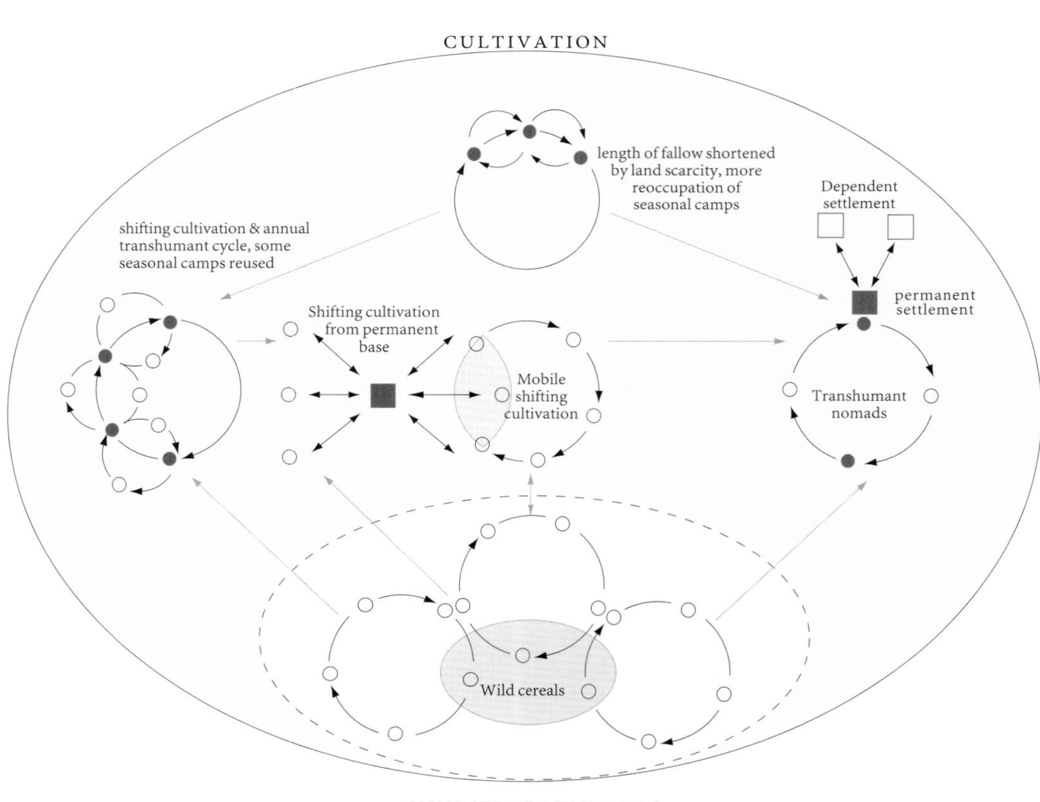

Temporary camp
Seasonal camp
Permanent settlement
Dependent Settlement
Area of friction

used point to a mixed economy of agriculture and animal husbandry as the basis of rural economies (cf. Pullar 1977). Figure 2 shows how this operated in the third and second millenniums BC. The resemblance to contemporary transhumant and nomadic forms of land use in the high mountains of Iran is striking.

The traditional nomadic way of life in Iran as described above is however changing under the impact of several powerful influences, namely degradation of the natural environment, population pressure, expansion of the road network and a series of land reform measures. Deforestation, changes in land use and overgrazing in many parts of the country have led to a critical reduction of the natural vegetation cover, exposing the soil to wind and water erosion. One effect is that slopes are being gullied by rain and snow-melt. The increasing rural population encroaches on traditional pastures for agricultural purposes and diminishes the traditional economic basis of nomadism. The development of roads in many parts of the country has brought about an increased use of trucks and pickups. These developments have greatly reduced some nomads' transportation function in society. And finally land reform measures under the Shah, and other legislation, have greatly reduced the nomads' traditional mobility. Actually, in some ways the improvements in transport have helped the nomads. For instance, road transport of sheep and goats has helped to put an end to permanent quarrels with villagers over grazing rights during migrations, and to circumvent the legal measures that affect their mobility.

The nomads' way of life is changing at an ever-increasing pace under these pressures, and new forms of social structure and spatial behaviour are appearing. Large tribal segments are moving into the cities; mixed economies are appearing; there is sedentarisation in either yaylaq or qeshlaq; and traditional migratory patterns are being abandoned due to the transformation of grazing areas into farmland. The German geographer Hütteroth (1973) has attempted to develop a general model of the causes and mechanisms behind the changes taking place in the types of nomadism and semi-nomadism found in the mountains and plateaux of south-west Asia, and some of his findings are shown in Figures 4 a–c. They point to the fact that traditional mountain nomadism is changing from a mobile to a more or less semi-sedentary life-style almost everywhere in the mountain belt of south-west Asia.

PUSH AND PULL FACTORS FOR NOMADIC SEDENTARISATION

Figure 3

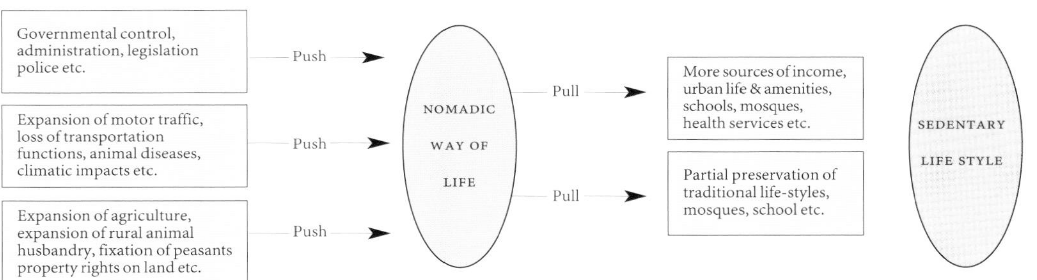

There are both push and pull factors (Figure 3) at work in the causes and mechanisms of change. Push factors are what force the nomads to change their traditional life-style, and pull factors are what attracts nomads and leads them voluntarily to give up their mobile way of life in favour of an urban or rural existence. The main push factor is the government's efforts over a long time to sedentarise the nomads. Bloody military campaigns, especially under Rezā Shah (1925–41), have been carried out in order to break the power of the nomadic tribes and to enforce their sedentarisation. Under Mohammad Rezā Shah (1941–79) the effects of the so-called 'White Revolution' had a tremendous effect on the remaining forms of nomadism. The transfer of land to village ownership especially led to a considerable expansion of agriculture and to an increase of rural shepherding comparable to Hütteroth's 'short-range semi-nomadism of mountain villagers'. This development was bound to cause conflict with the nomads, whose traditional land rights and uses were thereby severely threatened.

The urban pull factors include not only the broad range of urban infrastructures such as schools, hospitals, mosques, hamams and other services, but also the opportunities for jobs of different kinds and professional careers. The pleasant distractions of urban life are also a major pull factor for many nomads.

The rural pull factors influence those nomads and tribal people who prefer rural environments. For them village life offers a great number of positive attractions. Besides the basic public installations such as schools or mosques there is the chance to preserve at least some elements of traditional pastoralism. For example, they can continue animal husbandry on a reduced scale, including even the use of the traditional yaylaq or qeshlaq. This means that for at least part of the year they

MODEL OF MOUNTAIN NOMADISM AND ITS STAGES OF DECAY (AFTER HÜTTEROTH)

Figure 4

MOUNTAIN NOMADISM UP TO THE MIDDLE OF THE 19TH. CENTURY

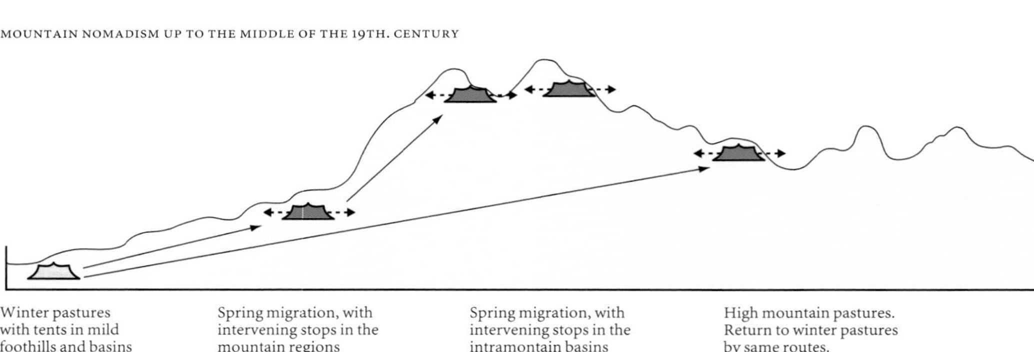

Winter pastures with tents in mild foothills and basins

Spring migration, with intervening stops in the mountain regions

Spring migration, with intervening stops in the intramontain basins

High mountain pastures. Return to winter pastures by same routes.

Tents	Houses
summer	
winter	
year round	

Form and direction of migration in spring

- Whole tribe or village
- Owner of large flocks & families
- Individual flock owners

DIFFERENT STAGES OF DECAY OF MOUNTAIN NOMADISM

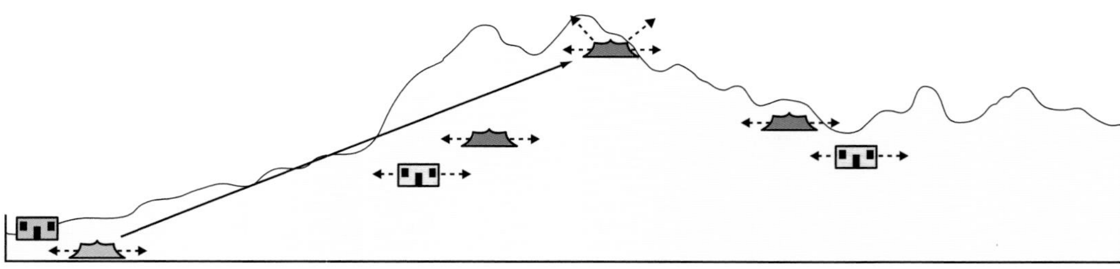

Fixed settlements with agriculture in the foot hills: first by poorer tribal groups or by wealthy families after land purchase

Partial sedenterisation in the mountains or at their fringes with changes towards forms of semi-nomadism

Some groups maintain mountain nomadism

Partial sedenterisation in the mountains or at their fringes with changes towards forms of semi-nomadism

ADVANCED STAGE OF DECAY OF MOUNTAIN NOMADISM

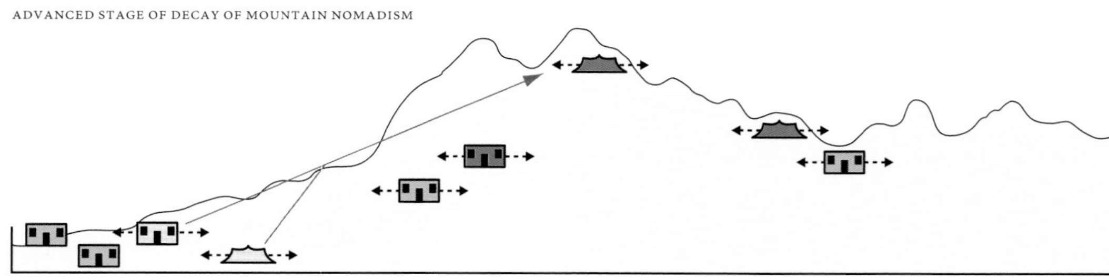

Fixed settlements in the foothills amidst or close to other population groups. Some families only have a fixed winter settlement and in summer migrate with their flocks and tents to the mountains. Other families continue to live in tents summer and winter either for lack of opportunities to settle or because they trade as hawkers

Settlement in the mountains associated with yaylaq peasantry: animal husbandry with firm summer houses

Settlement in the mountains associated with a yaylaq peasantry: animal husbandry with tents

can live traditionally, although growing competition for grazing rights from the short-range semi-nomadism of mountain villagers and pastoralising peasants poses a severe threat to this form of adaptation to present-day pressures.

Traditional nomadism displayed great variability and its reduction to the few basic types of Hütteroth's model (Figures 4 a–c) is a necessary but questionable simplification. In other words nomads are so versatile that typologies of their activities are difficult, if not impossible. Any attempt at formulating a model of nomadism has to take account of the versatility of the different nomadic tribes in their use of land, their ability to alter their patterns of migration and the differing ecological and economic circumstances they encountered. In short, the model has to encompass

PHASE MODEL OF NOMADIC SEDENTARISATION

Figure 5

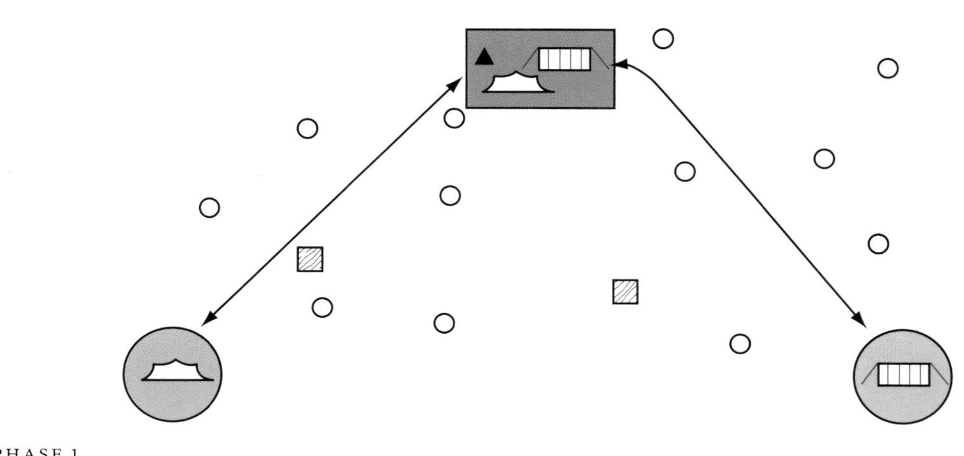

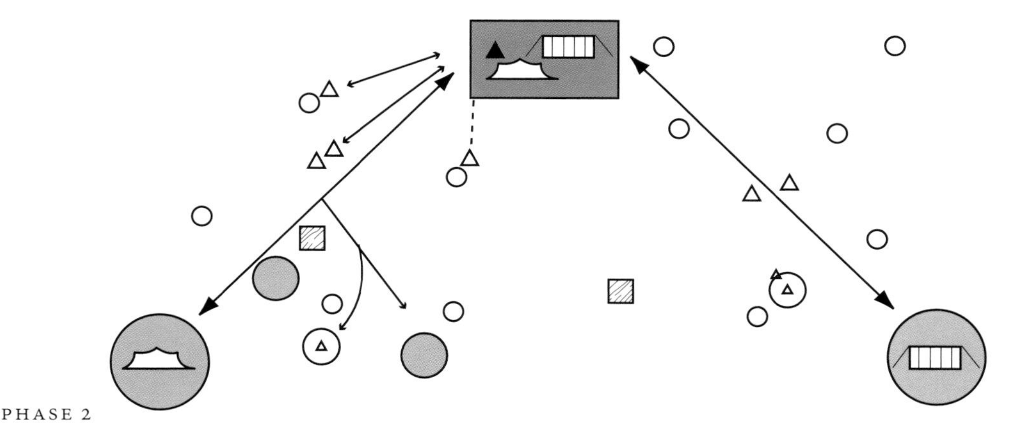

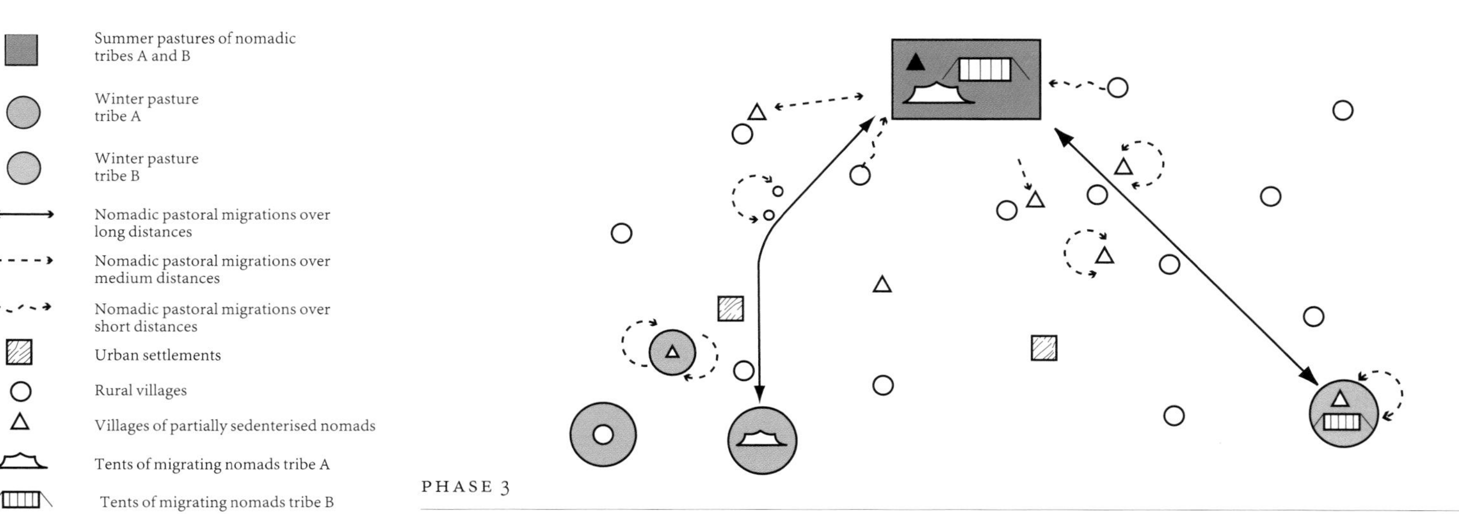

the nomads' potential for 'virtually infinite recombination' (Dyson-Hudson 1972: 26) of these different variables.

Nevertheless in practice such efforts of categorisation are useful, and in this introduction to the subject an attempt is made to represent the decline of Iranian mountain nomadism in the form of a three-phase model, into which such variables as migrational behaviour, settlement forms and patterns and economic activities are incorporated (Figure 5). The intention is to summarise the general evolutionary trends of recent tribal developments in Iran.

Phase 1 represents 'pure' or real mountain nomadism in which the nomads have no specific and pronounced contact with villagers or city dwellers. It is really Figure 4a in another form. In this phase migrations of up to several hundred kilometres are made between the summer pastures in the mountains and the winter pastures in the lowlands. The tent is used for housing all year and animal husbandry is the means of livelihood.

Of course this picture of traditional mountain nomadism is also too simplistic. The nomads have always engaged in other economic activities besides animal husbandry and have never been completely without contact with settled people. Actually these activities and contacts were essential to their existence and survival as nomads. They produced and sold their milk, cheese, meat and carpets in the cities and bought in the bazaars the tea, sugar, iron tools and other things they needed and could not do without.

Contact with settled people during migration was almost unavoidable, and was not always friendly. There were quarrels and fierce fighting over grazing rights and trespassing on agricultural land. And the central government again and again interfered with the nomads, often forcing whole tribes to settle down or transferring them to other parts of the country sometimes for political reasons (Perry 1975).

Phase 2 describes the partial breakdown of traditional nomadism, which is brought about by the encroachment of agriculture on to traditional pastures, the development of animal husbandry by settled villagers and the attractions of urban life. In this phase migrational behaviour, settlement patterns and economic activities are varied and combined in many new and different ways.

Migrational behaviour is particularly affected by the encroachment of agriculture. The nomads are forced either to look for alternative grazing areas or to develop new forms of economic relationship with the villages and towns. This is particularly true in the low-lying areas of qeshlaq, where scarcity of grazing can become very severe, causing the originally extensive tribal areas to shrink into a number of isolated pockets of grazing separated either by villagers who have occupied the winter pastures with their own herds, or by settled tribal families. In the face of these difficulties the nomads are increasingly forced to settle during the winter months. The tent is abandoned in favour of solid housing built either on traditional camping grounds along the tribal migration routes or in new settlements in qeshlaq itself, or on the fringes of rural villages—or even in towns. Tents remain the predominant form of housing in summer pastures.

As the areas of available pasture shrink, the nomads reduce the size of their herds. Consequently their income level falls and they have to find other ways of making a living. New and varied forms of economic activity begin to appear. They turn their own pastures into fields or combine traditional mountain nomadism with different agricultural activities. These activities can include seasonal wage-labour for landlords, a broad range of combinations of agriculture and animal husbandry and informal cash earning activities in towns and cities. These economic adaptations promote a willingness in the nomads to change from a migratory to a sedentary life-style and to settle permanently (Figure 5, phase 2).

Phase 3 represents the more or less complete breakdown of traditional mountain nomadism. This stage is reached when the land in yaylaq is transferred to other uses than pasturage or when competition from rural animal husbandry reduces the area of grazing available to the nomads to a critically low level. When this happens the last bonds of tribal unity are broken, traditional migrations cease and the socio-economic structure of tribal life collapses. The collective life of the tribe is replaced by that of individual families who little by little become members of the predominantly rural peasant society around them. Figure 5 (phase 3) represents this final stage, showing how permanent rural settlements increase in number and density while migrations take place over short distances with small flocks, taking on an almost transhumant character.

INTEGRATIVE DEVELOPMENTS OF PEASANT AGRICULTURE AND NOMADIC ANIMAL HUSBANDRY IN IRAN

Figure 6

Since the 1960s, attracted by the possible economic returns, Iranian villagers and city dwellers have steadily increased the size and number of their herds, thus eroding the traditional territories of the nomads. As a result, the nomads have themselves turned to agriculture in the hope of boosting their own incomes. Both developments have led to increased use of the limited and fragile land of the pastures, increased competition between these two peoples, and even hostilities. It seems, then, that in Iran the traditional mountain nomad and traditional peasant farmer, who originally had very dissimilar life-styles, are moving towards more or less identical forms of land use and patterns of agriculture in combination with transhumant animal husbandry (Figure 6). Indeed, this process has already gone so far in some areas that it is becoming almost impossible to guess the historical origin of a particular rural household.

Whatever the ultimate fate of nomadism in Iran, whether extinction or some form of limited survival, it is still important to the economic life of the country today. Large areas remain heavily dependent on the nomads' production of meat, cheese and yoghurt, and their sheep wool and carpets are in high demand.

It would be very regrettable if this way of life disappeared. Contemporary life would be so much the poorer in the absence of these vividly colourful and picturesque people (their outward appearance a stark contrast to the hardships they face in supplying their needs). Moreover, the disappearance of their wonderfully skilful combining of the limited resources of summer and winter pastures, without destroying either, would leave us lacking a much-needed living example of how to exist without overtaxing natural resources. Sadly, current trends and developments seem to be against this survival.

THE BAKHTIĀRI

Jean-Pierre Digard

Making a goat-skin container. Having soaked the goat skin in a solution of oak bark to tan the leather, she is about to clean it and scrape off the hairs. She wears typical items of jewellery: a long chain with glass beads hanging from the pins used to fix the veil to the headband, a necklace with cowrie shells, bracelets and rings. Winter camp at Susan, north of Izeh, 1986.

TERRITORY AND WAY OF LIFE

The Bakhtiāri and the Qashqā'i are the two largest tribal groups (*il*) of Iran. The Bakhtiāri tribe numbers about 600,000 members, of whom about a third were nomads in the 1970s. They are Twelver Shi'ites, and speak Lori, which like Persian is part of the north-western group of Iranian languages. Settled Bakhtiāri are to be found in the towns, and in many of the farming villages, from Feridān and Chahār-Mahāl to Esfahān, and in Khuzestān as far south as Ahvāz. Other settled members of the tribe, and nomads in particular, live in the tribal area (*khāk-e il-e Bakhtiāri*) which covers approximately 75,000 square km from the River Dez (from Shushtar and Rāmhormoz) in the west, as far as (but not including) Dārān and Shahr-e Kord in the east, including the great bend in the Kārun River and the upper reaches of the Zāyandeh Rud.

The traditional Bakhtiāri way of life is an example of the Turco-Iranian great nomadism that arose in the Zāgros mountains from the thirteenth century onwards, following the Mongol invasion. The present pattern for this way of life, or at least the pattern it followed until very recently, was established in the eighteenth century as a reaction to growing fiscal and administrative pressure from the Iranian authorities.

The Bakhtiāri nomads move between high summer pasture (*eylāgh*) on one or other side of the Zardeh-Kuh range (highest point 4,548 m, 15,000 ft) and winter pasture (*garmsir*) in the western foothills of the Zāgros, on the edge of the plains of Khuzestān. The ecological frontier of the two zones corresponds roughly to the course of the River Bāzoft. Bakhtiāri territory therefore belongs to two administrative provinces—the summer pasture land to the Chahār-Mahāl and Bakhtiāri province and the winter pastures to Khuzestān.

The distances covered in the main seasonal migrations (*bār*) vary according to the subtribe involved, but can cover as much as 300 km. They take place in spring, when the nomads go up into the mountains, and in autumn, when they descend. There is more grazing to be found on the spring migration and it takes place in more favourable climatic conditions. The journey lasts 15 to 45 days and the pace of travel is more leisurely than the autumn migration which takes 8 to 30 days.

The itineraries followed never vary. Only eight to eleven passes (marked *a* to *k* on the map) through the Zāgros are negotiable, according to season, and the nomads set up their encampments at the same places in them each time. These routes are famous for their extreme awkwardness. They lead across snow-bound passes, through narrow rock-strewn gorges, where the animals have to be hauled through one by one, over steep ridges where the rock has been polished smooth over the centuries by their regular passage, and across rivers (the Bāzoft or the Kārun) swollen in spring by melted snow from the mountains, which they must swim or cross on rafts constructed from branches strapped to inflated animal skins. All of these cause innumerable accidents to the tribesfolk and to their animals.

Each stage is short, seldom more than 10 km a day, because the animals need time to graze as they go. Once everything is packed up and the pack animals are laden, the women and a few men go on ahead to install the next camp and set up the kitchen. Sometimes in the autumn they may find that the water source in their chosen spot has been polluted or has unexpectedly dried up, in which case they have to go on to the next stopping place, which might be in another direction, hastening their step to reach it before nightfall.

The seasonal transfer is always made necessary by the cold and snow up on the *eylāgh,* the summer pastures, from October to April, and by the great heat and drought that hold sway in the *garmsir* (literally 'hot spot') from April to September; in addition, the grazing in both places is exhausted after several months of intensive use. This is why, in spite of the difficulties, each trip is usually awaited with impatience and undertaken with cheerfulness. The transfer represents a transition to better things and to new surroundings, a temporary break in routine which is accompanied by festivities, new and unfamiliar encounters, and a renewal of sociability.

This movement of the whole group is true nomadism, as distinct from transhumance, which consists of the transfer of flocks with their shepherds only. The economic activity of the tribe, and in particular animal husbandry (see below) hinges entirely on this nomadic cycle. Until a viable replacement for nomadism is found, such as the accommodation of flocks in one place plus the cultivation of fodder crops, and direct or reverse transhumance, it remains the only method of maintaining stock raising in the region at a relatively satisfactory level.

SOCIAL ORGANISATION

One of the singular features of Bakhtiāri social organisation is the subdivision of the tribe into interlocking social units, which segments lineages into an exceptional number of different levels. Each tent houses a conjugal family (*khānewāda*). An encampment (*māl,* a word used to designate both the encampment itself and the possessions gathered together into the encampment) comprises 3 to 12 tents and represents the extended family (*tash*, *owlād*). While they are on the move, related camps group together in nomadic units (*tira*) of about one hundred people. The *tira* are grouped into *tāyefa*, of which the largest, the Mowri, the Bābādi or the Gandali, number about 25,000 members, and the *tāyefa* are grouped into *bāb* or *buluk*. Each *bāb* belongs to one of the two *bakhsh* or *qesmat*, Haft-Lang and Chahār-Lang, which form the Bakhtiāri tribe (*il*).

The whole is often quoted as representing a patrilineal system of descent. In reality the groups making up the different levels are not all of equal value and do not carry equal weight in the general organisation of the tribe. The basic social units (from the conjugal family to the *tira*) are extended families, whose individual members are classified according to three basic principles.

PRINCIPAL SUBDIVISIONS OF THE BAKHTIĀRI

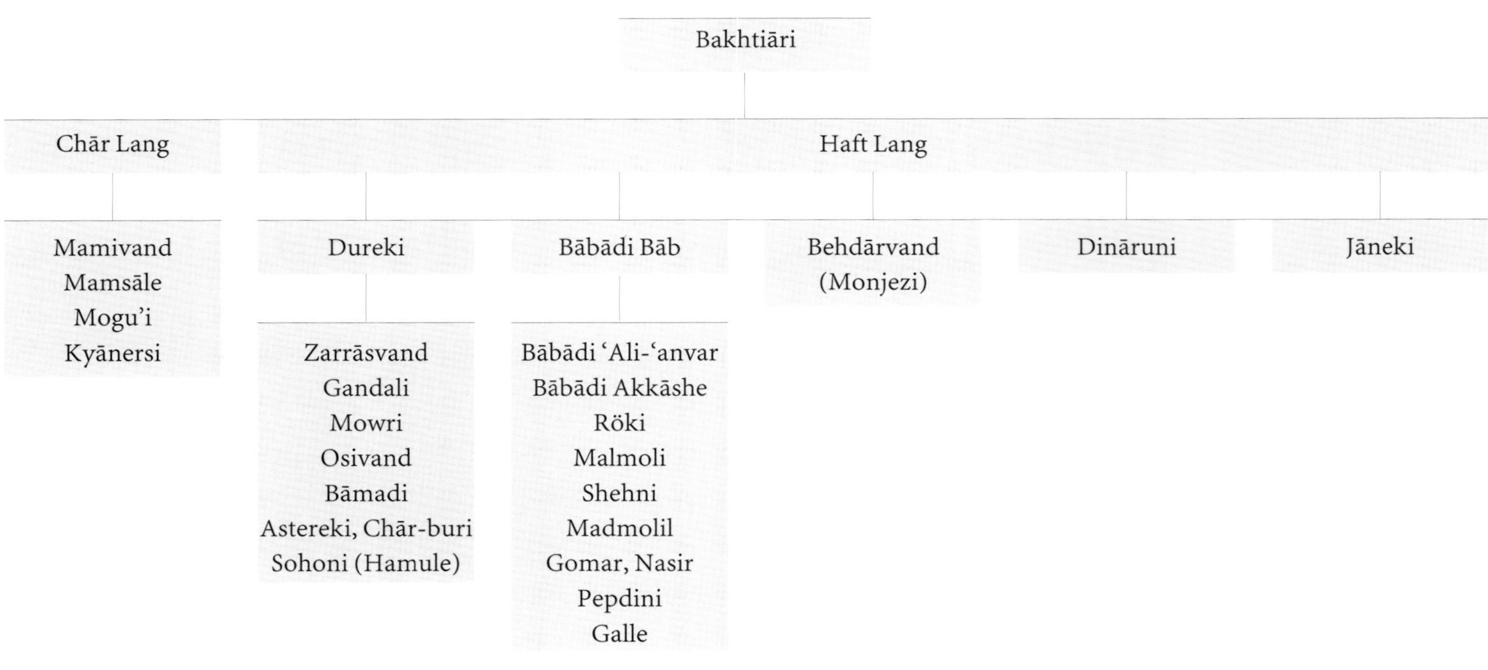

1. The rule of patrilineal descent (or patrilinearity) dictates that membership of the group is transmitted from father to son,
2. A preference for marriages between patrilateral parallel cousins, the offspring of two brothers (i.e. marriage between a man and his father's brother's daughter, *tātezā* in Lori). This preference amongst the Bakhtiāri has been shown to be put into practice in 18–43% of instances, varying according to which group is concerned.
3. Residence requirements obliging the bride to move from her father's to her husband's home (virilocality) or the home of her husband's father if he is still living in his parental home (patrilocality).

The social units described above provide real security and strength in cases of conflict between groups, and mutual support in daily agricultural labour. Minding the animals, shearing, milking, sowing and harvesting are all undertaken collectively by the male members of each encampment, or of each *tira* when they are on the move. Nomad camps and *tira* are scattered autonomous units living separately from one another. The fact that they are scattered means that water sources and grazing are not subject to too much pressure. This is one of the most important factors in the survival of Bakhtiāri society.

Presumed blood relationships play an important but to some extent indirect part in the definition of the largest units (from the *tāyefa* to the *il*). At this level most genealogies are imaginary, answering the Bakhtiāri need to express an *a posteriori* justification of such events as a change of political affiliation in terms of blood relationship. These large units only rarely function as support groups. For instance when there is serious conflict the preferential relationships that bind some of the units carry an obligation to come to each other's assistance. These relationships are known as 'blood of the cudgel', *khin-chu*, from the expression *khin ze chu pöy niemon*, 'blood never fades from the cudgel'.

The large units also fulfil a permanent role in the integration of the basic units, in particular their territorial integration. Despite the independent nature and dispersal of their camps, the members of the basic units are willing to move to another pasture if one has been over-grazed or to alter their route if a pass is obstructed. This mobility is guaranteed by the existence of the large social units, to which large tracts of land belong—land that may either have been appropriated collectively or may be in inalienable joint ownership. The use of the land is divided between the lineages.

ORGANISATION AND POLITICAL HISTORY

Another distinctive feature of Bakhtiāri tribal organisation is the existence—apparently very unusual in lineal systems—of a highly centralised and hierarchical political system. Until the 1950s, power was entirely in the hands of an *ilkhāni* (supreme chief of the tribe) assisted by an *ilbagi*. Later, power was distributed pyramidally through the various levels of society between the *kalāntar* of the *tāyefa*, the *katkhodā* of the *tira* and the *tash*, and the *rish-safid* (white beards) of the *owlād*. These leaders looked after law and order, dispensed justice and acted as intermediaries between the tribe and the outside world in general, and with the Iranian authorities and their agents in particular. Their most vital function, however, and the one with the most serious consequences for the Bakhtiāri, was to co-ordinate the migration of the nomads and to arbitrate in disputes resulting from pressure on grazing land and water sources during migration.

Originally performed as a service to the tribe, this function later became a source of economic and social privilege (access to the best grazing land, patronage, etc.) which favoured the emergence of a khan class as distinct from the simple nomads designated by the name *lor*. This is not the same as the ethnonym Lor given to the tribes inhabiting Lorestān, the neighbouring region to the north-west, on the far side of the River Dez. Once the tribal political structure had shifted away from its original function as a co-ordinating body it turned progressively into a means of exploitation and control, with its own system of taxation and troop conscription and led to the formation of political units (*basteh*) operating on behalf of the khan.

The gradual concentration of Bakhtiāri tribal authority was also favoured by external factors. One of the most influential of these, from the medieval period onwards, was the granting of crown lands (*khāleseh*) by the Iranian central government to the khan for his sole use as a reward for loyal service, military in particular. Unlike the tribal lands that were acquired collectively and used for pastoral purposes, these privately owned lands could be cultivated, and their ownership was

A group of men wearing their best clothes assembled for an audience with a chief near Shimbar, the mid-point of their migration route, 1987.

undoubtedly responsible for the semi-monopoly over agricultural produce, cereals in particular, enjoyed for years by the Bakhtiāri leaders. Many nomads were completely dependent on them for food. The economic influence that possession of these agricultural lands allowed the khans to exert over the tribe was further reinforced by the tribe's regular need to dispose of any demographic surplus it might have. Pastoral nomads facing disaster, who would otherwise be condemned to exile, were able to find settled employment on these estates, and provided the land-owning khans with a plentiful, inexpensive and exceptionally submissive labour force. These employees were 'subject' (*ra'iyyat*), as distinct from the simple nomads (*lor*), who might be very poor but who were technically free. These settled labourers were the poor relations, the victims of the nomadic agro-pastoral system, but at the same time were one of the key factors in its survival.

A second key element in the creation of an independent Bakhtiāri tribal authority was direct intervention by the Iranian government in the appointment and dismissal of tribal chiefs, especially from the eighteenth century onwards. In an attempt to achieve greater control of the tribes and the provinces, the Qājār Shahs drew up a system of indirect government that relied partly on the tribal khans, whose authority was officially sanctioned. They were invested with new powers: the administration and maintenance of law and order, tax collection and the levying of troops for the Shah's army. As long as they remained loyal to the ruler they were heaped with honours, but at the slightest lapse they would be mercilessly hunted down. As a precaution, the Shah would hold one or more members of the family hostage at his court.

Thus the last great Chahār-Lang chief, ʿAli Mardān Khān, was declared an outlaw (*yāghi*) and taken prisoner in 1841, leaving the way open to his Haft-Lang rivals, one of whom, Hoseyn Qoli Khān, was appointed *nāzem* of the Bakhtiāri by the Shah in 1862 and *ilkhāni* in 1867. However, in 1882 the Shah became uneasy at the power Hoseyn Qoli Khān had acquired and had him assassinated and replaced by his brother Emām Qoli Khān (nicknamed Hājji Ilkhāni). From then on, almost until the abolition of the title of khan by the Iranian government in 1956, successive descendants of one or other of the two brothers were the leaders of the tribe. This was also the origin of the division of the Bakhtiāri into partisans (*bastegān*) of the Ilkhāni or the Hājji Ilkhāni—a division which, paradoxically and in spite of appearances, had the effect of protecting the unity of the tribe from the schemes and intrigues of the central authorities. The *basteh* were formed between 1894 and 1912 following a series of agreements reached by the two branches of the khan family. The representation of each family within the *basteh* was monitored regularly to check that its members were being recruited from both lineages equally, thus ensuring that neither family became too dominant. This avoided a split into two warring groups within the tribe. To sum up, the *basteh* had the double aim of preventing the families of the great khans (*khavānin-e bozorg*) from losing control of power, and of preventing one branch of the family from gaining more power than the other. This method of monitoring factionalism is undoubtedly one of the most original features of Bakhtiāri social organisation, and has no exact parallel in any other society in the world.

Shaving is a rather new fashion and mainly confined to the younger men. The moustache is commonly regarded in Iran as an outward sign of adherence to the traditional values of Islam.

right
A Bakhtiāri man in traditional dress. The beard and moustache are as much a feature of Bakhtiāri cultural identity as their distinctive clothing.

The third and last factor reinforcing the power of the Bakhtiāri khans was the British presence in Khuzestān from 1857, initially in connection with their Indian interests. The building of the Lynch Road between Ahvāz and Esfahān, via Izeh and Ardal in the southern part of Bakhtiāri territory, and in 1908 the discovery and early exploitation of oil at Masjed-e Soleymān, deprived several thousands of nomads of their traditional winter pastures. The Shehni, who still constitute the majority of the Bakhtiāri population of Masjed-e Soleymān, lost their lands in this way. All these events, however, were a godsend for the *khavānin-e bozorg*. In exchange for guarantees of safety for the oil installations and personnel, the ruling families received about 5% of shares in the First Exploitation Company, and benefited over more than twenty-five years from the profits of the Anglo-Iranian Oil Company. When the company ceased trading in 1951, they received compensation. Once the Bakhtiāri leaders had been won over by the British with the promise of economic and political advantages—and this was strongly criticised in Iran—they could if the need arose be relied on for support against the central authorities. In 1907–9 Mohammad ʿAli Shāh Qājār failed to appear as committed to the support of British interests as he had previously been and was obliged to submit to the imposition of a constitution. Then, under pressure from a contingent of five thousand Bakhtiāri cavalry and other troops sent to storm Tehrān in July 1909, he was forced to abdicate. The military assistance of the tribal khans was subsequently rewarded with several ministerial portfolios, and they were even given the opportunity, which they let slip in the end, of seizing the throne of Iran.

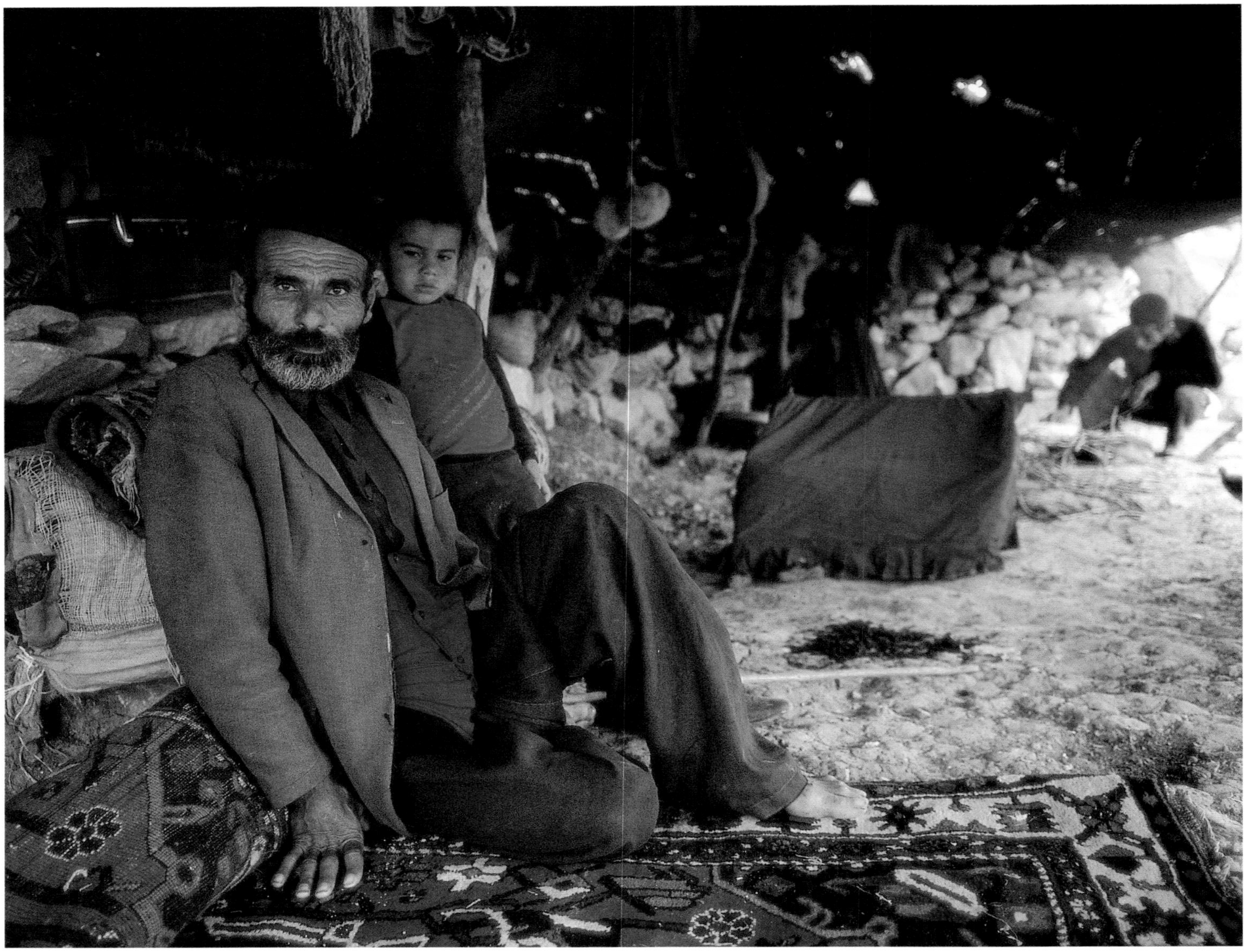

above
Inside the black tent the area to the left (looking in) is reserved for the men. Seated on a knotted-pile carpet this man leans against the low stone wall (*chol*) with its pile of bedding and saddle bags at the back of the tent. At the other end is the hearth. In the centre is a child's cradle covered with a green cloth. Winter camp north of Izeh, 1986.

below
Vertical section and plan of the Bakhtiāri tent (*bohon*) showing the position of the canopy (dashed line) and the tent poles (dots) in relation to the low stone wall (*chol*) and baggage-pile at the back of the tent.

1. *pisha*
2. *estin*
3. *chol*

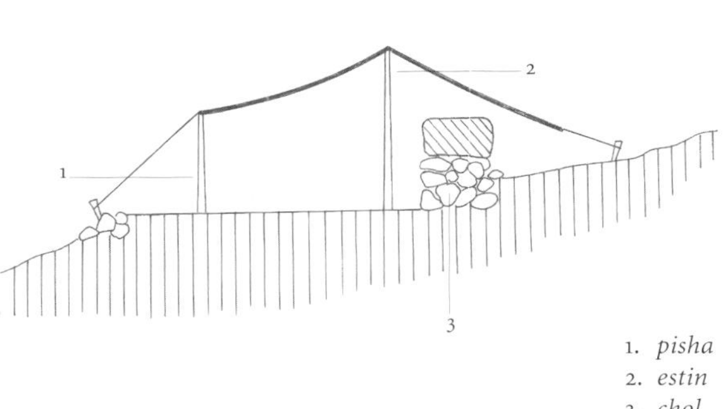

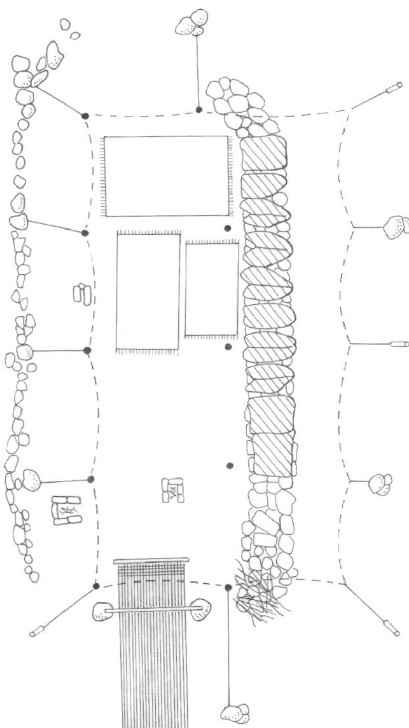

In conclusion, the position of the Bakhtiāri khans was recognised formally by two external bodies, and they benefited greatly from this recognition. They were able to reinforce their power over their own region whilst making inroads into the political machinery of the central administration. When disputes with the Shah arose, they had at their disposal an army worthy of serious respect and capable of highly ambitious military feats which they did not hesitate to use when the need arose. In the eyes of the tribe, these conflicts increased the prestige of the leaders and served their ambitions in the arena of national politics, furthermore it assisted them in the acquisition of new land from the neighbouring village communities. It would be true to say that over the sixty-three years from 1862 to 1925, the date of the accession of Rezā Shāh Pahlavi, the Bakhtiāri tribal chiefs constituted a state within a state in Iran.

DWELLINGS

The object most closely associated with the nomadic way of life, and indeed its most recognisable outward symbol, is the tent. Someone with an experienced eye can take one look at a camp and tell you exactly what season it is (in summer the tents are light and open, in winter massive and well insulated); the social status of the occupants (10 to 12 tents indicate a chief's encampment, 2 to 5 simple nomads), and their economic status (spacious tents with more than 10 poles, and in good repair, for the rich; 2 to 3 poles, with darns and patches all over, plus a couple of additional huts, for the poor).

The traditional Bakhtiāri tent (*bohon*) consists of a black canopy made of strips of goat-hair fabric stitched together. The strips run parallel to the longer edges of the canopy which is held up by two rows of vertical poles placed directly on the ground. One row runs along the front edge of the tent and raises it; the other, a row of longer poles, runs along the middle, dividing the canopy into two sections. The back section descends to the ground over a low stone wall (*chol*). The stability of the canopy depends on its tension, which is maintained by guy-ropes fastened to large stones or to pegs hammered into the ground.

Some camps include the occasional white cotton tent of the European type (*chādor*). They are not the norm, however, and they generally indicate the presence of camp members from one or other extreme of the social scale. Depending on their size, ornamentation and internal arrangements, they may either house powerful nomad leaders or be the dwellings of Kowli (gypsies) and Qorbati, who act as 'service' nomads and are generally despised.

The mountains in the centre of tribal territory, which are extremely steep, provide natural caves (*eshkoft*), used in winter either to house flocks, or, with a few improvements, for human habitation. Holes are made in the walls of the cave and stone walls are built across the entrance, leaving a doorway.

In western areas, where reeds are abundant in the winter grazing lands, some Bakhtiāri build during the summer months a light, oblong reed hut (*lawka*), or they use the reeds to construct a double sloped roof for a small dwelling with low stone walls (*kapar*) inhabited during the coldest winter months. Many Bakhtiāri, with ill-concealed scorn, declare these homes to be 'fit only for Arabs'.

The reed-covered hut with low stone walls (*kapar*) used in winter, shown in plan without roof and vertical section.

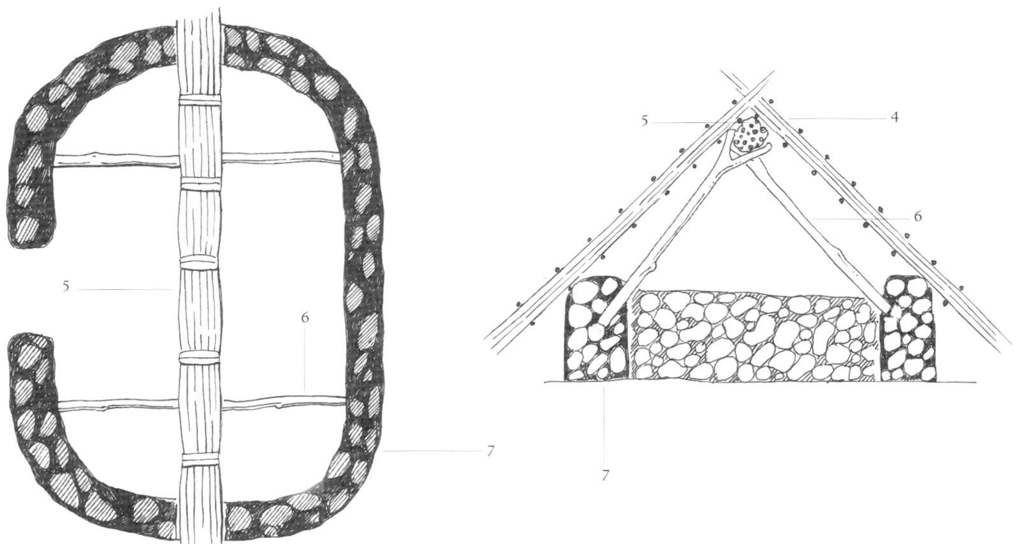

4. *safkh-ney*
5. *rek*
6. *āghö'i*
7. *chir or tifāl-bard*

above
Musicians from a nearby village make music for the festivities at a wedding in Dastenā, near Shahr-e Kord, 1991.

below
A shepherd boy playing an end-blown flute near Godār-Landar in 1985. He wears the *shaw-kolā*, a brown, beige or black felt cap, the characteristic male head-covering for all ordinary Bakhtiāri nomads.

Nevertheless, they are not unfamiliar with houses (*hāna* or *khonwa*, depending on which branch of the tribe they belong to) since settlement campaigns have been directed at them from the 1930s onwards. Their houses have high walls made of stone or cob and flat roofs made of wood covered with earth. Occupancy of a house need not necessarily indicate that nomadism has been abandoned, as there are many Bakhtiāri nomads today who move between two houses, or between a tent and a house. The gradual disappearance of the black tent, on the other hand, can be attributed more to the increase in the price of the goat hair needed to make the canopy than to the settlement of nomadic peoples. During the 1970s, goats were the target and victims of a peculiarly ill thought-out policy for the protection of grazing lands.

Dwellings that cannot be dismantled, like converted caves, houses and huts, define inhabited space very precisely. In a tent, on the other hand, inhabited space equals the surface covered by the canopy, though it merges with the outside world. It is worth considering this fact in relation to some of the most characteristic aspects of the social life of the nomads, which combines a highly cohesive life inside the tent with a great receptiveness towards visitors from outside.

The arrangement of the inside of the tent is more or less the same everywhere. The right-hand side (looking out) is usually the domestic area (*keyvānu*) allotted to the women and young children. Here can be found the hearth, stocks of fuel (wood and dried animal dung), skins containing water and yoghurt, sacks of flour, tea and sugar, and the loom. This side is always very busy and animated, and has the familiar clutter to be found wherever there is intense activity. The other side (usually the left), the area reserved for the men (*lāmerdon*), is furnished with carpets, rugs and cushions for entertaining guests in a dignified manner. The separation between the two areas is sometimes—but only sometimes—indicated by a moveable partition, rug or curtain. The furnishings, like the tent, have to be flexible and portable. Goat skins (*mashk*) are always preferred to pottery containers, and sacks and saddle-bags (*khorjin* or *hurzhin*) to chests. The containers are lined up with the bedding on the low stone wall which marks the back (*bala*, literally 'up') of the tent.

Each Bakhtiāri tent typically houses a nuclear family, a couple and their children and, in economic terms, is the consumption unit. Except when they are on the move, a group of from 3 to 20 tents forms a *māl* (camp). Each camp houses an extended family and forms a semi-autonomous production unit.

DRESS

Children, both boys and girls, usually only cover their upper bodies with a short jumper or jacket, and their heads with a bonnet or cap. On the back of these garments where the children cannot reach them are stitched or pinned things supposed to protect them from illness and accidents: innumerable little trinkets, beads, bezoars, a little bell, a piece of rabbit skin, a hawk's talon, or a wolf's tooth. At about six or seven they begin to wear clothes appropriate to their sex, but right up to adolescence and marriage these are but pale imitations of their parents' clothing.

Bakhtiāri men wear clothing that makes them identifiable at a glance, and they attach strong symbolic importance to it. Nevertheless the different items comprising the whole can vary quite widely depending on the wearer's age, his social status, and the branch of the tribe to which he belongs. Bakhtiāri dress has also changed with the passage of time. Clothing reforms were sometimes imposed on the tribe in the past, most recently under Rezā Shāh (1925–1941). Fashion also plays its part in the way tribespeople dress, as with everyone else.

The male Bakhtiāri costume consists of the following basic elements: a felt cap, a shirt and jacket, a cloth belt, wide trousers and rope-soled shoes. Nowadays the small beige or brown felt cap, known as the 'night cap' (*shaw-kolā*), is the most widely favoured. It is worn by the young, the shepherds and all the simple nomads (*lor*). Older men, or men of a certain standing, up to and including the chiefs, prefer the *kolā-khosrowi* which is a taller, almost cylindrical black hat. The great khan wore a white one in former times. In addition to its symbolic and protective functions, the *kolā* has a variety of uses. It can be used as a drinking cup, for concealing money pinned to the inside, or it can be used to attract the attention of someone in the distance if waved like a flag at arm's length.

One of the most characteristic elements of masculine Bakhtiāri dress (though not exclusive to this tribe) is the *chughā*, a knee-length, straight, sleeveless jacket made of natural wool, cream coloured with vertical stripes in indigo. Nowadays the *chughā* is often worn over a western jacket

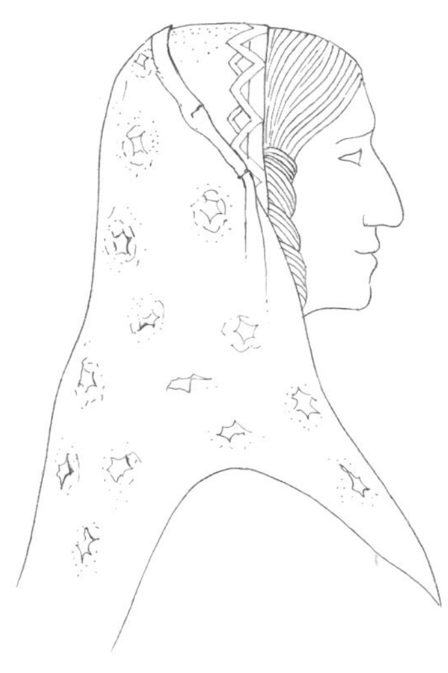

The veil (*meynā*) is pinned to the back of the headband (*lachak*) and is drawn forward under the chin to cover the chest.

above
The long diaphanous veil of the Bakhtiāri, which is attached to the head band, does not hide the face or hair but frames the face. The headband is tied under the chin with two ribbons.

right
That this young girl is wearing the *lachak* and *meynā*, probably indicates that she has reached puberty. North of Masjed-e Soleymān, 1985.

(*kot*). In the past the *chughā* was restricted to Lorestān, only spreading to the Bakhtiāri in the 1940s when it replaced the *gabā*, a kind of crossover coat with a seam at the waist, which had been banned. Today the most elegant *chughās* are called *chughā-livasi*, from the name of a village in Lorestān which is famous for making them. Traveller's tales from before the First World War describe a high-collared shirt, buttoning to one side, called a *joma*. This has disappeared completely and been replaced by the western-style shirt (*pirhan*) which can be bought in the shops.

The most distinctive garment worn by the Bakhtiāri is the very wide pair of trousers (*shawlār-goshād* or *tombon*) made of black cotton and measuring at least 120 cm round each leg. These are worn over a pair of striped or light coloured under-trousers (*zir-shawlār*), often simply pyjama trousers. Often, for the sake of economy, young people and shepherds wear just the under-trousers. The symbolic importance of the wide black trousers is so great to the Bakhtiāri that they prohibit their use by the Qorbati, artisans who are not members of the tribe and whom the Bakhtiāri despise. The Bakhtiāri give the pejorative name 'straight trousers' (*shawlār-tang*) to anyone not belonging to the tribe. The trousers are held up either by a large leather belt, or, more commonly, by a wide band of rolled white fabric (*shāl*); the folds of this are used for the storage of everyday objects (pipe, knife). In former times the *shāl* was always worn over the over-garment (*gabā*), but this is only done nowadays during energetic games, at work or at any moment when the flapping panels of the over-garment might cause a problem.

Two distinct silhouettes can be identified. One is characterised by the tall, black, cylindrical felt hat, the wide black trousers, with a jacket and a blue and white sleeveless *chughā-livasi* hanging free over his white waistband. This would be a leader, or a rich man uninvolved in manual tasks. The other can be identified by the small felt skullcap pressed well down on his head, coloured striped under-trousers often rolled up so as not to hinder his walking or running, and the sleeveless blue and white *chughā* crossed over and tied firmly round the waist with the cotton band. This is

An extended family on their downward migration. Dogs with docked tails and ears cool off in a roadside puddle. Near Shimbar, Autumn 1987.

the silhouette of the simple nomad (*lor*), who has to be equipped to do a variety of different jobs. These two distinct styles of dress are not so much based on any important difference in the clothes themselves as on modifications of the way they are worn, according to the economic position of the wearer—thereby demonstrating one of the fundamental features of Bakhtiāri society.

Lastly, there are the espadrilles (*giva*), traditionally worn by the Bakhtiāri. The top is made of knitted cotton and the sole of strips of compressed cloth. The sole is reinforced by a leather heel and at the front by a leather point which curls back over the toes. Unfortunately these *giva* are not made within the tribe and are very expensive. Nowadays they are increasingly replaced by factory-made moulded rubber shoes (*kashf-lāstik*) costing a quarter the amount but having a disastrous effect on the feet, particularly in hot weather.

To these basic items should be added a number of garments that have a specific use, like the felt capes and coats (*abānemet, kordin, shenel*) worn by shepherds in the mountains to protect them from rain and cold. Fur coats (like the *pustin*, worn all over eastern Iran) are unknown to the Bakhtiāri.

Bakhtiāri women have never succumbed to city fashions. For instance, they have never worn the veil (*chādor*), which covers the head and body right down to the ankles, and which at different times has been both forbidden and, under the Islamic Republic, imposed. They still refuse to wear it except when they have to go into town. Over the centuries their dress has shown far less variation than the dress of their menfolk.

They wear a very characteristic head-dress, consisting of two linked elements: (1) the *lachak*, a velvet headband decorated with mirror-work that covers the top and back of the head and the ears, and is held in place by two ribbons tied under the chin; (2) the *meynā*, a veil 2–5 metres long and 1 metre wide made of light, brightly-coloured, diaphanous material. One end of the *meynā* is pinned to the back part of the head-band, then drawn forward under the chin to cover the chest. It is then brought across to cover the shoulder and round the face to be fixed once more to the headband behind the

right
The characteristic elements of women's dress are the velvet headband, veil, long-sleeved blouse and full, ankle-length skirt. Summer 1985; snow still lies on the ground.

below
The traditional cotton espadrilles (*giva*) are expensive and being worn less and less. Their place has been taken by factory-made moulded rubber shoes.

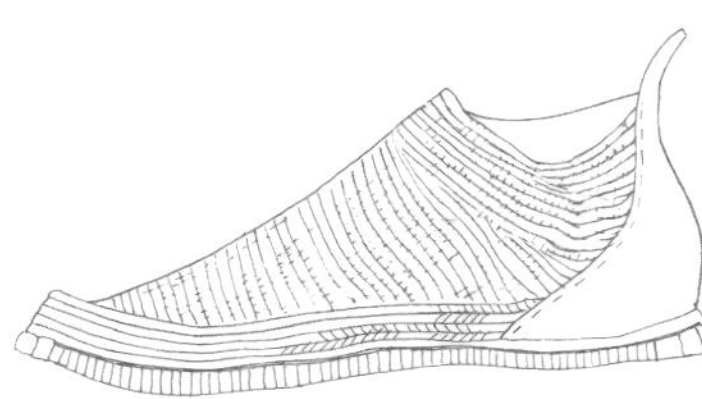

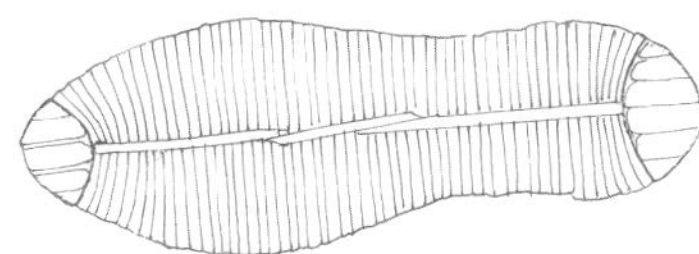

head. The veil worn by Bakhtiāri women—and this detail has always amazed visitors from Iranian towns where the *chādor* is worn—does not hide the face or hair. The hair is parted in the centre and twisted into two coils that meet under the chin, making a further frame for the face.

Women in mourning temporarily replace the headband and veil with a simple *kuluki*, a square of black material with a red or green border. This is folded diagonally in two, worn on the head with the point at the back, and fastened under the chin like a headscarf. The *kuluki* is also worn over the headband and veil to hold them in position when the women are working, milking animals, for instance. Folded diagonally and rolled, it is worn across the forehead and tied behind the head like a headband.

On their bodies Bakhtiāri women wear a long-sleeved blouse (*jowa* or *pirhan*) reaching to below the knee, slit in front to permit breast feeding and on either side at the bottom so that they can walk. Beneath the blouse an ankle-length skirt (*tombon-zanuna*) is worn. The skirt is extremely full, sometimes 8–10 metres round the hem, and gathered at the waist. In winter a sleeveless waistcoat (*jelezgha*) or a velvet jacket shaped like a cardigan (*kolejā*) completes the outfit. Sometimes both are worn together. Women never wear the *chughā*.

Amongst Bakhtiāri women, social class is not demonstrated by different clothing but by the cleanliness and condition of their clothes and the quality of the fabric they are made of. Other social indicators are the amount and value of ornaments worn, which include mirror work and coins stitched on to the headband and jewellery in white metal which, except for the rings and bracelets, is designed to be fastened to the clothes. Clothing ornaments include a long chain linking the pins used to fix the veil to the headband (*bandsizan*), pendants worn at the temples, hooked on to either side of the headband (*taksari*), and pendants knotted to the corner of the veil (*gusaredasmāl*). These flowing, brightly coloured clothes, which tinkle at the slightest movement, give the tribal women an unforgettable dignified and playful charm.

Milk soon goes bad so all of it is quickly made into yoghurt. The fermentation takes place overnight, and one of the first jobs in the morning is to make butter. The cream is not separated from the milk, as is usual in Europe, but made by churning the whole-milk yoghurt. The churn, a goat skin container suspended from a tripod, is swung to and fro until the butter separates from the buttermilk–a time-consuming job. Near Godār-Landar, 1985.

right
The basic ingredients of every meal are flaps of bread, yoghurt, tea and sugar. On the south-eastern slope of Zardeh Kuh near Bāzoft, Spring 1985.

FOOD

The basic foodstuffs eaten by the Bakhtiāri every day, sometimes to the exclusion of all other nourishment, are bread, dairy produce, raw onions and hot sweet tea.

The bread is made from whole grain flour (*ār*), the wheat (*gandom*) being ground on the spot, either in water mills (*āsyāw*) set up under river banks or, as is becoming more and more common, in diesel-powered grinders (*makina*), or even, amongst the poorest nomads, by hand on a stone mill-wheel (*bard-ār*).The wheat is stored in sheaves or as grain so that flour can be milled as and when it is needed. The bran is never separated from the wheat, the bolting of flour being unheard of.

Every day the women in each tent make the amount of bread that will be needed that day. A leaven is added to the dough (*khamir*) in the form of either a handful of dough from the previous day or a small cube of *gārā* (see below under dairy produce). The dough is then kneaded by hand for half an hour and left to rise for a couple of hours on a large copper dish (*lagan*). After this the real bread making begins. The woman making the bread squats on the ground near a hearth. On her left is the dish of dough, in front of her on a cloth (*sorfa*) is a circular wooden board with short legs cut from a solid piece of wood, the *towsi*. The hearth, on her right, is covered by a circular iron griddle, slightly convex in shape, the *towa*. This stands on a circle of stones with gaps between them to allow fuel to be added to the fire during the baking. The best fuel for baking bread is dried horse dung, which burns slowly and steadily, without flames, and maintains a constant temperature.

The cook sprinkles a little flour around the wooden board standing on the cloth. Then she makes balls of dough, the size of a fist, and places them in the flour. Each ball is then stretched over the board to the size of a pancake, and wrapped round a small rolling pin (*tir*), held in the right hand, and then rolled and patted and patted and rolled and turned repeatedly with deft strokes. Once the dough has been stretched to the limit of its elasticity it is rolled one last time round the rolling pin and then unrolled over the convex griddle to cook. Then another ball of dough is tackled. Each new flap of bread is spread over the griddle on top of the others and the whole heap is turned over to allow it to cook. Only one side of each flap of bread comes into contact with the griddle, and each piece is cooked only for the time that it takes to make the next piece. The pieces of bread have to be rolled out very thin so that they cook completely and the cook has to work fast so that they do not burn.

The bread described above is called *patir*. Other types exist but this is by far the most popular. The Bakhtiāri consume an average of 100 kg of *patir* per person per year. It is certainly delicious-tasting bread, and it has other features that make it convenient for the nomadic lifestyle. It serves

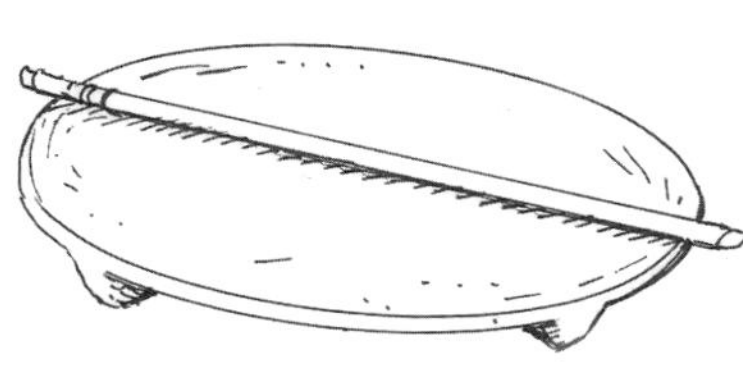

The iron griddle (*towa*) and wooden bread-rolling board (*towsi*) with rolling pin (*tir*).

both as a tablecloth and as a plate when spread out in front of the assembled diners, and folded into a cone it can be used as a spoon. If there is any left over at the end of the meal it is used as a napkin to wipe the mouth and hands.

The Bakhtiāri hardly ever drink milk (*shir*) as such. However, milk is the basic ingredient of a whole range of products with a variety of properties and uses, which all share the advantage of keeping well in spite of the very unfavourable conditions that prevail: heat, lack of hygiene, and so on.

The first of these products, the one from which the Bakhtiāri make all the others, is yoghurt (*māst*), which is obtained by adding rennet (*māya*) from the stomach of a new-born lamb or yoghurt made earlier, to warm milk. One kg of milk yields almost the same amount of yoghurt. Some of the yoghurt is eaten as it is and the rest is used for making other products.

The yoghurt is churned for hours in a large goat skin (*mashk*) slung under a wooden tripod; it separates into butter (*kareh*) and buttermilk (*dugh*). Ten kg of yoghurt gives approximately 1.5 kg of butter and 8.5 kg of buttermilk. The buttermilk makes an excellent drink which can be diluted with water and seasoned with salt, or with powdered wild celery leaves. The most elegant way of serving it is in a hollowed out block of ice.

In order to preserve it, the butter is melted at once, boiled, skimmed, put into a pot and allowed to cool and solidify. This clarified butter (*rowghan*) is the fat normally used for cooking.

When buttermilk is salted, boiled and the liquid is drained off, it gives casein solids (*kashk*), which, when formed into balls and dried in the sun, are easy to store and transport. It requires 10 kg of buttermilk to make l kg of *kashk*. The *kashk* balls can be mixed with water and give a white liquid with a very pronounced flavour (*āw-kashk*); mixed with bread this provides the dairy element of the diet in autumn and winter. The liquid drained from the buttermilk, which is both acid and very salty (*āw-namak*), is heated and evaporated until a yellowish paste (*gārā*) is left. This also has a very strong flavour and is used for cooking or as a raising agent for bread.

Milk has to be turned into *māst* and then into the other products as soon as milking is over. If it is left to stand it goes bad very quickly. The activities described above make up part of the daily routine

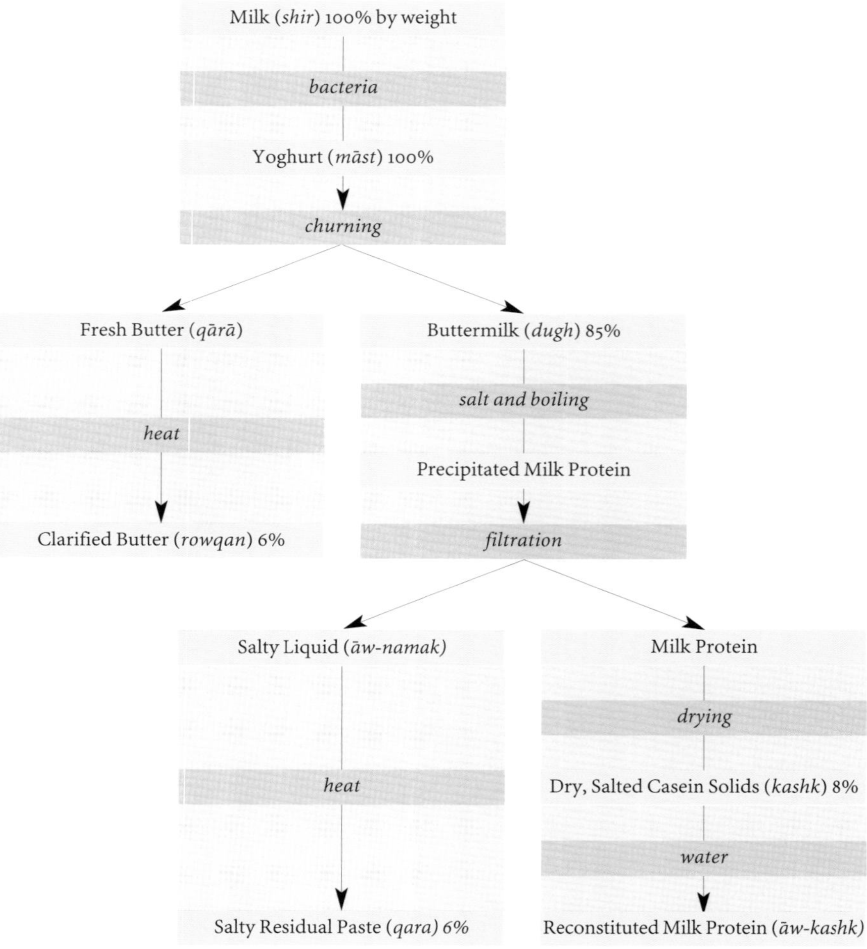

Bread is made from a lightly risen dough. Large flaps are rolled out on a wooden board and baked over the fire on a convex metal griddle placed directly on the hearth stones. The fuel preferred for baking is dried horse dung. Near Emāmzādeh Boveir, April 1985.

of the Bakhtiāri women, particularly from February, when lambing begins, to July, when the sheep and goats cease to lactate. All these milk products are made within the family and are strictly for family consumption only. Nothing is sold, except occasionally clarified butter, which is expensive to buy. There is no worse insult amongst the Bakhtiāri than to call someone a 'yoghurt seller' (*māst-forushi*).

Not much needs to be said about the other basic foodstuffs of the Bakhtiāri, onions and sweet tea, except that they are not produced by the tribe, and their purchase therefore constitutes a considerable outlay for most of the nomads. Onions (*pyāz*) are indispensable; they are the major fresh vegetable input in the Bakhtiāri diet. Tea (*chö'i*) and sugar (*gand*) are just as vital—though for a different reason—they are associated with sociability. The offer of sweet tea constitutes the most modest hospitality, and even the humblest Bakhtiāri tent has a kettle of water constantly on the boil over a charcoal fire, in readiness for the preparation of the precious infusion. Many nomads spend as much in a year on tea (an average of 12 kg per person) and sugar (120 kg per person) as they do on wheat. This amounts to 25–50 percent of total expenditure in the poorest families. Consumption of tea and sugar is an excellent indicator of the different standards of living within the tribe, and may be twice or three times as much in the families of the chiefs, where visitors have to be entertained frequently.

Variety is given to these basic elements of the diet by the addition of foodstuffs picked in the wild: celery, mint, wild plums, mushrooms, blackberries and other berries—all vegetables and fruits that can be eaten either fresh or dried. Then there is game for those with guns, honey, eggs and salt (see below). Cultivated vegetables and fruit, apart from onions, pomegranates and sometimes dried pomegranate seeds, are virtually unknown.

Rice and meat in a stew (*khoresht*) or grilled on a skewer (*kabāb*) are foods for feast days and are not the norm. The rarity with which home-grown meat is consumed is by no means exclusive to the Bakhtiāri. All nomadic societies dedicated to animal husbandry adhere to the same practice, for sound economic reasons. The slaughter of animals is avoided unless an accident or advanced age make it inevitable. The products obtainable from living animals—milk, wool or hair—are preferred to their meat or skin.

The Bakhtiāri eat three main meals a day, and men and women eat together unless there are guests present. Everyone sits on rugs around a cloth. The sheets of bread are spread first, to be followed by the other dishes that have been prepared. People serve themselves. Cutlery is seldom used, and is not necessary; they eat with the right hand, using a piece of bread to pick up food. Tea, drunk before and after the meal, requires special utensils, small cylindrical glasses (*estekhān*) with a capacity of 100 ml and china saucers (*zira*), which are stored with the tea-pot (*ghuri*) in the padded recesses of a solid wood casket (*hezār-pisha*) that protects the ware from impact while it is being transported from one place to another. The tea, which is served boiling hot in the glass, is often drunk from the saucer where it has been poured to cool down. A piece of sugar is held in the mouth as the tea is drunk. The end of a meal heralds another pleasure, tobacco (*tutun* or *tambāku*), smoked in a pipe (*chopogh*) or, more and more frequently when funds permit, cigarettes (*sigār*).

TRANSPORT

Transport is obviously of the utmost importance to any nomadic society, and the words written by an anthropologist about the Murngin of Australia could equally be applied to the Bakhtiāri: 'The criterion governing the choice of objects acquired and retained permanently by their owners is the ease with which they can be transported'. The Bakhtiāri however are not quite as uncompromising as this. The advantages to be had from owning certain immovable items, such as a house, a silo or a water mill, or items that are difficult to transport like the swing plough, almost always outweigh any other considerations. Nevertheless, it must be true to say that mobility and ease of transport are two criteria that have influenced the overall development of Bakhtiāri material culture, and this applies also to loans from other cultures. The objects in daily use by the Bakhtiāri bear witness to this. They are light and collapsible, or made of flexible, pliable materials. They are also adapted for carriage by animals or humans which are the only modes of transport available to the Bakhtiāri since the terrain is mountainous and it is difficult to build communication routes accessible to vehicular traffic.

Human porterage is limited to light loads and short distances, and is the exclusive domain of women, who are responsible for the daily chore of fetching water, the camps being deliberately set up at a respectful distance from the water source. They also gather wood when there is any to be had, otherwise cow dung and dried droppings are used. Water skins and bundles of firewood are carried on the women's backs, tied up with a strip of woven cloth (*veris*) which goes over the shoulders. During migration the women carry any children too young to walk or ride in a cradle. The *torba*, a simple cloth pouch with shoulder straps, in which shepherds carry their food and belongings, is the only example of a bag made to be carried by humans.

The rest of their belongings are carried by horses, mules, donkeys or cattle, each having an appropriate size of load. Donkeys (*har*) and mules (*qāter*) carry the same loads irrespective of their sex, with the exception of female donkeys in an advanced stage of pregnancy. Male mules are gelded, as are male donkeys not needed for breeding purposes. The gelded horses (*yābu*), considered unfit for riding, also carry loads. Although the use of cattle for carrying probably preceded the use of horses in this part of the world, oxen (*vārzā*) and cows (*gā*) are employed only occasionally, most often during migrations, when all means of transport have to be pressed into service. Their load-bearing capacity is generally recognised to be inferior to that of most equines. A cow carries 30–40 kg, an ox up to 90 kg, a donkey about 60 kg, a horse 90 kg and a mule 150 kg. The load sizes have less to do with their relative strength than the trouble each type of animal has in keeping its balance when the going through the mountains gets steep. The same kind of consideration partly explains why the camel, whose load-bearing capacity varies from 180 to 240 kg, is not used by the Bakhtiāri. Turkish (-speaking) camel-owning groups from the Esfahān area do come to spend the summers with the Bakhtiāri, but they do not migrate with them. They take the less precipitous southern route via Ardal and Izeh.

When pack animals carry loads, a protective layer in the form of a rug or pack-saddle is placed between the load and the animal's back. For saddle-bags or the tent a simple blanket (*jol*) suffices. It is held in place by a strap round the animal's rib cage, a belly girth and a crupper. In fact, the rug protects the saddle-bag from the animal's sweat, which is particularly important if the pack includes valuable weaving. For hard, angular loads that might injure the animal, the *pālon* is preferred.

The confusion of people and animals is typical of the migration. Riding on a laden mule, a woman supports a child on the load in front of her and carries another in a cradle on her back. Spring migration near Monar, 1985.

A mule is ready to depart, its load secured by a tablet-woven strap with a wooden buckle. Beneath the blanket covering the load a number of brightly coloured weavings are visible. Members of the Bāmadi clan are renowned for paying particular attention to their woven goods; even the mule's tail brace is richly decorated with tassels and mother-of-pearl buttons. The different layers of the woman's costume are well seen here. Spring migration near Doāb 1985.

above
A woman carries her baby in a wooden cradle strapped on her back. The decorative band used for this purpose is made by the process of tablet- or card-weaving, a particular technique still in use by the Bakhtiāri. Bābādi clan on the Monar pass, May 1985.

below
A woman nurses her baby by the roadside. Children too young to walk or ride are carried in a wooden cradle. Spring 1984, between Bāzoft and Doāb.

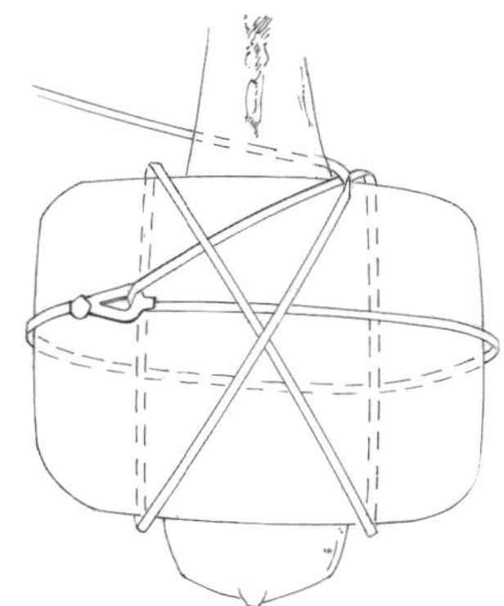

The method of securing a load by means of a strap with a wooden buckle (*hacha*).

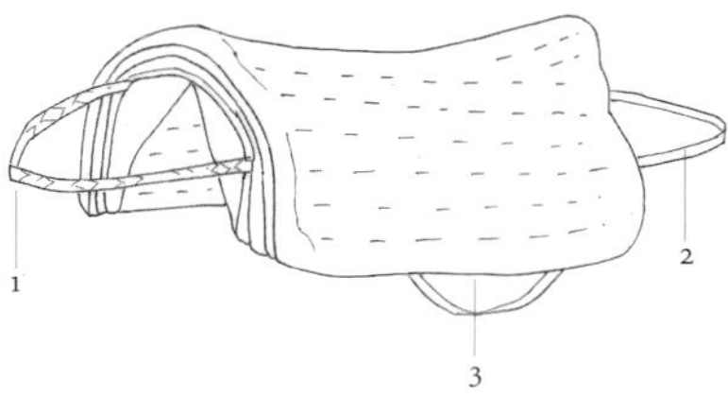

Quilted saddle cloth (*pālon*) for hard loads.
1. *runeki*
2. *varband*
3. *zirtela*

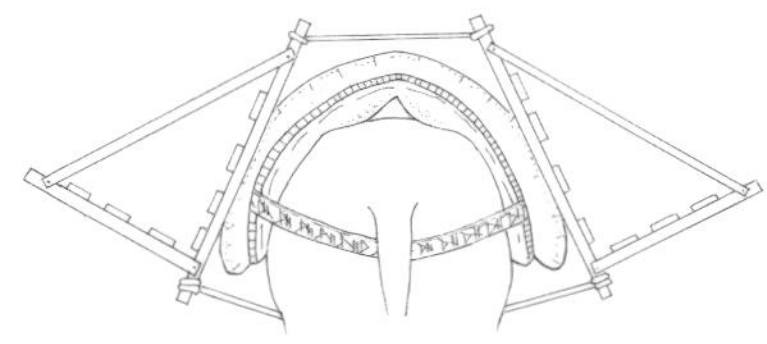

Wooden containers (*mafal*) for carrying stones and rough loads.

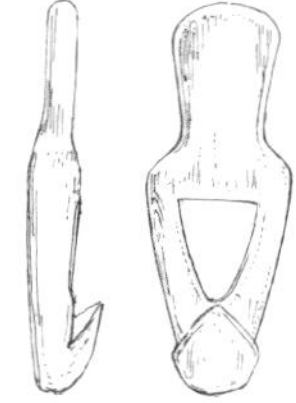

Wooden buckle (*hacha*) for fastening straps.

The *pālon* is a quilted cover stuffed with felt. Wooden containers (*mafal*) can be placed on this for carrying stones and suchlike.

The nomad's most essential piece of luggage is the saddle-bag. These bags all conform to the same design. The two ends of a strip of woven fabric are folded back and stitched to form pockets. When the saddle-bag is full the pockets hang on either side of the animal, on its flanks. The Bakhtiāri use three types of saddle-bag for different purposes. Each has a different quality and decoration. The *shalla* is a rough bag, without ornament, sometimes woven from cotton cord, which is used for transporting wood, goat skins and stones. The *hur* is also rough and simple, but of better quality. It is made of tightly woven wool and is used mostly for carrying grain and flour with the pockets stitched shut. The bag is placed on end, one of the short sides is unstitched and it is filled. When the contents are needed the long side is partially unstitched and the food is taken out as and when required. The *hurzhin*, used for the storage and transport of personal belongings, is the most elaborate of the bags. Three different types of weaving are used in its manufacture (see below) and it is embellished at the front with tassels (*mangul*), and bands (*noftorband* or *varuna*) decorated with beads and mother-of-pearl buttons. At the back of the bag there is a strap that can replace the crupper on the saddle, or be used in addition to it. Each pocket is fastened independently by loops (*kilit*) that pass through slits in the outer panel of the bag and are secured by a padlock (*qolf*).

The saddle-bag is placed on the animal, over the pack saddle. The whole load is kept in place by a tablet-woven strap (*veris*) with a buckle in the form of a piece of wood with a hole in it (*hacha*) at one end. The strap is passed through and then wound round the load in the opposite direction, otherwise it would have to be wound round the animal. The triangular part of the *hacha* fulfils the same function for the strap that passes under the animal (see diagram). The pack-horse harness is completed by a halter consisting of a woven headband (*awsār*) with tassels on it, a nose band consisting of a metal chain, and a lunge. The lunge is wound around the collar when the animals are in large caravans, and they are then controlled by the human voice.

All equines, and sometimes cattle, can carry people on their back with the arrangements described above: a halter, lunge and a rug to sit on. A rider can even perch on top of the saddle-bag; it is quite a common sight during seasonal migrations. The most favoured method of transport—and, together with hunting, the Bakhtiāri's favourite occupation—is horse riding (*savār*). For this, stallions (*asb*) are preferred; they are naturally livelier than mares or geldings and always available. Saddle horses, known generically as *māl*, which means wealth or material possession (in Lori *irom bā māl* means 'I'm going on horseback'), are invested by the Bakhtiāri with a glamour far exceeding their practical worth. The Bakhtiāri are keen and fearless horsemen. However, since war ceased to be an ongoing preoccupation, riders are inclined to choose mules for their docility and sureness of foot, qualities much appreciated during long journeys. Mules have the added advantage of being able to be used for other tasks as well.

As is usual when horses are needed for utilitarian purposes, the breaking-in process is summary and adapted to the requirements of the tribe, mainly travel, raiding and games on horseback. Apart from a few mules trained to amble, Bakhtiāri mounts are only required to move at the gaits natural to them in the wild; walking, galloping or, exceptionally, trotting. If greater speed is required, Bakhtiāri horses do not increase their gait but move to a faster one, a trot or a gallop. The bit (*aviza*) used by the Bakhtiāri is the Arab ring bit. The traditional saddle (*zin*), made of solid wood with a strong pommel and fitted with Arab broad-soled stirrups, has disappeared in favour of the flat British cavalry saddle. Spurs are not used. Instead, a whip with a short handle and three plaited leather thongs is carried. A movement of this away from the horse's body will generally procure a change of gait. All the horseshoes have a full sole, though only the front hooves are shod.

The almost complete absence prior to the 1980s of engineered roads or tracks through the mountains, even in the steepest, most dangerous passes, has been mentioned already. This absence is experienced most cruelly at river crossings, and particularly in spring when the rivers are swollen by melting snow. The antique bridges built by the Atābak in the thirteenth century are derelict now. One of them, between Dasht-e Gol and Iveh on the Kārun, has been replaced by a 'monkey bridge', a steel cable stretched across the river and known by the Bakhtiāri as a *jarra*. Only two modern bridges are known to me and both have been constructed on the edge of the tribal area so cannot therefore be used during migrations.

The family possessions have been prepared for the next stage of the journey after a stop near Doāb . The black tent (*bohon*) is being loaded onto a mule and in the foreground are two *hurzhin* filled with bedding and other soft goods. Bāmadi *tāyefa* on the spring migration, 1985.

The crossing of the Kārun, the broadest and swiftest river in the region, is done on rafts called *kalak* (from the Turkish). These rafts are constructed along lines that have not changed since ancient times. They consist of a layer of sticks and branches lashed to inflated goat skins (*mashk*). Women, children, very young animals and possessions are heaped on top. Those remaining, men and beasts, hurl themselves into the water and attempt to reach the other bank as best they can. Sometimes they are carried several hundred metres downstream. These river crossings are amongst the most climactic moments of the migration, packed with drama and, unfortunately, with casualties caused, often, by sudden contact with the freezing water.

ANIMAL HUSBANDRY

Animal husbandry is by far the most important productive activity pursued by the Bakhtiāri and, through the feeding of the animals and their protection from climatic extremes, the activity most closely connected with the nomadic cycle. Because of the way they have adapted it to their particular way of life, Bakhtiāri animal raising is flourishing. Their flocks are larger, better looking and more productive than the flocks of the settled tribespeople. At the same time, however, nomadic pastoralism is a highly vulnerable activity which with difficulty survived repeated attempts to replace it with a settled lifestyle during the twentieth century, and which, during the 1970s, was the target of a particularly absurd rural 'development' programme (see below).

Bakhtiāri animal husbandry concentrates on sheep (*gusfand*) and goats (*boz*). Most nomads depend on these two types of animal to provide their basic cash income, which derives from the sale of meat on the hoof and, when necessary, clarified butter, and to provide a large part of their nourishment in the form of dairy products and, occasionally, meat. These animals also provide the raw materials for their handicrafts, wool, hair and leather. Lambs and kids are born in the winter, in about February. After they have been fattened in the summer pastures, male animals not wanted

Spring migration near Monar in 1985. Marking the sheep with henna has a symbolic significance beyond that merely of identification.

1. Jingle (*qor*)
2. Small bell (*tirik*)
3. Bronze bell (*tārāk*)

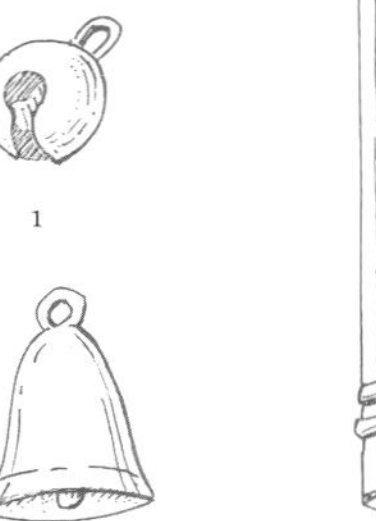

for breeding are sold off in the autumn to cattle drovers (*chupdār*) working as agents for the slaughterhouses and butchers in the neighbouring towns. Ewes and nanny goats are milked for human consumption until June. This chore, which needs no other tool than the hands, belongs exclusively to the women. On the other hand, sheep shearing is an exclusively masculine activity because by tradition only men may use sharp tools. The wool is used to make warm clothing, saddle-bags, and other useful items. Goats are also shorn and the hair is used for weaving the fabric for tents and for making felt. Shearing takes place in the spring, after the migration.

The sheep, which belong to a very hardy breed called Lori, with fat tails (*domba*) and very aquiline noses, are distributed very unequally. Some nomads have flocks numbering several hundred, some none at all. This situation is brought about by the fact that some flocks provide products for commercial purposes rather than for home consumption. The flocks are thus the centre of pastoral activity, and the source and the reflection of social inequality. The reverse is true for goats because nearly everyone possesses at least a few goats. In Bakhtiāri terms it could be said that the goat and not the cow is the 'poor man's sheep'. Goat products are less commercial, but the goat is a hardier animal and supplies more milk than the sheep. The liveliness and pranks of the goats play a vital part in the hurly-burly of a nomad encampment.

To put it politely, the quality of Bakhtiāri cattle is not outstanding. Cows (*gā*) are fairly numerous but small in size and not very productive. Blame for their mediocrity can be assigned to the practice of systematic castration of the strongest males to turn them into working oxen (*vārzā*). Some of the Arab groups integrated with the Bakhtiāri (Arab-Kamari, literally 'mountain Arabs'), who live permanently in the winter quarters, specialise in the rearing of buffaloes (*gāmish*); buffalo milk is very rich in animal fat and is widely appreciated. Until the First World War, these buffaloes used to be driven as far as the eastern flanks of the Zāgros mountains where they would be sold to Armenians from Feridān and Chahār-Mahāl for use on their farms.

As has been shown, the Bakhtiāri also breed horses, a local breed improved by Arab stock, as well as donkeys and mules, for agricultural activities, threshing and, less frequently, ploughing,

Flocks are led by rams or castrated billy goats (*sehis*) chosen for their height and imposing horns. They are trained to respond to the human voice and wear a large bronze bell (*tārāk*) with a deep note, which serves as a kind of badge of office. The other animals wear a small bell (*tirik*) or jingle (*ghor*) which in addition to providing a kind of musical accompaniment to the life of the flock can alert the shepherd to abnormal movements at night and can help to locate any animals that have become lost. Near Zardeh-Kuh, spring migration 1985.

transport and riding. However, unlike their southern neighbours the Qashqā'i, they do not own any dromedaries. The only camels to be found in this area of the Zāgros mountains belong not to members of the tribe but to Turkish groups, who are permitted to use Bakhtiāri lands for transhumance from Chahār-Mahāl. They are the Laraki from around Gandomān and even villagers from Chāl-Shotor, Riz, and Gholām-Khāst near Esfahān.

BAKHTIĀRI LIVESTOCK HOLDINGS IN 1979

SMALL DOMESTIC ANIMALS		LARGE DOMESTIC ANIMALS	
goats	551,000	donkeys	60,000
sheep	824,000	cows	203,000
horses	40,000		
mules	101,000		
TOTAL	1,393,000	TOTAL	404,000

Other domestic animals, though less numerous than those discussed above, nevertheless play a very important role in Bakhtiāri affairs. Chickens (*morgh*), to be found scratching around almost every tent, live on what they can find and supply the nomads with eggs and a small quantity of meat, enough for the appropriate dignified entertainment of moderately important guests, without the sacrifice of a sheep or a goat. During the migration these fowls are perched on top of the load borne by an ox or an ass, attached by the leg or enclosed in a cylindrical wicker basket (*korok*). At overnight stops, the chickens are let out to feed, then rounded up the following morning by dint of noisy and highly comical pursuit just before the caravan moves on.

Dogs (*say*), which have no economic value and are thoroughly despised by the Bakhtiāri, are nevertheless omnipresent. Each tent owns two or three. They are huge beasts with longish hair, generally white, beige or buff or sometimes black. They breed freely and their appearance is quite variable. The Bakhtiāri never touch the dogs directly because they consider them to be physically impure (*najes*). Once I was rebuked for playing with a puppy still too young to be frightened of human beings. The dogs learn very early what to expect from their masters which amounts to the minimum nourishment needed to build up their loyalty. It consists of rough bread (*nuwāla*), scraps of rejected food, sometimes stolen food. Furthermore they are stoned and beaten if they come too close to the tents. In exchange for this they demonstrate unfailing ferocity and are swift to attack any man or animal trespassing on their domain, barking endlessly at the slightest movement or noise. They play an important part in guarding the camps and defending the flocks though they are not used as sheep dogs are in the West for their aggressiveness would endanger the animals' lives.

The Bakhtiāri method of rearing herbivorous animals consists mainly in knowing how to keep the animals in a flock, knowing how to handle and move these flocks and how to modify the composition of the flocks in order to achieve a particular result.

Reproduction takes place rather freely. Once the surplus males have been got rid of by being sold for slaughter (sheep), or by being castrated and put to work (the male goats to lead the herd, the pack horses and oxen to the plough), the male or males selected for breeding are let loose amongst the females at a moment which will ensure that their young are born at an opportune time. For the small animals at least, parturition must be over before the spring migration which takes place at the end of March or beginning of April.

The critical period in the breeding of sheep and goats falls between the time when births begin and the moment when weaning is completed. Twenty per cent of young born alive die during this period. A close eye has to be kept on everything at this time; the young must be helped to feed, the weakest amongst them must receive additional food and adoptive mothers and babies must be found for the animals who have lost one or the other. Later, when weaning is taking place, the young are kept on the immediate outskirts of the camp where they gradually learn to graze whilst the mothers are taken to the pastures by themselves. Suckling takes place only twice a day, morning and evening, after milking. Nomads almost always favour this technique of separating the flocks, rather than using mechanical weaning devices such as muzzles or halters with spikes. They consider that these devices slow the pace at which the young learn to graze, or make mothers aggressive towards their young and decrease their maternal skill. Both these disadvantages are serious ones in a system where no other food apart from mother's milk is available for the herbivores except what grows naturally.

Bakhtiāri flocks therefore are fed mainly by grazing on natural pasture land. In natural conditions such as those pertaining in the Zāgros mountains, this means that the basic method of feeding flocks is nomadism. Depending on the size of the flocks, the distance travelled by the animals

MAXIMUM NUMBER OF SHEEP PER HECTARE OF PASTURELAND

TYPE OF PASTURE	NUMBER OF SHEEP IT CAN SUPPORT
High mountain	2.0
Degraded high mountain	1.0
Steppe vegetation	0.5

almost always exceeds the distance travelled by the humans. Even if ten or twelve sheep or goats can easily find food within a radius of a few kilometres around the camp, the same will not be true for flocks of several hundred animals. These flocks are forced to undertake two transhumances in addition to the normal nomadic migrations: one from the summer camp to the nearby alpine pastures, and one from the winter camp to the surrounding plains. Some of the larger flocks travel more than 1200 km per year.

The distance covered by the animals depends on the quality of grazing land available; the poorer it is, the larger the surface area required.

The animals are not scattered throughout the available pasture land all the time, but move about in clusters (called *rama* for horses, *galla* for the sheep and goats) grazing as they go. *Rama* and *galla* can both be translated as 'herd' or 'flock'. In general it is the combination of constraints governing movement and grazing that determines the maximum size of the flock. When the grazing is not particularly abundant, the animals at the front take the best of the vegetation. Those following behind always tend to move forward to the same level as the leaders, so that a grazing flock moves in line abreast, in a straight line or an arc perpendicular to the direction in which they are travelling. However, this disposition of the animals is not really satisfactory for flocks more than 300 strong, because of the unevenness of the terrain. A *galla* could therefore be defined as the largest flock in which sheep can derive the greatest benefit from grazing natural pastures, without getting in each other's way.

The problems of grazing are different for goats (when they are not mixed in with the sheep). Goats are less numerous than sheep and are rarely to be found in flocks of more than fifty. They are also far less fussy about their food than sheep. They can eat virtually anything including thorny bushes (*khār*) and nothing is beyond their reach. Because goats can find food in places which sheep have already abandoned, goats are brought in to graze after the sheep have left and are kept longer in one place. So it is not so much the goats themselves as the use made of them that causes damage to the local vegetation. In fact, in the particular case of the Bakhtiāri region, the goat might be regarded as having an advantage over all other animals where the rational exploitation of pasture land is concerned: no other domestic animal, not even the sheep, can reach the high peaks and scale the sheer cliffs to exploit what they have to offer. Without them it is estimated that about a quarter of the surface area of the tribal lands would be used exclusively by wild herbivores, particularly by wild goats.

Leaving aside the donkeys and mules, which can make do with the most unappetising food, such as huge thistles so big and prickly that men usually beat them with a stick to break them up, it is the large animals kept by the Bakhtiāri that come off worst as far as food is concerned. To increase their chances of finding something appetising to eat they are given much more freedom to roam than the smaller animals. Their diet is frequently supplemented with a mixture of barley (*jow*) and chopped straw (*kā*) served in rough wicker baskets (*salah*). Other essential dietary supplements are salt (*nevek*) when the salinity of the pastures is insufficient (in Khuzestān the grazing is salty almost to excess), and of course water (*āw*) either in a trough (most often a hollowed out tree trunk) fed by a spring, or a river to which the flocks can be led to drink, and even to bathe if the weather is hot.

For obvious reasons, the nomads regard the occasional provision of vegetable foodstuffs other than those found in natural pasture land as a welcome addition to the animals' diet, but never as a

A family group having breakfast at a summer camp near Shurāb, April 1984. The canvas tent-cloth is used by poorer nomads as a cheap alternative to the woven goat-hair canopy.

long-term substitute for grazing. 'Extensive' in the fullest sense of the word, Bakhtiāri animal husbandry makes no use of stalls or stables. Because the nomads leave the cold places (*eylāgh*) before it gets really cold and the warm places (*garmsir*) before it gets really hot, they do not need buildings to protect their animals from extremes of climate. When need does arise there are plenty of caves (*eshkoft*) to provide shelter.

Enclosures are on the whole non-existent, or very small. Low walls of stones and thorn brush mark out a *bār-band* round certain tents, where horses can be enclosed at night, or a *kola-barra* where kids and lambs can be penned in whilst their mothers are being milked. It is unusual too to see animals tethered or on ropes, except, for example, saddle horses when they are being ridden. If it is preferred that the animals do not stray too far from the camp then a semi-hobble

below
Semi-hobble (*do-daste*).

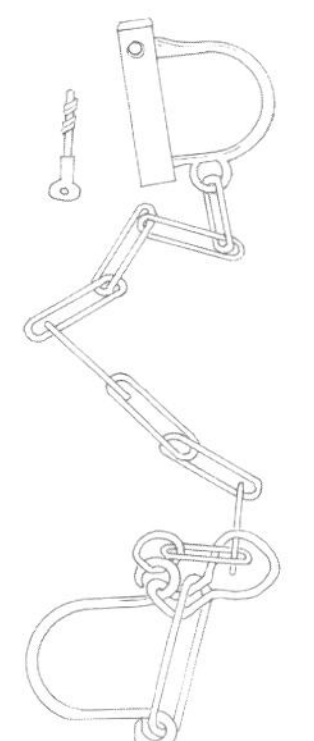

(*do-dasteh*), looking rather like handcuffs, is clamped on to the front legs. This slows their pace without preventing them from grazing.

Prolonged enclosure or tying up of animals would require the provision of alternative fodder, and is not compatible with the nomadic style of animal husbandry. The latter can really only be practised properly on groups of completely free-roaming animals; the whole art of nomadic stock breeding is to allow full rein to the animals' gregarious instincts, and then to exploit this instinct to its fullest advantage. It is known, for instance, that one of the principal features of gregariousness is the habit shared by various herbivorous mammals of meeting and moving in a group under the leadership of one or more if its dominant members. Most Bakhtiāri techniques for minding and moving animals represent the application of this principle; the movement of the leaders is controlled and this controls the remainder of the animals as well. One basic method of achieving this (particularly with horses) is to identify the leader of a band, usually a stallion or an old mare, and to place a semi-hobble on the leader's front legs. A second method, used for the small animals, involves the imposition of a leader or several leaders, trained in advance and familiarised with human beings. Leaders of the flocks, castrated billy goats (*sehis*) or rams (*dobor*) are trained to respond to the human voice by being rewarded with salt, for which they have a great liking. The animals are chosen for their height and for their large, imposing horns. Their haughty gait and the way they carry their horns is exaggerated with a few little accessories: tassels, amulets, a large bronze bell with a dignified ring (*tārāk*), which is a kind of badge of office. Each flock of two to three hundred beasts will have four or five of these leaders, always moving together and constantly watched by the rest of the flock; a movement from them is enough to make the whole flock move.

Successful animal husbandry therefore depends primarily on an expert and extensive understanding of the natural world and of animal behaviour, and those in possession of such knowledge constitute a specialised work force: grooms (*ramakhon*), herdsmen (*gāgelon*) and shepherds (*chupon*). Shepherds in particular assume great importance and bear heavy responsibility on account of the number and the value of their sheep, and also because these animals spend several months of the year guarded by them alone, in pastures far distant from the camps. Shepherds are armed with a club (*gorz*) and a sling (*kivom*) and are accompanied by their dogs (*gallepā*), which are born amongst the flocks and are distinct from the dogs in the camps.

The shepherd's expertise is passed down orally and by example. Apprenticeship begins very young, at eight or nine. Good shepherds are highly prized, the more so as these days they are becoming scarcer. This is partly attributable to the spread of education, which tends to divert school-age children away from traditional careers. It must also be said that the job of the shepherd, although rewarded by a wage that is relatively high by Bakhtiāri standards (generally 10 per cent of the annual increase in male lambs in the flock), is a particularly thankless and restricting one. It may not require the same sustained physical effort as agricultural labour, but minding the flocks demands constant vigilance and availability. A shepherd's life is an extremely isolated and uncomfortable one. Many shepherds give up when they marry, and many marry late—at over thirty if they are very poor—in order to have time to save up the 'price of milk' (*shir-bahā*), the sum given to the fiancée's father in compensation for the marriage.

Notwithstanding the vigilance of the shepherds and the ferocity of their dogs, and in spite of the fact that animals are branded with a hot iron, or by having their ears cut, theft remains very common. In fact it is almost a national pastime, or at any rate an activity whose status is, to say the least, ambiguous. Sheep-stealing is unanimously condemned and severely punished—the ancient khans used to have the ears of those they caught cut off—however the thieves themselves enjoy an enhanced social status. When a sheep owner who has been robbed manages to trace the perpetrator of the crime, he has to prove, by giving an exact and very detailed description of the stolen animals, that they belong to him. The thief would subsequently be dishonoured (it is considered) if he did not then acknowledge his crime. Thief and victim negotiate the return of the spoils; usually the thief manages to extract a promise from his victim that he will withdraw from further proceedings.

More than any other activity, Bakhtiāri animal husbandry demonstrates that the idea of 'material culture' in isolation is absurd because in addition to the tools and objects, a whole range of knowledge and expertise contributes to 'material culture'. Without it, the tools and utensils are lifeless and deprived of meaning.

right above
Ploughing in summer quarters using a swing plough drawn by a pair of oxen.

right below
In their summer quarters the Bakhtiāri use a one-handled plough; either the *khish-mostārom,* a type found in the region of Isfahan (*left*), or the *khish-takdasti* which is found in Kordestān and the Hamadan region (*right*). In their winter quarters they use the two-handled Mesopotamian plough (*khish-bāhi* or *khish-dārpāzani*), an extremely ancient type found throughout Khuzestān (*bottom*). The wooden parts they make themselves; the metal plough-share is made by visiting gypsies.

AGRICULTURE

Nowadays, most of the Bakhtiāri cultivate wheat for human consumption and barley for the animals (wheat accounts for 75 per cent of the harvest). Their cereal crops are dependent on rain and are planted on very poor soil. More and more of the grazing land is being ploughed up. Yields are between 300 and 700 kilograms per hectare.

The soil is fertilised naturally by the excrement of the animals put to graze on the stubble, and during fallow years. Once the rains arrive, the soil is ploughed with a swing plough (*khish*), drawn by a pair of oxen or, less commonly, two mules or horses. The animals are harnessed together to a double yoke (*joft*) placed over their withers, in front of or over a roll of cloth that acts as a collar. The word *khish* (plough) is also used to describe the area that can be ploughed in one day by such a team. The Bakhtiāri use a one-handled plough in the summer pastures and a Mesopotamian twin-handled plough in the winter pastures. They generally plough only once a year, sowing broadcast in front of the plough (60–70 kg of seed per hectare).

Crops are harvested with a sickle (*dās*). The stalks are seized below the ears with the free hand and then cut about 30 cm above ground, the sickle being drawn towards the body. The higher the stubble, the longer the animals can spend in the fields after the harvest, with better manuring as a result. The sheaves are gathered and piled up using wooden pitchforks—either the two-pronged *daker*, made from a forked stick, or the *ganger* with six to nine prongs which are fixed to the handle with strips of untanned leather (the leather is applied wet and tightens as it dries). The threshing floor (*kharmen*) is a specially prepared circle of beaten earth, 10–15 metres in diameter. Threshing is achieved by driving a line of horses, mules and donkeys round and round the threshing floor, with the donkeys in the centre and mules and horses round the edge. A man walks behind the animals singing, shouting and gesticulating to stop them slowing down and eating the ears of wheat. This technique of threshing by trampling is peculiar to the nomads and called *ākhon* or *holey* by the Bakhtiāri. Settled tribespeople prefer to use a tribulum (*chom*), a wooden sledge dragged behind an ox. The underside of the sledge is armed with stones embedded in the wood.

After about fifteen hours of this treatment the threshing of a medium-sized stack is complete. Next the straw is separated and what remains is winnowed with a pitchfork. The fine straw, husks and grain are tossed in the air, the grain falls down vertically whilst the lighter chaff is blown a little farther away by the wind. Unwanted elements are subsequently removed by sieving, and are then picked out by hand.

What is truly unique about Bakhtiāri agriculture is the fact that cultivation takes place in both summer and winter pastures simultaneously. This gives rise to perpetual movement between fields, which naturally exerts a strong influence on the nomadic cycle. In the summer pastures the nomads do the sowing at the beginning of September, just before the autumn migration, and harvest and thresh the crop when they return in June–July the following year. In the winter pastures however sowing takes place at the end of October, the time of the first rains and shortly after the nomads' return. The crop is harvested at the end of their stay. Even though early varieties of cereals are grown, which ripen in five months, the timing of the harvest often makes it necessary for several men from each camp to stay longer in the winter quarters and to catch up with the migration on foot. In this case the threshing has to wait until the following year when they return. Although this system of cereal cultivation is typical of the nomads, it could not be successful without logistical support from the settled members of the tribe who keep an eye on all the property too big to be transported (such as ploughs) and, in the winter quarters, the sheaves of wheat waiting to be threshed.

below
Double yoke (*joft*) used for ploughing with oxen. It is placed over the withers in front of a roll of cloth which acts as a collar.

below right
The method used for harnessing mules to the plough.

1. *lidin*
2. *lidinband*
3. *jar*
4. *jājar*
5. *dārkhish*
6. *gawādār and hamekash*
7. *jol-kachal or kachal-band*
8. *joft*

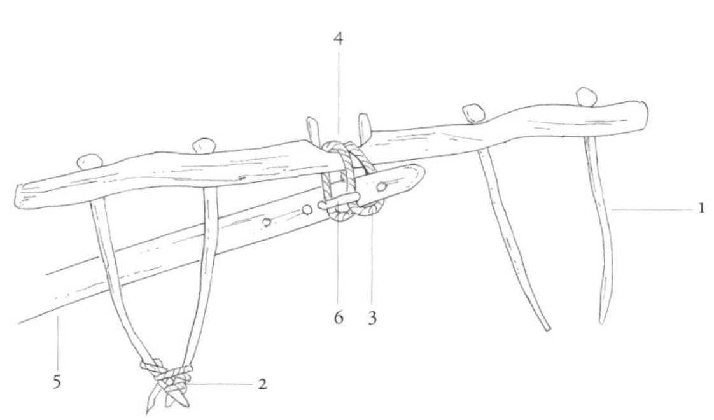

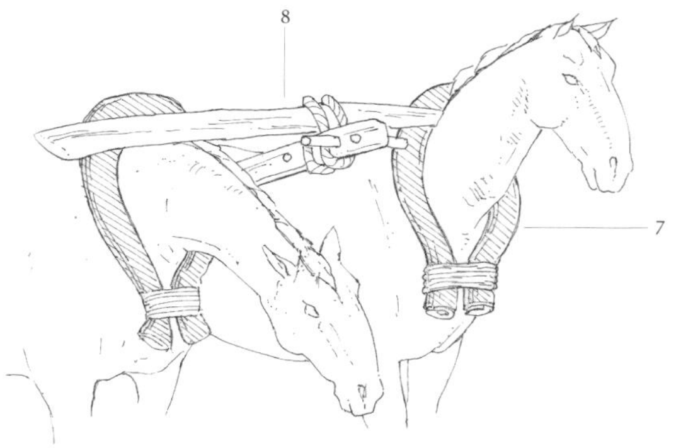

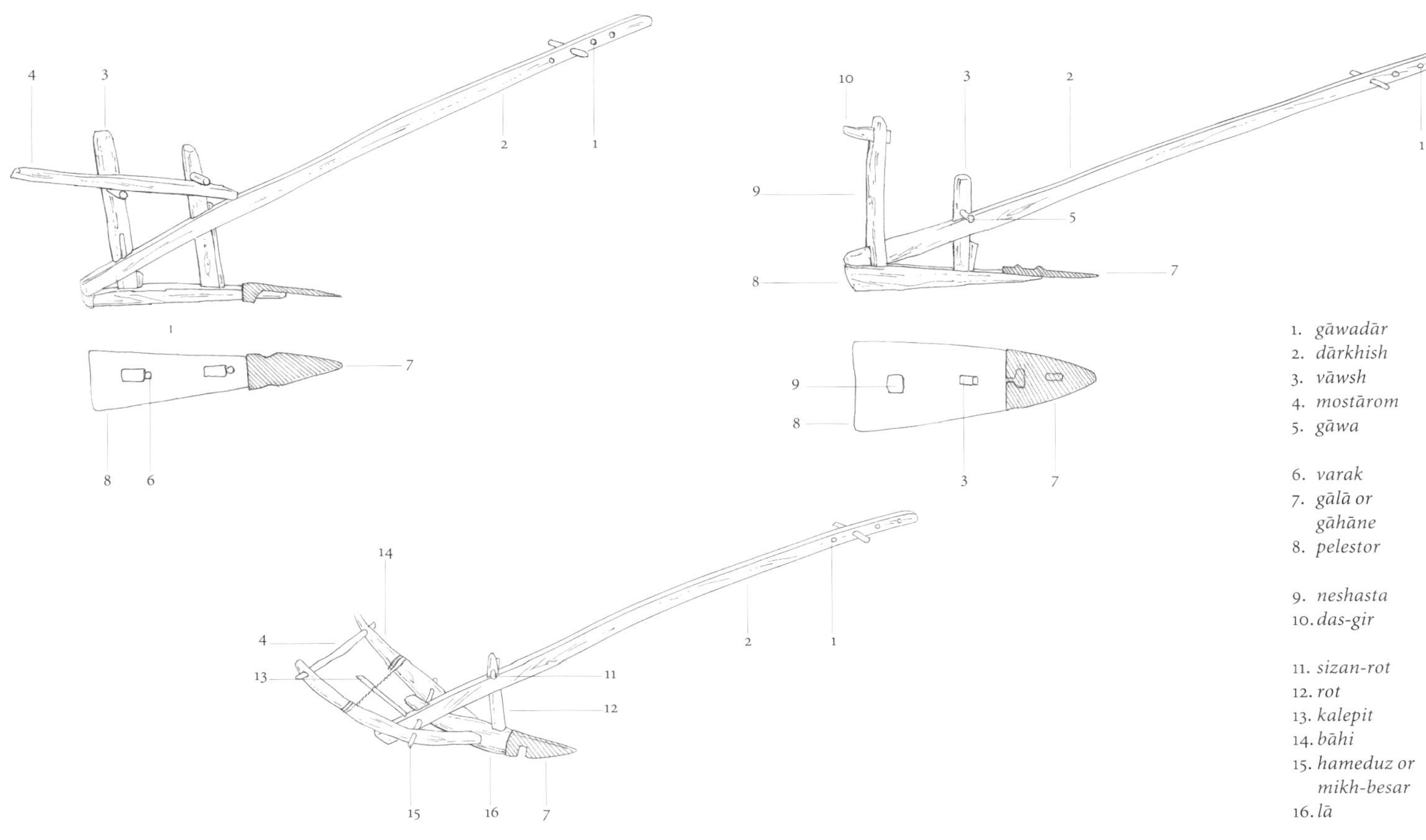
1. *gāwadār*
2. *dārkhish*
3. *vāwsh*
4. *mostārom*
5. *gāwa*
6. *varak*
7. *gālā or gāhāne*
8. *pelestor*
9. *neshasta*
10. *das-gir*
11. *sizan-rot*
12. *rot*
13. *kalepit*
14. *bāhi*
15. *hameduz or mikh-besar*
16. *lā*

HUNTING AND THE GATHERING OF WILD FOOD

Supplementary food is provided by hunting and the gathering of edible plant food, such as berries and mushrooms. The Bakhtiāri are passionate huntsmen, going after gazelle in the winter quarters, wild goats in the summer pastures and game birds and wild boar in both places. They also gather plants for non-culinary use; in the old days dyestuffs were of special importance. Some of these wild products are sold and fetch very high prices: gum tragacanth (*zidi*) and especially *gaz*, which we know as manna, a sugary substance used in confectionery. Salt (*nevek*), an important element in the diet of both humans and animals, as has already been mentioned, occurs naturally in the water of some of the rivers in the tribal area. Groups living near these rivers extract it by evaporation and sell it in blocks (*ārā*) weighing 18 kg. All these activities dovetail neatly and convivially into the nomadic cycle and demonstrate the close relationship between Bakhtiāri society and the environment that supports it.

Hunting deserves special mention. The position it occupies in the Bakhtiāri psyche really bears no relationship to its economic importance, which is quite modest in terms of the provision of meat and the elimination of predators and competitors for the food required by the flocks. Hunting resembles riding in this respect. It is interesting to note that Bakhtiāri oral literature celebrates high deeds of hunting (*shekāl*) and war (*jang*) with the same passionate intensity. Favourite epic poems portray a hero who, after many vicissitudes, comes to offer his war booty in homage to his leader, or the game he has killed while hunting to his beloved. Both activities share a destructive finality, require the same kind of skills (pursuit, tracking, encircling, ambush or lying in wait), and involve the use of a horse and rifle, both of which have an aura of prestige. Success in hunting as in war (at any rate in Bakhtiāri terms) presupposes such qualities in the protagonist as familiarity with the environment, cunning, physical endurance, skill and accuracy in the handling of weapons, courage when dangerous animals (wild boar, bears, panther) are his prey, plus efficiency (and elegance) in the sense of wanting to get as close as possible before taking aim. Game may be valued principally for the skill needed to get close to it (wild goat) or to shoot it on the wing (partridge). Hunting therefore provides an excellent training for war, and in the absence of war offers men an outlet for expressing aggression and an opportunity to prove themselves in a way appropriate to their attitudes and ideology.

The Bakhtiāri are passionately keen on weapons. Nomads never go anywhere unarmed, even short distances (for instance from one camp to another), though the arms may be just sticks. Some of their clubs are terrifying. The most widely used club—and the shepherd's main means of defence—is the *gorz*. This is a shortish stick (80 cm), bulbous at one end, with a diameter of 5–6 cm; the bulbous end is polygonal in section and its edges are sharpened. These edges are sometimes protected and reinforced with sheet metal nailed to the wood. A good *gorz* is made of extremely hard wood (wild almond) cut from a solid block; it can weigh several kilograms and cost as much as a high-quality pair of rope-soled shoes. As a weapon the *gorz*, which is used with both hands, is evidently very ancient; the word is used in Ferdowsi's *Shāh-nāmeh* (tenth century) to refer to the club of the hero, Rostam.

The sling (*kivom*) is probably as old and as widely used. Shepherds use it to direct their flocks, as well as for frightening off wolves. Children learn to handle it from an early age and achieve an alarming level of skill.

The earliest documentary evidence of the possession of firearms by the Bakhtiāri is a portrait of the first *ilkhāni* of the tribe, Hoseyn Qoli Khān, who died in 1882, showing a muzzle-loading flintlock gun. After the Constitutional Revolution of 1906–11, the Bakhtiāri were able, according to Sardār As'ad, another leader, to muster the fire power of 150,000 foot soldiers and 25,000 cavalrymen. Their arms came from various sources and gave rise to a flourishing arms trade and a substantial amount of smuggling. The supply of guns was for years a pre-condition for any political agreement with the tribe. The British were amongst their most solicitous purveyors of weaponry from the end of the nineteenth century onwards, and the Germans during the two world wars. Up to the beginning of the 1960s, the Bakhtiāri arsenal was in fact a virtual replica of the Iranian military arsenal, and for a very good reason: between 1914 and 1953 the number of guns falling into tribal hands during skirmishes with the regular army has been estimated at about a hundred thousand (not counting machine guns, anti-tank weaponry, etc.). One type of gun seems to have been particularly appreciated by the Bakhtiāri , a Czechoslovakian model made in the town of Brno. The word *bernow* currently used by them describes any kind of military gun (as opposed to the *dolile-tahpor*, the hunting gun with two barrels), and an adjective derived from the same word is applied to humans, animals and objects alike when they are remarkable for their beauty. The Bakhtiāri marksmen have always had a reputation for speed and accuracy even in the least favourable conditions. In a sharp-shooting exercise called a *geyghāsh,* performed from the back of a galloping horse, a good shot is one who, with a quick left and right, hits a target or prey behind as well as in front of himself. In cemeteries in the tribal area many of the graves have a gun carved on the headstone to commemorate the skill of a dead marksman.

Crazy about arms and quick to resort to them, the Bakhtiāri inevitably began to be regarded as a threat by the Iranian authorities. Their disarmament has been the cornerstone of the tribal policy of successive governments in Iran since the Second World War; except, that is, for the first few governments who tried to appeal to tribal 'patriotism' and to involve them in national defence. In fact, the disarmament of the tribes only really began in 1957 and was not achieved (officially, at least) until the later 1960s. No policy implemented by the Iranian government in tribal lands has excited such enduring anger and such active opposition from the tribes as the disarmament policy. The length of time taken to implement it demonstrates this. Furthermore no policy has proved so ineffectual; the speed with which military weapons reappeared amongst the Bakhtiāri at the outbreak of the Islamic revolution illustrates the point clearly enough.

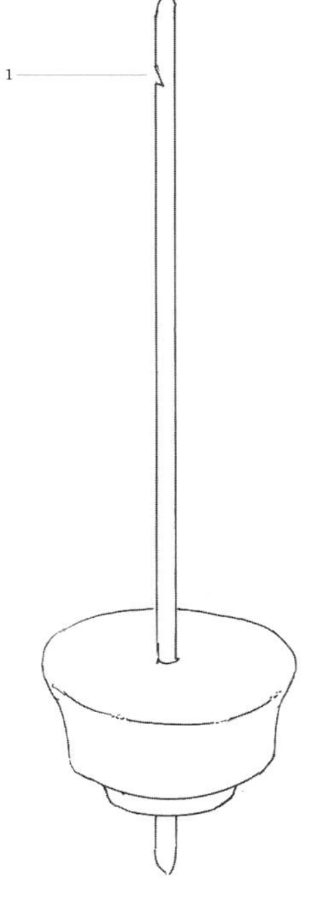

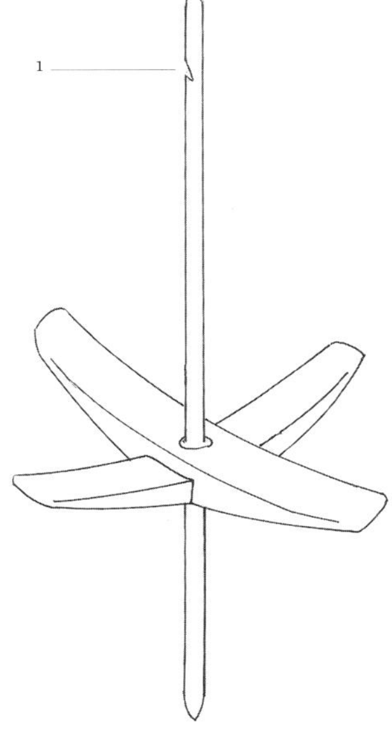

A light spindle (*dik*) for spinning fine yarns and a spindle with removable cross-arms (*parra*) for spinning coarse yarns.

1. *list*

CRAFT TECHNIQUES

The craft techniques practised by the Bakhtiāri tend to be at a simple level. Some techniques, like basket making and leather work, are represented by only two or three rough products: the cylindrical basket (*korok*) used to transport chickens, the flat basket (*salah*) used for feeding straw and grain to herbivorous animals, the goat skin (*mashk*) used to hold liquids, water, yoghurt or *dugh*. Metal work is not practised at all by the tribe. The few metal objects indispensable to the Bakhtiāri way of life (ploughshares, stirrups and bits, kitchen utensils) are provided by non-tribal craftsmen, Qorbati or Kowli. The Bakhtiāri neither make nor use any pottery.

By contrast, their textiles are surprising for their diversity, richness and technical complexity. In this respect the Bakhtiāri certainly belong to Muslim civilisation, described by the historian M. Lombard as a 'textile civilisation'. The nomads use only sheep's wool (*pashm*) and goat hair (*mi*) from their own flocks. However, woollen wadding (*kazal*) is delivered to Qorbati artisans, the *nemetmal*, to be made into felt (*nemet*).

When the animals have been shorn, the wool and hair are washed several times in running water. The Bakhtiāri attribute the brightness of their carpets to the action of this water. Goat hair is combed using a special comb (*shonwa*), which consists of a plank of wood equipped with a parallel double row of metal teeth on the upper edge. The person using it has it on the ground in front of them with the prongs vertical. Wool, which is softer than goat hair, is beaten with a stick to disentangle the fibres rather than being combed.

The spinning of goat hair and sheep's wool alike is done with a hand spindle. The most popular spindle in current use is the *parra* that can be taken to pieces. Wool or carded goat hair is wound round the spinner's left forearm. Strands are pulled out with the fingers and twisted by the rotation of the spindle, which hangs on the end of the yarn. When the spindle is about to touch the ground, the yarn is wound diagonally round the crosspieces and the spinning movement is started again. The *parra* provides a method of spinning quickly. Another type of spindle, the *dik* is preferred for finer yarn; its rotation is slower and steadier. It is handled in the same way, the spun yarn being wound round the stem of the spindle. Women using the *dik* sometimes allow the nail of their left thumb to grow unusually long. They then pierce a hole in it through which they draw the strands of wool and thus control the thickness of the yarn as they spin. When the spindle is full the yarn is wound into a tight ball, or a hank if it is to be dyed. Reels and bobbins are not used.

The production of dyestuffs for wool was in the past an important activity. As late as the 1940s and 1950s, a few Bakhtiāri carpets could be found with up to twelve colours: black, blue, two different greens, brown, beige, white, two reds, pink, orange and yellow. Nearly all were made using natural ingredients. The white and sometimes the beige and brown are natural undyed wool. Most of the other colours were obtained from decoctions of plants picked by the women in the mountains.

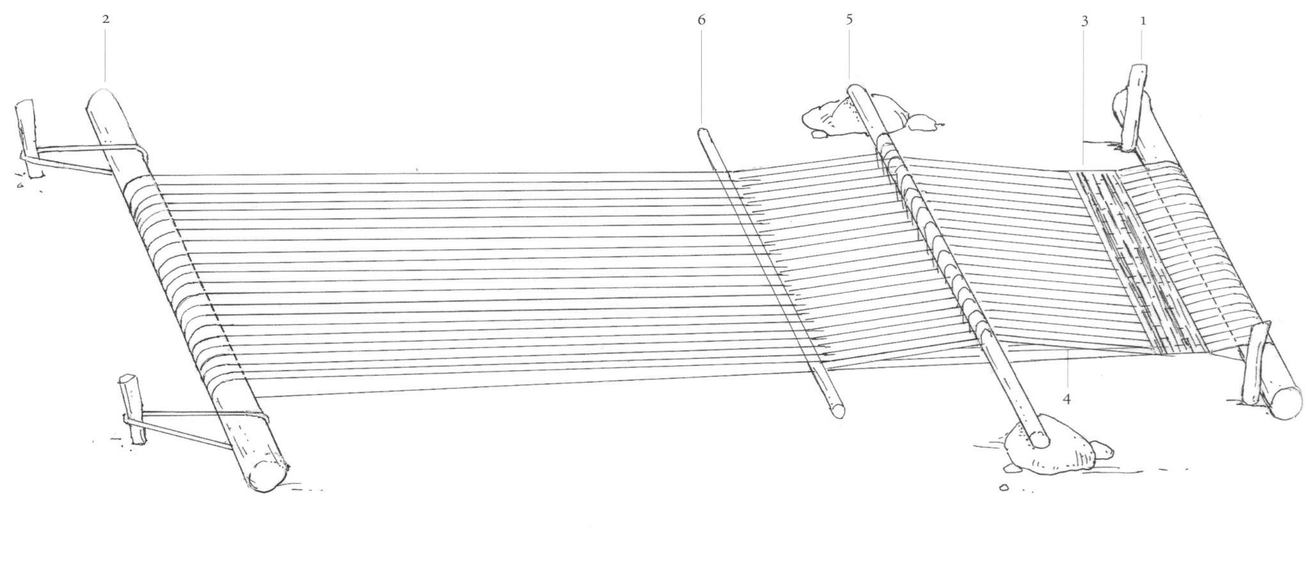

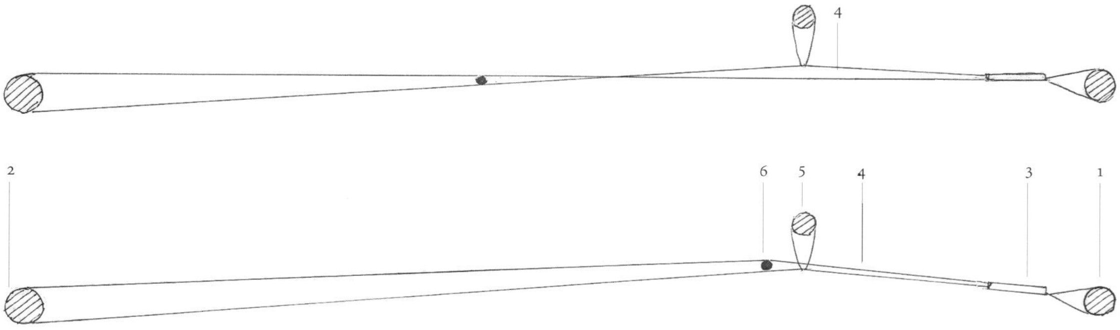

1. breast beam (*bonzom jelow*)
2. wrap beam (*bonzom - pain*)
3. cloth
4. shed and counter shed
5. heddle rod (*chu - piz*)
6. shed stick (*posh - piz*)

right
Straps and narrow bands are made by the process of card- or tablet-weaving. The warp threads, which are the length of the finished strap, are attached to pegs in the ground, the further one several metres away outside the tent. The shed is produced by rotating 'cards' (*duwāl*) made of leather (seen lower left), and the wefts are compacted with a wooden sword-beater (*chapat*).

left above
A horizontal ground loom in use.

left below
Diagram of the horizontal ground loom (*tamdār*). The breast beam is held in place by two pegs. The tension of the warp (*reshtan* or *cherk*) is maintained by the action of tying the warp beam tightly to two other pegs. The heddle rod (*chu-piz*) rests on two stones and the shed and counter shed are formed by moving the shed stick (*posh-piz*) as shown in the drawing of a loom in longitudinal section.

The spun wool would be treated with sheep manure prior to being dyed. The albumen brightened the colours and helped to make them fast. Nowadays these techniques have almost completely disappeared, and the settled artisans who dye wool for the Bakhtiāri use only chemical dyes.

Weaving itself (*bāf*) is a vital element of the Bakhtiāri economy because it transforms home produced raw materials, wool and hair, into such goods as straps, saddle-bags, rugs, clothes and tents for local consumption. It is also the only activity that is exclusively feminine.

For making girths (*veris*) the Bakhtiāri use a card loom; the technique is known as tablet weaving. This is a simple type of weaving, transitional between the making of cords and braid and the weaving of fabric. The cards are of hardened cow-hide, 5–6 cm square, with a hole pierced in each corner. A warp thread passes through each hole in a number of plates (10 to 20, according to the width of girth required). The threads are stretched between two pegs hammered into the ground, as far apart as the length of girth required. The plates are aligned so that they hold the warp threads apart in two layers and the weft thread is passed between them. The weft is packed down with a knife about 30 cm long made from a single piece of wood (*chapat*). The plates are rotated vertically a quarter of a turn each time after the passage of the weft, and each thread appears at the top one time in four. Very varied geometric patterns can be produced, and if each plate is moved separately, patterns of the utmost diversity can be woven. In addition, the rotation of the plates twists the warp threads four by four, producing a warp-twined effect which is very characteristic.

All other weaving is done on large horizontal, single heddle looms (*tamdār*), as used, with few variations, by all the nomads in the Middle East. The looms are simple, easily taken apart for transporting and therefore well adapted to the itinerant life.

Three different types of weaving are produced on this loom. The commonest is *sāde-baf* (literally 'simple weaving') which corresponds to our plain weave (one under, one over). The warp and weft of these fabrics are of the same material, wool for the men's jacket (*chughā*), goat hair yarn for the tent fabric. The two other types of weaving are the 'soumak' and the knotted carpet. For these the

right
The saddle bag (*hurzhin*) is used for storing and transporting personal belonging. It is made on the loom in a single piece and then folded (see dotted lines below) and sewn up at the sides to form two pockets.

below
Three different weaving techniques are used: (1) plain weave for the inner panels, (2) weft-wrapping or 'soumak' which the Bakhtiāri call 'animals' for the outer panels and a small square on each inner panel, and (3) knotted pile at the bottom where the bags rest on the ground (*pella*). The *hurzhin* is completed by the addition of tassels and closure loops (*kilit*).

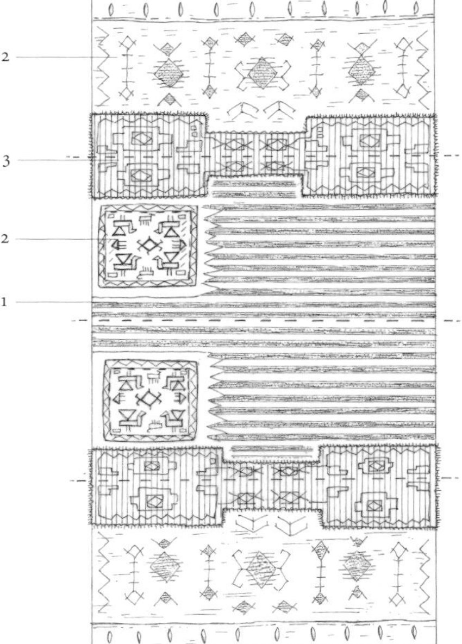

warp (*shiligh*) is cotton and the weft (*khoma*) wool. 'Soumak' and 'kilim' should not be confused. The Bakhtiāri weave the former but rarely the latter. The term 'soumak', which is familiar to western flat-weave collectors, is not a word they use, and there is no Lori equivalent for it. When the Bakhtiāri talk about this type of weaving they use the name of the finished product—*hurzhin* (saddle-bags), or *ley*, the long strips used to cover the saddle bags at the back of the tent. Alternatively, they use the name of the patterns woven into the fabric, *nashq-gāmasisi* (animals) for the saddle-bags and *nashq-botishā'i* (geometric patterns) for the *ley*. The Bakhtiāri use the Turkish knot for knotted-pile weaving (*qāli-bāf*), which they use on the bottom of the saddle-bag (*pella*) and for piled rugs, (*qāli*).

The saddle bag, *hurzhin*, used to carry and store equipment and personal possessions, is perhaps the most interesting type of Bakhtiāri weaving because it demonstrates in one object three techniques described above: (a) plain weave for the inner panels, (b) 'animals' for the outer panels and (c) knotted pile at the bottom where the bags rest on the ground.

Carpets made by the knotted-pile technique for use on the ground vary according to the thickness of the materials used and the delicacy of the work. As its name implies, the *khersak* (from *khers*, 'bear') is coarse, and the Bakhtiāri too regard it as an inferior product. The pile is long (3–4 cm), and the decoration scanty and rough in outline.

The *qāli*, or knotted-pile rug after which the technique is named, is a much finer piece of work. Most Bakhtiāri carpets can be recognised easily by the motifs woven into them. The middle of the carpet is divided into squares measuring about 20 cm a side (*kheshta*, 'bricks'), and each square bears a semi-figurative motif almost always based on plants such as cypresses and weeping willows, each distinct from the next but of more or less standard design. The border of the carpet usually has a floral motif in the form of a continuous garland or a succession of medallions or both. All these motifs can be woven without being drawn beforehand because they are traditional. The quality and refinement of the *qāli* varies enormously; the average knot count is between 900 and 1,800 per square decimetre.

The saddle bag (*hurzhin*). Each pocket is fastened independently by loops that pass through slits in the outer panel of the bag (*below*). The end loop is secured by a padlock (*qolf*).Saddle bags are usually embellished at the front with tassels (*mangul*), and bands (*noftorband* or *varuna*) decorated with beads and mother-of-pearl buttons. At the back of the bag there may be a strap (*dineka*) with a padded crupper dock (*rofida*) that can replace the crupper on the saddle, or be used in addition to it.

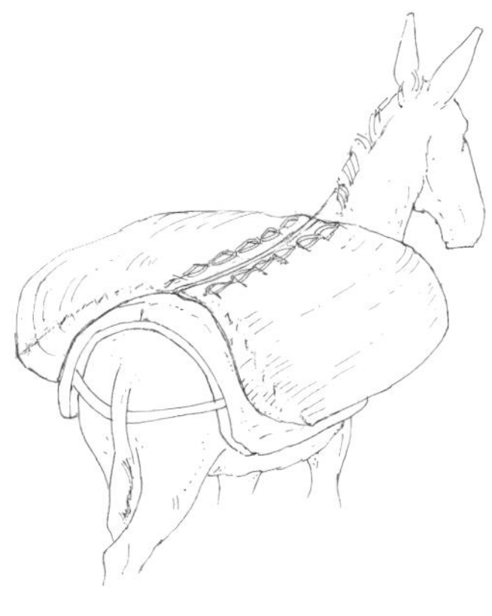

The closure loops (*kilit*) pass through slits in the outer panel of the bag. The end loop is secured by a padlock (*qolf*).

The majority of Bakhtiāri carpets therefore are not very fine compared, for instance, with carpets from urban workshops like Kāshān, which seldom contain less than 2,500 knots per square decimetre. Their manufacture nevertheless requires a considerable investment of time and money for most nomads. To illustrate this, I include here some figures relating to a carpet whose manufacture I was able to monitor in October–December 1969 at Qal'eh-Barān (Khuzestān) in the *tāyefa* of Gand-ʿAli. This was a piece of average weight and size (1.72 by 2.30 metres) and an average of 1,210 knots per square decimetre, and so fairly typical of this kind of product. The materials required were 21 kg of wool, at a cost of about 130 rials per kg. Other expenses were: 260 rials for dyeing the wool and 510 rials worth of cotton for the warp and the selvages. The actual weaving was done by one woman who took 147 days to do a total of 736 hours work (this represents an average speed of about 650 knots per hour). The carpet was finally sold in town for 5,500 rials (then worth about £30).

These figures explain the relative scarcity of high-quality tribal rugs, and the almost total absence today of the highest quality tribal rugs of all, the *bibi-bāf*, which only the daughters of the khan (*bibi*), had the means and time to produce because they had domestic help with the household tasks. The *bibi-bāf* were large (3 by 4 metres and more), and of high quality, sometimes as many as 5,000 knots per square decimetre. They would take several months of full-time work and the assistance of hired weavers. The weaving of *bibi-bāf* in the tribes more or less ceased in the 1930s when the great Bakhtiāri khan families were eliminated by Rezā Shāh's regime. The work was revived with varying success at a later date, notably at Chāl-Shotor, in the Shahr-e Kord region. These days it is carried out in workshops in village communities, because there are few nomadic families now who can release their womenfolk from the normal domestic chores long enough for such a time-consuming craft activity. The history of the *bibi-bāf* is doubly interesting therefore for the light it throws on an evolutionary process that may have affected many skills in the past.

Every other product or service required by the Bakhtiāri is supplied by the shop-keepers (*dokondār*) in neighbouring towns and villages (Gandomān, Ardal, Fārsān, Shahr-e Kord and Dārān for the summer pastures; Dezful, Gotvan, Lāli, Masjed-e Soleymān, Izeh, and Rāmhormoz for the winter quarters), or by specialised trades people who are not members of the tribe but who travel with the nomads: shoemakers (*givekash*), tailors (*khayyāt*), felt makers (*nemetmāl*), blacksmiths (*āhangar*), joiners (*takhtkash*), barbers-cum-circumcisers (*dallāk*), and musicians (*tushmāl*). All these tradespeople, and particularly the Kowli (gypsies), who make small utensils like spindles, carding combs, beating combs for weaving and sieves, are, as has been noted before, more or less scorned by the Bakhtiāri who give them the generic name of Qorbati (strangers).

The Bakhtiāri system of production is thus both socially and technically specialised, in that it has been adapted to a particular environment. It may be more productive than other systems, but it is also more vulnerable.

EPILOGUE

MATERIAL CULTURE AND THE FUTURE: ELECTIVE BUT STEADY ASSIMILATION

The 'material culture' described in broad outline above is not immune from change. Its origins may be hidden in the mists of time, but it is not immutable. The Bakhtiāri, like every other social group, are subject to change, and as they change, the techniques used by them and the objects surrounding them change too. Whether we like it or not, this is the case. Changes occur in different spheres, in response to different pressures.

The contact established and maintained by the Bakhtiāri with the West since the arrival of the British in ʿArabestān (the former name of Khuzestān) in the mid-nineteenth century, is one of the most remarkable features of the tribe. Paradoxically, however, the Bakhtiāri, in sharp contrast to their neighbours the Qashqā'i, have remained one of the least 'westernised' tribes in Iran. This is largely due to their geographical location, far from the main communication networks and large towns in the area. The Bakhtiāri absorbed Western influence in part through direct contact, first with the English and later, to a lesser extent, with the Germans during the two world wars, and in part indirectly, via the tribal policies the Iranians attempted to impose from 1925 onwards based on Western models. Western influence affected many aspects of Bakhtiāri life, producing a range of effects, some insignificant and some fraught with consequence.

Curiously enough, direct contact seems to have had scant influence on the Bakhtiāri, and to have produced only a limited number of isolated borrowings from Western material culture. The massive military presence of the British Army and the display of goods and equipment of all types at British oil installations on the very borders of tribal territory should not be forgotten. But the paradoxical lack of influence can largely be explained by the distance the British, with their indirect rule, managed to preserve between their installations and the Bakhtiāri tribe. This distance was also painstakingly maintained by the tribal chiefs who were intermediaries between the tribe and the outside world and could not be circumvented. Their instinct, easily understandable, was to hang on to the political and material advantages to be gained from such imposing neighbours. From the British period onwards the great Bakhtiāri chiefs, or at least some of them, could be said to have become westernised; some, like Hājji 'Ali Qoli Khān Sardār As'ad whose role in the Constitutional Revolution has already been mentioned, even spent long periods in Europe. For the great mass of nomads, however, cultural borrowings were again few and modest in scope, and were limited to material items and their accompanying vocabulary. However, these borrowings did not all assume the same significance and meaning, nor did they all provoke the same consequences for Bakhtiāri society. Analysed from this angle, three situations or categories can be identified.

The first category includes the borrowing of techniques or materials to replace existing, more rudimentary and less efficient Bakhtiāri ones. The adoption of the new techniques and materials brought about definite advances in productivity or efficiency without significant consequences for the host society. Into this category come, for example, paraffin lamps, including the hurricane lamp with a wick (*chelāgh-markabi*) and the pressure lamp (*chelāgh-turi*), whose spread sounded the death knell (for obvious reasons of efficiency) of the old-fashioned oil-lamp (*chelāgh-pisuz*). Similarly the English cavalry saddle, with its metal pommel and leather seat, replaced the solid wood Bakhtiāri saddle. The *zin-e inglisi* was more comfortable to sit on and, besides, materials for its construction could be had more cheaply than materials for the traditional saddle, which was cut from a single piece of wood. At this time the destruction of woodland in the tribal areas was already far advanced.

A second category of borrowings consists of items that answered the same need for efficiency and productivity, but had more serious consequences for Bakhtiāri society, even if it was only because they were unequally distributed within the tribe. A good example is provided by breech-loading firearms (*tahpor*), and then automatic rifles which superseded the ancient muzzle-loading *puspor*. Modern weapons, obtained either as spoils of war or by purchase at exorbitant cost, have always been distributed very unevenly through the tribe. They have generally been owned by groups that are powerful already or by groups linked by birth or by political persuasion (*basteh*) to the khans. Modern weapons certainly made their contribution to the crucial structural changes that took place at the turn of the twentieth century.

A more recent example (from the 1960s) but just as significant was the abandonment of a number of water mills (*āsyāw*) in favour of modern diesel-powered grinders. These grinders, imported from Italy, are known as *makina* by the Bakhtiāri. They grind wheat less finely than the water mills, but give a better yield, up to 1,800 kg of flour per 24 hours, as opposed to the water mills' 1,000 to 1,100 kg per 24 hours, and it seems that increased yield makes the higher overall price acceptable. Their real attraction lies in the fact that they do not depend, as the traditional mills do, on the proximity of a watercourse with a regular flow. Whereas many *āsyāw* virtually cease to function during the summer season, a *makina* can be set up anywhere and can function round the clock, providing that fuel and, sooner or later, spare parts are available. At any rate, compared with the other equipment used by the Bakhtiāri, the *makina* is a large and complex machine that has to be installed by specialised workmen from outside the tribe, and requires a big outlay of materials and wages. The Bakhtiāri maintain that these grinders give them the same amount of trouble as do the pump-operated oil lamps! One diesel mill that I observed being installed in 1970 had to be carried, in pieces, from Lāli to the place in the mountains where it was to be installed; 60 men were needed to transport it and it cost its owner a total of 45,000 rials at the time. The *makina* requires the attention of two or three people full-time, and there are always expenses to be born (fuel, spare parts, etc.). Because no co-operative community organisations exist to satisfy consumer needs in this respect, the high cost has, through a well-known process, favoured the concentration of grain milling facilities in the hands of a privileged few, most of them khans or, nowadays, *kalāntar*.

An elderly woman on the upward migration to the summer pastures with one of the numerous camp dogs. 1985.

A third category of borrowings share one overall characteristic: they answer no particular need apart from the human need (which also exists in Bakhtiāri society) to imitate the behaviour of the upper classes. Even though they contribute nothing towards 'progress' as such, they can take hold just as firmly as the more obviously indispensable borrowings, and can sometimes modify behaviour quite considerably. Tea is an excellent example. The traveller H-R. d'Allemagne has left an interesting eye-witness account of Bakhtiāri attitudes to tea in 1907:

"Tea and coffee are unknown to the common people, and, as their chiefs explained, their use is avoided as far as possible because it makes people dependent on other countries for the supply of tea itself and of sugar, not to mention the glass and china that have to be brought from Europe at great expense" (d'Allemagne 1911, IV, p. 181).

The chiefs' concern was most admirable; the truth, of course, was different. The chiefs' main aim was to remain the sole beneficiaries of the tangible manifestations of friendships lavished on the Bakhtiāri at the time in far from disinterested fashion by the English. Things have certainly changed because, as has already been shown, most nomads, even the poorest, drink large quantities of tea and consider it a necessity of life even though its purchase sometimes demands great sacrifice. The Bakhtiāris remember the end of Rezā Shāh's rule as a 'period without tea or sugar'.

To close this rapid inventory of Bakhtiāri borrowings from the West, a fourth category exists which is somewhat separate from the other three, but just as instructive. This category consists of Western items that have been tried and rejected, or have been only partially assimilated by Bakhtiāri culture. Most striking is the example of the Merino rams introduced hopefully by several important Bakhtiāri stockbreeders in the 1950s, to improve the quality of the wool produced

A newly married woman wearing a red *meynā* on her way to visit settled relatives living in a nearby village. Her husband rides in front and her mother-in-law by her side. Doāb, summer 1984.

by Lori sheep. This was a complete failure for two reasons: first, the Merino rams found mounting the Lori ewes awkward because of their fat tails; second, and even more importantly, the lambs born from the Merino-Lori cross did not have this fat appendage. In the eyes of the Bakhtiāri, it must be noted, the fat tail plays an essential role in the value of the sheep, for aesthetic as well as for culinary reasons.

The other examples are not as clear-cut as this one. The white Western tents (*chādor*) which some of the chiefs make a point of preferring to the black goat-hair *bohon* are a case in point. Tent snobbery dates from the arrival on the scene of the Anglo-Iranian Oil Company, and, as so often in such cases, comes with a ready-made attempt at justification for such a preference. The Western tent is esteemed to be cooler, or more weather-proof, or lighter than the traditional tent. In actual fact, in addition to its high price, it has the disadvantage for the average Bakhtiāri user of being open only on the two short sides (ends). The full opening along the whole of one side of the tent, or three sides including the long one, is a feature of the traditional tent that governs to a great extent its entire interior lay-out, as well as the way it faces and its position in relation to the other tents in the camp. This is why the Western tent has had only very limited success with the Bakhtiāri. Its use is confined to accommodation for guests, or for a co-wife, as an adjunct to the main goat-hair tent of some of the chiefs.

European dress (three piece suit plus soft hat or cap) has also only met with limited acceptance, though for a different reason. Under the pretext of modernisation, the replacement of traditional dress with European dress was made compulsory by the law of 28 December 1928. The Bakhtiāri, unlike other tribes such as the Qashqā'i, never resigned themselves to giving up their felt hat, blue-and-white striped jacket and black cotton trousers, the main items of masculine attire which are imbued with strong symbolic value. They only kept two items from the days of Rezā Shāh: the European jacket (*kot*) and the waistcoat (*jelazgha*), useful for their numerous pockets and the fact that they can be worn under the sleeveless jacket.

Bakhtiāri culture has been highly selective in its choice of borrowing from the West, guided by a variety of criteria such as efficiency and compatibility. The resulting westernisation affected the chiefs much more than the simple nomads at large; in fact to talk of westernisation of the Bakhtiāri tribe as a whole is really an exaggeration. The only major consequence of westernisation for Bakhtiāri society has been to accentuate the difference between the *khavānin-e bozorg* and the rest of the tribe.

From the beginning of the reign of Rezā Shāh in 1925 the problem of cultural assimilation assumed new and weightier proportions; that date signalled a complete break in relations between the Iranian administration and the tribes. After a long period of 'controlled hostility', during which, in spite of their disagreements (violent at times), the tribes were an integral part of the Iranian state, a new era of marginalisation and deprecation began which amounted almost to the deliberate eradication of nomadism and the tribes. This was pursued in the name of modernisation by a centralised 'modern' government, 'modern' signifying at that period 'westernised'.

The new ruler, Rezā Shāh, waged a particular campaign against the Bakhtiāri, whose power, organisation and way of life he judged to be incompatible with the modernisation of the country along European lines. He pursued threefold aims:

1. detribalisation by arresting and sometimes executing the leading khans, and confiscating their possessions. The khans were replaced by officials who were put in charge of tribal affairs and administration.
2. removal of their culture through a whole series of measures designed to harass: for instance forbidding them to wear beards or traditional dress, by which the Bakhtiāri set such store;
3. enforced settlement; the nomads had to choose whether to live henceforth in their winter quarters or in the summer pastures. Once they had made their choice, the army prevented them moving from one area to the other by patrolling the migration routes.

This enforced settlement, to judge by its results, could easily figure in the category of rejected efforts at westernisation defined above. Under pressure from the Allies, Rezā Shāh had to abdicate in 1941 in favour of his son Mohammed Rezā. Taking advantage of the turmoil caused to the machinery of state by the Second World War, the nomads reverted at once to their traditional migratory way of life. From his point of view, Rezā Shāh's tribal policy ended in failure. Apart from introducing farming and makeshift dwellings, which were nearly all later abandoned, it caused nothing more than the temporary disruption of the pastoral system; however, it succeeded in reducing the poorest nomads to penury.

After two decades of temporisation and experiment, Mohammed Rezā Shāh (who in 1951 married Sorayā Esfandyāri, the daughter of a Bakhtiāri khan) pursued a tribal policy in the 1960s that differed from that pursued by his father only in the methods he adopted. On the advice of American experts in agrarian reform (who had gained all their experience in Latin America) his government applied a policy of 'indirect' settlement. His method consisted in attacking nomadism not head on, but by the more devious means of undermining the economic institutions and social infrastructure of the Bakhtiāri. The land reform law of 1962 led the way, particularly affecting the great chiefs whose lands stretched right to the edge of tribal territory.

The nationalisation of forests and grazing lands in the mid-1960s did even greater damage. On the pretext of protecting the environment, owners of flocks were obliged to obtain individual permits which only allowed them to graze their animals in certain specific areas. This law introduced a system that bore no relation to the Bakhtiāri nomadic pastoral system, and furthermore it was totally inappropriate for the ecological structure of the Zāgros mountains. The new system was based on the individual use of communally owned land, and thus did away completely with the best that the tribal institutions had to offer, namely co-operation in their use of the land and communal use of springs, pasture land, migration routes and other natural resources. At the same time government officials and government propaganda attempted to instil into the nomads a sense of shame about their way of life and customs, which were presented to them as hopelessly archaic; only 'modern' methods of production and consumption were worthy of a great nation like Iran.

What is the situation like now, a decade after the institution of the Islamic Republic? It is an indisputable fact that the Bakhtiāri are completely (or almost completely) settled and detribalised. Only transhumance (the movement of flocks with their shepherds, not to be confused with nomadism) can be seen there now. The tribe has lost its cohesion and its traditions have fallen into disuse.

How and why was the Islamic Republic able to achieve in a decade what the Pahlavi dynasty had failed completely to achieve in half a century, and not for want of trying? A variety of theories could be advanced, all testifying to yet another change of direction in official Iranian tribal policy. However, one thing is certain: in the case of the Bakhtiāri (unlike the Qashqā'i) repression played only a minor role in the matter.

The main factors, almost entirely attributable to the deeds of the 'struggle for reconstruction' (*Jehād-e sāzandegi*), are fourfold. Firstly, new institutions, tribal councils (*shurā-ye 'ashāyeri*) were set up at local level in which people who had had no role to play in the traditional power structure (young people, 'simple nomads') were able to participate. Secondly, stock rearing, the main occupation of the tribe, was ideologically reassessed and was given practical assistance and protection. Most importantly, the cultivation of grazing land and of nomad routes was forbidden, and marketing systems were set up. These measures helped to win the support of the simple nomads, who were solely engaged in animal husbandry, and who had access only to the tribal lands held in common. Thirdly, grain storage facilities were provided so that those who had access to agricultural land could store their harvest. Finally, an unprecedented amount of energy was invested in the development of communications (roads, bridges, telephones) even in the most inaccessible areas, in social services (housing, electricity, health) and in the distribution of food and consumer products (co-operative stores). The effect of these four factors has proved far from insignificant. It is well-known that nomads are willing not to build up their herds (and thus avoid overgrazing) if they have easy access to cereal feeds and other consumer goods. Now, thanks to the implementation of the above measures, *a settled life appears more attractive to the Bakhtiāri than their former nomadic life*. Not all the problems have been solved, however. Social inequality persists or has appeared within the tribe, and this may in time be a source of new conflicts. There may be unexpected consequences such as individualistic behaviour by members of the tribe, or, to put it bluntly, the development of a 'dole' mentality; those excluded from the new power structure may display resentment and vengeful tendencies. Given the instability of pastoral systems in crisis

At Gotvand, a large village between Masjed-e Soleyman and Shushtar, a nomad family is in the process of settling. The tent is still used but surrounded by a wall. Soon more solid structures will be built in the enclosure.

conditions, these factors (and others too numerous to list) could constitute the same number of potential threats to the new order as the problems they have solved.

Are the Bakhtiāri (which ones?) more happy as citizens of the Islamic Republic than they were under the Pahlavis, or as clients of the British? It would be difficult to say. Anyway, the changes they have been going through recently have been more profound than anything that they had gone through before. Until recently nomadism was the central feature of their lifestyle, the lynch pin around which their material culture, economic activity, social organisation and even their value system and perception of life revolved. The suppression of the nomadic lifestyle will probably provoke, sooner or later, profound modifications in the Bakhtiāri social and cultural fabric. Even if it is not always immediately obvious, the gradual loss of Bakhtiāri culture stands in bizarre contrast to the few isolated borrowings of material culture in the previous period. Is it correct to talk in terms of massive westernisation, or the wholesale destruction of Bakhtiāri culture? Such strong terms do not really apply yet, for although many nomads are not immune to a certain 'westoxication' (*gharb-zadegi*), manifested in the high and often unjustified esteem in which they hold everything made abroad (*sākht-e khārej*), they are demonstrably less affected by it than are most Iranian city-dwellers. We should also try and avoid the romanticism which is prevalent in the West whenever nomads are mentioned. Can we seriously deplore the loss of Bakhtiāri culture if this is the price to be paid for even the most modest improvement in their living conditions?[1]

SACRED SPACES AND POTENT PLACES IN THE BAKHTIĀRI MOUNTAINS

David H. M. Brooks

The Bakhtiāri are a partly nomadic people living in the Zāgros mountains of south-west Iran who migrate twice-yearly, in spring between their winter and summer pastures, and back again in autumn.[1] The journey can be anything up to 250 miles (400 km) for many Bakhtiāri and last anything up to six weeks depending on the prevailing weather conditions. In the course of these migrations they cross several chains of mountains, the highest with peaks of 14,000 ft (over 4000 metres) and snowbound passes at 12,000 ft (3500 metres), rivers and high snow-fields. It is an extremely hazardous undertaking.

Approximately a quarter of a million people and several million animals—horses, donkeys, sheep and goats—travel to the summer pastures on four main migration routes of varying difficulty. These routes lie along cliff faces, across fast-flowing and icy-cold rivers, through gorges and ravines and over snow-covered mountain passes swept by whistling gales. There can be dust storms with temperatures of up to 120 degrees in the foothills, rain storms, electric storms, sub-zero temperatures and sudden blizzards. The people facing these hazards are of all ages and conditions. There are old men and women crippled with rheumatism and arthritis, the newly born, pregnant women, children, as well as the young and healthy. Accidents happen, animals, and sometimes people, fall down cliff faces, drown in the rivers and freeze to death. Tribal fights break out, people are maimed or killed and camps (*māl*) are raided by sheep thieves.

The winter pastures are in the low-lying hills of Khuzestān. The nomads' stay there is brought to an end by the onset of spring. When soaring temperatures desiccate the grazing they move their herds of sheep and goats, migrating through progressively higher pastures in an extremely mountainous environment, up and over the highest range to their summer pastures in Esfahān province.

The nomads stay in their summer pastures for approximately four months, moving slowly down the mountain slopes as their animals exhaust the grazing, and in the autumn, when the grass stops growing and before the higher mountain passes become impassable with snow, they return along the same narrowly defined routes to their winter pastures. The conditions on this migration are very different from the spring. The summer sun has burned most, often all, available grazing and the animals go hungry. The tempo of travel is much quicker than in the spring, with the increasingly hungry and weakening animals being pushed as fast as possible through the mountains. The rivers are lower in the autumn and are no longer such a hazard.

As can be seen from this rather brief description, the nomads' survival depends on their knowledge of these dangerous mountains, on their ability to predict and cope with the weather, and on the need to maintain a keen vigilance as they move. Experience is essential to cope with the vagaries of the environmental and climatic conditions, which vary from year to year. On the migration, daily decisions have to be made about when to move, how far to move, and the possibility of a sudden change in the weather. Rain, snow, or dust storms can reduce visibility to zero, make movement impossible, and may lead to total disaster. Caught in a storm on an exposed cliff face, unable to proceed to a more sheltered spot, whole herds of sheep have been lost in one night. Every migration presents its own unique conditions, and, even under the best circumstances, animals and people are lost.

After successfully negotiating a particularly difficult passage of the Monar pass, people place stones on boulders at the edge of the track as the token of a vow or pledge made for safe delivery from danger. May 1985.

Members of the Bābādi clan crossing the Hezār Chāmeh, the pass of a 'thousand hazards', a difficult and dangerous passage in the northern part of Bakhtiāri territory which has to be crossed to reach their summer pastures. 1960s.

THE SIGNIFICANCE OF STONES

The Bakhtiāri world is one of stone. On the grand scale, the landscape they cross on their spring and autumn migrations consists of rock, the mountain chains, their cliff faces, dramatic gorges and ravines. On the smaller scale, boulders, stones and pebbles of every size abound everywhere, impeding the nomads and their many animals. The footing is always awkward, often dangerous, and sometimes deadly. The pack animals and horses suffer particularly badly. They get not only stones under their shoes but frequently debilitating wounds on their forelegs.

The several migration routes could be made easier, at least temporarily, if the stones were cleared, but the nomads rarely do this. In the early twentieth century, the government officials continually complained to the khans, or tribal chiefs, for their failure to keep the southern Bakhtiāri trade route clear of stones for the muleteers bringing produce through the mountains between Khuzestān and Esfahān.

Stones (*bard*) figure in many aspects of Bakhtiāri life. Stone-strewn ground (*chul*) needs to be cleared when it is brought under non-irrigated dry cultivation. Where wheat is cultivated beside the migration routes, protective stone walls are built to prevent damage by passing flocks. Stones are also commonly used to mark boundaries. Circular walled structures (*cher*), open to the skies, a couple of metres in diameter and approximately 4 feet (1.2 metres) high are built for storing straw or grain, or used as pens for young lambs and baby goats.

Stones are laid out on the ground to form a firm dry base onto which saddlebags, saddles, the variety of containers for all the household equipment, and bedding are piled, and then covered by blankets or woven carpets to form the back of the tent. This stone base is about 3 feet (1 metre) wide, possibly two layers thick and roughly 15–20 feet (4.5–6.0 metres) long depending on the size of the tent. On the migration tents are often not actually pitched unless the weather is bad or the camp group of up to a dozen tents is staying on the same spot for several days. Camp sites (*wargāh*) which are regularly used year after year have these stone bases permanently laid out, sometimes even three-sided,

Fording the River Bāzoft. At the time of the downward migration in autumn, the water levels in the rivers are much lower and less of a hazard than in the spring. 1960s.

The 'Road of the Women' (*rāh-e zan*) which winds along the face of a cliff and in places is so narrow that people and animals must walk in single file.

like a permanent ground plan, over which the tent is pitched. At either end of the pitched tent, stones can easily be added to build up side walls and the gaps stuffed with available greenery to protect the household better from wind or rain. More elaborate back and side walls may be found in the longer stay summer pastures with built-in cupboard spaces, the tent forming the roof.

Stones have many other uses in daily life. For example, on migration, when pegs cannot be used, the tents are often tied down to heavy stones which are also used to supplement the tent pegs at other times.

High in the mountains suitable boulders one or two feet high are selected to grind wheat or acorns into flour. (Acorns form an occasional supplement to the diet in times of drought and among the very poor.) The grinding, which is done with a stone rolling pin (*bard ār*), wears a hollow in such boulders.

There are also hearthstones. The hearth (*chāla*) of each tent, a square- or triangular-shaped depression dug in the ground, is built up with three sizeable stones (*chālmeh*) which form a firm-sided base for cooking pots, and support for kebab sticks. There are two, sometimes three hearths in the tent, one or two in the women's part for cooking, and another in the men's side. These hearths are the centre of tent life and they all have *chālmeh*. The men's hearth is used for entertaining, for tea making and grilling kebabs. Oaths are sworn on the hearth and on the fire (*ātesh*) in it, and in a sense respect is formally given to it as the heart of the family. A hearthstone is believed to have power in itself, and all three are used by the women in a curative ritual performed in the case of sudden and unexplained illness. The intention of the ritual, which is called *chālmeh bori* (*bori* is the imperative of *boridan*, to pull or take away), is to pull the disease out of the body. Men are not allowed to carry it out, and while many Bakhtiāri men typically express scepticism about its efficacy, there is no attempt to stop it being performed.

The ceremony is performed by an old woman. She lays the patient flat, and starting at the head, moving towards the feet, she touches the patient's forehead, nose, mouth, chin, chest, hips, knees, ankles and toes, saying alternately '*borid*' then '*naborid*', '*borid*', '*naborid*' (take away, don't take away) at each subsequent touch from top to toe. The patient is touched with seven different items in turn. After the toes have been touched with a loud '*borid*' to take the disease away, each is 'thrown away'. The items are: bread, sugar, salt, a bunch of roots (*riseh*), a gun, a large cooking pot (*tik*) and the three hearthstones (*bard-e chālmeh*). If a gun is not available, a heavy club (*gorz*) is substituted. The disposable items are actually thrown away, while the hearthstones, club and pot are symbolically put aside. A prayer for health is also uttered at each place touched on the body. The seven items are considered the most important in the life of the nomads. To complete the *chālmeh bori* exorcism, and to bring additional efficacy and merit to the ritual, a chicken or perhaps a goat is sacrificed and the meat shared by everyone in the camp.

Stones are thrown both to 'encourage' recalcitrant animals, and to prevent them from straying too close to the edge of a dangerous path.

STONE THROWING

This is a prized accomplishment for the Bakhtiāri. They throw them in a variety of contexts, usually with quite astounding skill and, on occasion, lethal accuracy. Some people have the reputation for hitting hawks in flight and bringing down other birds on the wing. The stones they throw can be heard whirring through the air.

Stones are used as an aid to the control of pack animals and flocks on the move in the mountains. With their help stray or runaway animals are manoeuvred back to safer parts of the sometimes dangerous pathways and cliffs. Collapsed and heavily laden animals are mercilessly encouraged to their feet with thrown stones the size of fists to prevent them blocking narrow pathways. Fights over collapsed and blocking animals are common, so stones are readily used to force unwilling or frightened cows in particular to move on.

Children learn to throw stones very young, at two or three, by tormenting the tent dogs. By the time they are seven or eight they are skilled stone throwers and adept at herding young lambs and baby goats and controlling their energetic baby flocks.

Unlike some other cultures, including our own, dogs are not used in sheep herding. The shepherds are totally incredulous at descriptions of sheep dogs and roar with laughter in total disbelief at the notion of competitive sheep dog trials. Bakhtiāri dogs are either tent dogs or dogs for guarding the sheep against thieves and wild animals, particularly wolves. (Wolves have become quite a problem since the Bakhtiāri were disarmed in the 1960s.) Tent or camp dogs guard their owner's tent and their own individual territory round it. These dogs are fed only by their owner and rarely leave the immediate environs of the tent. They rush ferociously at any stranger arriving at the camp. They also clear up the human baby excrement in the camp and it is common to see a mother hold out her very young child for it to defecate straight to the dog.

These dogs, although serving a useful guarding function, are a major nuisance in camp life. Their incessant barking, their bickering with each other and mock attacks on familiar members of the camp cause irritation and children endlessly throw stones at them. This stone throwing is explicitly encouraged by the adults to train the children.

On approaching a strange nomad camp, the experienced visitor will arm himself with several stones, and, even if he doesn't, he has only to bend down to pick up a handful of stones as the camp dogs streak towards him barking ferociously for them promptly to turn tail and run howling back to the tent. All this of course alerts the camp members to the approach of strangers. Throwing the stones and really hitting the dogs is regarded as perfectly acceptable by the owners and limping dogs with misshapen legs are a frequent sight.

The dogs that guard the sheep are larger, tougher dogs trained to be ferocious and are well

A watchman on guard near Emamzādeh Boveir. At some points of the migration it is difficult to guard the flocks adequately, and thieves lurk about on the look-out for a chance to steal animals or goods. Some nights all the men of the camp will join the watch, talk loudly about guns, and throw stones from time to time into the darkness to scare off any would-be robbers. April 1985.

thought of and better fed than the scavenging camp dogs. Their ears are cropped, and sometimes the tail is docked, to avoid them being grabbed by a wolf. They work with the shepherds guarding the flocks at night. Thieves abound and the flocks on the move are particularly vulnerable high in the mountains.

Sometimes the flocks are brought into the camp site itself for protection, but more usually they are settled away from it. Some nights all the men of the camp will stay with the shepherds to try and discourage thieves. Along with the dogs other stratagems are used at these times. There is loud talk about guns to discourage any possible listener and periodically stones are thrown energetically into the darkness on all sides of the flocks. It is not uncommon for stones to be thrown at the defenders as disgruntled thieves give up. The discovery of an ongoing theft, which happens regularly on the migrations, inevitably provokes dangerous and damaging stone throwing, with stones whistling through the night at alarming speeds. Smashed teeth, mangled lips and head injuries are a common sight.

A rather frightening game is played among Bakhtiāri youths. They set up two sizeable stones about 50 metres apart and two youths each stand in front of a stone and proceed to throw pebbles to hit the stone 'defended' by his opponent. The winner is the one who hits the other's stone most often. The game is as much a test of courage as of skill since to defend successfully means not only distracting the opponent with one's body, thus hoping he will miss, but also the possibility of being struck. Most Bakhtiāri games tend to be painful and teach skills required in nomadic life, as does their stick dancing. Sometimes in the stone-throwing game the pebbles from each side collide in mid air with a loud crack, which is regarded as honours even.

More serious conflicts than these competitive stone-throwing games take place regularly between camp groups, sub-tribes, or between nomad and peasant, and can result in fatalities. It is by no means uncommon to see several dozen furious Bakhtiāri men and women throwing stones at each other in deadly earnest over some dispute or other. When hundreds of people are struggling to get on to the next valley over critical and dangerous mountain passes, tension is inevitable, and when animals fall, collapse or get in each other's way, a conflict is easily sparked.

Thrown stones also play a part in the rituals involved in the *Pir Ghār*, the Shrine of the Cave, described below, and have a religious rather than purely practical or learning significance.

STANDING STONES

Small cairns of stones (*chālkuh*) mark particularly difficult points on dangerous cliffs or mountain passes, or places of bad luck (*bad bakht*) where animals regularly fall. One cliff face is so bad and steep that only women and the flocks can use it, while the pack animals and the men accompanying them go a longer route over the top of this particular mountain range. This path is called the Rāh-e Zan or Road of the Women, and is a pathway no broader than a person's body with a sheer drop beside it of more than a thousand feet into the valley below. The women have to scramble down it as best they can. Cairns of single stones or piles a foot high are built on overhanging boulders to mark danger spots where women have fallen to their death. They serve to alert the migrating women, who mutter prayers as they pass to avert the danger, and make a salaam or greeting to pay respect (*ehterām*) to the person who placed the stone markers or built up the cairn. Placing such a warning is regarded as a meritorious act, and by acknowledging it the passing women hope to avert the danger to themselves. The risk of accident is very much increased for those women who are either carrying young children, babies, young lambs and baby goats or are heavily pregnant.

While discussing difficult routes, mention must be made of the Hezār Chāmeh (the Pass of a Thousand Hazards). This pass is high up in the mountains and on this particular migration route roughly marks the boundary between the winter and summer pasture areas of the Bakhtiāri tribes. It is also locally known as the pass of vultures and thieves. During the spring migration in particular, when there are thousands of very young lambs and goats with the flocks, both vultures and eagles circle high in the sky at this pass, waiting for pack animals to fall and feasting on their corpses when they do. Thieves habitually hover round the top of the pass itself because the animals are strung out in single file and are extremely difficult to protect until the entire flock is over the top. Stones fly, tempers break, mistakes are made and fights are common. The pack animals struggle fearfully on this pass, hauling their loads up what seems an endless mountainside, appallingly difficult underfoot. The boulders on either side of the path at the top of this pass mark the most spectacular views forward to the summer pastures. They are strewn with single stones, which express thankfulness that the pass is over, and the end is in sight, although many days of travel still lie ahead.

One of the most potent places on the Rāh-e Monar (the Monar Road), the migration route used by many of the Bakhtiāri, is the Monar mountain, which gives its name to the whole route. The Monar is one of the most formidable obstacles the nomads face on their migrations. Its potency as a place comes not only from its rugged grandeur and difficulty, but because several very important intertribal conflicts with many deaths took place there, in both the ninetenth and the twentieth centuries. It was on this path that one of the leading Bakhtiarwand khans killed the leading Duraki khan, Ja'far Qoli Khan, *circa* 1836, a killing which marked major shifts in the internal balance of power in the Bakhtiāri polity and the beginning of the rise to power of the Bakhtiāri khans in the twentieth century, as well as territorial changes among the sub-tribes.[2] More recently, intertribal conflict in the 1940s resulted in deaths and feuding. The Bakhtiāri have vivid songs about such fights on the Monar.

The Monar is a mountain chain in itself, with the path to be negotiated running many kilometres along the sheer cliff face before eventually winding round and over to the other side of the mountain. In places the path is barely wide enough for an animal, and its surface worn slippery smooth by the passing feet of generations.

It usually takes virtually a whole exhausting day to travel the rocky approaches to the cliff, winding higher and higher. The ascent proper begins under the overhanging cliff face with the valley many hundreds of feet below. In places the pack animals have to be led nose to tail and coaxed out towards the very edge of the path. There is much danger for the heavily laden donkeys, particularly

Tents are pitched over low stone walls which serve as a dry base for the baggage at the back of the tent. Additional walls may be built up at the ends of the tent as a wind-break. Some camp sites are used year after year. Spring 1964.

the ones carrying the goat hair tents, because the bulkiness of the loads can cause the animal to bump against the cliff face and upset its balance. The panicked braying of an overladen donkey crescendoing into a scream as it tips its load, loses its balance and tumbles over the edge into the valley below is not uncommon. Shrieks of noisy horror and despairing ululation by the women accompany such disasters, the animal dead and its load virtually irrecoverable.

In the spring heat the noise and sight of the Bakhtiāri on the march are overwhelming and make the Monar one of the most notable places in this region. There is shouting, the wailing of children (sometimes tied to the backs of the already overladen pack animals), the barking of dogs, the spitting of goats, the tinkling of animal bells, the complaints of women uncomfortable in a whistling wind, the continuous smell and splashing of animal droppings, the laughter of girls taking the opportunity to flirt with passing youths, and the movement of hundreds of nomads and thousands of animals, nose to tail, strung all along the mountain face as they struggle to the other side.

On the approaches to the Monar, and along the path itself, are many cairns (*chālkuh*). As on the Rāh-e Zan, cairns along the cliff face, on boulders right at the edge of the tortuous pathway, mark danger spots and places of bad luck. The stones are supposed to be instrumental in averting the bad luck. There are other cairns of significant stones on just about every sizeable boulder on the upper approach slopes to the Monar pass itself. In places they form a wall on top of the boulders, and particularly around three 'sacred' trees in whose branches stones are also placed individually. These three trees are virtually solid with stones, and festooned with strips of rags tied to every twig and branch. Each stone and rag (*hokm*, religious command) represents a vow (*nazr*), or is a token of a pledge to remember, thank or honour the memory of the long-dead saint whose shrine (*emamzādeh*) can be glimpsed glistening far below by the side of the mountain.[3]

The nomads invoke the help of this saint for a safe passage across the Monar. The women tear rags from their skirts or the veils hanging from their backs and tie them on with a muttered prayer, perhaps vowing to call a future child after the saint ('Abdollah) or asking him for safe passage or to intercede in some general problem. Both men and women put stones in the trees after first pressing them to the forehead and kissing them three times. Twigs broken off other trees can also be inserted into the branches of the 'sacred' trees. Many however completely ignore the trees or laugh at those who tie on rags and insert stones.

Above the path where these trees are to be found, overlooking the valley far below, are several cairns that each comprise a single tall, narrow stone with one or two more stones on top. These are pointers to the shrine below. They look like sentinels, and indeed are called custodians or guardians (*motavalli*) of the shrine. This is both a potent and a sacred place for many of the passing nomads, particularly for the women. If a woman is pregnant on a migration, at this place she will undoubtedly place a stone and tie a rag to invoke Pir 'Abdollah's help for a safe delivery of her child. *Motavalli* form a particular class of cairn and I describe them and the shrines in the next section.

Lastly, there are stone lions (*bard-e shir*). These stylised sculptured lions stare out from numerous isolated Bakhtiāri graveyards in the many valleys of the Zāgros mountain chains. Sometimes singly, sometimes in clusters, they proudly mark the graves of important men, in particular of warriors who have died in battle. Some are so old they have fallen on their sides and the names and dates of the fallen hero are now faded. Others are very recent, shining white, with mouths open in ferocious grins, eyes, mouths and fangs picked out in contrasting black.[4] The sides of the lions are carved in relief, some with horses or a horse and rider, some with rifles or a wild goat. Other older lions show pistols, swords and daggers[5] and mark the graves of warrior heroes of the past. Many travellers in the region, from Sir Henry Layard in the 1840s and Mrs Isabella Bishop in the 1880s, to many more in recent times, have mentioned these stone lions. They have struck the imagination, not least because such sculptures are rarely found outside this part of the Zāgros. The oldest lion mentioned in the literature, dated AD 1643/44 (AH 1053),[6] is in the graveyard at Dizak on the edge of the Bakhtiāri territory in the summer pastures. Others deep in the mountains are dated AD 1789/90 (AH 1204) (H. Wright 1979: 20, 27). These vigilant lions represent bravery, manliness and male prowess in riding, hunting or fighting, and are permanent visible symbols of the most highly prized male qualities. They stand testament to what all Bakhtiāri men aspire to be.

The lion, symbol *par excellence* in Iran of bravery, was once common on Bakhtiāri territory in the winter pastures of Khuzestān. Layard has several stories of lion hunts and encounters with them

right
A lion gravestone at Susan, north of Izeh, probably that of a warrior. Carved on its flank are a gun, dagger and axe.

left above
A chicken takes a ride on the spring migration at the Monar pass. May 1985.

left below
Stone lions in a mountain graveyard

(Layard 1894: 185–9). In his study of the lion rugs woven in Fārs, Tanavoli mentions the finding of a lion's tooth in this area as late as 1963 (Tanavoli 1978: 23, 24), although the lion is thought to have been extinct for much longer than that. The word for lion, *shir*, is used for hero, and is attached to the name of individual men, most famously perhaps to Shir ʿAli Merdun (ʿAli Merdun the Hero), about whom songs are sung. The lion as metaphor for hero is well-known in Iranian literature, and is of course one of the terms used for ʿAli the revered son-in-law of the Prophet. Thus both as metaphor and symbol the lion represents a potent image of heroism for the Bakhtiāri.

It is also used in rare cases to signify powerful, even aggressive women in the term *shirzan* (lion woman). This term is never accompanied by the individual woman's name. She is known as a *shirzan*, or in the past as *shir bibi*, *bibi* being the title for a high status woman belonging to the leading khans. One such *shir bibi* was Bibi Mariam, the mother of the Shir ʿAli Merdun mentioned above. The nomads maintained that ʿAli Merdun inherited his heroic qualities from his mother, a particularly independent and dominant woman early in the twentieth century. The linguistic use of lion, the symbol of maleness, for a woman clearly signifies the unusual and anomalous qualities of such women. The paradigm for the term *shirzan* is Zeynab, the *Shirzan* of Karbalā, the daughter of ʿAli and sister of the martyred third Imam, Hoseyn, who is so central to Shiʿi Islam.

The *bard-e shir*, or stone lions, figure in a particular ritual for men who are not complete men, i.e. cowards (*tarsu*). Several nomads described this ritual to me, although they suggested it was very rarely done because there were not many cowards among the Bakhtiāri! Something very similar is to be found in Mrs Isabella Bishop's book of her travels further north in Bakhtiāri territory (Bishop 1891, 2: 75, and 1892: 13). The coward is taken by his friends to the graveyard on a night of full moon[7] and, while saying prayers to the dead hero, passes seven times under the stone lion, between its legs. A prayer is supposed to be said for every 'circumambulation'. The afflicted man is also supposed to crouch under the lion and pray for bravery (*deliri, shojāʿat*). I was assured it worked. This potency to bring about a transformation, to cure an affliction, is more usually the prerogative of

A *seyyed* visiting a nomad encampment. The *seyyeds* are the guardians or custodians of the local shrines who provide for the religious needs of pilgrims. Itinerant *seyyeds*, often impoverished, visit nomads in their area to dispense blessings in return for food or money.

sacred places, of the *emamzādeh* or shrines scattered irregularly in the mountains. It is however primarily women who visit shrines.

According to B. A. Donaldson there was in the past a carved lion outside the city gates of Mashhad. Childless women, i.e. incomplete women, came to pour oil upon it 'and to walk or crawl under it, hoping that by so doing they may become pregnant' (Donaldson 1938: 24). Such women in Bakhtiāri territory more commonly visit a particular shrine. Fertility is regarded of course as the supreme value of women.

SACRED STONES

Sacred stones are carried by impoverished, itinerant *seyyeds*, who are the guardians of a shrine. The polished, shell-shaped stones are wrapped in cloth and produced by the *seyyed* for blessing passing nomads. Such ragged and illiterate *seyyeds* travel round the camp groups as the nomads pass through the area or valley in which the shrine is located. A person to be blessed is first tapped on the shoulder several times with the stone which is then pressed to their forehead and lips while the *seyyed* murmurs a blessing. In return he gets a coin or two, a plateful of flour, a handful of sugar, and possibly some salt. Usually, when such a *seyyed* arrives he is greeted by the camp dogs with what seems to be particularly ferocious energy and he makes an undignified entrance thrashing frantically at the bounding dogs while the Bakhtiāri in the tent make little attempt to hide their laughter, and none to control the dogs. However casually he is treated, the *seyyed* is always given something to eat, and most people accept what many of the men obviously regard as a very doubtful blessing.

A profoundly sacred stone in the foothills marks the place of a footprint (*qadamgāh*) of the revered Imam Rezā, the eighth Imam, buried in Mashhad. It is the only example in these mountains, although many others are found elsewhere in Iran. On top of a smooth stone ground there is a large, partly shaped stone several feet high with a niche carved out of it near the top. Inside the

niche is a copper 'hand of Fatema' (*panjeresti*) and an inscribed stone covered with rags. Those who wish, put their hand into the niche while making their request of Imam Rezā, and in return for his help they make some sort of vow, for example to visit a nearby shrine.

Close to this site is a place for making vows (*nazargāh*) set beside a huge tree. It consists merely of a dozen or so large stones set in a wide circle about 10 feet (3 metres) in diameter with a stone lintel making a doorway between two of them. Cloth strips are slung between the other stones. It was said that death would follow if the stones were touched or the tree cut. The Imam Rezā is thought to have once had lunch on this spot and the tree grew. It now blossoms with strips of coloured rags, the votive offerings of a multitude of women.[8]

The guardian stones (*motavalli*), mentioned earlier, function as markers or signs of a neighbouring shrine. While the shrine may be invisible, located in a sheltered defile or up a side ravine, often at a water source at the foot of the mountain, the *motavalli* are located on slopes and are easily visible to passing nomads. Depending on the terrain, these tall sacred standing stones can be either close to the shrine to whose presence they stand witness, or several kilometres away. They are up to 1.5 metres high and constructed of tall narrow stones balanced one on top of another like a column, quite distinct from the cairns of small stones described above. They serve to orient the nomads in the direction of the shrine, and their minds towards its presence. On passing these guardians, the women drop their heads and unobtrusively make a salaam, greeting the particular saint and acknowledging the presence of the shrine. A prayer is muttered *sotto voce* as they search carefully among the foothills to catch a glimpse of the signalled shrine, and success is accompanied by a distinct sigh of pleasure at the merit so achieved. Such places are known as *salāmgāh* (Lambton 1971b). Men do not bother, being sceptical of such matters, but the *motavalli* are never ignored completely.

Like the sacred trees on Monar, the *motavalli* are said to belong to their particular shrine. The source of their potency, their religious worth, comes from association with the shrine and ultimately from the holy figure whose place it is. There are dozens of these shrines scattered in the mountains, and thousands in the villages and cities of Iran. In the immediate vicinity of the Bakhtiāri shrines are found numerous cairns, and any trees are solid with stones and fluttering with rags. Usually several *motavalli* stand on the neighbouring slopes, and all of this together intensifies the vibrant potency of these sacred places, which generally have graveyards beside them, some with stone lions.

SHRINES

Pir Ghār (the Shrine of the Cave) is, as far as I know, unique among the sacred places in Bakhtiāri territory. Here a combination of political, religious and natural elements has created a small but potent place of local power. The deep cave is located at the foot of a cliff in the summer area of Chahār Mahāl, in the mountains above the village of Deh Cheshmeh (the Spring Village), beside the source of a spring that irrigates the fields below and provides the water for the village. Settled peasant villages lie along this valley, which also forms a pasture area for several Bakhtiāri subtribes. The village was previously owned by Sardār Za'far, one of the most important of the leading families of khans once dominant in Chahār Mahāl. On the cliff face near the entrance to the cave are three panels carved in relief, one recounting the history and deeds of this family of khans, one the role played by the Bakhtiāri in the constitutional revolution in Iran *circa* 1910, and the third a partial genealogy of the khans. The shrine is in the cave, which is full of recesses and tapers to a funnel that disappears up into the cliff.

The story goes that a holy man (*pir*), whose name has long since been forgotten, went into the cave to pray, but never reappeared. He vanished and was never seen or heard of again—a pale echo perhaps of the twelfth Imam, the Hidden Imam. This is the only shrine which is nameless, all the others being named after a dead holy man, or in one instance holy woman.

Beside the cave entrance an area has been cleared and flattened, making a platform where those coming to the shrine, tribal or peasant, can rest and eat a ritual meal beside the gurgling stream if they wish. As at most shrines it is mainly women who come, to ask the holy man to intercede and grant them their request for recovery from illness, for health for themselves and particularly for their children.

Inside the cave, slung from wall to wall, is a rope of amulets, copper bells, woven material, rags, safety pins and blue beads. Just below one end of this rope, which is slung about three feet off the ground, is a large honeycombed rocky recess filled with solidified candle wax and ablaze with candles lit by the women who come with their requests and vows (*nazur*). The recesses above it are black with greasy smoke from the many candles that have burned here. For a wish to be granted, it is believed, the petitioner must throw up to seven stones at the cave walls, and one has to stick in a crevice or recess. If all the stones fall, then it will not be granted.

This cave shrine is thought to be particularly efficacious for healing sick babies and young children, who are brought into the shrine and passed over and under the rope of copper bells either three or seven times, a quasi-circumambulation. Afterwards an animal is slaughtered, ideally a goat, and the meat is distributed among the local poor. The shrine is very popular with the villagers of this region.

The term *emamzādeh* (descendants of the Imams) is used to designate both the shrine itself and the descendant of a Shi'i Imam, who is always named. There is not always agreement among the Bakhtiāri as to precisely who these descendants are, particularly in the case of smaller and more localised shrines. Those of doubtful descent are often more commonly called *pir*, meaning ancient or old, as for example in the case of the cave shrine mentioned above. In Iran most shrines are associated with relatives of the eighth Imam, Rezā, who was killed in what is now the pilgrimage city of Mashhad in AD 818. Many of the Imam's relatives were in Iran, or travelling towards Mashhad when he died. Some were also buried in Mashhad and his descendants' tombs are found all over Iran.

The Bakhtiāri believe that three of their dozens of shrines are connected with close relatives of Rezā, two with his brothers and one with his sister. Another sister's tomb, the shrine of Fatema, is in Qom and is one of the major pilgrimage centres in Iran. It is widely believed among the nomads that these three relatives were on their way to visit the eighth Imam when news came that he was dead, and that after hearing it they stayed where they were in the Bakhtiāri mountains and later died there. These *emamzādeh* are by far the most well-known shrines among the nomads. Their authenticity is not doubted and they are regarded as being particularly sacred.

The activities associated with the three major *emamzādeh* are more elaborate, and the catchment area of visiting pilgrims much wider than is the case with the other *emamzādeh*, which are familiar only to those who either live part of the year relatively near them or who pass them on their migration routes. Shushtar, a small market town close to the edge of Bakhtiāri territory in Khuzestān, their winter area, has approximately eighty such shrines, while Shirāz, a major city in the south of Iran, has over a hundred (Betteridge 1981). Many people are sceptical about them, although most acknowledge they must be the shrines of holy men.

There is a degree of specialisation among even the small shrines, and each has a miracle (*mo'jez*) associated with it. The degree of belief in these miracles ranges from general acceptance in the case of the major shrines to downright scepticism for some of the more local ones. Attendance at the minor shrines is almost exclusively a female activity. When migrating, the nomads rarely visit the shrines they pass.

The resident *seyyeds*, guardians or custodians visit the camps collecting flour, cash sometimes, sugar and tea for performing services such as burial when needed. Several of the small shrines have living descendants of the Imam resident at them. These descendants now form small lineages and are part of the Bakhtiāri polity. They do not migrate and do not own any territory. Some *seyyeds* are literate and even well-versed in the Koran. At at least one shrine the resident *seyyeds* are given a proportion of the locally grown wheat in return for providing religious services when called upon. In the southern reaches of Bakhtiāri territory lies the area controlled by a sub-tribe (*tāyfeh*) of *seyyeds* called Mashā'ekh, who trace their descent back through fourteen generations to Seyyed Sāleh, reputedly a son of Musa, the seventh Imam, father of Imam Rezā. There is a shrine called Emamzādeh Sāleh near their territory, about which I have no information. Most of the minor shrines have associations with either domestic or wild animals, thus connecting the sacred world with the natural. In this connection, stones, trees and wellsprings have already been mentioned, as have wild animals like lions and wolves.

Shāhzādeh Mahmad Dināvar is a minor shrine, of local interest, in the upper Bāzoft valley near Zardeh Kuh, the highest mountain in the region. The shrine is called after Shāhzādeh Mahmad who is reputed to have brought Islam to this region. The name Dināvar means bringer of religion.

The saint is in fact buried in Shirāz. His descendants, known as Sheykh-e Ravāti, form a *tāyfeh* and have their summer pastures here, as well as a few small hamlets. The Ravāti guardians look after this shrine and vehemently claim that it performs miracles.

As proof, they told the following story about a wolf to an audience of migrating nomads. Wolves are a real danger in the mountains and there are many stories and proverbs about them. This one is often told to children to stop them being afraid of wolves: "An old woman in Bāzoft was out with her goats. A wolf took one. She wailed and called loudly on Shāhzādeh Mahmad for help, asking only for the wolf, not for the return of the goat. That very day the wolf came into the village like a donkey, never opening its mouth. Children could ride around on the back of the wolf without being harmed and *gusht-e gorg be chāleh* (wolf meat in the hearth), they killed it."

The audience greeted the tale with raised eyebrows, solemn nods and winks. The sceptical reception led the indignant Ravāti sheykh to turn to one of those present and remind him how the previous year they had been out watching others fruitlessly hunting two ibex (*pazan*) on the opposite slope. The other had turned to him and asked why, when he was a sheykh, he wasn't helping. So the sheykh called on Shāhzādeh Mahmad Dināvar, saying if he did not help he would no longer believe in his power and would stop making prayers (*nemāz*) to him. Almost at once the two ibex ran almost literally into the arms of the hunters and one after the other they were killed. The sheykh had turned triumphantly to his companion and said that now he too must believe and he must be given a gift (*nazr*) because of the vow. He was given one of the ibex, to be distributed among the Ravāti.

To contain and deflect danger, children wear tied to their upper arms little amulets (*telesm*) made of a green cloth with the hair of a wolf sewn inside, or, if they can get one, the claw of a panther (*palang*), also reputedly found in the mountains. These amulets consist of 'the wild' wrapped up in and contained by 'the sacred' (green is the Prophet Mohammad's colour and symbolises the sacred). A living baby wolf may sometimes be buried in the courtyard of a house, thereby, it is hoped, preventing an adult wolf entering it, not an unknown event. That wolves can in fact be coped with is apparent in the proverb 'when a wolf becomes old, the dog laughs'.

This recounting of a deal made with the saint is typical of the *nazr* made at *emamzādeh*, a sort of *quid pro quo* where, if the saint grants the request, the pilgrim will do something in return, in this case continue to believe and serve the shrine.

This particular shrine is concerned with relations with wild nature, and both tales illustrate its help in controlling, in the first case, danger, and in the second, a source of food. When called upon, these religious *emamzādeh* provide help for the Bakhtiāri in their encounters with wild nature.

Pir Ahmad (Bedal) (Ahmad the Guide) is a shrine on the other side of the mountains in the winter pastures in Khuzestān, in the region of Andekā. The *sādāt* (plural of *seyyed*), or descendants of the Imams, of this shrine are called *mārgir*, catchers of snakes (*mār*). The shrine is especially for snakes, and the *sādāt* of Pir Ahmad have the power to protect people from snake bites, and from their effects. Not all snakes in the region are poisonous, and few are deadly, but it is thought that their poison is more concentrated, and thus more dangerous, during the hot dry summers. Pir Ahmad is said to be crawling with snakes, but they never bite or harm even the children of the *sādāt* resident at the shrine. Snakes are believed to congregate there in great numbers on auspicious days and the *mārgir* are said to eat some of the thirteen types of snake they claim swarm round their shrine.

These *mārgir* are a familiar sight in the mountains. They travel around the camps of the nomads and the settled hamlets and villages with a bag of snakes and will perform a protective ritual for those who wish to make a gift to the distant *pir*, in return for food or cash, flour or even wheat. The *mārgir* takes a snake from his bag and lays it on the back of the neck of the supplicant, who holds the head of the snake while the *mārgir* holds the tail. An invocation for protection is made to God (*khodā*) asking for the intercession of Pir Ahmad. If the subject is afraid, then he or she holds the *mārgir's* hand, who then holds the snake by the head and pronounces the appropriate prayer. As I was an unbeliever, the visiting *mārgir* said it was necessary to wind the snake right round my neck while I held its head and he the tail. As he was mumbling the incomprehensible prayer the snake bit me on the back of the hand. The quick-witted *mārgir* claimed that because this happened just as the secret prayer was being said, I would come to no harm. Apart from a slight swelling, this proved to be the case. He sucked the wound, spat out the 'badness' and said another prayer. They themselves get bitten sometimes but are never harmed.

The shrine of Pir Shāh Alborz with its ancient oak tree, in the village of ʻAlikuh. 1960s.

The *mārgir* claimed that fear of snakes is worse than even the most dangerous bite and he recited a story familiar to the members of the camp group about how a man was sitting under a tree talking to a *mārgir* when a snake crawled down the tree above him and bit him on the head, without the man seeing what had bitten him. He merely brushed away what he thought was a mosquito. The *mārgir* said nothing. Some days later, the same two were sitting under the same tree and the *mārgir* told the man he had been bitten by a snake without realising it. The man promptly dropped dead.

The theme of protection against the dangers of the wild, and the necessity of not being afraid, is again clear, reinforcing familiar values of bravery and discernment held dear by the Bakhtiāri.

Pir Shāh Alborz is a well-cared-for shrine with a magnificent old oak tree beside it in the Bakhtiāri village of 'Alikuh, deep in the mountains. Associated with this shrine, far away on the opposite side of the valley, on the upper slopes of the mountain, is a strange discolouration shaped like a huge camel. Camels, though common among the Qashqa'i tribes further south, are very rarely seen in the more precipitous Bakhtiāri mountains. The guardians of this shrine, who reside in Masjed-e Soleymān, in the winter area of Khuzestān, are the keepers of an ancient document, some said inscribed on a sheepskin, from the time of Nāder Shah (*circa* AD 1746) giving title deeds to the land on which the village of 'Alikuh stands as reward for the role a particular Bakhtiāri played in Nāder's armies during the siege of Qandahār in present-day Afghanistan. These title deeds have ensured the continuing settlement of the members of his *tāyfeh* in this fertile area, in spite of concerted attempts to dispossess them by the leading khans at the turn of the twentieth century and later. The *sādāt* in possession of this document (*raqam*) were able to provide protection from the illegitimate force (*zulm*, a central theme in Shi'i Islam) being used against the tribesmen. The khans gained some support within the village and such was the dissension that many deaths occurred and many houses were destroyed. About half the inhabitants were forced to migrate for at least a decade. Such was the result of attempted oppression (*zur*), it was pointed out.

Pir Baraka is a typical mountain shrine in the winter pastures in Khuzestān. It is hidden up a defile, and instead of the more common dome has a tall conical structure on top of a rectangular mausoleum, or room (always kept carefully locked). The saint died in the south and is 'remembered' in this spot. There are no resident *sādāt*. The shrine is surrounded by a pathway lined with cairns, and has several trees thick with stones and flying the usual streamers of rags. The accompanying graveyard has a stone lion of indeterminate age. The shrine is thought to be specifically for sick cows, which are brought here. *Eh Barakeh, gāv (gusaleh) namord: ye pas be narzet* ("Oh Pir Baraka, do not let the calf die, one leg belongs to you as our vow"), is the prayer. One quarter of the calf, or the value of a quarter, then belongs to the shrine. The exchange is both a cure and a protection against illness.

Pir Boveyr is another conical shrine close to the Monar mountain range. This shrine however has resident guardians, the *sādāt*, who live in three or four houses beside the shrine, but also go out visiting the passing nomads. There are several stone lions in the graveyard, with swords and old muzzle-loading guns (*puzpor*) carved in relief on the sides. The shrine is located by a small water source at the head of a twisting defile and specialises in horses, donkeys and all pack animals. The loss of a pack animal is always a severe blow to the nomads, since without enough pack animals they cannot move their household equipment—in extreme circumstances cows are pressed into service.

Their pack animals often have fearsome open wounds on their shoulders, the result of heavy loads rubbing on them. These debilitating wounds are treated with liberally applied hot poultices of grasses and herbs boiled to mush and mixed with antiseptic ashes from the hearth fires. The nomads' horses suffer from periodic plagues and are often wounded in accidents. Pir Boveyr is regularly asked to help: *Ya Boveyr, asb-om khu basheh* ("Oh Boveyr, make my horses well"). Practical means are combined with sacred means in the attempt to cure the animals.

Emamzādeh Bābā Za'id, to which a narrow winding path eventually leads, is a shrine built high up on a mountainside right in the middle of tribal territory. Bābā Za'id was an old hermit. Down in the broad valley floor there are two sacred trees, festooned with rags and heavy with stones, standing as markers of this shrine. The shrine itself is built literally round a large oak tree. A few households of completely illiterate and impoverished sheykhs belonging to one of the major Bakhtiāri sections huddle here on the mountainside beside this tree shrine. Women coming to this shrine circumambulate the trunk of the tree inside. This shrine is particularly associated with sanctuary (*bast*), although ideally this is a property of all shrines. The sheykhs here also play a role as mediators in intertribal conflicts, historically very common in this particularly broad and lush valley. To stop the fighting they throw their turbans (*foutāh*) amongst the combatants. The conflict stops (again ideally) and the process of negotiation can start. On the winding path, lines of cairns and trees with rags tied to them mark the way. It is characteristic of the nomads' ambivalent attitude towards such impoverished sheykhs that they commonly steal what little wheat the latter manage to grow down in the valley, leaving them to eke out their meagre diet with acorn bread.

Pir Bauruzemun or Pir ʿAli Rezā is a well-thought-of shrine in the winter pastures on the road to the Monar. It has the typical conical structure on top of the rectangular tomb room and several rooms for visiting pilgrims. It is surrounded with evergreen myrtle trees (*murt*) which 'smell sweet', oaks (*balut*) and judas trees (*arghaman*). There are resident *sādāt* nearby and the shrine is well looked after. It is believed to be genuinely associated with Imam Rezā and women come here who do not produce children, or who have difficulty bearing live ones.

Visiting shrines in Iran is called *ziyārat* (to pay a visit). Women making *ziyārat* commonly stay at least one night and sometimes as long as a week. A pilgrim will bring with her food for several days and she is usually accompanied by other women. She must lay a small, new, folded green cloth under one of the trees in the graveyard and leave it there during the night. If by the end of her stay a myrtle leaf falls on to her cloth, then her fervent wish to bear a child will be granted. If it does not then she will not. She gives the resident *sādāt* the usual offerings of flour, tea and sugar, and the green cloth, and if in fact she does subsequently successfully bear a child, she returns the following year with money for the sheykhs to fulfil her *nazr*.

Thus, at this shrine incomplete women hope to be made whole, and so fulfil their most important role in Bakhtiāri society, the bearing of sons. They ask the saint to intercede on their behalf by reciting *Eh khodā, ye kor bede be mo, oulad nadorom* ("Oh God, give me a son, I have no children"). This shrine functions for women in the same way as the stone lions do for cowards, incomplete males.

To be barren, or continually to miscarry, or to have one's children die one after the other, is not only a personal tragedy for the afflicted woman but a social disaster for the husband. A man's personal and social identity is critically tied to the fertility of his wife, to the physiology of women. A man must have children, preferably sons, in order to be fully adult—a complete man. A man whose wife fails to provide him with sons will inevitably find his future diminished and he will marry again. To be the mother of sons is the ideal of every woman, as it ensures a future for herself. Thus both men and women have a particular interest in this *emamzādeh* and a man is unlikely to complain even if his wife stays there several days.

The following three shrines are the ones associated with authenticated close relatives of the eighth Imam, Rezā, and scepticism about them is very poorly regarded by most Bakhtiāri.

Emamzādeh Shah Qotb od-Din,[9] also known as Pir ʿAbdollah, lies in the valley within sight of the Monar pass, and is the shrine which is the power source of the three sacred trees mentioned earlier. Qotb-od Din (Pole of Religion) is identified as a son of Imam Musa, and thus brother of Imam Rezā. There are resident *sādāt* here, and in the disturbances of 1952 they gave sanctuary to several rebels (*yāghi*) attempting to rally support for the then Prime Minister of Iran, Mossadegh. However, the shrine is most famous for a rare rain-making ceremony (*darkhāst-e bārun*) that is held there, and it is the only time that large bodies of men are involved at any shrine.

After an extended period of extreme drought the political chiefs (*kalāntars*) of the sub-tribes (*tāyfeh*) whose territories are most affected may ask for this ceremony to be held. They and their followers gather at the shrine and collectively ask the resident sheykh to perform the ceremony. Each *tāyfeh* provides a bull (*pel*) for sacrifice. The sheykhs are asked to erect the *bard-e* Shah Qotb od-Din, two large cone-shaped heavy boulders which lie normally on their sides. An elderly sheykh is chosen to erect them. He has to be as old as possible because it is believed that the one who stands these stones erect always dies very shortly after. I was repeatedly told that this was a certainty and that the rain would come when he died. The boulders are then laid down on their sides again. The rain is regarded as this shrine's miracle (*moʿjez*).

A large sum of money (20,000 tumāns [about £800] was mentioned to me) is given in exchange for this conscious death, willingly carried out by the selected sheykh on behalf of the tribesmen. The money is carefully and exactly collected through the attendant kalāntars and is called *hin pil*, blood money, for the sheykh who will die. Such blood money is normally paid for blood spilled and for killings in the course of feuds between *tāyfeh* . The blood money is then distributed amongst the sheykhs with the bulk going to the immediate family of the elderly sheykh. The ritual is very rarely performed, I was told, because of the seriousness of the consequences for the resident sheykhs.

Emamzādeh Soltān Ebrahim is the only one in the mountains said to be visited by thousands of pilgrims (*ziyāratkon*), some very illustrious. The saint of this shrine is another son of the seventh Imam, Musa. In January 1878, Hoseyn Qoli Khan, the paramount chief (*Ilkhāni*) of all the Bakhtiāri tribes until his murder by the government in 1882, made a pilgrimage to Soltān Ebrahim's shrine, staying for several days.[10] The shrine is not at all easily accessible, being in a gorge on the south side of the river Kārun. The pilgrims cross by a rope swing bridge (*jorreh*) in baskets in which they sit. Frightened pilgrims tie themselves in (Sardar As'ad 1909: 219). Three of these *jorreh* (possibly *charak*) at this part of the river belong to the *emamzādeh*. There is a sizeable community of his descendants, the *sādāt* of the shrine, now living in a village near it. They were exempted from taxes and any service during the period in the nineteenth century when the khans were dominant (Sardar As'ad 1909: 530). Its principal attraction is a relic, the skin of a gazelle (*āhu*) a thousand years old with verses written on it, to which miracles are attributed.[11] The sick come to this shrine and wrap themselves in the ancient skin in the hope of a cure. They say prayers, pay money and sacrifice sheep, which are given to the *sādāt*.

The *sādāt* or sheykhs are all regarded as being of Arab origin, being descendants of the seventh Imam, and in the two shrines just discussed, descended from actual siblings of the revered eighth Imam, Rezā. They are now incorporated into the Bakhtiāri tribal system, and some, like those of the Soltān Ebrahim shrine, have flocks, migrate and cultivate some wheat.

Finally there is the shrine of Pir Khātun Haleb, reputedly a sister of Imam Rezā, the only female saint in this part of Iran. It is situated near the village of Sarpir in Chahār Mahāl, right on the edge of Bakhtiāri territory. Perhaps because of the extensive settlement in the region, both peasant and Bakhtiāri, this shrine specialises in the ceremonies associated with *Tāsu'ā* and *'Āshurā* on the 9th and 10th of the month of Muharram, commemorating the death of Hoseyn, the third Imam, who is so central to the emotional and religious life of Shi'i Islam. The central ritual of Shi'ism is the commemoration of his martyrdom.

This shrine has two storeys, the lower one accessible only to women. This inner and lower room is said to contain a thousand-year-old log of wood on which is carved a history of the area from long ago (*az qadim*). Men are barred from the inner sanctum. The shrine thus links purely local elements, the ancient log, with the wider world of Shi'i Islam in the most direct way.

These last three shrines are felt to be distinct from the rest of the lesser shrines because they are believed to be 'authentic', and as such more potently sacred than the others. They are far more famous among the tribesmen than the others, which are strictly local. There are similar, lesser, 'inauthentic' *emamzādeh* in other parts of the Bakhtiāri and neighbouring mountain regions.

While only a few Bakhtiāri have made the pilgrimage (*hajj*) to Mecca, many more have made *ziyārat* to the central Shi'i shrines, to Mashhad, to visit the tomb of Imam Rezā, and to Karbalā in Iraq, the site of the tomb of the martyred Hoseyn. Social and political status as well as considerable religious prestige come to those who have made such visits. Other meritorious religious acts are the making of *ziyārat* to local shrines, making *nazr* with gifts of flour, tea, sugar and sacrificial animals, and contributing to the upkeep of shrines, whether local or central.

In 1873, possibly as a consequence of a destructive earthquake in parts of the Bakhtiāri summer quarters, Hoseyn Qoli Khan, the *Ilkhāni*, sent an artisan to Karbalā to decorate the inner sanctum of the tomb of the Imam Hoseyn with mirror mosaic (*ā'ineh kāri*) (Garthwaite 1983: 148). The worker returned three years later having expended the then not inconsiderable sum of 6,000 tumans on the mirror work of the '*haram* of Seyyed al Shuhadah', the inner sanctum of the 'lord of the Martyrs', one of Hoseyn's major titles (Garthwaite 1983: 152).

Tragically, the wanton destruction of the shrines of Karbalā was reported early in 1991. It was done, during the aftermath of the invasion of Kuwait, by Iraqi forces fighting against the Shi'i uprising.

'The most damaged shrine is the tomb of Imam Hoseyn ... sprays of machine-gun fire mark the wondrous glass works, and marble pillars in the inner sanctum of Hoseyn's tomb' (Evans 1991). As we have seen in Iran as well, on several occasions, politics is no respecter of the sanctity of religious shrines.

TATTOOING

Finally, a rather different technique for protecting oneself from illness and dangerous forces—the once very common strategy of tattooing the body. A dark green-blue is used for all types of tattoo (*khāl*) against arthritis. For instance, large dots are tattooed on vulnerable ankles, knees and elbows. A hot tea glass, for suction, is placed over such dots, while the tattoo is still bleeding, in order to 'draw out' the arthritis from painful and swollen joints (*kāpeh koftan*). Dots are tattooed at the corners of the mouth and eyes and on the cheeks and lips to protect the vulnerable and visible orifices of the face. This is a very popular practice among women, but only rarely does one see men with blue dots on the face. Sometimes, again for protective reasons, the more isolated of the nomad women have their eyebrows tattooed right across the forehead in a thick, unbroken line, which, along with kohl on the inner eyelid, dramatises and emphasises their beautiful dark-green eyes (*sauz-e ti-e kol*), and is a practice once much admired by the Bakhtiāri. The chin and neck are often tattooed with several different designs. Ankles and wrists may have a line circling them to protect the legs and arms from harm, while some have the word 'Allah' etched protectively round the wrists. These permanent markers too provide protection while also being thought enhancements of a woman's beauty.

The colour of the tattoo is achieved by combining vegetable, mineral, wild animal and human elements: a dark-green herb mint (*pineh*) which is put in a thirst-quenching mixture of yoghurt and water (*dugh*) to enhance its flavour; the sooty residue collected from the inside of the paraffin lamps they use (*did-e cherāgh*); the bile of wild game (*zahlu-e shekal*), an ibex or wild goat for example; and finally the breast milk (*shir-e pistun*) of a woman recently delivered of a female child. These four items are mixed and boiled together, then kept for four days, to let the colour deepen. This mixture is brushed onto the part of the body to be tattooed, and the tattoo is made by continually pricking the skin with a needle, drawing blood, until the mixture takes. The result is a greenish-blue tattoo.

This mix, which combines bile, an inedible part of a wild animal, with mother's milk, an edible, life-giving substance associated with fertile women, is considered a suitably balanced concoction to provide a permanent protective marking against all those unknown forces that can harm the vulnerable women in the mountains.

SUMMARY

The themes which emerge from this discussion of Bakhtiāri encounters with the sacred are those of averting misfortune, of protection against the natural dangers of their mountainous habitat, of cure—the transformation from illness to health—and of help with the problems of the female life cycle with an emphasis on fertility and those times of a woman's life when she is most vulnerable—during pregnancy, childbirth, and when nurturing small children.

Stones are employed for protection against the practical hazards faced on migrations in a number of ways. People throw stones at dogs, wolves, thieves and each other in games and in conflict. They are built into protective walls and containing structures. They form a solid base for their worldly goods to lean against at the back of their tents. Cairns mark danger spots on mountain paths and indicate the presence of a sacred place. As well as being signposts to the shrines they are a link to powerfully protective, long-dead descendants of the Imams, whose tombs symbolise their permanent potency in the world. Stones, the embodiment of permanence, are also used in rituals as disparate as the individual *chālmeh bori*, the cure of sudden illness, and the collective rain-bringing ritual at Shah Qotb od-Din, which transforms deadly drought into life-sustaining rain for the community.

Entering the sacred space of an *emamzādeh* is, it is hoped, curative by itself. *Ziyārat*, or visits, are regarded as being beneficial to the women, many of whom confessed quietly to enjoying such breaks from their tedious and often arduous daily work, as well as to being sure they would feel better, be cured, become pregnant, or deliver safely. Deep scepticism and cynical disregard for the potency of these *emamzādeh* is common among the men, but they rarely discourage a woman from making a *ziyārat* if she thinks it necessary.

By circumambulation one wraps oneself within sacred space and round a sacred centre, the tomb in the shrine, thus consciously locating oneself as close to the sacred source as possible. An echo of such circling round a sacred centre was seen within the Pir Ghār, the Cave Shrine, where babies were passed over and under the rope of charms seven times. Another such echo is in the ritual cowards undergo by the light of the moon, that friend of lions, when they pass repeatedly under the legs of the heroic stone lions and crouch within the aura, the memory, of the dead hero, praying for the transformation of their deficient manhood into heroism. The action of wrapping and containment is seen also at *emamzādeh* Soltan Ebrahim, where the sick enclose themselves in the ancient gazelle skin, praying for health. The wrapping of snakes round nervous necks by *mārgir seyyeds* continues the theme of wild nature contained by the sacred. Likewise the protective amulets have symbols of wild natural power—the hair of a wolf or claw of a panther—sewn up in cloth of the sacred green colour. Tying rags and placing stones in trees, themselves natural symbolic surrogates of the sacred shrines, is a means of wrapping a gift-pledge (*nazr*) within the sacred force field of the *emamzādeh*, thereby establishing an individual relationship with the long-dead saint. The pilgrims present their specific and personal circumstances, and the saint's help is evoked, to protect, cure and thus transform their state of being, their very lives.

Just as the sacred encloses and wraps round an ancient log, a tree, a sweet-smelling myrtle leaf, individual Bakhtiāri consciously journey into these sacred places, their *ziyārat* locating and establishing them in a personal relationship with powerful, dead, sacred intercessors. Thus they reverently wrap themselves in sacred knowledge, within sacred space, contained by this protective power sourced in God, in order to acquire aid in the practical daily struggles and circumstances of their nomadic lives. Knowledge of sacred spaces and of sacred places thus comes to form an essential part of the practical mastery by Bakhtiāri of their life in the mountains.

Our tombs are in the hearts
of our partisans and followers.
Sabzewari.

A Hasanvand woman bakes bread on a metal griddle over an open hearth. Near Pol-e Dokhtar, 1985.

'WHEN WE HAD STRENGTH': THE LURI MYTH OF A GOLDEN AGE

David Bradshaw

When I first arrived in Luristān in 1975, the tribal-nomadic system that had once dominated the province to the virtual exclusion of settled life was in terminal decline, and the tribal system that traditionally underpinned pastoralism had lost most of its meaning. The head of the tribal office in Khorramābād, the provincial capital, which kept count of migration permits, estimated that fewer than 50,000 of Luristān's total population of 700,000 were still nomads.

I wondered what kept the Luri nomads going when it was obvious in my meetings with them that they sensed they were out of tune with the times. Many had come to see themselves as oddities and were embarrassed, even ashamed, to talk with an outsider about their migratory way of life—an attitude that mirrored that of the state officials who regarded nomadism as an anachronism which had no place in the 'Great Civilisation' ostensibly being built in an Iran that looked to the west in everything. For most Lurs, doing well no longer meant accumulating a big herd of sheep and goats, but owning a business in town. The friends and relations they admired most, and were the young nomads' role models, were those sharing in the economic boom which convulsed Iran in the 1970s.

The general answer is poverty. Although most of those nomads I met wanted to settle down in Khorramābād, whose population had trebled to 100,000 between 1950 and 1975, or in villages where they had family ties, many suffered near-penury and few if any had enough money to buy a building plot in town; and the village lands could barely support their present populations, never mind new settlers. *Faute de mieux,* they were obliged to carry on migrating each spring and autumn between winter pastures in the south-west and summer pastures in the north-east with their herds of sheep and goats, their mules and horses, their chickens in baskets and their wolf-like dogs.

The Lurs, buffeted by change and faced with a decline in their fortunes, were strikingly nostalgic; confused by the present they romanticised their past into a nomadic golden age.

Looking back to the times before Rezā Khān (later Shah) suppressed their independence, as he did that of every other Iranian tribe, they recalled better days, when, as they put it, 'we were free' or 'we had strength'. They spoke nostalgically of the days when most men were armed and power came from the barrel of a gun; when they were so strong that the writ of the governor appointed by Tehran extended little further than the walls of his stronghold, the Falak-o-Laflak in Khorramābād; and when men scorned the settled life and nomadism ruled. The men then were brave and honest (a common complaint of modern Lurs was that a man's word could no longer be trusted) and the nomads rich and prosperous.

In those glorious times, I was told, the tribes were like extended families, and the tribal leaders were 'fathers' to their tribes. For the Lurs of 1975, their lost past was the best of all possible worlds.

The description of Luri nomadic society given by western visitors to Luristān in the nineteenth and early twentieth centuries contradicts much of the idealised image modern Lurs have of it. Far from being a time of probity, it was one of treachery, when oaths meant little: guests were often slaughtered by their hosts against all traditions of hospitality; tribal leaders exploited the tribesmen; and life for the majority meant poverty, insecurity and uncertainty.

But is the western picture reliable? Until the 1930s the dangers of travel in Luristān were such that western visitors were few and their visits short. Moreover, most suffered one way or another at the hands of the Lurs and were ill-disposed to them. Nevertheless, many of them were what might be called trained observers—diplomats, military men and scientists—and made careful and minute observations. Therefore, it is probably true to say that their writings give a more accurate picture of what life was really like than the highly selective folk memories of the modern Lurs. It is my aim to present these two views side by side in order to show what can happen when the real past is subjected to the myth-making process.

To hear the Lurs talk, their land had been dominated by tribal nomadism since time began, but although they had many legends about their origins, they had little accurate knowledge. Most adult men could recite their pedigrees to a common ancestor half a dozen generations back, but were unable to quantify exactly when this individual lived. For example, the Beiranvand tribe, with which I lived for some time, claimed that they and the Bajulvand were descended from 'Beiran and Bajul', 'two brothers' who had 'come from Arabia Hejaz'. In fact there was an element of truth in their claim, in that the first people calling themselves Beiranvand and Bajulvand arrived in the region from the Mosul area around 200 years ago. The Beiranvand did not know this, nor did such details appear to matter to them. 'Nomadism', as Arnold Toynbee (1947: 168) wrote, 'is essentially a society without a history'.

On the question of how long nomadism has dominated Luristān, the evidence actually shows that the province supported a thriving *settled* population for most of its history. Luristān, sandwiched between Kurdistān and Bakhtiāri, is a sheaf of ridges running north-west to south-east and rising in height from the Mesopotamian plain to the Iranian plateau; Garrin Kuh in the north-east is over 13,000 feet (4,000 metres) high. Much of the land is hostile to man. Expanses of bare rock reduce the soil cover and the terrain is barren and eroded where soft and porous rocks come to the surface, yet the rugged mountain slopes provide grazing for livestock. Between the ridges lie fertile valleys which are drained by the Seymareh, Karkheh and Kashgān rivers. Here and there the valleys widen out into well-watered plains perfectly suited to agriculture—Khaweh, Alishtar and Horud in the north, Khorramābād and Jaidar in the centre, Hulailan, Tarhan and Rumishgan in the south. Between November and April westerly winds bring rainfall of at least 12 inches (250 mm) a year (the minimum for rain-fed agriculture) and frequently three times as much. The natural vegetation is a mixture of alpine-type pasture and 'Zagrosian oak forest' (a mix of dwarf oak, elm, maple, walnut, almond, pistachio, pear and pomegranate, with poplar, willow, alder and ash in the moister ravines) (Bobek 1968: 185).

Luristān's geographical position, between Mesopotamia and the Iranian plateau, made it an important thoroughfare from the earliest times. The archaeological record shows that from at least the second millennium BC Luristān supported a mix of settled agriculture and livestock herding—transhumance, if not nomadism as such (Moorey 1973: 17; Stein 1940)—the bias being towards settled agriculture. Since those far-off days the mix of agriculture and pastoralism has shifted in accordance with prevailing economic and political conditions. Archaeological sites in Luristān are 'astonishingly close together'; the place was probably more densely settled in antiquity than it is today (Thrane 1964: 167). The ruins of Sassanian cities at Saidmarreh, Rudbar, Sirwan and so on, Sassanian bridges at Pol-e Kalhur, Pol-e Dokhtar and elsewhere, and the remains of ancient roads and canals testify to former prosperity. Later, Arab geographers wrote of Luristān's flourishing economy and largely sedentary population.

This settled prosperity seems to have lasted well into the era of the princely dynasty of Atabegs, who ruled Luristān from the twelfth to the seventeenth century, and if any time was Luristān's 'golden age' this was probably it. However, by the mid-eighteenth century the settled life in Luristān had largely vanished, and most of the (probably much reduced) population were nomadic herders of sheep and goats, though growing some grain and other crops in their winter and summer quarters. Nomadism dominated even in places that once supported towns and villagers.

Modern Lurs had no folk memory of this 'bedouinisation', and of how the complicated system of rights to land use in winter and summer quarters and along the tribal road (*il rah*) was established. As far as they were concerned, nomadism was a fact of nature and had not 'developed' at all.

The process of bedouinisation was probably linked to the political and social insecurity which followed the massive invasions of Turkish and Mongol nomads into Iran in the middle ages. Old histories record how Luri farmers took to pastoral nomadism after the fashion of their conquerors 'so they were not exposed to the violence of whosoever first came upon them' (de Planhol 1968: 414).

The anarchy into which Iran was plunged by the Afghan conquest of 1722 probably helped to entrench tribal nomadism in Luristān, while the tribal displacements practised for military or

A young married woman of the Hasanvand sub-tribe. 1985.

punitive reasons by successive Iranian shahs may also have played a part. In Luristān, for example, many of the leading tribes are relatively recent arrivals: the Selseleh group of tribes—which includes the Hasanvand, Yusufvand and Kulivand—was moved by Shah 'Abbās from Mahidasht to Luristān. The Beiranvand and the Sagvand were both moved to Shirāz, the Beiranvand by Nādir Shah, the Sagvand by Karim Khan Zand, but both managed to return to Luristān, where they established themselves by appropriating lands from neighbouring tribes, and absorbing some of them. One can imagine that such movements, and the land struggles they involved, helped to undermine security. The supremacy of nomadism in Luristān was, as Irons (1974: 635–8) has shown it to be amongst the Turkmen, a defensive mechanism against insecurity.

Insecurity was, by the start of the nineteenth century, the hallmark of Luristān. 'Many of the tribes live in a state of open rebellion' while some, 'confiding in the fastness ... subsist almost entirely by the plunder of travellers,' wrote Major Sir Henry Rawlinson, who passed through Luristān in 1836. 'The men seem to consider robbery and war their proper occupation, and are never so well pleased as when engaged on a foray,' remarked Rawlinson, who, despite having the protection of a regiment, came close to losing his life to 'these ruffians who make no more account of cutting a man's throat than a sheep's' (Rawlinson 1839: 55). A few years later Sir Henry Layard judged the Lurs to be 'less under the control of the Persian government than any other part of the Empire'. The tribes, Layard observed, were notorious for their plundering propensities, particularly the Delfan and Selseleh.

next page
Goats are extremely hardy and can find grazing in places impossible for sheep. Though less commercially valuable than sheep they provide more milk for home consumption and are thus the mainstay for poorer families living at the level of subsistence. 1985.

'The country they inhabit can seldom be traversed in safety either by single travellers or caravans'. Villages outside Luristān, in the Silakhor plain near Borujerd, were fortified against Luri attacks, though the tribes seemed undeterred: many lay ruined as a result of Luri raiding expeditions (*chapaws*) (Layard 1846: 4).

The plundering of caravans and villages was a sordid business, yet it has lived on in Luri memory as a heroic activity. Modern Lurs, who felt 'colonised' by Tehrānis and other administrators in Luristān who generally looked down upon them (I often heard Tehrānis refer to them as 'dirty people'), enjoyed recalling times when they, 'the Lurs', had bested these outsiders, and were feared by them.

What the Lurs recalled as a 'golden age' of national unity was actually a nightmare of instability and danger. The tribes in the old days behaved as abominably towards each other as they did towards outsiders. Tribe fought tribe and clan fought clan for grazing land and plunder. Blood feuds were endemic. Tribal leaders worked for their own narrow self-interests and rarely for the greater good of their tribes, and they oppressed the common tribesmen mercilessly.

The Lurs themselves were not entirely responsible for this state of affairs. Appalling government throughout the Qājār period (1794–1925) ensured that the insecurity that led to the domination of nomadism was prolonged, and that there was no period of stability in which the settled life could recover. Qājār 'administration' helped to dissolve the bonds of Luri society and compound tribal anarchy.

From the twelfth to the seventeenth centuries, Luristān had its own rulers, the Atabegs, a dynasty of semi-independent princes. The last, Shahverdi Khan, was murdered by Shah 'Abbās around 1620 and replaced with a rival chief, Hoseyn Khan, who was given the title of *Wali*. At the end of the eighteenth century the central government wrested Luristān east of the Kabir Kuh—'Pish Kuh'—from the *Wali's* control, though he and his successors continued to rule west of the Kabir Kuh—'Posht Kuh'—with a degree of autonomy that varied in proportion to the strength of the governor of Kermānshāh until the last *Wali* was deposed by Rezā Shah in 1928. The tribes of Posht Kuh generally acknowledged the overlordship of the *Wali*, although his authority was often weakened by feuding within his own family, instigated or encouraged by the government.

At first Pish Kuh came under the jurisdiction of the governor of Kermānshāh, but around 1840 it was transferred to that of the governor of Isfahān. He usually appointed a local governor who based himself in Khorramābād when he was not following the tribes around in order to keep a watchful eye on them. Without exception these governors were a disaster for the region. They cared little for the interests of the Lurs, or for improving the resources of the province. Instead they pursued three aims: the collection of the taxes assessed by the government in Tehran (plus of course the personal pickings or *modākhel*); the safety of trade routes across the province; and the preventing of any tribal leader from becoming too powerful. They often failed in the first two, only occasionally succeeded in the third, but triumphed in the fourth.

The governors' general failure to achieve their aims resulted from the quality of the armed forces at their disposal. The governor had his own little army made up of recruits from the tribes and sometimes supported by a regiment from outside. However, these troops were usually anything but disciplined, and were ill-trained, ill-fed, ill-clothed and ill-led. They were simply no match for the Lurs, even though the tribesmen may not have been specially good fighters, despite the tales of heroism told to me around Luri camp fires in the 1970s. It was inevitable that such forces would fail to cow the tribes. In 1891 a French scientific expedition sought out a governor who had gone south 'to punish the brigandage of some Lur chieftain' and found the governor's camp 'surrounded by rebellious nomads and in a very precarious position'. The governor nevertheless had the aplomb to give the Frenchmen letters of safe conduct addressed to all the Lur chiefs, 'even those who were at that moment engaged against him' (de Morgan 1894: 29).

On the rare occasions when the governor could call upon a half-decent force the Lurs were usually sent packing. In 1908–10 the Beiranvand devastated the Silakhor plain and raided as far as Borujerd, Nahāvand and Malāyer. They defeated a punitive expedition under the governor, Montasser ad-Dowleh, in 1910. The following year a force of 2,000 Bakhtiāri levies under a new governor, the Bakhtiāri chief Amir Mofakham, put to flight a Beiranvand force twice its size. '[The Beiranvand] had scarcely fired a shot when, on their chief Fazil being killed, they fled

Unprecedented rainfall has caused these Lurs from the Kohgiluyeh region to cover their tents as best they can. Winter camp near Dehdasht, 1984

precipitately and made no further stand. Their tents were looted and their women dishonoured shortly afterwards' (Wilson 1912: 37).

The governors managed to rule by a combination of intrigue and periodic full-scale campaigns. By offering the prospect of revenge on some rival tribe and promising gifts and honours (the Lurs had a curious weakness for honorary titles and robes of honour) they could usually usually count on rallying a fair proportion of Luri tribal leaders to their side. By playing off one tribe against another a governor was thus usually able to get his way: '... their want of unity rendered them totally unfit to oppose [the governor]' (Layard 1846: 3). When taxes went unpaid for years, which was often the case, the governor would launch a full-scale military campaign to 'loot' the unpaid revenues from the recalcitrant tribes. In 1884 a Sagvand chief, Hajji 'Ali Khan 'described his tribe as being impoverished by government exactions which they were unable to meet; certainly none of them were wealthy and many were poor, where all should be rich' (Bell 1885: 9).

It must not be thought that periodic taxation left the Lurs relatively well-off. The chiefs oppressed and taxed the common tribesmen as hard as, or harder than, the government, and it was not uncommon for men to leave one tribe for another because of the severity of their leaders' exactions. 'The rebelliousness of the Lurs,' concluded one visitor, 'must simply be taken to mean that, being unable to meet excessive demands, they resist them' (Bell 1889: 466).

Governors took extreme measures to keep the roads open, but the results were usually short-lived. Sometimes they would take hostages from the tribes as guarantees of good behaviour and sometimes they would deport persistent offenders. In about 1904, the governor of Luristān and the *Wali* of Posht Kuh joined forces to seize several headmen and 500 families of the Direkvand tribe, whose depredations had closed the road north from Dezful, and deport them to Posht Kuh, where they remained for four years (Wilson 1912: 26). More usually they would round up headmen of the guilty tribes and summarily execute them. In 1881 the Zell os-Soltan, a son of the shah and governor of Isfahān, went to Khorramābād to pacify the tribes. 'After several days [his forces] captured

A 'weaning bit' (*kāwor*), used when young goats continue to attempt to suckle even after they have been weaned. It is used because kids butt the udder with their head to cause milk let-down and the sharp points of their growing horns can cause injury.

The look of this young mother at the entrance to her tent conveys something of the legendary ferocity of the Lurs. Shrinking resources and the growing competition for grazing, caused by a rapid growth of population, have caused some Lur groups, notably the Selseleh and Bairanvand, to adopt an extremely aggressive approach to the preservation of their territory from the intrusions of outsiders. Near Kuhdasht, 1984.

Asad Khan Beiranvand and Sardar Khan Sagvand, along with five of their brothers, and executed all of them. [The Zell' s forces] plundered their camp and seized their property, and those remaining fled and came to Arabistan to the Bin Lam' (Garthwaite 1983: 165). In 1891, the governor, Seif ol-Molk, opened the road from Borujerd to Khorramābād, which had been cut 'by plundering tribes', with a terrible execution. 'Thirteen men chosen from amongst the notables of the tribes had their right wrists slashed; they bled to death, and two others were shot. This example pacified the valley of Ho-roud' (de Morgan 1894: 28).

Given this climate of government and chiefly rapacity, it is hardly surprising that the tribesmen themselves indulged in looting whenever they could. Much of the looting was directed against caravans crossing the province. The caravans, with thousands of mules and horses, would march at night lit with torches and with an armed guard of 50–100 horsemen. However, 'at the least attack the government horsemen disappear with the muleteers. The soldiers die of fear through the whole journey and the merchants must pay danger money which doesn't encourage trade' (de Morgan 1894: 213). The tribes would negotiate tolls (*rahdāri*) with the caravans in return for a promise of safe passage across the mountains, but the promises were often broken. In 1904 the Mir Baharvand bound themselves on sealed Korans to conduct two British officers, Major Douglas and Captain Lorimer, from Dezful to Khorramābād and back for 200 tomans. On the return journey the two men were attacked and badly wounded by their tribal escorts and stripped of their possessions. The Mirs' excuse was that they had sealed Korans only for the outward journey, and that their guarantees of safety for the return were verbal only, and therefore non-binding. After the attack on Douglas and Lorimer the governor rounded up senior Mirs and fired one of them from a gun. Such examples had no lasting deterrent effect.

The plundering propensities of the Lurs were not only, or even primarily, directed at outsiders. Other tribes, other clans of the same tribe, and even families of the same clan, were considered fair game for plunder. Most blood feuds arose when men were killed in the act of, or defence against, robbery: the Lurs did not believe that defending property from theft justified the shooting of the guilty party. When someone was killed, 'Compensation is exacted, but according to no fixed scale, the sole criterion being the strength of those who make the demand, and the ability of the weaker party to pay. Blood is only exacted for blood when there is no chance of obtaining its pecuniary equivalent' (Wilson 1912: 27).

The talk around Luri camp fires in the 1970s often turned to the subject of tribal leadership, it being a sore point amongst modern Lurs that many of the khans had become rich landowners, whilst most common tribesmen were landless. Modern chiefs were compared with those of the past, mostly unfavourably. The latter, I was often told, looked after the tribesmen 'like their own sons'. Here again was an idealised folk memory that disregarded the facts.

For a start, there was enormous tension between the tribal leaders and the common tribesmen, for a variety of reasons. Tribal leadership was usually contested by several individuals, each of whom might enjoy the allegiance of one or more subdivisions of the tribe, the clans or *taifehs*. That allegiance had to be earned; how long it would last depended upon the chief's prestige, which itself relied upon his ability to defend the tribesmen and their lands from enemies and provide them with opportunities for plunder. The chiefs passed their lives in a series of intrigues and alliance-making, or *dastehbandi*, to increase their power and prestige, avoid taxation and maximise their revenues; the pacts were often cemented with marriage alliances.

For their part, the tribesmen did little to attract their leaders' kindness. The authority of the khans over the common tribesmen, or *rayat*, was uncertain. The clans, which were made up of extended families claiming (often fictitious) common ancestry, enjoyed a degree of autonomy unusual in comparable Iranian tribal societies, and rarely acknowledged any authority higher than that of their clan leader (*kadkhoda*), whose own position was often contested. The *rayat* frequently ousted their khans altogether. 'I doubt whether there is a man, even among the so-called headmen, who can really control half a dozen others, and it is in consequence virtually impossible to make any binding agreement with them' (Edmonds 1922: 340).

One visitor reckoned that the Luri system 'more nearly assimilates to the spirit of a confederated republic than of a great feudal aristocracy' (Rawlinson 1839: 109). In fact, it was close to anarchy, and exhibited a particularly severe degree of disorder when compared to that prevailing among other nomadic groups, such as the Bakhtiāri and Qashqa'i, where large integrated tribal confederations controlled both agricultural villages and pastoral nomadic groups, and powerful chiefs were able to limit lawlessness.

The final horror in this situation was the part played by the government. The governors of Luristān made it their business to keep the tribes divided, to weaken the khans and make tax collection easier, which had the overall effect of dissolving still further the bonds of tribal society and increasing insecurity. Before Rezā Shah, Luri society was more completely atomised than perhaps most other comparable Iranian tribal groups.

Given this state of affairs, it is not surprising that the turmoil was repeated at the tribal level. By convention the Pish Kuh Lurs are divided into four 'groups'—Delfan, Tarhan, Selseleh, and Bala Gariveh. Outsiders sometimes referred to these groups, incorrectly, as 'confederations', but they were geographical rather than political divisions. Of greater practical political significance were the two dozen or so tribes—Hasanvand, Beiranvand, Sagvand, Direkvand, and so on. However, even at this level it was rare for a tribe to be completely unified under a single leader, or khan; nor did the tribes remain fixed and permanent entities.

On rare occasions a charismatic leader did manage to weld several Luri tribes together under his single leadership. One who did was Nazar 'Ali Khan, chief of the Amrai tribe, who became the principal figure in Luristān around the turn of the century. His story is worth recounting. Born in 1860, 'he commenced his upward career by stealing a horse, then a rifle, then some money, with which he collected a band of fellow thieves, who by their daring and successful raids soon enriched themselves at the expense of their neighbours' (Wilson 1912: 15). He defeated his cousin in a struggle for the leadership of the Amrai, and thereafter, though never having large forces at his command, managed, through guile and a facility for alliance building, to bring most of the tribes of Tarhan and Delfan, and some of the Selseleh, under his influence. Sometimes Nazar 'Ali fought against the governor, at others with him. In 1899 he was imprisoned and bastinadoed in the palace garden at

A gravestone with what appears to be a hunting scene, in a graveyard belonging to Hasanvand Lurs.

Khorramābād by the governor, 'Ain ad-Dowleh, thus 'eating both chains and the stick', as he put it. In 1903, he was hunted by governor Salar ad-Dowleh but managed to evade capture. In 1907, he gave Salar ad-Dowleh refuge when the latter rebelled against the Shah, and married off a daughter to him. The following year a new governor, Nezam as-Saltaneh, declared him a rebel, but Nazar 'Ali seized the Nezam and imprisoned him in Khorramābād. Nazar 'Ali was 'a great opium eater, but a man of character and energy who knows how to rule and how not to pay taxes' (Wilson 1941: 167). He nevertheless performed enough services for the governor to collect a string of titles: Sardar Akram, Fath-e Lashkar, and in 1910 he was made 'Wali of Pish Kuh'. His power died with him, though a son of his was prominent in one of the last Luri rebellions against Rezā Shah.

The tribes were constantly in flux, growing by assimilating members from other tribes, or splitting and declining, sometimes disappearing altogether, through absorption by other tribes, or through settlement. For example, the Yusufvand, Kakavand, Ittivand and Qaid Rahmat tribes declined in strength and prestige as their members settled in large numbers in villages north and west of Luristān around the turn of the century.

Clans, or individual tribesmen, might leave one tribe to join another, if better opportunities for plunder were offered, or if the oppression of their leaders became insupportable. In the late nineteenth century, the Direkvand grew by absorbing members from the Beiranvand, Sagvand and Hasanvand, who had been attracted by its success in milking the trade route from Dezful to Khorramābād that crossed its lands; at one point the newcomers made up fully one-quarter of the tribe. In the 1900s, the Beiranvand themselves became the biggest and most feared tribe in Luristān, some 10,000 families strong, because its successful and virtually unresisted raiding expeditions on the Silakhor plain and the towns of Borujerd and Nahāvand drew new members. Smaller neighbouring tribes, such as the Dalvand and Qaid Rahmat, allied themselves closely with the Beiranvand; given time, they too might have been fully absorbed into the Beiranvand tribe. Tribes which grew by accretion would often expand territorially at the expense of less powerful or declining tribes.

The towns and villages in Luristān also led a precarious existence. In fact, Khorramābād was the only town in the province. At times during the nineteenth century its population fell to as little as 2,000 and probably never rose above 5,000, compared with 15,000 for Dezful and over 20,000 for Borujerd. Its bazaar was poor, and prices, because of the difficulties of importing goods, were two to three times those of Dezful.

Villages were limited to favoured areas. One such was the Khorramābād plain, under the walls of the governor's fortress, but it was no guarantee of safety. In better times, as in 1836, the plain was 'a richly cultivated district thronged with villages and gardens' (Rawlinson 1839: 97), but when times were bad, as in 1917, the villages 'were all ruinous and deserted' (Edmonds 1922: 340). And even at the best of times the villagers were poor, 'being exposed to the attacks of the Hasanvand, Sagvand, and Beiranvand. These, not happy simply letting their flocks have free rein in the fields of the settled villagers during their migrations, also demolish their houses and steal their sheep, goats, cattle and mules' (Rabino 1916: 9).

Outside the Khorramābād plain villages were rare. In 1877 one visitor estimated that there were only thirty-six in the whole of Pish Kuh (Houtum Schindler 1879: 84). There were some upon fertile plains, Alishtar, for example, but even there most of the land was given over to grazing: 'the great body of the plain, however, is pasture ground, and I'liyat encampments were scattered over its whole surface' (Rawlinson 1839: 100).

Settled agriculture was linked to the fortunes of the towns and villages, of course. It was very restricted in bad times and cautiously expanded when governors were strong. For example, in 1899, during the rule of governor 'Ain ad-Dowleh, many Lurs were 'giving up their tents and becoming *deh-nishin*', though they are despised for it by the bulk of the tribesmen' (Durand 1902: 233). 'The settled are despised by the nomads and are considered by them to be degenerate,' wrote one visitor, who went on, 'This sentiment is but one of envy. The life of the *deh-nishins* would attract all did not the counterbalancing fear of exactions and increased taxation serve to force them into a mode of life less under government control' (Bell 1884: 82).

In these circumstances the resources of Luristān, especially its fertile land and its advantageous geographical position, were grossly underexploited. This was hardly the 'best of all possible worlds'.

Pastoral nomadism was the basis of the Luri way of life. North and east of the Kabir Kuh, which divides Luristān into two, the tribes of Pish Kuh—Hasanvand, Beiranvand, Sagvand and others—would migrate in autumn from the summer quarters (*sardsir*) in the mountains and valleys of the north-east to the winter quarters (*garmsir*) in the valley of the Seymareh or the plains north of Dezful. A few tribes wintered in the Silakhor plain near Borujerd. When the sun desiccated the southern grasses and melted the snows in the north, they would return to the north, along migration routes between 150 and 250 miles (240 and 400 km) long. These 'long-range' Luri nomads would pass *en route* through the lands of the Papis and other short-range nomads who occupied the central Pish Kuh and whose summer and winter quarters were contiguous.

Colonel Bell joined the Sagvand on migration in 1884, moving north with them in a series of short stages 7–12 miles (11–19 km) long. No villages were passed, and no other tribes were seen 'as our tribe was, as it were, making a forced passage through the lands of inimical fellow tribesmen'. However other tribesmen certainly were around, if unseen, and robbed the migrating column incessantly (Bell 1889: 471–3).

In 1899 Durand observed the Sagvand on migration: 'All the morning we had passed a stream of the Sagvands marching to their winter quarters—a long line stretching as far as we could see—thousands of sheep and goats and small cattle and donkeys and some ponies—they looked poor—but cheery enough—the men wild ruffians—some armed—the women with long side locks—dark indigo clothing mostly—open in the front showing the breasts—a few were pretty and mounted on mules or ponies with good carpets—favourite wives doubtless' (Durand 1899: 15). This description was more or less still valid (except for the cattle, which are no longer taken on migration) eighty or so years later.

The population was small, and may well have fallen during the century. In 1836 Rawlinson estimated the Pish Kuh Lurs at 44,000 families—perhaps some 220,000 people—and those of Posht Kuh at 12,000 families. In 1884 Bell reckoned that there were 210,000 Lurs in both Pish Kuh and Posht Kuh together, whilst in 1913 Rabino estimated the tribes of Pish Kuh at some 31,000 tents, or some 150,000 people.

The tribespeople lived in black goat hair tents, whose size and furnishings varied according to the owners' wealth, and they relied mostly, but not exclusively, on the milk, meat, wool and hair of their flocks. They grew barley, wheat, maize and opium mainly in their summer quarters, 'but partly through apathy, partly through fear of the exactions of their chiefs, the Lur cultivates only as much as he needs' (Rabino 1916: 6). They also gathered wild fruits and nuts and large quantities of acorns that they ground into powder to bulk out wheat flour when making bread (or even to replace wheat entirely in hard times when wheat flour was scarce).

The tribespeople enjoyed few friendly contacts with the Iranian plateau, which was regarded by the Lurs as potential spoil, but a few tribes wintered in the Silakhor plain near Borujerd and there was some trading of surplus livestock, butter, cheese and wool with settled people: de Morgan reckoned that most of the wheat the Lurs ate was bought in exchange for wool (de Morgan 1894: 28). The Lurs also supplied Borujerd, Nahāvand and Kermānshāh with charcoal, and exported mules famous for their strength and hardiness (Rawlinson estimated that 1,000 were exported annually), gum tragacanth, cherry wood pipes, the skins of otters (once found in all of Luristān's rivers), and pomegranate juice (de Bode 1845: 256). Luri horse trappings and large woollen bags (*hurs*) were also sold. In exchange the Lurs bought food, utensils, guns and cartridges.

Western travellers to Luristan reported much poverty. E. M. Durand, who visited Luristan in 1899, was told by Mir 'Ali Khan, a Sagvand chief, that 'the Persians bully them and starve them and drive them into robbery'. Durand had to admit that the Lurs he saw seemed 'miserably poor' (Durand 1899: 216).

If anything, the chronic state of anarchy in Luristān worsened during the twentieth century, especially after the promulgation of the constitution in 1906, which paralysed government throughout Iran because it created confusion between the power and authority of the central government and the governors of the provinces. 'Indeed in the mouth of a Lur the word *mashruteh*, "constitution", is simply a synonym for "disorder". He will say, "So-and-so is making constitution", i.e. he is playing Old Harry somewhere' (Edmonds 1922: 342). The government attempted to impose some indirect control over the tribes by appointing Nazar 'Ali Khan *Wali* of

Pish Kuh and acting governor, but he was resisted by many tribes and by leading Khorramābādis. The Lurs referred to this as the time of *khod-sari* (do-as-you-please).

Because of the unrest the routes through Luristān were closed between 1917 and 1924. The last governor to attempt to penetrate to Khorramābād until the coming of Rezā Shah was Nezam as-Saltaneh in 1915, and his force, which included a large contingent of Swedish-trained gendarmerie, was subsequently totally defeated by the Lurs. Visitors at this time painted a particularly grim picture: 'There is nothing in Luristān upon which one can build. There is no confidence in the present, no pride in the past, no hope in the future, no patriotism, except within the narrow limits of the tribe ... no bond of religion, for Islam is weaker here than anywhere else in Persia and nowhere strong. Oaths are valueless, and where anarchy is rife even self-interest is not an easy chord to strike' (Wilson 1941: 262).

Yet in Luri memory this period was the apogee of the golden age.

The anarchy continued until 1924, when Rezā Khan, soon to be Rezā Shah, moved to subjugate the turbulent Lurs and open the road through Luristān to the semi-autonomous province of Khuzestān, whose oil riches he wanted to bring firmly under Tehrān's control. In April that year he sent a message to the tribes to say that their security was 'assured', and that they could therefore hand over their arms to their 'brothers in the armed forces' who would 'be your protectors from now on'. The message continued: 'Even the wild black Africans are on the road towards progress and improvement. It is not becoming that you, the sons of an ancient country like Iran, with its illustrious historical civilisation, should wander over desert and mountain like predatory animals. You must give up that nomadic and tent-dwelling life. Follow the proper and noble way of life of your ancestors, who built, furnished and improved their surroundings and who lived in towns' (Wilber 1975).

Motor roads were built through Luristān, and along them came a mechanised army with trucks and heavy guns which the deeply divided and lightly armed Lurs could not match. Chains of police posts were established. Tribes which resisted paid a heavy price, their leaders executed or imprisoned in Tehran. The tribespeople were slaughtered and looted. The army imposed harsh rule, outlawing traditional Luri dress, shaving the Lurs' long beards and hair, ripping up their tall felt hats and coats and forcing them into 'European' clothes and peaked 'Pahlevi hats' with the shah's portrait printed on the lining. Forced settlement, from 1929 onwards, caused great distress, especially to those, like the Beiranvand, whose summer and winter quarters lay in the north and extreme south of Luristān respectively.

A visitor in 1936 wrote of the 'exceedingly primitive look' of the 'reed houses and mud hovels' built by the Lurs to replace the tents which had been burned. 'That [settlement], so beneficent on the whole, must involve serious hardships for the quondam nomadic tribal population can scarcely be doubted' (Stein 1938: 327–31). Freya Stark, who was there in 1931–2, felt that the Lurs' character had changed, that 'Something of the tribesman has gone, something of the peasant has crept into their manner' (Stark 1934: 180).

That a myth of a golden age could grow out of this terrible history truly amazed me. There was certainly no arguing about it with the nomads and I could only listen in wonder at the tales they told.

Ploughing north of Yāsuj in spring 1986. These slopes were once forested and the roots of the trees are left in to stabilise the soil. If the soil is shallow-ploughed, some of the trees can regenerate. With tree cover at the present level, soil erosion is almost certain to occur.

BOYER AHMAD

Erika Friedl

The Boyer Ahmad region is famous all over Iran, but until recently few outsiders had travelled there and there was little information against which to measure the tales of great beauty, wilderness, inaccessible mountains, daring hardy tribesmen and danger. The local people say Boyer Ahmad has everything: warm and fertile river valleys with villages built on hills formed from layer upon layer of the ruins of earlier villages; quiet, oak-covered hills and mountains where camps of black goat hair tents dot pastures amidst thousands of sheep and goats; wide, flat, dry basins surrounded by dark mountains and rocky outcrops of eroding limestone; high passes and steep gorges; snow-capped peaks and cold springs in the Zāgros; hot, shadeless plains where oases are the only green patches in the sand and huge bonfires of burning gas on the horizon mark the presence of oil wells. There are hot winds and long, slow rains, and a steady rhythm of colour changes marks the passing seasons: white and blue in the snowy winters, lush greens in spring, yellows and parched browns in summer and autumn.

Boyer Ahmad lies at 30°N and 51°W, to the south of the main Zāgros range. Mountain ranges running roughly north-west to south-east cut the area into parallel valleys connected by passes. Despite its difficult terrain, the area seems to have been settled since Achaemenid times, and archeological evidence—ruins, pottery and tools—suggest there were flourishing villages and towns where now only small hamlets exist and transhumant herdsmen live, who, until two decades ago, used neither pottery nor the wheel. The area, part of a tribal province, covers some 8,000 square miles (20,000 square km) and borders on Bakhtiāri country, the pastures of the Qashqa'i and other, smaller tribes with whom the Boyer Ahmadi share many cultural features. The largest town is Yāsuj in the north-east of the province, a planned administrative centre singularly lacking in charms but set in a beautiful landscape. Within twenty-five years, mostly through immigration, it has grown from a tiny settlement of a few families in mud-brick houses and branch-huts into a sprawling city of cement houses and wide dusty streets with nearly 40,000 inhabitants. The other administrative centre, Deh Dasht, in the south, next to the ruins of an earlier town on an old important trade route between the Gulf in the south-west and Isfahan to the north, is also growing fast. Over the centuries, this caravan route and its supporting villages have flourished and declined as control over the area by the central government has waxed and waned.

About 200 years ago, in the absence of strong governmental controls, a few small tribes in central Boyer Ahmad formed a confederacy with a khan for leader. The confederacy rapidly expanded its territory and soon controlled all of what is now Boyer Ahmad. In this turbulent phase of Boyer Ahmad history, local trade routes were abandoned, buildings and bridges fell into ruin, orchards grew wild and many old agricultural villages were destroyed. However, in their turn these highly mobile tribal groups started to found their own villages, which grew wherever political and economic circumstances allowed. For example, Sisakht, below one of the highest peaks of the Zāgros, was founded by a few households in the former summer pastures of a small transhumant tribe about 150 years ago, and has grown by immigration and a high birth rate into a small town of nearly 4,000 people.

Some 140,000 people now live in Boyer Ahmad, including many outsiders, and their ways of making a living have diversified. For most people, grass and animals, woods and water, no longer provide a livelihood but are only a backdrop to other commercial or administrative activities. The remaining pastoralists and farmers are using all of Boyer Ahmad's ecological niches to the fullest, be it lush grazing for the herds in near-inaccessible high valleys in the summer, when the lowlands

above
The valleys of Boyer Ahmad are extremely fertile, yielding up to three crops per year. Areas formerly used for grazing by nomads are now coming under the plough as a result of increasing pressure from a rapidly growing settled population.

previous page left
These bare hills, once covered with oak forest, are now criss-crossed by the tracks of grazing animals. Soon the green flush of the spring grass will be gone and the thin top-soil, with no vegetation to stabilise it, can easily be washed away. Soil erosion and the loss of fragile ecosystems are now major problems in many parts of the country. Between Yāsuj and Dehdasht, 1985.

previous page, right above
The pressure of a growing population on limited resources has caused devastating deforestation in Boyer Ahmad, a region once rich in oak forests. North of Yāsuj, 1985.

previous page, right below
Gathering *kangār*, a kind of thistle which is dug out of the ground just as it is breaking the surface. It is eaten with rice as the first green vegetable of spring thirteen days after *nowruz*, the beginning of new year. North of Yāsuj, 1986.

are desiccated by the scorching sun, or a sheltered valley offering feed for goats when all around is smothered in snow; be it generously fertile fields in the lowlands that yield three crops a year, or small orchards and vineyards perched on terraces on grey alluvial slopes watered from cold mountain streams by means of channels hewn out of rock.

In the past, there were other opportunities for fast, sure-footed men. Grandfathers remember night raids on their sheep and goat pens by neighbouring tribesmen and villagers, and their own robberies. They remember attacks on caravans and swift forays into settlements to the north and east of the tribal boundaries. (Boyer Ahmad is still thought of in Iran as a dangerous land of robbers and plunderers although the tribesmen have been disarmed and pacified for three decades.) More recently, Boyer Ahmad men have migrated to cities outside the area, and to the Gulf and Kuwait, and brought money, ideas and new ways of life back to their brothers. Nomadic tribesmen have founded settlements, and instead of traditional mud-brick houses with flat dirt roofs they build the stone and cement houses with corrugated roofs of the cities; people leave the tightly clustered villages and build new houses in their gardens, which surround the village. The cultural geography of Boyer Ahmad is changing rapidly as the population increases by leaps and bounds, and contacts with the outside world intensify.

The birth rate is very high throughout Boyer Ahmad, above 4 per cent per year in some places, and the population is fast outgrowing the region's capacity to support it. Emigration is increasing, although in fact the Boyer Ahmadi have been emigrating in a steady stream for several generations already, and have populated whole plains in neighbouring Fārs province. Most of these emigrants fled because of political instability at home, persecution by tribal chiefs, or lack of land and water. Old people and occasional travellers say that in the 1940s the area was one of clear streams, dense oak forests, an abundance of game and birds and lush meadows, with flowers everywhere and grass shoulder-high to sheep and goats. Twenty years later these had been replaced in many locations by bare rocks, polluted waters, garbage, naked, deforested, eroded hills and meagre, semi-arid steppes, especially around settlements. The game has been hunted to near-extinction by the tribesmen and, recently, sport hunters. The game wardens and foresters can do little to protect the land from the

A screen (*dafak*) which is used for hunting birds especially partridge. The screen, which is made from goat skin, is painted with a design which is thought to attract birds. The little animals decorating the screen are cut from cloth and stuck on. The hunter shoots through the hole near the top.

destructive effects of an exploding indigenous population, tourism and development projects.

There is now hardly a self-supporting village or camp, despite the invasion of more woods and pastures by the plough and increased yields of wheat, barley, corn and legumes through the use of machinery and chemical fertilisers. Everywhere in Boyer Ahmad, the proletarianisation of the countryside can be observed, especially where administrative centres and new roads with commercial establishments accelerate the transformation of a largely self-sufficient and producing economy to one that is increasingly service-oriented and market-dependent and is dominated by urban-oriented interests and urban-educated men.

The newest road in Boyer Ahmad is a wide highway through Yāsuj connecting Shirāz in the south-west with Isfahan in the north-west. Ambitious development projects like this accelerate the political, economic and cultural integration of Boyer Ahmad into the nation at large, continuing a process begun by Rezā Shāh in the 1930s. As a consequence of fifty years of integration, the importance of tribal identity, tribal politics and tribal interests is diminishing. Some forty tribes of varying size make up the Boyer Ahmadi. In the past these combined in shifting political alliances and patterns of hostilities that kept people poor, insecure, vulnerable and dependent on their political leaders. Although the tribes of Boyer Ahmad are of different origins, they are all Luri-speaking Shi'ites and share beliefs, rituals, places of pilgrimage, customs, life-styles and stories. These bind them to the territory, the smaller tribal leaders and, until recently, the house of the paramount khan. The last paramount khan was assassinated by the government in 1963 for insubordination.

In the past, tribal leaders were used by the government as administrators and tax collectors and as a result they developed into landlords and claimed services and tributes from the tribesmen, thus turning them into peasants. Some of these arrangements were successfully contested by the people during the 1965 land reform and now many former tribal chiefs are living obscure lives in poverty. Others, however, benefited from opportunities in mechanised agriculture and now control large land holdings in their own names. Commercial, capital-intensive sheep and goat ranching, mostly by outside investors, is reducing the economic choices of the indigenous tribal smallholders who own only small herds and cannot afford to hire shepherds or buy feed supplements for their animals.

Mount Dinā, one of the highest peaks of the Zāgros mountains, forms the natural border between Boyer Ahmadi territory to the west and Qashqa'i territory to the east. North of Yāsuj, 1986.

Traditionally, the Boyer Ahmadi seasonally migrated between their summer and winter pastures and survived on the yields of a mixed economy of agricultural and animal husbandry. Sheep, goats and a few cows, herded and managed by men, yielded milk products and wool which were turned into marketable cheese, butterfat and woven goods by women in highly labour-intensive processes. All these products, and the game the men got by hunting, were heavily taxed by tribal chiefs, so that often the people actually had to survive on food gathered by women in the wild, such as acorns (made into acorn-flour bread), wild vegetables, nuts and berries. Both men and women worked very hard from the age of six or seven. Food was scarce, life was precarious and the mortality rate high. In spite of nostalgic visions of fat sheep and blooming gardens, people remember these times with little fondness.

The division of labour was such that no man or woman could survive alone. However, because men were in control of all property (according to tribal law, women could not inherit), as well as of children, women were in effect cheap labour. Although women were of great economic importance, and were socially prominent in camp and village, the quality of their lives depended (and still depends) on the generosity and sensitivity of the men who are responsible for them. This state of affairs is supported by an ideology in which men, manliness and male attributes and activities provide the norms and ideals of human conduct, while women are considered weak and morally inferior caretakers of male property and interests. However, most women manage to exert influence over others through the manipulation of their indispensable services and of relatives, and by this means achieve some control of their own lives, but it is only a precarious kind of power.

Although life for the Boyer Ahmadi has changed drastically in many ways recently, relationships between the sexes have remained the same, or have even worsened. Many women lost their traditional economic niches when men sold their animals to pursue wage labour or white-collar jobs. Thus few women now spin wool on their traditional drop spindles, and yet fewer weave on the horizontal looms, because their woven bags and knotted rugs with colourful, geometric tribal patterns do not sell well in the urban, export-oriented market. Increasingly women are being reduced to home-makers and bearers of children, whereas formerly they commanded a wide range of skills. The formal education that has been available in many villages and tent camps for two decades has benefited women even less than men because the school curriculum is not tuned to the needs of rural tribal life; and local white-collar jobs for women are limited to a few in teaching and nursing.

Housekeeping is changing rapidly with the introduction of appliances (even in the tents, gas ranges, thermos flasks and gas lamps are standard features), new foodstuffs, piped water and electricity. City-style clothes are displacing the wide colourful skirts and long shirts of the traditional women's costume. In the money-oriented modern economy, women are more dependent on their men, the wage earners, than when they at least produced and controlled some of the available food, scarce as it was. Now even the traditional flat breads the women baked on convex griddles are being replaced by bread bought from city-style, professional (male) bakers.

After the revolution, contacts with the dominant, Islamic-urban culture intensified: new mosques were built and fundamentalist mores were disseminated from the 'pulpit', in schools and over loudspeakers. Traditional music was outlawed as non-Islamic. Thus singing, the playing of dance tunes on oboe and drum, the women's characteristic round dance and the men's mock-fight stick dance were all banned. Weddings, therefore, which used to be the most colourful, noisy and ostentatious community-oriented rituals, became quiet, private affairs, and the only unquestioned public appearances of women were as mourners at funerals and during graveyard visits on Thursday afternoons.

In song and proverb, the Boyer Ahmadi, men and women alike, praise the beauty of high mountains, cool springs, lush gardens, spacious tents, the hospitality of khans, their well-appointed castles, spirited women, brave young men, rifles and horses. In these songs they conjure the charms of a life-style that was admired by all but was reality only for the tribal chiefs and their families, and now is largely a romantic memory.

The Boyer Ahmad district in the early twentieth century was home to a powerful tribal confederacy of Lur nomads, the Boyer Ahmadi. In the late twentieth century, few all-year-round nomads remain, and those who manage to survive are under heavy pressure to settle.
Boyer Ahmadi women dress very much like their neighbours the Qashqa'i. Near Dogonbadān, winter 1985.

THE WORLD OF THE PEOPLE OF DEH KOH

Reinhold Loeffler

DAILY LIFE AND THE MAINTENANCE OF SOCIAL CONTROL

Deh Koh[1] is a pseudonym for one of the large villages of Boyer Ahmad whose people I have studied since 1965. It lies on a small, basin-shaped plateau some 7,000 feet (2,100 metres) up in the inner ranges of the Zāgros mountains in south-western Iran. The tightly clustered adobe brick houses are separated by narrow lanes within the village but present a virtually unbroken wall on the outside—a reminder of the region's violent history.

Agricultural land, orchards and vineyards surround the village on all sides. Beyond these are rugged mountainsides partly covered by oak forests which serve as pastures for the villagers' flocks of sheep and goats. During spring and summer, those households with more than 15–20 animals maintain them by means of a transhumant-type organisation in which both sheep and goats are taken to pasture from outposts in the mountains which are periodically relocated. In the winter months, only the hardy and frugal goats can be kept in such outposts, while sheep have to be stable-fed in the village.

In former times the community was dominated by a local landlord, a tribal chief who had manoeuvred himself into his powerful position by manipulating government influence and tribal alliances. Under his oppression everything beyond their bare survival needs was extracted from the villagers. Their response was to keep production at a minimum, make no agricultural investments and avoid all elaboration—be it cultivative techniques, housing, tools, rug weaving, clothing, comforts or adornment—as this would only have invited more of the landlord's exploitation. The staple food of the time was a coarse bread prepared from the meal of acorns collected in the surrounding oak forests—food of such inferior quality that the landlord demanded no share of it.

By the mid-1960s government authority had divested the landlord of his power and people were able to keep what they produced. This new condition freed their desire to evolve from the abject poverty in which the traditional system had kept them and gain the means to send their sons to high school, the only avenue of social mobility open to them. This ambition drove the rural population—characterised in the literature as inert and resistant to change—to work with almost monastic dedication and exert themselves to the limits of their capacity. They rapidly extended agricultural cultivation to the limits of the community's territory, and increased their herds as fast as possible, which made the maintenance of herding outposts necessary all year round.[2]

Their hard, back-breaking yearly cycle of labour allows no let-up. In spring and summer, the men start their day of agricultural toil by first light and work in the scorching heat with hardly a break until sunset at whatever the season calls for—the cleaning and repair of irrigation channels, the cultivation, harvesting and threshing of wheat and summer crops, the cutting of a nutritious mountain grass (*jāshir*), indispensable as winter fodder, the managing of herding outposts in the high pastures and their periodic relocation in the mountains surrounding Deh Koh. Occasionally a man will make the three-hour trip up to the high pastures to cut a fresh supply of firewood for his household there and to take milk products down to the village. The main autumn and winter chores are harvesting grapes and making trips to lower villages to barter them for rice, ploughing and sowing wheat fields, cutting firewood, clearing new fields, digging new irrigation channels and taking turns with other men in manning and supplying specially sheltered winter outposts for the goats, a task which entails extreme hardship as the men and pack animals struggle across mountain passes in deep snow.

In the northern part of the Boyer Ahmad district are the Bahme'i, a Lur tribe having many features in common with their neighbours the Bakhtiāri. This Bahme'i girl is filling a goat skin container with rainwater. Near Rām Hormuz, October 1984.

The women too start early. In summer they manage the herding camps some 2,000 feet (600 metres) above the village and they sometimes begin work as early as 3 a.m. The first of their daily tasks is the churning of butter in a skin bag, and the rhythmic sound they make ushers in the new day. When this is finished, the women boil the buttermilk to make curds, wash pots in the ice-cold mountain streams, milk up to sixty sheep and goats (this is done twice a day), spin wool, roll curds into small balls to dry in the sun, gather wild vegetables on the mountain slopes, cut, dry and store them for winter, and, in the course of all this, take care of their children. They are still at work after nightfall, boiling milk to be turned into yoghurt for next morning's churning.

There is almost no leisure. People are busy with their work 12–15 hours every day of the year except on two religious holidays and maybe a day or two spent at a relative's wedding feast. Besides these feasts, which take place solely in autumn because people find no time for them in other seasons, and an occasional visit to another house in the evening, there is no entertainment—there are no coffee- or tea-houses, no television, no seasonal feasts, no weekends (the day is not even broken by calls to prayer), and living standards—small houses, cheap clothes, scarce food, and no comforts—are extremely modest.

The multiple ties of kinship, friendship, neighbourhood, economic contracts, water-use groups and inescapable mutual interdependencies make Deh Koh a tightly knit community. In it there are no formal institutions like a village council, a circle of elders or mosque organisations with authority to regulate social behaviour as there are in other places. Instead, regulation is entirely by informal means that draw their power from the intense pressures a tight-knit community exerts on individuals to play the roles society expects of them and to conform to cultural and social norms.

The most common of these informal means of social control is the threat that deviant behaviour will become a matter of public talk, causing the offenders a loss of reputation (*ābru*) and giving them a 'bad name' or 'black face.' Another is the threat of sanctions: the refusing of help to offenders, or ostracism. Threats are themselves another means of control. If a husband neglects his duties, his wife can threaten to return to her parents, to stop working, even to kill herself—threats which have indeed been carried out. And there is the mechanism of positive reinforcement: a person conforming to the norms will be shown appreciation, offered help and, perhaps most important, given respect (*ehterām*).

The effectiveness of informal social controls in maintaining social order can be judged from their success in conflict management. In Deh Koh, when conflicts erupt between opposed parties, mediators and social networks have only the leverage of informal controls to work with. Nevertheless, the disputes are contained if not settled by these means, and serious violence is prevented. In fact, never in living memory has a quarrel led to more violence than an exchange of blows. This is quite remarkable considering the large size of the village (population 2,250 in 1971), the scarcity of resources and the growing population pressure. The efficacy of informal controls demonstrates the intensity of the constraints and conditioning to which individuals in Deh Koh are subjected.

However, informal means of social control are not effective in all areas of Deh Koh life. They seem to work quite well in the maintenance of work patterns, the prevention of serious violence and sexual offences, the segregation of the sexes and the generation of support, but not in the areas where vital interests are at stake. For instance, in the past it was considered an immorality to assist the landlord in his tyranny. Nevertheless, in spite of being fully aware of the wrong he was doing, a man might have felt forced to serve the landlord in order to protect his own family. And today, a person can, in the firm conviction of being legally right, pursue a claim that is an outright wrong in the eyes of others. Finally, social controls, however well internalised they are, tend to be ineffective when a person feels his or her behaviour will go undetected.

The frequently repeated experience of the villagers that social norms are violated, and their observation that this is widespread, has generated in them the view that people in general, but especially the people of the area, are inherently inclined towards evil. This is an important element of the villager's social experience. I was often told, 'You don't feel this, but when we are, for instance, ploughing along the edge of a neighbour's fields, it's as if some overpowering force makes us push the plough across the boundary.'

The people consider greed and untrustworthiness the most notable expression of man's inclination to evil. They argue that stealing and lying are part of his nature, as killing chickens is part of the fox's, and it is therefore foolish to expect people to behave any differently. These sorts of views are instilled at such an early stage in the children's socialisation that one of the first words they learn to speak is that for 'lie.' Later experiences again and again confirm what they have been taught: irrigation water is cut off, fruits are stolen from gardens, land is infringed upon, an earlier wife is left in poverty, evil gossip is spread and quarrels abound. Such events reinforce an attitude of suspicion and mistrust towards others. What a person says tends to be dismissed as a smoke-screen that hides 'the real truth.' The listener then reconstructs 'the real truth' as he imagines it to be.

Of course, the villagers acknowledge that there are also good people. There are those who give help when it is needed, those one can trust, those who take a loss for the sake of making peace in a quarrel, those who devotedly take care of old parents or a crippled husband and those who have risked their lives fighting the former landlord's oppression and bringing education to the village.

The black tent of a Boyer Ahmadi family near Dehdasht, late winter 1984.

But overall, they say, the drive to evil is there. They see its effects daily, and they have to be constantly on their guard and dissimulate their intentions.

These then appear to be the main components of the peasants' experience of life in Deh Koh: incessant and hard physical work, tight interdependent social relations and the feeling of being surrounded by people who, on the whole, are potentially harmful. How do they understand and make sense of these conditions? To answer this question, we have first to examine their ideas system.

THE WORLD VIEW

The basis of the world view of these people is belief in the all powerful and merciful God of Islam, who is conceived primarily in his aspects of creator, provider and ultimate judge.

They have no doubt of the existence of God. The wonders of what they see as his creation—the universe, wheat growing from a dry kernel of seed, the colour patterns on a kid's coat, the passage of night and day—cannot be explained otherwise, they feel.

Equally firm is their belief that God will provide. Misfortunes will ever come—in fact they have to come—but there is no need to worry because God will compensate for them. If, for example, the wheat turns out badly, inevitably the other crops will flourish or the flocks prosper. This does not mean, however, that one can just sit and wait for God to provide. No, man has to apply himself as well as he can. People say, 'One ought not to eat unless one is tired.' The relationship between divine grace and human agency is conceived in terms of the formula, put into God's mouth, 'From you the effort, from me the blessing.' Man has to put forth all his effort, nothing else will do, but God's blessing is equally essential, without it nothing else will prosper at all. This blessing cannot, however, be forced by any means. God gives what he wishes to give. This is one's lot, one's share (*qesmat*), and whatever it may be one has to be content with and thankful for it.

While there is uniformity of belief as regards God as creator and provider, there is great diversity regarding God's reward and punishment. Some say most of the retribution for wrongdoing takes place in this world, others maintain that most is left for the other world. Some are convinced that offenders will inevitably be punished in this world in demonstrable ways, others say that if this takes place at all we would not recognise it as such. Some claim that earthly conditions reflect God's reward and punishment, others see no connection between a moral life and earthly well-being. As to a personal divine judgement, some are so convinced of its reality they give detailed descriptions of it, while others—mainly those little exposed to formal learning and so ruled by sceptical mistrust and an earthy realism—reject the idea entirely, saying, 'Nobody really knows if heaven and hell exist or not.' But whatever their individual beliefs concerning reward and punishment in this life or the next, all are certain that 'Doing good will see good; doing evil will see evil.'

This leads us to social ethics. At the heart of the normative code are the injunctions 'work hard' and 'do good.' As to work, the villagers say that it is the aim and meaning of this life, and that they have been created to work to fulfil God's aim that there shall be life in this world. As for doing good, the injunction is expressed in the form of exhortations and prohibitions. Among the exhortations are such formulations as 'What is yours is also partly others', 'This heart has to have compassion', or 'As God gives us all this bounty, so we too have to give to others.' More specifically people are urged to share with others, especially when they have just received something; provide for those they are responsible for, including animals; help, care for, be kind to and have compassion for the poor, the weak, the old, the sick, the stricken, the lonely, strangers, orphans and the disabled; be co-operative and ready to do something for the community, like mediating a dispute; be ready to make concessions in a quarrel so that peace will be restored; be content and modest; and to give respect to whom it is due.

The prohibitions constrain people not to harm anybody or anything, be it by employing a child for economic tasks and so depriving him or her of an education, or by making the load of a donkey too heavy; not to be aggressive, use violence or get into a fight; not to oppress, steal, commit adultery or work laxly in the employ of others; not to lie, slander or insult; not to show off, display power or aspire to social prominence; and not to give family or community a bad reputation.

The peasants of Deh Koh see the sacred figure of Imam 'Ali as the exemplar of these ideals. Significantly, they see him not as the martyr or the heroic fighter, but as the epitome of the

right above
A Bahme'i family in their winter quarters near Rām Hormuz in 1984. The stone walls of their 'house' are actually covered by a tent cloth. When they leave for their summer camp near Dishmuk in the spring, the stone walls will be simply abandoned until the following autumn when the family returns.

right below
The winter tent of a Bahme'i family. The structure has an air of permanence and, now that the nomadic life is becoming increasingly difficult to sustain, it may not be long before this family settles and the tent cloth gives way to a more durable roof. Near Rām Hormuz, 1984.

peasant. 'Ali, they believe, worked his own fields, wore poor, coarse clothes, ate only barley bread and at night went out to spend his riches on the poor and needy while often going hungry himself. Relative to these ethical injunctions, orthodox ritual is considered of minor importance. Many people say they cannot manage the obligatory five daily prayers, which also require an unattainable state of ritual purity, and most feel unable to observe the dawn to sunset fasting during the month of Ramadan, especially when this month, which is tied to a lunar calendar, falls in the hot season. But generally, people expect that such neglect will be forgiven as long as they keep doing good. As to pilgrimages, including the obligatory one to Mecca, people think it is better to give the money to the poor instead.

To appreciate better the described system of social ethics, let us briefly look at it in perspective. It is obviously a variant of Islam, but clearly sets accents that are significantly different from orthodox versions. In the formal expositions of Shi'ite dogma and practice (*osul* and *foru'*), notions of God, the Prophet and the Imams, as well as rituals and prescriptions, receive clear prominence over a system of social ethics, and mullahs follow the same pattern in their preaching. If challenged, mullahs emphatically extol the importance given to ethical behaviour by Islam, but, as the villagers see it, that is not the thrust of their presentation of the religion. As one villager commented, 'The mullahs tell us to say the prayers and observe the fasting even if a man is so poor that he goes naked and hungry all day long!' Formal Islam gives predominance to the relationship between God and man, not to that between men, a preference which, for obvious reasons, has always suited the dominant classes, secular and clerical alike.

In contrast, among the inhabitants of Deh Koh the system of social ethics occupies the dominant, central position in their world view. Thus, when they define religion, a good Muslim, good and bad persons or behaviour, it is invariably done in terms of social ethics—work, sharing and not doing harm. This, they say, is the true Islam.

In the same vein, the villagers give ethical behaviour unequivocal priority over the fulfilment of ritual obligations. Prayers, fasting and pilgrimage are considered absolutely worthless if performed by a person doing evil or lacking compassion. The orthodox position, by contrast, is that each such behaviour is judged on its own merits, and that the fulfilment of ritual duties will eventually compensate for sins committed. In fact, by classifying prayers and fasting as 'obligatory' (i.e. sinful if not done), but compassion and helping as merely 'desirable' (i.e. not sinful if not done), orthodox jurisprudence clearly assigns to ritual behaviour an implicitly higher value than to ethical behaviour—exactly the opposite of local sentiments. To give expression to these sentiments people frequently quote the saying, 'Drink wine and burn pulpits, but do not harm other people.' The fact that they think—albeit erroneously—that this saying is a Koranic verse shows how convinced they are that their priorities are the truly Islamic ones.

The special character of the people's ethical system is also highlighted by the fact that it generates sensibilities regarding life which seem to be foreign to orthodox Islam. Thus, they regard the slaughtering of an animal—a perfectly neutral act by orthodox standards—as something that is, or may be, sinful, even if unavoidable, because taking a life is doing harm to another living being. It is out of the same sensibilities that, in the 1980s, they challenged the Islamic government's claim to be propagating the true Islam by prosecuting prostitutes while conducting the war against Iraq. 'Which is better,' they asked rhetorically, 'two young people having sex or tens of thousands of people being killed?'

We can only speculate as to the origins of this system of social ethics. It appears that it is generated and maintained by the experience of living in tightly knit, interdependent and reciprocal relationships. Its specific forms seem to be derived, on the one hand, from a popular tradition with roots perhaps going back to the Zoroastrian emphasis on social ethics, and on the other from Islamic concepts selectively adopted and assimilated. The result is certainly by no means a full-fledged peasant religion with a cycle of seasonal festivals celebrating growth, life, fertility and sexuality. It is nevertheless a system more congenial to the people's daily experience than orthodox Shi'ite Islam with its mixture of radical salvation theology, its celebration of martyrdom in holy wars and its obligatory rituals that not only carry little meaning for the people of Deh Koh but even entail often insurmountable hardships.

Boyer Ahmadi woman making bread. Winter quarters south of Dehdasht, 1986.

UNDERSTANDING AND CONTROLLING EXISTENCE

The villagers make sense of their daily existence by means of a philosophical system compounded of their system of social ethics and a tempered version of Islam. They see the world and life in it as created and sustained by God's bounty which emanates from him in a perpetual stream and manifests in a perennial process of genesis. It is man's destiny, they think, to take part in this process both as an actor and as a recipient. As an actor, his role is to work to provide food for himself and for others, and to have compassion and care for and help others and share his relative plenty with them. Thus, whether a villager thinks of himself as carrying out God's orders, as fulfilling the destiny he has been created for, as realising the only lasting value, that of serving people, as following the Imam 'Ali's sacred model, as helping to realise God's aim that there be life in this world, or as mirroring God's own outpouring of creation and benevolence—he feels his behaviour is grounded in ultimate realities and has intrinsic meaning.

As recipients, villagers see themselves as totally dependent on God's bounty and grace. The only meaningful attitude to adopt in this situation is for them to surrender unconditionally to His will and put their trust in Him and declare themselves thankful for and content with whatever He may give them as their share. This attitude brings about a calmness, a release from worry, and—as God's response to such submission can be expected to be compassionate generosity—a sense of ultimate safety and well-being. It is out of such deep feelings that they are moved to formulate short prayers on starting their work, such as the following: 'Oh God, I trust in you; let all beings, the birds, the worms, the ants eat from it, and give me my daily bread too. Everything is in your hands.' In such prayers they express how they see the world and their place in it.

The people of Deh Koh construct their self-images in terms of this system. They see their daily hard work, their providing, sharing and not harming others as quintessential good behaviour and themselves as morally good because they do these things. This view is not affected by their own perceived wrongdoings, which are usually justified in one way or another: some are declared trivial in relation to the total picture; others had to be done out of necessity; others were made unavoidable by prevailing conditions; and in quarrels they were in the right anyway. Furthermore, the concepts of their philosophical system are manipulated in a self-serving way to avoid possible reproach. Thus, in justifying their economic position, the more wealthy of the village say that they apply themselves to their work with utmost diligence, while the poor work laxly and without zeal.

In their turn, the poor insist that their condition is determined exclusively by God's inscrutable wish; their own work and morality cannot be blamed for it. Finally, people's failure to meet ritual obligations does not weigh heavily on them. Ethical not ritual excellence is what is of the essence for them. This shift away from ritual criteria, which they feel they cannot meet, to social ethics, which they are emphatic they fulfil better than any mullah, allows them to uphold their picture of themselves as good Muslims even in the face of being called bad Muslims by mullahs riled by their neglect of ritual, notably of course their refusal to pay the religious taxes (*khoms*, *zakāt*).

Thus, people maintain and defend their basic moral goodness, which allows them to expect God's blessing in this world and His mercy in the next—although not with certainty or as a right, to be sure, because that would run counter to their attitude of surrender as well as their ingrained scepticism. They also expect the respect (*ehterām*) and goodwill of the community.

These constructions of meaning and moral identity are of course intrinsically challenged by the acts of stealing, quarrelling and lying they witness day by day. If these acts went unpunished they would be rightful acts and the villagers' own work, moral behaviour and ethical views meaningless. Their belief in God's retribution, which they see manifested in concrete events, assures them that what they see as evil is indeed evil and will not stand unpunished, and that they were indeed in the right. Thus they not only gain a sense of ultimately prevailing justice but safeguard the integrity of their world view as well.

Lastly, their philosophical system provides the people of Deh Koh with what they take to be a means to influence events. As we have seen, at the core of this philosophy lies the assumption that what holds this world together is generosity, which is an imitation of God's bounty. It is God's bounty that creates and sustains life in this world, and it is man's providing and sharing that helps realise this process and makes social life possible. Generosity is therefore the supreme good and is what pleases God most and lets Him respond with favours, blessing and mercy. This notion forms the basis for the pervasive practice of giving alms and making vows. For instance, alms are given on the first day of every month for the well-being of the family, every Thursday night for the benefit of the dead, at the start of a journey for safe passage, after an ill-boding dream to ward off misfortune, and as a thanksgiving for escaping from danger. Vows to saints are made for the recovery of sick persons, for the success of children in school and at the end of the agricultural season as thanksgiving and petition for continued well-being. Of all the folkloric practices used to attempt to exert control over fate, these are definitely the most pervasive, and the little streams of generosity percolating through the social fabric impress on everyone the supreme goodness of giving and the validity of their ethical system.

EPILOGUE: DYNAMICS OF CHANGE

This philosophical system served people well. It made sense of their existence and, to a degree at least, reconciled them to the undesirable circumstances under which they were forced to live—the physical hardships and deprivation, the meagre and uncertain returns and the pressure of social controls in crowded quarters. However, they never came to like these conditions. They wanted a more restful life, a more stable income, better living conditions, more personal space and, above all, a better future for their children. Thus, when opportunities for change arose in the mid-1970s, they grasped them eagerly. Many took up seasonal employments in the cities, others turned to crafts and trade and the youth aimed for degrees from the newly-established local high schools to qualify for salaried government jobs. As a result, an unprecedented amount of cash flowed into the village and a modern, educated middle class appeared. At the same time, however, social relations were restructured by the national administration and, after the 1979 revolution, a politicised Islam strove to capture the people's souls with religio-political propaganda, calling for the sacrifice of lives whose sustenance people had always understood as God's aim and their own task.

So, as new spacious houses mushroom on former agricultural land, as close communal ties loosen only to give way to even more oppressive national ones, and as the noise of motor traffic drowns out the sharp cries of agricultural workers goading oxen from behind ploughs, the domestic sounds of thin wooden rolling pins knocking on bread-making boards and the slosh of yoghurt churning in skin bags, the culture and philosophy of compassion of these quiet, modest, hard-working people passes into history.

KURDISH NOMADS OF WESTERN ĀZARBĀIJĀN

Lale Yalçın-Heckmann

INTRODUCTION

Hill walkers and mountaineers who journey eastwards along the high ranges of the eastern Taurus mountains, over the barren hills and plateaux, and through the occasional narrow green valleys, gain the impression that it is totally uninhabited. In late autumn, when the brown hills look dry, as if nothing would grow, the impression is even stronger. Yet these seemingly empty lands are the home of the Kurdish nomads and villagers, and the traveller can have the shock of suddenly coming across an encampment of their black tents and be astonished to find it full of nomad women beautifully dressed in colourful, glittering clothes. They will probably be by themselves, waiting for the sheep and goats to be brought to them for milking by the men, who are away during the daytime grazing the flocks or cutting hay for fodder. The Kurds have a strong attachment to these harsh mountains, and their modest but colourful way of life and love of independence have often been described.

The Kurds form one of the largest ethnic groups in the Middle East. Estimates of their total numbers vary, but range from 20 to 25 million. It is not possible to be more exact because the countries in which they live often do not record ethnic background in their population censuses and because the criteria are not agreed.

Before the First World War their territory lay within the borders of three imperial states: the Ottoman, Iranian and Russian. Today it is divided by the boundaries of six states: Turkey, Iran, Iraq, Syria and the Republics of Armenia and Azerbaijan.[1]

KURDISTAN, THE COUNTRY OF THE KURDS

The word Kurdistān was first used in the twelfth century, for a province to the north-west of Hamadān created by the last Seljuk ruler, Sultan Sanjar. In the fourteenth century, according to Arab historians, the province had sixteen cantons, but in the sixteenth century Iran detached Hamadān and Luristān and reserved the name for the region of Ardalān, with Senneh (now Sanandaj) as its capital.[2]

In Iran today there is a province of Kurdistān in the area around Sanandaj, although Kurds also live in large numbers in the provinces of Western Āzarbāijān and Kermānshāh. There are also groups of Kurds living in Khorāsān, Kermān, Fārs, northern Luristān, Posht-i Kuh, Qazvin and Māzandarān. In Western Āzarbāijān they live in the mountainous regions of Orumieh (Urmia) (cantons of Ushnu, Mergewer, Dasht, Tergwer, Brādost), Salmās (Somai, Chāhrik), Khoy (Qotur, Aland) and Māku, where the Kurds live on the slopes of Mount Ararat.[3]

WESTERN ĀZARBĀIJĀN

The province of Western Āzarbāijān consists mainly of highlands and plateaux above 3,000 feet (1,000 metres). The border with the Republic of Nakhchevan follows the low valley of the river Aras, while the border with Turkey runs through mountains that rise to over 9,800 feet (3,000 metres). This region has a high rainfall and is one of the most fertile in Iran. The valleys that break up the highlands are densely populated by Āzari Turks, Kurds and some Armenian and Nestorian Christian communities. The Kurds along the border with Turkey are mostly settled in tribal villages and practise agriculture, though some live as nomads.

A young woman of the Jenikānlu section of the Jalāli tribe on the downward migration from their summer pasture near Dānānlu, north of Māku. Autumn 1986. The Kurds of this region are Sunni Muslims and speak Kurmānji.

A Kurdish summer camp in the extreme northern corner of Western Āzarbāijān at Ağrichay close to the Turkish border, 1986.

THE KURDISH LANGUAGE

This is a distinct language and belongs to the Iranian language group. There are three main dialects, with the linguists disagreeing to some extent about the degree in which they differ from one another. The first, north Kurmānji, is spoken mainly among the Kurds within Turkey, in northern Iraq and in western Iranian Āzarbāijān The second, Sorāni, (south Kurmānji) is spoken among the Kurds in Iraq who live in areas to the south of Bāhdinān and those Iranian Kurds who live in the province of Kurdistān. The third dialect, Gurāni (Zāzā or Dailami in Turkey), is spoken mainly by the Zāzā Kurds in eastern Turkey and by the Kurds in Kermānshāh in Iran.

The use of the Kurdish language is discouraged in the countries in which they live, particularly the written form. Turkey and Iran each have an official state language, the use of which is promoted in preference to all others. Thus, like other minority groups in these countries, the Kurds do not have the right to use their language in education. Moreover, to add to their difficulties, the Turkish Kurds use the Roman alphabet while the Iraqi and Iranian Kurds use the Arabic, so there is no literary contact between these groups. Because of their common alphabet, there is strong literary contact between Iraq and Iran in terms of 'illegal' publications and written communication. Turkish literary activity is more limited. Such problems contribute to the difficulty of unifying the Kurdish language.

Oral literature is rich among the Kurds and is very popular. Oral history, for example, often takes the form of epic poems and songs, and the ability to recite or sing them is looked on as an artistic achievement. Songs are also an important part of this oral tradition, and there are many types. Those sung at weddings and dances praise love and the beauty of women, while another type, the *lavje*, may have love as one theme but can include others, such as the blood feud, wars, heroes of the Kurdish uprisings, or the oppression of an agha or khan and the rebellion of a brave young man against him. The songs are learned by direct transmission from one person to another and from locally produced cassettes which are distributed across the state boundaries.

RELIGION

The Kurds in Western Āzarbāijān are mostly Sunni Muslims, whereas their neighbours the Āzari Turks, who form the major population group, are Shi'ite. There are Shi'ite Kurds living further south in Kermānshāh and Luristān. Various *tariqa* (religious brotherhoods) such as the Qādiri, Naqshbandi and Rifā'i are organised among the Kurds; their *sheykhs* and *morids* (followers) are often active across the state boundaries.

HISTORY

The Kurds are considered to be one of the oldest indigenous peoples of the Middle East. According to Vladimir Minorsky, 'about the period of the Arab conquest [in the seventh century] a single ethnical term Kurd (plur. Akrad) was beginning to be applied to an amalgamation of Iranian and Iranicised tribes.'[4] After this period, the tribes were organised under different Kurdish dynasties which competed with one another or collaborated with or fought against the surrounding Arab, Armenian, Boyid and Ghaznavid dynasties and rulers. With the Turkish conquest of Anatolia and the domination of the Turkish Seljuk dynasty in the eleventh century, the small Kurdish dynasties were wiped out.[5] During the thirteenth century, the Mongols invaded from the north and east and the whole region, where Kurdish, Turkmen and other tribes and peoples lived, was thrown into turmoil. For about three centuries from the sixteenth onwards, Kurdish territory became the arena for an intense rivalry and struggle between the Shahs of Iran and the Ottoman Sultans.

Sharafnāmeh, the famous work of the Kurdish historian Sharaf ad-Din Bedlesi (1596), gives the history of Kurdish dynasties of the sixteenth century, and lists the origin and dispersal of some of the Kurdish tribes of the Persian and Ottoman empires. According to this source, some Kurdish tribes lived in both Anatolia and Āzarbāijān. The Pāzuki and Domboli are examples of tribes appearing in both countries; similarly, the Brādost, another tribe in the north-west now living along the border between Iraq and Iran south of Shamdinān (now Şemdinli in south-east Turkey) is said to have resided formerly in lands lying west of Urmia.

The lands of the Kurdish tribes became peripheral to both the Safavids and the Ottomans after the border agreement of 1639, though the need to control the tribes did occasionally become a political emergency necessitating the assertion of central power. The feudal Kurdish princes

An elderly woman of the Hasow Khalaf section of the Jalāli tribe in a winter camp near Shotlu north-west of Poldasht close to the Aras River which forms the boundary with Nakhichevan. Late autumn 1986.

right above
Here a calf skin instead of the more usual goat skin is being used as a churn to make butter from yoghurt. Near Siah Cheshmeh, summer 1986.

right below
Women and children drawing water from a spring near their camp at Ağrichay close to the Turkish border, 1986.

therefore ruled more or less undisturbed until the political and administrative-military changes of the nineteenth century.

The first sign of Kurdish nationalism among the leadership, if not their followers, is considered to have been the revolt of Sheykh Obeydullah of Shamdinān (Şemdinli) in 1880.[6] Obeydullah, a Naqshbandi sheykh from a well-known Seyyed family, 'led many tribes of central Kurdistān in a large revolt, directed at first against the Iranian government and intending the establishment of an independent state'.[7] Initially, he was supported by the Ottoman Sultan. He succeeded in uniting Kurdish tribes on both sides of the Turkish-Iranian border, including some of the Nestorian tribes in Hakkāri, and took the area between Lake Orumieh and Van. With a force of 20,000 he attacked the towns of Mahābād (Sāujbolāgh) and Miāndoāb and killed most of the Shi'a Āzari Turkish inhabitants.[8] He was defeated by Russian and Iranian forces[9] in 1881 and returned to Turkey. The Sultan, under pressure from Great Britain, Iran and Russia, sent him to exile in Mecca, where he later died.

The next major revolt which affected the Kurdish tribes of north-west Iran was that of Simko in 1920.[10] Simko was the paramount leader of the Shakāk, the second largest tribal confederacy in Iran, which inhabited the mountainous region to the west of Salmās and Urmia. They were mostly transhumants or semi-nomads, spending the winter in mountain villages. Simko had such power that he successfully played the various political and military interests of the surrounding states against one another. He controlled an area from Western Āzarbāijān to the south of Sāujbolāgh (Mahābād) and collected taxes, especially in the years 1918–21, when there was a power vacuum in the region. Most of the Kurdish tribes, nomads and peasants of western Āzarbāijān took part in Simko's military campaigns. He was defeated in 1922, after Rezā Shah had come to power and organised a disciplined army.

There was another nationalist uprising in 1926–30 which began within the Turkish borders. The tribes of Heydarānlu and Jalāli, who inhabit the area both sides of the Turko-Iranian border near Māku, took part in it and the tribesmen who lived on the Turkish side fled to Iran. After this uprising Turkey adopted severe measures and forced both tribesmen and non-tribal Kurds to settle in different parts of the country. The Iranian regime deployed the army and forced ten thousand Jalāli tribesmen to settle in central Iran. The tribe was practically exterminated, according to Ghassemlou[11], and only a few came back in 1941 when Iran was occupied by the Allied forces and Rezā Shah had to abdicate.

In 1946 nationalist aspirations brought about the forming of the first and only Kurdish Republic in Mahābād. Shakāk tribal support for the Democratic Party of Kurdistān, which founded the Republic, was especially important and the Shakāk tribal chief Amr Khan was one of the three generals of the Republic's army.[12] However, the brief republican experience in Mahābād mainly involved the non-tribal, urban Kurds from the province of Kurdistān. It was violently suppressed by the Iranian government after less than a year. From the fall of the Kurdish Republic to the Islamic Revolution of 1979 the Kurdish tribes of Western Āzarbāijān were under the influence of the modernisation policies of Shah Mohammed Rezā, though they were less affected than other tribal groups, such as the Qashqa'i, Bakhtiāri or Shahsevan.[13] With the intention of increasing the security of farmers, Mohammed Rezā Shah interfered with nomad-sedentary relations and forced nomads to settle, which resulted in a fall in livestock production and the disuse of large areas of difficult terrain, especially at high altitudes. The Shah introduced western-style dress and conscription for men, literacy campaigns and the appointment of military governors.[14] His tribal policies also involved land reform measures, the abolishing of tribal khans and military control of nomadic migration. Nomadism became increasingly marginalised during this period.

POPULATION

At present Western Āzarbāijān is populated by various ethnic groups, some of which contain both tribal and non-tribal elements. For instance, among Turkish-speaking Shi'ites there are tribal groups like the Afshar and Qarapapagh, and non-tribal, mostly urban, Āzaris. As outlined above, some of the tribes of this region are known to have existed as far back as the sixteenth century. Nevertheless, even if the name of a tribal group is still the same, its internal organisation and norms have probably changed significantly over time.

In north to south order, the following Kurdish tribal groups live mainly in Western Āzarbāijān:

above
Washing clothes and dishes in a stream with mount Ararat in the distance. Ağrichay, north-west of Māku. Spring 1986.

right
Women of the Milān tribe engaged in domestic chores: preparing to make bread and washing dishes. At their summer camp, known locally as Tavreh. Spring 1989.

left above
Kurds of the Milān tribe having just arrived at their summer quarters with all their equipment are getting ready to set up camp. Tavreh north of Khoy, spring 1989.

left below
In the southern part of Western Āzarbāijān in the Naqadeh region are Kurds who migrate between the south-western shore of Lake Orumiyeh and a mountainous area south of Ziveh where there is a mixed population speaking both Turkish and Kurdish. Here a man holds the sheep for milking. Near Kanirash village, spring 1988.

Jalāli, Milān, Shakāk, Diri, Herki, Begzādeh, Zerzā, Bilbās. These groups are the largest. They usually take the form of confederacies with tribal sections and sub-sections. They all have sections and affiliated groups and individuals across the borders in Turkey or Iraq. The confederations have sometimes included more than twenty-four tribes and were traditionally divided into nomadic and settled sections. The best known examples are the Herki and Shakāk. The tribes have multiple internal and external criteria for group identity and membership, which is not surprising considering their internal divisions and varying historical and demographic patterns of development. This is discussed in more detail later.

SEASONAL LIFE

The terms 'nomad' and 'semi-nomad' refer to two types of pastoral production with mobility between summer and winter residences as a fundamental component of the annual cycle of food production. In Western Āzarbāijān the nomads live in tents in both summer and winter, whereas the semi-nomads spend the summer in tents in mountain pasture but live in village houses in the winter, which is long with heavy snow falls. Mostly they migrate between the high mountains on the Turkish-Iranian border and the villages of the high plateaux and river valleys to the east. The villages are mostly situated in fertile valleys and by rivers. Their economy is based on farming and animal husbandry, the most common animals being cattle, sheep and goats. The high mountain slopes are generally more suited to grazing by sheep and goats; cattle husbandry becomes the dominant form only where the grazing and market conditions particularly favour it.

With the onset of spring the focus of life begins to change from the village to the pasture camp. The young men take the animals to graze fresh grass, the women begin to gather mountain herbs, mushrooms and roots and the older men visit other villages and towns to exchange news and goods. By the time the summer activities are at their peak the villages are mostly empty, the villagers being constantly on the move between camp sites, fields, gardens, houses, villages and city. At no dwelling during this time can one find all the household members together. The children are wandering between the pasture and the village house (when they are not at a few day's distance from one another), the young women are mostly in the pasture tent, the older women are tending the gardens and fields in the village and the men are at or on the move between various sites for the purposes of work, trade or social obligations.

The summer camp is the dwelling place until early autumn of the young men, women and children. In early summer, depending on the distance of the camp site from the village and the availability of pasture, the first camp will be inhabited mainly by young brides and unmarried women. They milk the sheep and goats twice a day at peak season and carry loads of hay and wood down the hills on their backs.

The activities of summer are in general preparations for winter. Hay making may begin as early as April or May, depending on the altitude, climatic conditions and location in a particular area. Fodder is expensive in winter and households have to rely on their own labour and land resources to have enough to last the winter. The men cut the grass on the mountain slopes and make it into bundles which they leave to dry for use as winter fodder for the animals. Where the ground is steep and rocky they use a sickle, but where it is flatter and smoother they use the scythe. The men start at dawn and help one another in rotation, all working for one household each day. Cutting hay is very hard work and is a source of masculine pride. Men boast about their speed and skill in cutting the best grass in the shortest possible time. When there is a shortage of men in the household, the women help but they get little recognition for their contribution. Often the men are embarrassed that they need help and in public try to hide the fact.

Like the fodder, the major part of the produce from the fields and gardens is stored for winter. Only the surplus is sold in the market. The young male sheep and goats are sold at the end of the season, after they have recovered from winter diseases and gained weight. The income from their sale may be used for major items of expenditure, like the restocking of animals or to pay for a wedding.

The large social gatherings and festivities that take place during these months are prevented in winter by the weather, the state of the roads and the strain on economic resources.

The nomadic way of life is, and always has been, a symbiotic one. The nomad and semi-nomad sells his animals and their produce to the villager and in the market in order to have cash. The villagers

Women of the Otāblu section of the Jalāli tribe preparing to set up their tents having just arrived at their summer quarters. Near Kelisakandi, west of Māku, spring 1985.

hire out fields for grazing when the nomads pass by on their migration to summer or winter quarters. Peasants exchange their grain or maize for animal products such as cheese, butter or meat. However, this interdependency does not of course prevent competition for resources and power. For instance, formerly nomads used coercion to obtain and keep the grazing rights to certain pastures and hay sites, and according to historical reports villagers were much at their mercy. Now the pendulum has swung the other way. The nomadic groups are not as strong as they were and no longer act as a political and military force against agricultural communities, the state authorities or other competitors. The pastures have been progressively taken over for cultivation and 'pure' nomadism nowadays involves a complex network of relationships with the villagers and state authorities.

The semi-nomadic mode of life seems to be an adaptive solution to the present-day constraints on nomadism, but it is not an easy one. The practitioners have to master not only the strategies of nomadism but also those of agriculture. Nevertheless, for border regions where state control and penetration are limited in extent, such as in Western Āzarbāijān, semi-nomadism in a tribal setting can succeed and become a stable mode of life.

TRIBES, TRIBAL MEMBERSHIP AND LEADERS

It is first necessary to say what is meant here by the term 'tribe'. In much of the Middle East tribes are groups of people who claim to have kinship relations to one another, a common descent, common ancestors, who usually reside together and have common economic and political interests. Tribes vary from one another in size, area of settlement and the significance of their history. They may have sections and sub-sections, or may be organised into tribal confederacies, as has been the case in Western Āzarbāijān.

The most widely accepted criterion for tribal membership is descent, but there are others. Men and women belong to the tribal group of their father. If the mother belongs to a different tribe, the relation to her tribe is often considered of secondary importance, though not always insignificant. For instance, kinship ties to the mother's group become important if the group is influential, respected and wealthy. The tribal ties to affinal groups are usually crucial for political and economic relationships, for example, in trade partnerships or the formation of groups in a summer camp.

The other criteria for tribal membership are less clear and open to controversy. For example, residence in a traditionally tribal area usually amounts to tribal membership. In this Kurdish region especially, where there have been forced or voluntary migrations in times of war and peace, those who reside in a village which has a tradition of being tribal, or those who share their pastures, may claim membership of the same tribe even if common descent cannot be definitely established. The outcome of the claim can matter a great deal when the tribe as a political unit is strong enough to assert and maintain rights to certain pastures, hay-cutting areas and water resources. Tribes in Western Āzarbāijān are allowed, as in eastern Turkey, certain traditional rights of access to crown- or state-owned lands. However, these rights are mainly for the usage of pastures and do not amount to land ownership *per se.*

Other criteria for self-definition of tribal membership include dialect, clothes, head dresses, certain marriage practices, dances and handicrafts. Tribesmen also establish their own and others' identities from an historical perspective, using tribal names, places, heroes and events of the past. Hence, the Begzāde claim nobler ancestors in comparison to the Herki, and the Jalāli and Shakāki a particular history of nationalistic struggles in contrast to the tribes of lesser political significance.

The degree to which a tribe acts as a political and economic unit depends on its internal structure and the leader's political authority. Not all tribes have leaders. On the whole, a Kurdish tribe with a strong political leader is perceived by others to be 'stronger' or a 'real' tribe. Most of the leaders have to fulfil a variety of roles for the tribesmen, as brokers, mediators and translators, or even as their suppressors. In the economic sphere, for instance, failure to secure rights of access to certain pastures through coercion or other tactics, may result in their loss to other powerful landlords or through the politics of nationalisation.

Tribal leadership in the past is referred to as having been hereditary and selective. In each tribe there were lineages, and sometimes a large descent group as big as a tribal section (*taifa*), from which the leader was chosen. The leader's eldest son was normally expected to succeed him, but if he was considered unworthy other sons, nephews or close kinsmen would be considered instead. The decision

Women and children of the Milān tribe preparing to cook the vegetables they have just gathered in the wild. West of Khoy 1988.

was in the hands of the tribal elders' council (*ri spi*). This council could also unseat a leader by the symbolic act of putting his shoes outside the door while meeting in the leader's reception room.

The institutions of tribal leadership have changed greatly in recent times. If a tribe has a leader at all, he may be a landlord residing in the tribal village or an absentee landlord who is also the representative of a political party; he may also be a professional urban man, such as a doctor, lawyer or trader, living in town, delegating power to others in the countryside and performing the services of a broker and patron for the tribesmen in return for gifts, dues, loyalty and political support.

The leadership may also be divided between brothers. If there are three brothers, for instance, one brother may reside in the countryside and attend to pastoral production and the management of herds, while another may be a modern city professional who sends his children to modern schools and performs an intermediary role between the central state and the tribal periphery. The third, the youngest and probably best educated of the brothers, may represent the (often socialist) radical political wing of the leadership, sometimes even taking an anti-khan stand against the tribal leadership, thus addressing Kurdish nationalist and socialist revolutionary sentiments and politics within the tribe or for a wider clientele.

Today tribesmen are as heterogeneous as the society in which they live. Although nomads, semi-nomads and villagers constitute most of the tribesmen, there are also migrants and settlers in big cities who originally belonged to a tribe and for various reasons continue to cultivate their ties with it. However, the urban dwellers usually picture the 'typical' tribesman as a nomad who is part of a monolithic group—the 'tribe'—that acts in concert, a view that is partly a relic of the past when sedentary people had good cause to fear the nomads. Contemporary tribesmen do not conform to this image. Their contacts with tribal and non-tribal people and groups are not only numerous but on an individual basis that may actually have divisive effects on the larger tribal collectivity.

The semi-nomadic tribesmen of Western Āzarbāijān are firmly embedded in the national, social and economic life which is dominated by national state policies. These influences are clearly visible in their consumption habits: their simple black tents may be produced from goat hair by women using traditional methods, but they use motor vehicles for transport, pocket calculators to estimate the price of sheep and goats and expensive stereo cassette players to listen to their music.

A Jenikānlu family having breakfast in their tent. The elderly woman at the back of the tent is still in bed because she is sick. Near Avajigh, spring 1986.

MARRIAGE

In the tribal context marriage and weddings are highly important events and there are certain prescribed rules for them: a woman should marry a man from a family or tribal group whose status is equal to or higher than her own. Marriage within the tribe is the ideal, but in reality there are many reasons for marriages between tribes. In fact those between members of different tribes are socially more significant than those within the tribe, particularly when they occur between men and women of the ruling tribal elite, or between members of tribal leaders' families for such reasons as terminating a blood feud or a similarly long-standing enmity between two tribes, or for other political alliances.

A frequently expressed ideal is the marrying of a daughter to her father's brother's son. Though rare, it does sometimes happen. Actually, the definition of a paternal cousin is flexible, caused by the fact that paternal cousins of second, third or further degrees are all called father's brother's son (*pismam*).

Weddings are public events where the bride and groom's kin or tribal groups display their social standing. When there is little prestige involved, the weddings are modest, the preparations brief and only a few families contribute to the expenses. In such cases few guests are expected and the wedding lasts no more than a day and a half. The climax of the affair is the taking of the bride from her parents' house to the groom's, where joyful dances and a feast take place.

On the whole, wedding ceremonies are colourful occasions and are very much looked forward to by everyone. They are occasions for people, especially the young, to look their best and perhaps to find a suitable partner. The music and dancing allow sentiments to be expressed and emotions to rise. Women cry at the loss of a daughter to another family while others joyfully lead the dances on behalf of the groom and men show off their skills and abilities in singing and dancing. This display of emotions causes a lot of worry to those who are in charge of the proceedings.

A wedding has several parts. The first is the religious ceremony (*nikah*), which may be performed at the very beginning of affinal relations, soon after the agreement to marry has been reached, in order, some Kurds claim, to prevent the engaged girl from being kidnapped. At the completion of this religious ceremony the couple are formally considered to be man and wife, but they are not socially recognised as such until the wedding festivities have taken place.

After the religious ceremony, at the early stages of the wedding celebrations, the two groups hold a henna evening, where the bride-to-be puts henna on her hair, hands and feet. For this event

A woman of the Otāblu section of the Jalāli tribe setting up the bedding pile of her tent prior to erecting the canopy. Spring 1988.

a henna party is organised with singing, dancing and food. This is often a women-only occasion; women from the groom's family bring henna and present it to the bride's female kin, who host the evening and provide the women guests with small gifts and their children with sweets. The henna evening is more of an urban than a rural practice, although it is common for rural brides to put henna on their hands before the wedding. This practice is almost universal in the Middle East, and the symbolism involved is complex.

The date of the actual wedding is set at short notice, at the moment the two sides are satisfied that the negotiations are complete and enough visits and exchanges of gifts have taken place. When the bride's father lets the groom know that his family can come and get their bride, the wedding starts. The groom himself does not come to take the bride; the wife-taking party consists of the best man (*brazava*), who is in charge and is the main financer of the wedding, the groom's father and father's brother(s), and his other male and female kin plus neighbours and friends. When the groom's side arrives, the bride's family, kin and neighbours receive the guests, men and women being taken into separate wedding houses. The entertainments include the giving of small gifts and sweets to children, tea, food and, at intervals, dancing. For the bride's relatives this is not considered a celebration; their general sentiment is one of sadness at giving a daughter away, although she may be marrying her father's brother's son. The bride is expected to be sad and quiet, and her crying is appropriate if it is not excessive. Thus, although they are guests in this part of the wedding, it is the women and men from the groom's side that lead the singing and dancing, and emphasise their joy at receiving the bride.

The bride is ceremonially taken away by the groom's kin, with singing and dancing. If the wedding is at a pasture camp, she might be mounted on a horse, though in villages today the bride is taken with a convoy of cars. When she arrives at the groom's house the most lively and crowded part of the wedding begins. Some of the bride's kin may have accompanied her to the groom's house, but apart from them the wedding is mainly for the groom's kinsmen, neighbours and guests. Men and women are entertained separately and the festivities may last for two days. At the end of the festivities the bride and groom are taken to their bridal tent or room. Only after the marriage is consummated does the wedding come to an end.

Wedding ceremonies are occasions where many of the prevailing notions about gender are expressed. Women are expected to look pretty, and young women wear only bright colours—red, orange, yellow and white—while the older ones wear dark red, green, blue and purple. Married women wear a special type of head-dress (*kofi*). To sing and dance well are considered desirable skills for young women. Men, on the other hand, should look smart and self-confident and be able to talk wisely in public gatherings. Although Kurdish men and women in rural areas do not practise avoidance in any strictly Islamic sense, nevertheless, dancing together is thought to have potential for sexual arousal. Hence young men and women are carefully watched during weddings for the type of contact they have with one another. And if there is, for instance, an elopement in a village some time later, the couple are usually thought to have agreed to it during a wedding.

The Kurds have great admiration for beauty in women and men. Love for the beautiful beloved is a central theme in poetry and music. Women are often kidnapped by men and may be physically attacked and injured in the process. If the woman is known for her beauty, public opinion would be sympathetic to the kidnapper, even though violence is involved. Nevertheless, abducting a woman is a serious offence and is not tolerated, especially if it occurs between families from different tribes, when it can lead to inter-tribal conflict. The role assigned to tribal women, therefore, is that of being attractive and dangerous at the same time.

A large tent of the all-weather goat's hair type, for use in both winter and summer. Near Āshkhāneh, autumn 1987.

KURDS OF KHORĀSĀN

Notes by Mohammad-Hossein Papoli-Yazdi

TRIBES AND CLANS

The names Alvāry (Clavijo 1928), Chamshagazak, Shādlu (Iskandar Beg Munshi 1350/1971, vol. 1: 139–41), Za'farānlu, Shādilu, Amālu, Kywānlu (d'Allemagne 1911, vol. 3: 55), Kāvānlu, Amārlu, Qarachārlu, Jāni Qorbāni (Sani' al-Dawla 1301–3/1884–6, vol. 2: 356) are all mentioned in early texts, but no details are given. In 1990 twenty-five Kurdish clans, all nomadic, were living in the north of Khorāsān.[1] Although the clans claim to be tribes, they are not hierarchically organised. In former times, however, each clan had a chief. The Za'farānlu belonged to this category. Their last chief, Shāhpur Negahbān, died in 1960.[2]

After the land reform of 1962–3 most of the chiefs of settled clans severed relations with their tribes. In 1979, at the outbreak of the Islamic revolution, their only role was that of mediator between families, or between nomads and the administration. They were consultants rather than chiefs of a clan or tribe.

The following twenty-five names belong to recognised Kurdish clans:

Amārānlu, Bādlānlu, Bājkānlu, Bichrānlu, Bravānlu, Brimānlu, Hashtmarkhi, Hizlānlu (Izlānlu), Jirestani, Kavānlu (Kavkānlu), Kikānlu, Kurde-Hashtmarkhi, Malānlu (Malavānlu), Maliyān (Milānlu), Namānlu, Pahlavānlu, Qahramānlu, Qajkānlu, Reshvānlu, Sārkhāni, Shikharmirānlu, Sifkānlu, Topkānlu, Varānlu,

Some of these clans are subdivided into different families, for example the Topkānlu and Qahramānlu clans. The Topkānlu are divided as follows: Alu, Aqāmohamadi, Asheq or Doholzan, Karkānlu, Katu, Mohamadi, Mosākhāny or Farhādi, Noz and Samakānlu, and the Qahramānlu into the Gulvānlu and Qahramānlu.

The figures below are those of the Kurdish tribal population of Khorāsān at the time of the first census after the Iranian Constitutional Revolution (*Revue du Monde Musulman*, 1910, no. 12, pp. 491–2)

Kurdish tribes of Chenarān	4,760
Tribes of Jelvān	2,040
Tribes of Shirvān	16,200
Tribes of the Quchān frontier:	
Bilcharānlu	790
Kam Kānlu	1,170
Senduklu	1,320
Tribe of Jifān (Gifān) and dependency	5.500
Tribe of Kushkhāneh	4.160
Tribes of Jersān	1,620
Other places	5,790
Total	43 350

For a variety of reasons these figures should be treated with caution. First, the system used for taking the census was extremely primitive, probably largely conjectural. Furthermore, it is impossible to distinguish between the nomadic population and the settled population because when the Qahramānlu tribe is named, either the settled or the nomadic Qahramānlu may be intended. Both originate from the same tribe. The censuses of 1956 and 1966 did not record the ethnic origins of the inhabitants of Khorāsān and it is therefore impossible to estimate the proportion of Kurds present in the total population.[3]

Preparing to load the camels for the spring migration. Qahremānlu clan, near Bojnurd 1984.

The census of 1966 gave the total 'mobile' population of Northern Khorāsān as 11,406 people—Bojnurd 6,861, Quchān 580, Mashhad 1,403 and Daragaz 2,562 (SAR 1966). The meaning of the term 'mobile' is not clear. It could refer to nomads, or alternatively it could refer to homeless migrant workers coming to work in the sugar-beet plantations, particularly in November when the census was taken. There were no official figures for the nomadic population of Khorāsān before 1979. The 1976 census gives the nomadic population of northern Khorāsān as 1,128 families (i.e. a total of 5,443 people). During the Shah's regime the extent of the nomadic population, and nomadism in general, was concealed as far as possible. De Planhol comments as follows:

'Although the number of true nomads remaining in Turkey may only be in the tens of thousands, in Iran there must certainly be more than a million, the ridiculously low number given in the 1956 census (247,000 nomads), which fails to include for example the nomads of Baluchistān. should not deceive us.' (De Planhol 1968: 198).

In 1979 the number of Kurdish nomads in Khorāsān was estimated at around 12,000. During the summer of 1979 the total number of nomadic encampments in northern Khorāsān was 352.

According to the most recent census in 1987 there was a total of 3290 Kurdish families (17,000 people) leading a truly nomadic way of life in the north of Khorāsān.

TERRITORY

The book *Matla al Shams* (Sani' al Dawla 1301–3/1884–6, vol 1: 156, 157, 158) tells us that the northern region of Khorāsān was first divided between the different Kurdish clans during the reign of Shah Sultan Hoseyn (1694–1722).

Nowadays the Kurds in the north of Khorāsān spend the summer in the mountain pastures of Hezārmasjed, Binālud and Shāhjahān and the winter in the plains of Sarakhs, Pasakuh and Daragaz and in the Turkmen steppe as far east as Chāt. They have spread right across the north of Khorāsān from east to west and even occupy part of the eastern Turkmen steppe. Historically, areas like Sarakhs, Pasakuh and Daragaz had been thought of as Kurdish winter quarters ever since the reign of Shah 'Abbās I. The eastern part of the Turkmen steppe and the valleys north of Bojnurd, inhabited mainly by Turkmen, seem to have been frequented by Kurds as well over the past few decades.[4]

The Kurds are known to have been living in the plains of Gorgān at the time of Shah 'Abbās (Iskandar Beg Munshi 1350/1971, vol. 1: 580). Today, eighteen villages in Māzandarān and Gorgān have names containing the word 'Kurd' (Ministry of Defence 1329/1950), for example Kurde Kuh, Kurde Mahalah, Kurde Asyāb and so on. Apparently, however, the Kurds had no access to the area between the Atrak and the Gorgān rivers until the 1930s, nor, of course, to the eastern part of the Turkmen steppe.

Iskandar Beg Munshi (1350/1971, vol. 1: 580) states that at the time of Shah Tahmāsp the area between the Atrak and Gorgān rivers was inhabited by a variety of Turkmen tribes. P. M. Sykes arrived in Samalgān via Bandar-e Gaz, Chāt and the Turkmen steppe during the winter of 1893–4. Sykes' route across the steppe follows the present-day winter quarters of the Kurds almost exactly. He did not, however, come across any Kurds, and said that the area was Turkmen country as far as Samalgān (Sykes 1902). Rabino, the British Consul in Rasht from 1906 to 1912, wrote that 'the areas below are the permanent home of the Yamotes, whose name has never previously been recorded: 1. The frontier post of Moravah Tapah on the southern bank of the Atrak, 72 English miles north-west of Bojnurd, 2. The frontier post of Yaghālām. 30 miles from Jāksar.' Nowadays these three places are in the winter quarters of the Kurds. Rabino adds, 'There are endless conflicts between the clans of Guglān and the Kurds of Bujnurd.' This shows that the Kurds did not gain access to the Turkmen steppe before 1920 (Rabino 1928).

I believe that the Kurdish claim to have been using the pastureland in the Turkmen steppes for the last seventy years is a reliable one. A number of them say that before 1930 their clans spent the winter in the grazing around Daragaz and had their summer pastures in the mountains of Hezārmasjed, and that for the last seventy years they have wintered in the Turkmen Sahrā region and migrated in summer to the mountains of Shāhjahān. Today the villages in the eastern part of the Turkmen steppe are peopled almost exclusively by Turkmen. The Kurds simply spend the winter in the pastureland of the region.

THE SEASONAL DIVISION OF ENCAMPMENTS

The summer encampments are divided as follows: 42.4 per cent in the mountains of Hezārmasjed, 47.7 per cent in the mountains of Shāhjahān and 9.9 per cent in the pastures of Binalud. This has been interpreted as demonstrating that Shāhjahān, which has only recently become a home to the Kurds, is more attractive as a summer camping ground than Hezārmasjed, the earliest centre for the Kurds in northern Khorāsān. The great majority of those spending their summers in Hezārmasjed belong to the semi-nomadic Kurdish tribes, or to other semi-nomadic tribes such as Turkic-speaking inhabitants of Jarf.

The winter quarters are more widely dispersed than the summer quarters. In winter, the encampments of the true nomads in the north of Khorāsān are located in five different areas. Turkmen Sahrā 44.6 per cent, i.e. 157 out of 352: the Sarakhs Pasakuh region 43.8 per cent, i.e. 154 out of 352; the Daragaz area 5.4 per cent, whilst Sabzavāra and Esfarāyan only attract 4.8 per cent. There are only five encampments, 1.4 per cent, in the Mānah district beside the river Atrak, halfway between Shāhjahān and Turkmen Sahrā.

The lead camel in a caravan is always led by a girl or young woman and is equipped with a handsome harness. It is given a neat load which is covered with a specially woven cover, the *plās-e Kurdi*. One can tell from its lips and face—seen better in the detail opposite—that it is a cross between a female Arab dromedary and a male *bughur*, the Central Asian or Bactrian two-humped camel. The first generation cross, *māyeh* in Kurdish (*mādeh* in Persian), is the preferred animal for heavy transport since it is tolerant of cold, is good on rough terrain and can carry a larger load than either of its parents. The bag (*tubrah*) suspended from the front camel's load contains basic food for the journey.
On migration to their winter quarters near Marāveh Teppeh, autumn 1987.

THE MIGRATION, CAMELS AND THEIR EQUIPMENT

On the migration, women usually lead the camels, linking them together in groups of three or four. Young women are given priority in leading the first camel of the caravan and are expected to make the entire migration on foot. A man would never take the halter of a camel except in emergencies, for example if a camel were to bolt. Although women may ride horses, they ride camels and donkeys only in exceptional circumstances such as illness, however it is acceptable for old women to ride donkeys. Camels are led by means of a plaited woollen lead rope about 5 metres long attached to the metal ring of the harness. The harness (*afsār* or *avsār*) is made of sheep's wool and consists of three main parts: the *qusheh afsār* which is a nose band (*qusheh*) consisting of parallel plaited cords with a plume in the centre; a woven head band some eight spans in length and four finger-breadths wide which passes around the back of the camel's head and is joined to the nose band by a metal ring; and the *pardeh afsār* which consists of tasselled cords hanging down from the head band on both sides of the camel's head.

Head bands are woven on a loom and decorated with a variety of patterns using the weft-wrapping technique. Both ends of the head band near its attachment to the harness ring are left plain. This part is known as the root (*shalcheh*). There are differences in the harnesses worn by camels depending on their position in the train. The harness worn by the lead camel is more ornate than that of the others. Its *qusheh afsār* has six cords rather than three, and the *pardeh afsār* is decorated with more numerous tasselled cords. The lead camel in addition to having a good-looking harness is further distinguished by having a neat load covered by a specially woven cloth decorated with tassels. The harness of the last camel in the train has a small metal device between the lead

top
The lead camel of the camel-train seen opposite. The nose band (*qusheh afsār)* has six bands and the set of tasselled cords hanging from the harness (*pardeh afsār*) is particularly ornate.

centre
The nose band of this camel is simpler than the one above, having only three separate cords, and it is therefore not a lead camel. The *pardeh afsār,* the set of tasselled cords hanging from the harness, is also simpler. On migration to winter quarters near Marāveh Teppeh, autumn 1987.

bottom
Kurdish women normally cover their mouths, so this woman, seen without her veil, is in some unusual circumstances. The red and black silk kerchief tied over her headscarf indicates that she is married. Her face is not tattooed in any way. This practice is not common among the Kurdish women of Khorāsān, indeed they disapprove of it. Qara Meydān, near Bojnurd, autumn 1986.

rope and the ring, known as an *aqabkesh* (pull-back), which plays an important role in controlling it. Six little teeth are cut into the lower part of the *aqabkesh* which, when the lead rope is pulled, dig into the skin of the camel's face. When the camel slows down and falls behind, the *aqabkesh* acts as a spur to increase its speed and catch up with the camel in front. This device facilitates the work of the person at the head of the caravan and avoids the need for an additional driver at the rear.

If the lead camel is a female, the others will also be females. The Kurds do not normally use bull camels, though, on the rare occasions when they do, all the camels are bulls because controlling them during the rutting season when there are females around is very difficult. Everything possible is done to prevent two crossbred camels from mating, since the offspring are weak and the birth will sap the mother's strength unnecessarily.

DRESS

Amongst the Kurds of Khorāsān, women's dress differs depending on age and marital status. For example the woman on the left on p. 167 (centre) with the yellow skirt with the plain violet silk kerchief on her head is unmarried whereas the woman on the right, with the red skirt with the striped hem, has tied her veil in a manner that indicates she is newly wed. Up to the age of eight or nine, girls can wear what they like, but after the age of nine, they are obliged to wear tribal costume.

The style varies from one clan to another. Among the Bajānlu younger women tend to wear yellow or red velvet skirts decorated with bands of seven colours. They make the skirts from bought velvet, sew on the bands of seven colours, and sew patterned material inside the hem. The hems of the skirts of older women, on the other hand, are decorated with striped or plain material. Amongst the Topkānlu, unmarried girls wear velvet skirts decorated with seven colours while older women wear plain red skirts. Varānlu girls wear skirts of dark blue velvet with white flowers, and married women plain dark blue. Finally, among the Sifkānlu, unmarried girls do not wear velvet at all, but material patterned with red flowers on a white background. In any case, each clan can be recognised by the colours worn by the women. Underwear consists of a plain cloth undershirt with long sleeves the front of which is decorated with zigzag pattern

A woman's head-dress has three components: the *bonhāni*, a cloth directly covering the hair so that the visible head coverings do not get dirty; a white shawl (*chahārqad*), consisting of a piece of unsewn white cloth 300 by 90 centimetres, which covers the head, mouth, shoulders and upper part of the body (left, top); and a silk kerchief (*rusari*), usually made in Yazd (plain violet for unmarried (left, top) and black and violet for married women (left, bottom and p. 171)), which is worn on top of the head over the *chahārqad* as the outermost layer. Unmarried girls never wear the colour black.

To keep their hair in place, women use a clip (*pan*), visible (left, top) as a black, red and yellow band on the right of the young woman's face; being unmarried, she has allowed a lock of hair to fall down over her forehead. This would not normally be an acceptable style in a married woman. In the old days, before the introduction of clips, women plaited their hair to keep it in place. On p. 168 the woman on the right is wearing a Turkmen headscarf. These are bought in the market and to wear such a scarf is considered an expression of modernity. It should be noted that this woman has some of her hair protruding from under her scarf which is not the usual practice among married women.

All women have to veil their mouths and for this reason the circumstances of the woman seen left are unusual. Normally, women do not wear the *chādor* or at least they used not to. However, on p. 170 a number of the women are seen either to be wearing the *chādor* or have tied a scarf around their necks. This is because of the presence of strange men. Since the Islamic revolution, this custom has become more strictly observed.

The men generally wear normal town clothes consisting of jacket and trousers and these days they tend to be second-hand. Until American-style overcoats became popular, most men wore the blue air force coats bought from army-surplus stores, and even now Kurdish men can be seen wearing them. These coats were popular because they were woollen, could be worn over several layers of clothing, and had extra pockets. Older men usually wear knitted woollen hats without a brim; the traditional Kurdish hat is no longer worn. Kurdish men gave up wearing tribal costume about 60 years ago.

left
Two women from the Za'farānlu clan north of Shirvan, summer 1984.

right
Setting up a temporary camp site on the migration to winter quarters near Marāveh Teppeh. Yekkeh Se'ud, north-west of Bojnurd, autumn 1987.

right top
The women have begun to unload the animals. Unloading camels is women's work, whereas loading is work shared by both sexes, and tightening the cords over the load is men's work. The women first spread a striped cloth known as a 'Kurdish plas' (*plās-e Kurdi*) on the ground, on top of which they place quilts and other things. A felt cloth remains on the first camel's back with an ordinary striped *juvāl* beneath, of the type used for storing household items and cooking utensils like pots and pans.

right centre
The camels have been unloaded and turned loose to graze. The women have chosen a place to pitch the tent and have collected stones 10 to 15 cms high and arranged them on the ground about half a metre apart. Two rows of boards placed on the stones act as a platform for their belongings. This arrangement keeps the sacks of foodstuffs and bedding away from the ground and allows air to circulate beneath them. This must be a temporary camp-site, otherwise they would be clearing away the stones and preparing the ground properly as a *yurtgāh* for a stay of two or three months.

right bottom
Two women are setting out their belongings on the wooden boards. In unloading the equipment, they place the bundle of quilts on the boards first, since they do not need supporting. They then place a felt on the boards and prop the *juvāls* against the bundles. This type of *juvāl*, finely worked and valuable, they call 'Turkish'. These *juvāls* contain the clothes and household items and are stacked front to front and back to back. This is to prevent their decorated face from being damaged by coming into contact with the coarse weave of the back of its neighbour. Likewise, when they are loaded on camels, their backs must always be against the camel's side, with the patterned side outwards. Once the finely woven *juvāls* have been stacked, they add the coarser 'Kurdish'-type *juvāls* containing foodstuffs (see p.173).

left above
A family group inside a tent. The sacks set out on the left will contain animal feed such as barley. They are stored horizontal, whereas sacks with stores for human consumption like flour, wheat and other grains are kept standing up so that their contents are more readily available. At the back of the tent, behind the man's head, the bedding stack is visible. The carpet on the floor the tent is of felt and its design is typical of Quchān work.
The colours of the women's dresses show that all three are married. The man next to the woman on the right of the photograph is sitting so close to her that he must be her husband. Kurdish men are usually clean-shaven; the beard and his coat may indicate that he recently served in the war.

left below
The winter housing (*khānicheh*) of a poor family dug into a hillside near Oqchi just south of the Turkmen border, 1985. The floor is covered with felts and a knotted pile carpet. Neither of the women is wearing tribal dress and the bedding stack is covered with some kind of blanket rather than a traditional weaving.

THE TENT

The tent of the Khorāsān Kurds is rectangular in plan. The interior of the tent is divided into several sections, as follows: the first section, at the back of the tent, is the family's living area, where they sleep and eat. Bedding and other household items are stored on one side of this section. The second section, the middle of the tent, contains a small stove for making tea. Here the men sit, drink tea and chat. The third section, which is not usually spread with rugs, is where people leave their shoes and dump such things as horses' harnesses and shepherds' cloaks for the women to tidy up after them. The fourth section is right under the front flap (*bargav* or *pishmāl*). This is where the tent's work, for example boiling milk or beating *telem*, is carried out in winter. Of course, in warm weather these activities go on in the open air. The entrance to the tent is at one corner of the rectangle, to one side of the front flap.

The tent canopy is made by sewing together a number of long, narrow panels, each about 12 metres long and about a metre wide, which span the width of the tent. The number of panels sewn together side to side determines the depth of the tent. The width of the panels varies from clan to clan as follows: Qahramānlu: 1.20 metres, Hashtmarkhi: 1.10, Hizlānlu: 1, Bādlānlu: 0.85 to 1, Zharaf Mountain clans: 0.40 to 0.60, Qazi Kurdish villages: 0–0.50 metres. New panels are usually added at the front of the tent, and old ones removed from the back. A family will normally only be able to renew part of the tent each year depending on its finances and the energy of its women.

The canopy is supported by sets of four poles running parallel to the front of the tent, and the number of sets of poles determines the depth of the tent. The poles at the centre are longer and those at the sides, known as *geluchak,* are uniformly shorter. Likewise the poles at the entrance are shorter than those in the centre.

In Northern Khorāsān all parts of the tent canopy except for the front flap (*bargav* or *pishmāl*) are made of goat's hair. The *bargav* is made of wool and never sewn to the tent itself but fastened by a sort of hook. This is because in cold weather the preparation of all the food, including the dairy products, takes place under the front flap, and goat's hair cloth constantly sheds fibres whereas the woollen *bargav* does not. The flap is removed in warm weather to improve ventilation, and for ceremonies such as weddings so that those sitting inside can look out.

The main factor limiting the size of a tent is weight, which must not exceed the capability of the animals to carry it, traditionally the camels. The Bactrian camel (*bughur*), the female Arabian-Bactrian cross (*māyeh*) and the single-humped Arabian dromedary (*arvāneh*) can comfortably carry 250 kilos. This corresponds approximately to the weight of a tent with twelve panels. Some rich families own two or three tents. These have to be carried separately. Very large tents can be made by sewing the panels together. There are a few families whose tents remain either in the winter or summer quarters all the year round.

In winter, a pit is dug to a depth of about 80 cm, the sides smoothed down, and the tent pitched inside. Alternatively, stones may be piled up around the tent to a height of about 80 cm. These techniques protect the tent against cold air. A low earth wall is also piled up round the tent with a shallow ditch to channel off rain water. In recent years the Kurds have been making increasing use of light, small, cotton tents while on the move between summer and winter quarters.

THE KHĀNICHEH

The housing of the poor is the *khānicheh* or *khāncheh* (i.e. little house). Villagers who have only just started the migration and do not possess many animals may live in huts of this type in the spring. Examples can be found in the Persian-speaking villages of Pazangān, in Pamakuh near Kalāt Nāderi. To make a *khānicheh*, a pit is dug about 5 x 3 metres in extent and 1.5 to 1.8 metres deep. The surface is then levelled, but no other floor or foundation is laid. Shelves and recesses are made in the sides of the pit which are then smoothed down with wet mud. Three such shelves can be seen in the photograph. Two, about one metre above the ground, provide space for household items like pans, bowls, glasses, dishes etc., while one other, in the lower left hand corner of the picture, stores water-flasks. The bottom of this type of shelf is slightly hollowed out. The pit is roofed simply by laying thin sticks across it and covering them with old tent panels, sacking or polythene. In some areas, though, they use wood and tiles to make a better roof than the one shown here.

Wedding celebrations near Qoreh Meydan, late summer 1987. The front flap of the tent has been lifted so that those sitting inside can see the festivities. Weddings are one of the few occasions when restrictions on social contact between the sexes are relaxed.
The elderly man in the left foreground is carrying a baby; Kurdish men do sometimes hold their young sons in their arms which is something not done in Turkmen society. The casual posture of the older woman on the right would be regarded as frivolous and vulgar in a younger person and would not be tolerated.

THE WEDDING

Girls from migratory Kurdish clans usually marry later than their village counterparts. The reasons are economic. The cost of a wedding amongst the migrants is on average three times as much as in the villages. A girl is regarded as an important source of labour for the family and fathers try to delay their marrying as long as possible. The Kurds have a high birth rate.

Unmarried girls may speak to anyone male or female, but married women are forbidden to speak to men other than their relations. However during wedding festivities there are hardly any restrictions on social contact between the sexes. Both men and women can participate in the same dances, although they cannot dance one man with one woman. The dances do not have a formal structure and there can be more men than women or vice versa.

During the celebrations the custom of *shābāsh* is prevalent. *Shābāsh* is an abbreviation of the words *shād bāsh* (i.e. 'be happy'). The custom can be encountered at all types of ceremonies but is particularly popular during weddings when there is dancing. The favourite time is when the 'lovers' (as the musicians are called) are playing a soft and mellow, rather than a fast and rhythmic, tune and the women are dancing side by side in a circle. In such dances, the *qushmeh*, a sort of double-piped flute, is favoured, rather than loud instruments like the *zernā* or the drum. The *shābāsh* is organised by an individual known as a *shābāshchi*.

While the women are dancing, any of the spectators can give the *shābāshchi* a sum of money for delivery to a particular woman or girl as a token of admiration or courtship. Often relations send such tokens: fathers to wives or daughters, uncles to nieces, brothers to sisters, cousins and so on.

On receiving the *shābāsh* the *shābāshchi*, taking care to hold up the gift so that everyone can see it, announces, in a loud voice, in Persian (or the local Kurdish or Turkish dialect): '*Ay, shābāsh, shābāsh. Ey hamisheh 'arusi bāshad*' (Eh shābāsh. May there always be weddings). '*Jibhā hamisheh por az pul bāshad*' (may pockets always be full of money). '*Labhā hamisheh khandān bāshad*' (may lips always be smiling). '*Gusfandhā por-e shir bāshand*' (may sheep be full of milk). '*Kanduhā por-e-gandom bāshand*' (may stores be full of wheat). '*Omrhā tulāni bāshad*' (may lives be long). '*Sāheb-e 'arusi salāmat bāshad*' (good health to the host). '*Polow-ye 'arusi por gusht bāshad*' (may the wedding dish be full of meat)..

After each line, those present echo the last words with '*Ey bāshad*'. All this is accompanied by jokes and comments to amuse the spectators. The *shābāshchi* then announces: 'Lords, gentlemen, ladies. Mr X has given Mrs or Miss Y, or Mrs A has given Mr B the sum of 500,000 tomans' (here the *shābāshchi* names a sum greatly in excess of the real amount given). Then, folding the money, and dancing in time with the melody, he approaches the recipient, male or female, and moving along with them, either ties it to the woman's scarf or, if a man, slips it into his pocket, announcing the name of the sender as he does so. Of course, young men also send *shābāsh* to girls they fancy, and sometimes girls do the same for boys. On rare occasions, the boy will take the *shābāsh* direct to the girl he loves. However, a girl would never deliver a *shābāsh* directly to a boy, but would always use the *shābāshchi*.

right
A married woman knitting a hat; significantly she is wearing her skirt inside out. This is a sign of mourning. It is not customary amongst the Kurds to wear black during mourning since the colour is thought unlucky. In this respect the culture of the Khorāsān Kurds differs from urban practice. Near Bojnurd, winter 1986.

WEAVING

The Kurds of Khorāsān have until recently been prolific weavers. Changing patterns of land use, impoverishment through natural disasters such as the winters of 1968–9 and 1972–3, shortage of fuel, and the use of motor vehicles to transport animals have all had their effect on the weaving culture of the nomads. Impoverishment has led many families to sell their weavings and settle while others have put their weaving skills to use by making non-traditional items for sale.

Among the most important of the traditional weavings is the *plās-e Kurmanji* or *plās-e Kordi* (see opposite). This is a warp-faced fabric woven as a long strip on a horizontal ground loom. The strip is then cut into pieces, usually four, which are joined side to side to form a large cover. The Kurdish *plās* is one of the mainstays of the wedding trousseau. Every girl must weave one. On the wedding-night the *plās* functions as a curtain separating the bridal chamber from the rest of the tent. This is its most important use for the newly married bride. A finely woven *plās* can also be used to cover the load of the lead camel in a caravan, or, indeed, in the case of very rich people, of all the camels in the train. In short, the *plās* is a symbol of wealth and social status. Each panel of a finely woven top quality *plās* takes about 240 woman-hours to make. Thus, a complete four panel *plās* can be expected to take 960 hours or nearly four months at eight hours a day.

For storing foodstuffs coarse-woven *juvāls* are used (see opposite centre). This type, woven entirely out of wool,designed to be carried by a camel, is too big for other animals to manage.

A Qahremānlu woman weaving on the horizontal ground loom. Near Bojnurd, summer 1982.

Although they can be made at any time of year, the commonest time for weaving *juvāls* is during the autumn. This type takes about 90 hours to make. Finer woven and more richly decorated *juvāls* are used for clothes (see p. 167, bottom). Although not essential, a finely woven *juvāl* for storing clothes would normally form part of a girl's dowry when moving to her husband's home. Like all weaving operations, this work is exclusively undertaken by women.

Another item in constant use, especially as a mark of respect for guests, is the cloth in which bread is wrapped (*sofreh-ye parchkin*). Because of the reverence in which bread is held, a bread-cloth must be woven from the wool of the camel, an animal which is correspondingly revered. As camel wool cannot be dyed, the cloth itself is always of natural colour. The bread-cloth seen opposite is a warp-faced plain weave with patterns known as *gol-e Topkānlu* which have been worked in knotted pile and weft wrapping, using sheep's wool and bought cotton yarn. As a consequence of the spread of plastic cloths, the *sofreh-ye parchkin* is now little used and rarely made. They take about 50 hours, or 6 days to make. The camel's wool is collected in the summer by the women when the camels moult. Some parts of the camel are also shorn at the same time. The wool may not be used for making any item that will be trodden on or come in direct contact with the body.

top
Detail of a bread cloth.

centre
Detail of a coarse-woven *juvāl* used for storing foodstuffs

bottom
Detail of a woollen *plās-e Kurmanji* or *plās-e Kordi*

THE TORKASHVAND OF WESTERN IRAN

Eckart Ehlers

INTRODUCTION

There have always been small unclaimed tracts of land between the territories of the larger tribes of western Iran which, by acting as buffers, have helped to diminish conflicts between the powerful tribes of the Zāgros, such as the Bakhtiāri and the Lurs. These 'no-man's-lands' attracted those lesser tribes and tribal groups which had no large grazing grounds or suitable and undisputed migratory routes, and provided them with excellent pasturage at least during their migrations.

The Torkashvand is one of the many small nomadic groups in the western highlands of Iran that have had to adjust themselves to their powerful neighbours (the Lurs in this case) and get the best out of the limited land resources available for their herds. The Torkashvand were forced into peripheral areas for their summer and winter pastures (*yaylaq* and *qeshlaq*). They actually managed to make their combination of yaylaq and qeshlaq economically viable, but only by means of long and tedious migrations (up to 150 miles [250 km] and lasting several weeks) in spring and autumn. Their traditional summer pastures were on the Alvand Kuh, an isolated mountain range near Hamadān, and they originally migrated through the valleys, basins and defiles of the Zāgros to their winter quarters near Gilān-e Gharb on the Iraq–Iran border. Now, however, these lands have been occupied and the Torkashvand's use of them is a matter of dispute.

The Alvand Kuh was the last Torkashvand territory to be disputed. This range is about 30 miles (50 km) from west to east and 12 miles (20 km) from north to south, and its highest peak is 11,745 feet (3,580 metres). The heavy winter snow cover and the great number of good springs provide its foothills with sufficient water for irrigated agriculture. Villages now surround the base of the mountain and the nomads have to search higher up for their pasture.

The lush high summer pastures of the Alvand Kuh are the traditional yaylaqs of the Torkashvand and the Yarımtoglu, both comparatively small tribes numbering approximately 300 tents each. The Laki-speaking Torkashvand pastured their sheep and goats in the north-western part of the range, while the Turkish-speaking Yarımtoglu occupied the south-eastern. Until the late 1960s both were able to follow their traditional nomadic life-style without too much difficulty. Since then, political, social and economic changes in the larger world, such as population growth in the villages and towns around the foot of the mountain, and especially the great Iran–Iraq war of the 1980s, have increasingly affected them.

LIFE IN THE 1950S. A NOMAD'S ACCOUNT

I learnt much of the history of the Torkashvand's difficulties by talking to one of their leaders, Ahmad 'Ali, in the Alvand Kuh in the middle 1970s, when the so-called 'White Revolution' had put new stress on the nomadic tribes, especially the smaller ones. He was leader (*kadkhodā*) of the Rahmati, one of the dozen or so subtribes (*tireh*) making up the Torkashvand. The Rahmati were by far the biggest subtribe, which meant that Ahmad 'Ali had an especially important role within the tribe. At the same time, because of their size, they had suffered most from the changes he described, so many indeed that it was almost impossible to keep up their old way of life.

I visited his tent high in the Alvand Kuh, at about 8,200 feet (2,500 metres), one bright September morning. The sheep were still in their overnight corrals but some flocks, accompanied by one or two men and wildly barking dogs, were already moving towards the nearby slopes where they would spend the day as they had for more than three months, browsing on the pasture now depleted by steady grazing and the dry summer. The nomads had rotated pastures over the months, and even moved their tents and corrals, but the great number of herds of

A woman from one of the Turkic-speaking tribes whose traditional summer pasture is on Mount Alvand (Alvand Kuh) where a number of lesser tribes with no large area of land available to them can find grazing for their flocks. These tribes include the Laki-speaking Torkashvand and the Turkic Yarımtoglu. To reach their winter pastures these tribes have to migrate through the territory of the Lurs whom they resemble in their dress. 1985.

considerable size, and the growing competition from the villagers for pasture, was putting increasing stress on the land. Over tea Ahmad 'Ali described the Torkashvand way of life during the 1950s, when he was a child:

"When I was a boy my father was the kadkhodā of the Rahmati. Then the Malijāni, Ghurkāh, Solaimāni, Moshed, Rahmati, and all the other subtribes used to live more or less close together. I remember that at the time we all had our winter pastures near Gilān-e Gharb, close to the Iraq border. It was a long way from here, a hundred and fifty miles [250 km] and more, but it was nice down there. Our tents were stretched out over a broad and gently sloping plain at the western foot of the Zāgros. The temperatures were pleasant, although of course it sometimes snowed or rained, which was good for the pastures. Most of the time it was quiet. It was the lambing season and mild temperatures were essential for the survival of the new-born animals.

"Yes, the stays in qeshlaq and yaylaq were good, but the migrations between them were the worst part of our life, and for the animals too. We were sixty to seventy days on the road. We had a traditional migration route but there were always troubles and problems on the way. First, there were disputes with the villagers whose settlements and fields we had to pass or cross. They wanted us to pay for grazing rights on their harvested fields, for the use of their water or for damage we were supposed to have caused. Then there were troubles with the herdsmen of other tribes through whose territories we had to pass. They too wanted us to pay, often for the same reasons as the villagers.

"We numbered several hundred people and several thousand animals, so just imagine the chaos at the narrow crossings in the Zāgros and in the few places in the narrow valleys there where we could stay overnight, or maybe even a few days in order to rest!

"Our worst times were in the cities, small towns and large villages we either had to pass through or by, places like Gilān-e Gharb, Māhidasht, Kermānshāh, Bisotun, Kangāvar or Asadābād. There was nowhere to stay with the animals, no escape from the trucks and cars. Goodness knows how many sheep and goats were killed by reckless drivers! And how hostile the people were, treating us like robbers and uncivilised barbarians! They threw stones after us and nobody—no policeman, no soldier, nobody—was willing to protect us! And don't forget we did the journey twice, first from qeshlaq to yaylaq between mid-March and the middle to end of May, and then again from yaylaq, the Alvand Kuh, to qeshlaq between September and mid-November. No wonder that quite a few of us Torkashvand, and other tribes as well, started looking for another way of life."

Ahmad 'Ali then went on to give his account of the first big changes in the tribal way of life in 1950–5, when a good part of the tribe's winter grazing grounds near the Iraqi border had been made into 'King's Land' and developed as farmland.

"More than twenty families of the Rahmati, some of them close relatives, including my uncle, had received land and settled there together with members of other clans. But those without land had nowhere in winter to graze their sheep and goats or set up their tents. Quite a few subtribes, and even some families of the Rahmati, had to look for new winter pastures. At that time one could still find them in the remote small valleys and basins of the Zāgros that had been empty land between different tribes. The tribe now only came together in the summer in the Alvand Kuh, and it was the happiest and best time of year for all of us. These are the times we all remember."

Ahmad 'Ali's account was substantiated by the anthropologist Jacob Black-Michaud, who was working in Luristān in 1969–70: '... the Torkashvand in about 1955 ... were motivated by mounting population pressures and a consequent steep rise in grazing fees to reorient their migration routes along a north-south axis through Luristān' (1986: 38). While this statement holds true only for certain sections of the whole tribe, these events certainly mark the beginning of the land problems of the Torkashvand and other tribes of the highlands of Iran, namely decreasing availability of pastures, be it in yaylaq, qeshlaq or, worst of all, in both places at the same time. They also mark the beginning of the breakdown of the tribes' spatial behaviour, social ties and traditional economies. For many nomadic tribes in the highlands of Iran—and Ahmad 'Ali agreed—the years between 1950 and 1960 marked the definite end of their traditional societies and economies, which had always had to adapt and adjust themselves to changes in the larger world, but had never been faced with the loss of their pastures.

CONTINUITY AND CHANGE SINCE THE MID-1970S

By the mid-1970s the life of the Torkashvand had changed dramatically. Rapid population growth in the villages and towns, the expansion of rural settlements and agriculture, and an increase in the number of the villagers' flocks of sheep and goats, had greatly contributed to a further deterioration and even partial collapse of the nomadic structure. There was hardly a tent on the high pastures of the Alvand Kuh that had not been affected, according to Ahmad 'Ali and others.

Here it may be appropriate to record the powerful Lur tribe's opinion of the Torkashvand, as recorded by Black-Michaud, an impeccably sharp observer of nomads and nomadism in western Iran in 1970: 'All Luri nomads ... look down upon the Torkashvand, who may be rich in flocks, but who are really *nādār,* since they have no landed property' (1986: 88). The scornful term *nādār* literally translates as 'have-nots'. The Luri economy, on the other hand, has been aptly described as an 'agro-pastoral combine', because it is based on a traditional combination of agriculture and animal husbandry. This economic dualism coincided with a social dualism, since Lurs have followed a settled life-style for a long time, while the rest remained mobile and migratory herdsmen. The lack of land was something Ahmad 'Ali returned to over and over again.

"The change of our pastures near Gilān-e Gharb into fields was the beginning of our troubles. After that tribal unity and solidarity just broke up. Now there is a confusing variety of life-styles, of economic activities and migrational patterns within the different subtribes, and even within families. Frankly, I've lost track of it all, but I'll tell you what's happened to us Rahmati, and we're typical of all the other subtribes of the Torkashvand.

"Well, just look around. This is our family's traditional tent site. We've been coming here as long as I can remember, so for me this is home, at least during the summer months. We've been lucky so far. We're one of the few families that have kept their traditional yaylaq. We used to be surrounded by other Rahmati tent groups, but that was a long time ago, when the whole mountain was still ours.

"Some years ago the Shah in Tehrān decided there should be a land reform and much of the land here, including some of our traditional pastures, was handed over to the villagers at the foot of the mountain. They expanded their fields into our pastures, increased the size of their flocks and forced us not only to retreat into the highest parts of the Alvand Kuh but even to give up some of the land we still considered ours. They came with police, and once even with soldiers, so finally we had to give in.

"Now everything is mixed up. Rahmati tents are in at least seven or eight different parts of the Alvand Kuh or neighbouring areas. You will find members of our subtribe, among them quite a few of my relatives, in the high valleys of Shahrestāneh, Artiman, Kashāni and Oshtorān—all in the Alvand Kuh—and now there are Rahmati in the mountains of Nahāvand and in other ranges south of it."

The Shah's so-called 'White Revolution' was the second big change the nomads experienced. The changes in land ownership affected both their winter pastures and the areas along their traditional migration routes. As the amount of available pasture shrank, more and more nomads were forced to consider giving up their traditional way of life and settling down, but the problem was where. Selling their herds would provide some money for the purchase of land, but it was scarce and prices high. The villages hardly had enough for themselves, in spite of the land reform, and the large landowners would not sell, and in fact tried to acquire even more.

The Rahmati and the other subtribes of the Torkashvand developed a number of strategies to cope with the situation. Besides spreading over a greater number of small isolated qeshlaq locations than before, quite a few tent groups tried to settle along the traditional migration routes. By 1975 the Rahmati, who were typical of the tribal groups at the time, had winter pastures not only near their traditional qeshlaq in Gilān-e Gharb, but also near Sar-e Pol-e Zahāb (where they rented what was formerly their own land from a newly-established farm corporation), and at different sites near Bisotun and Kangāvar. They also had winter pastures, near Andimeshk in Khuzestān and near Khorramābād, Pol Dokhtar and many other places along their routes to the west and south. Other groups moved into such towns as Asadābād, Shahābād and Karend or such cities as Hamadān or Khorramābād. They took up jobs of different kinds, mostly as unskilled labourers, and soon amalgamated with the urban population or moved on to Tehrān. In short, tribal unity and solidarity were severely affected in these years, as was the traditional economy.

A young Torkashvand girl and an older woman. The Torkashvand are often classified as Lurs because they dress in a similar fashion and come in close contact with them. However, their language is Laki which is considered to be a dialect of Gurāni Kurdish with some admixture of Lori. They may be the relic of an earlier Kurdish population that was once more widespread in the region or simply nomads who migrated away from their ancestral territory long ago.
Near Hoseynieh, north of Andimeshk, February 1986.

As mentioned above, the Lurs always looked down on the Torkashvand. They acknowledged their wealth of sheep and goats, but derided them for being poor in land. Whilst the judgement is unkind, it is of course a true statement of the facts. Their economy was based solely on their flocks of sheep and goats, their sheep providing milk, butter, cheese, yoghurt, wool and meat. The goat hair was used for the production and repair of their tents, and the wool for bags and other receptacles, and sometimes even for simple mats and rugs. As a rule, the Torkashvand tried to bring the size of their flocks to the point where they had a surplus they could sell, and mostly they sold as many animals as the flocks would reproduce. This money, together with some income from the sale of milk and milk products, enabled the Torkashvand to buy wheat and fodder crops from the villagers and necessities such as pots, pans and kettles from the urban bazaars, and sometimes even some 'luxuries' such as shoes, garments or even sweets. The flocks were their main source of income, and indeed they were quite wealthy, but by the mid-1970s the situation had changed dramatically.

By 1975, the Torkashvand had not only dispersed into a great number of summer and winter pastures, but quite a few had given up pastoralism altogether, and others partly. Those in this latter category frequently adopted a kind of semi-nomadism. They reduced the size of their flocks and migrated only once a year, the season being decided according to the availability of and access to pasture. The rest of the year they stayed where they had settled along their migratory routes, in either newly-erected houses or even whole villages located in small side valleys, on narrow river terraces or on tiny flat plateaux along mountain slopes. These locations and their environs could support small herds for only a limited time each year. Although attempts were made again and

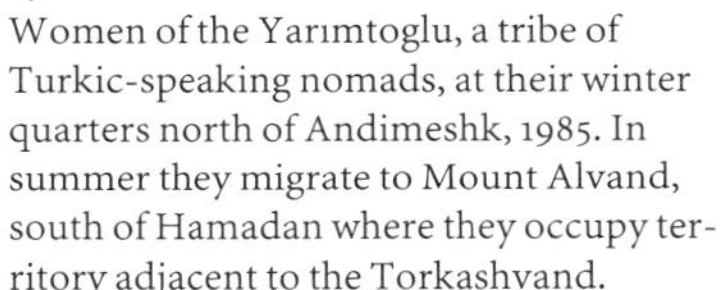

Women of the Yarımtoglu, a tribe of Turkic-speaking nomads, at their winter quarters north of Andimeshk, 1985. In summer they migrate to Mount Alvand, south of Hamadan where they occupy territory adjacent to the Torkashvand.

again, agriculture proved to be more or less impossible. Those nomads who tried to settle on the fringes of existing villages also ran into difficulties. In most cases quarrels and conflicts were the consequence, although a few attempts, especially where settled former tribal members offered hospitality, may have been successful and made integration into a rural environment possible. The new settlers were treated as intruders and competitors, which is of course what they were. Most small villages had hardly enough land to sustain their own inhabitants, and the addition of only one family and its animals in many cases had a severe effect on the limited resources. In these circumstances settlers were often forced to look for additional sources of income and ended up in a mixed economy that was neither nomadism nor agriculture. After the loss of their traditional winter pastures near the Iraq border, some Torkashvand families settled down near Sahneh, halfway between Hamadān and Kermānshāh.

After a long search and much controversy with the villagers they founded several 'winter villages'. These were located either far away from the rural settlement (very often right on the edge of the village's territory) or high above them (see figure p. 180), and many of the sites had neither water nor public facilities such as schools or mosques. Their inhabitants, deprived of their viable herding economy, developed different strategies of survival. First of all they tried to spin out the grazing season around their winter settlements as much as possible. They got their herds out of their mostly subterranean winter stables as soon as possible in spring, often even when snow still covered the ground, and kept them outside as long as possible in autumn. In summer, the greater part of the families migrated to the yaylaqs of the Alvand Kuh. Those left behind tried to plough the stony land of the mountain slopes around their winter quarters hoping to produce at least small quantities of grain. They also helped the villagers whenever and wherever possible in exchange for a few bushels of wheat and barley. In late summer and autumn, the harvested fields could then be used as additional grazing areas for both peasant and nomadic flocks, but only after the straw and chaff had been reclaimed (mostly purchased) as winter fodder. However, in many cases all this was not sufficient to sustain the semi-nomadic households and quite a few members of the families therefore looked for jobs and additional sources of income in nearby towns and cities. They worked as casual labourers in the booming construction and building sector, and as hawkers, pedlars, watchmen and carriers, and part of their small monthly incomes helped to establish a kind of minimum economy.

A third survival strategy, besides that of founding 'part-time settlements' and integration into existing villages, was the erection of seasonal camp sites at the periphery of towns and big cities. For many months of the year Hamadān and Kermānshāh especially, but also other cities such as Khorramābād, Dezful or Andimeshk, were surrounded by nomad camps, Torkashvand among

RURAL AND NOMADIC FORMS OF LAND-USE ON THE KUH-E ALVAND AND THEIR CHANGES THROUGH LAND REFORM

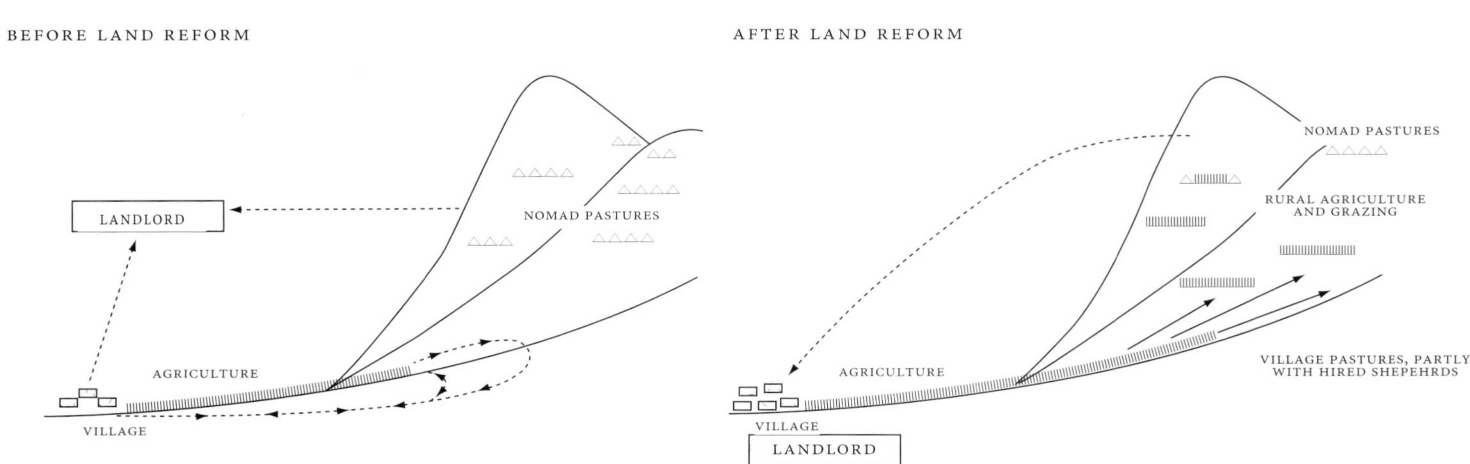

them. Here the nomads could sell their scanty surpluses of milk, yoghurt or meat at relatively high prices. More important, however, they had access to a variety of urban trades and professions. The camps at the urban fringes unquestionably proved to be the most decisive factor for change from a nomadic to a settled life-style, be it in town, city or countryside. During this time of change in the 1970s animal husbandry remained the dominant economic resource in almost all Torkashvand households, whatever the size of individual flocks. The level of wealth or poverty was determined by the number of sheep, not goats, the total number of fertile and pregnant ewes being crucially important. Sheep as the basis of the traditional nomadic household serve three purposes, which are, in order of importance, (1) the production of milk and milk products, (2) the production of meat and (3) the production of wool. The sizes of flocks are mainly adjusted to the ecological potential of the pastures, and in recent years the average size may have fallen due to the constraints discussed above.

The Torkashvand flocks are managed in exactly the same way as those of the Lurs. Black-Michaud (1986: 43) gives the following description:

"Ewes run with the stud rams from early August until mid-October—that is, from the earliest date at which they are in oestrus after the final cessation of milking ... Most lambs are dropped between late December and early March. Until early April all the milk is left to the lambs, which are suckled twice a day at dawn and dusk. The lambs never run in daytime with their dams but are kept protected for the first three or four weeks of their lives in the shelter of a hemispherical construction of withies inside the living tent. The lambs thereafter continue to spend nights under cover of the tent, but in a more open fold, until camps begin to move northwards at any time between mid-March and early April. When, prior to the migration, they are already well established, they are formed into a flock with the sexes mixed and are grazed as such until the beginning

A woman from one of the Turkic-speaking tribes whose summer pastures are on the slopes of Mount Alvand. On spring migration near Tuyserkān, 1986

of July. Only then are the female lambs incorporated into the existing ewe flocks and the males grouped separately for fattening and sale at eighteen months."

As a result of the changes the Torkashvand have undergone, a house may be a lamb's first shelter rather than a tent, and the herds may be split on the high pastures, the ewes and lambs remaining close to the tents, at least until the end of the milking and suckling period, while the male animals migrate daily to the higher and more remote parts of the mountains. Again Black-Michaud's description of the Lurs exactly describes the Torkashvand position on the Alvand Kuh:

"From arrival in the high pastures until weaning in early July suckling only occurs once a day after the ewes have already yielded most of their milk to their human owners. Milking takes place daily at 11 a.m. or noon from early April onwards. Around 15–20 May a second daily milking is instituted at 2 or 3 p.m. From mid-July the supply of milk begins to tail off, and the ewes are again milked but once a day until, in mid-August, only a few female goats are still giving a very little milk."

Milk was and is the staple 'crop' of the Torkashvand, and it is still the most important single product of the summer camps. Milking and milk processing are exclusively female tasks, as are cooking, baking or fetching water, while herding is men's work. Milk is hardly ever used as such, but serves as the basis of a variety of products. Most of it is processed easily and rapidly overnight into yoghurt (*māst*). Most of the yoghurt is sold to nearby towns and cities, often through urban dealers and middlemen who set up their camps among the nomadic tents in yaylaq. The remaining milk and yoghurt is refined into a variety of products: clarified butter (*roghan*), a kind of curd cake (*kashk*) and finally a delicious and highly prized fresh cheese (*shirāz*) which is in great demand among urban people.

The sale of animals for slaughter has always been a major source of income for nomadic households, and holds true for the Torkashvand. The nomads prefer to sell yearling rams and ewes past

above left
A woman from one of several Turkic-speaking tribes whose summer pastures are on Mount Alvand. Chālanchulān, 1985.

above right
Torkashvand shepherd wearing a felt mantle (*kapanak*), 1986.

left
Torkashvand father and son, February 1986.

opposite above
The tent of the Torkashvand is similar to that of the Lurs. Here canvas takes the place of a goat hair canopy. 1986.

opposite below left
Setting up a reed screen as a temporary shelter. Torkashvand, autumn 1987.

opposite below right
Detail of a tent screen made from reeds and cane bound together with goat hair and secured in place with a woollen band. Torkashvand, 1987.

A pair of large saddle bags ready for loading. Torkashvand, Rahmati tribe, near Andimeshk, on the way to summer pasture on Mount Alvand, 1986. In view of the fact that the language of the Torkashvand belongs structurally to the Kurdish dialects, it is interesting to note that the design on the face of this large, knotted-pile storage bag is one found on Kurdish weavings in both eastern Turkey and Khorāsān.

their breeding age. In general, approximately a quarter to a third of the average viable flock size are potential slaughter animals. The actual figure for any individual flock varies according to its size, its gender composition and the environment in which the animals live, and harsh winters, extreme aridity, lack of water and disease can drastically reduce the number. There can be further considerable losses from negligence, theft, wild animals or other avoidable causes.

The animals are most often selected and sold at the end of the summer grazing season, but there are secondary peaks of animal sales at New Year (i.e. 21 March) and the time of *Eyd-e Qorbān*. Selling during migration does happen but is not common. Occasionally urban traders and middlemen come to the summer pastures to buy, but the best prices are got from urban dealers and butchers at the edges of large cities. Meat eating is not an everyday occurrence among the nomads. It is reserved for a few special events like New Year or marriage, or when an animal is very sick and about to die.

The third source of wealth from animal husbandry is wool. While its value may be small in comparison to those of milk products and meat, wool production is nevertheless important. Shearing takes place at the end of the winter season, when a thick dense fleece has developed. The average production is 2–4 lbs (1–2 kg) per animal. A lot of the wool is sold in urban markets, but often the Torkashvand exchange it for commodities in the urban bazaars or give it to villagers in exchange for grazing rights. The hair they get from their goats is used to make their black tents, carrying straps, sacks and bags. The residue of the wool is occasionally sold or exchanged for cleaned and spun wool that is used to weave *gelims* or small carpets.

Weaving is practised only to a limited extent among the Torkashvand, and in fact carpet weaving, which is carried out only by women and children, has come to a stop in the current absence of city-based tourists, the main purchasers. The households in which the carpets were produced used to get a small income from the work.

The changes in the Torkashvand way of life since the late 1960s have of course mirrored the

Washing hands before breakfast after a night of very heavy rain. Canvas is used for covering the tent in place of goat hair by poor nomads. The new-looking felt mantle he is wearing remains warm even in the rain. Torkashvand near Hoseynieh on the way to their summer camp on Mount Alvand between Hamadān and Tuyserkān. February 1986

overall political and socio-economic changes in Iran during this time, and for the Torkashvand have meant a profound restructuring of their entire traditional economy. For example, the Torkashvand, in common with many other tribes, have entered into relationships with villagers and urban dwellers that are different from the traditional ones so far described in this chapter. One of the more common of these new liaisons is the mixing by the nomads of village- or city-owned flocks with their own herds, and even the shepherding of them, in return for a number of the new-born lambs plus a share (usually half) of the milk, its products, and the wool. It need hardly be said that it is the settled Torkashvand in particular who look for such arrangements, especially shepherding, and if they do find them they entrust their own flocks to their migrant kin. By this they not only hope to uphold their traditional claims to their pastures in yaylaq—and sometimes even in qeshlaq—but they secure an additional form of income to supplement their meagre livelihood. These arrangements can also benefit the nomads. They receive a share of the herd's products and do well if it flourishes, and very often are granted grazing rights in those villages along the migration route from which their charges have come.

As part of their efforts to adjust to the changes they were faced with, the Torkashvand tried to move in the direction of 'agro-pastoralism' and attempted to become like the Lurs, who, it will be remembered, scorned them as landless 'have-nots'. Unlike the Lurs, however, they could not claim any land or territories as their own, and vacant land did not exist. There were areas whose ownership they could have disputed but the tribe was too small to engage in such struggles with any hope of success considering the forces ranged against them. Denied the Luri solution, they were forced to look for other economic survival strategies which, on the whole, were at the cost of spatial dislocation, the dissolution of tribal society and the deformation of their traditional economy. In other words, the Torkashvand have been going the same way as so many other small and large tribes in Iran, namely from a migratory tribal nomadism towards a final sedentarisation within a rural or urban environment via different forms of agro-pastoral combinations.

above
Torkashvand on their way to their winter camp near Pol Dokhtar, autumn 1987.

right above
On migration. The mules are carefully decorated with distinctive fringed tack. Torkashvand, near Khorramābād, spring 1985.

right below
Breast-feeding on the move while caring for a second child and a kid. Torkashvand, February, 1986.

AND TODAY ...?

Apart from the rapid growth of the rural population, three events have particularly affected the Torkashvand in recent years: the Islamic Revolution, the Iran–Iraq war, and the influx of refugees from the war in Afghanistan.

First, the Islamic Revolution of 1979. Without doubt its impact has been much stronger in the villages and cities than on the nomads, but it has affected tribal societies because there has been no attempt to address the pressing problem of land ownership. The new government has neither acknowledged the results of the Shah's 'White Revolution' and its land reform nor initiated reversals of its decisions; nor has it developed new agricultural policies that consider the nomads' interests and potential. Second, there are the lasting effects of the long, fierce Iran–Iraq war, which have had particular impact on the Torkashvand. As mentioned before, their traditional winter grazing grounds were located near the border with Iraq, and of course these border areas were heavily affected by the war, like so many others in mountainous western Iran. Air-raids badly damaged the villages and cities and the inhabitants left their homes and fled into the country thus putting even more pressure on the limited land resources.

And third, there has been the impact of the Afghan refugees. While most of them came into the eastern part of Iran, quite a few have also trickled into the west where they have settled down at the margins of the villages and cities and taken over many of the auxiliary jobs and functions that once belonged to the Torkashvand and the other nomads.

However, the biggest threat to fast-changing nomadism is the rapid growth of the rural population. The high birth rate, which has even increased since the Islamic Revolution, has resulted in an ever-mounting pressure on rural land, which is exacerbated by the refugee problem. The figures in the table below demonstrate the dramatic population increase of eight villages located at the south-eastern edge of the Alvand Kuh. Their almost frantic growth changed some of them from villages to small towns, and they are representative of the trend in the other rural areas the Torkashvand used.

	1956	1966	1976	1986
Abaru	1,443	1,822	2,289	3,162
Arzānfud	1,817	2,247	2,706	2,914
Azandaryān	3,037	3,633	4,881	7,346
Deh-Now 'Aliābād	839	1,016	1,339	1,765
Gonbad	1,634	1,751	2,238	2,611
Mangāvi	811	993	1,217	1,608
Oshaq	981	1,195	1,491	1,713
Varkāneh	779	947	980	1,011

Such a rapid increase in rural population implies a corresponding increase in the pressure on the land. This means that it is harder and harder for the nomads to find the necessary pre-conditions for their life-style, though some people are of the opinion that nomadism has undergone something of a renaissance since government control became less repressive. It remains to be seen if this view is correct or not, but it is not unlikely. Nomadism is an extremely versatile life-style that is well-suited to the arid rugged mountain environment of western Iran. Its mobility and capacity to combine remote locations into an entirely successful form of animal husbandry gave the nomads—at least in the past—a viable economy and a good living.

When I revisited the Hamadān area and the Alvand Kuh in 1990 and 1991, there was nothing to be seen of either Ahmad 'Ali, the Rahmati or the Torkashvand in general. I wondered what had happened. In September 1992 I went again to the Alvand Kuh and still could find no sign of them until I stopped at one of the winter settlements they had established over twenty years ago along their migration route between yaylaq and qeshlaq. It lay a few hundred metres off the main road between Hamadān and Kermānshāh near Sahneh.

Not much had changed since my previous visit in 1975. There were almost as many tents as before and the winter houses too were much the same. Many of them were empty as it was still early, and most members of the *tireh* of the Malijāni preferred to live in them as long as the summer

A winter settlement of the Rahmati branch of the Torkashvand close to the main road between between Hamadān and Kermānshāh near Sahneh seen in 1975 (left) and 1992 (right). For the three years prior to 1992 they had been prevented from grazing on the Alvand Kuh because the high pastures had become seriously degraded

temperatures permitted. Many of my friends recognised me and I felt immediately at home. Over a glass of tea they told me their story.

What I learned was that they had not been allowed on the Alvand Kuh for the past three years. The great pressure on the land—to a degree from themselves, but even more so from the villagers at the foot of the mountain—had seriously damaged the natural ecosystem of the high pastures. Overgrazing had led to catastrophic destruction of the natural vegetation and the 'desertification' of large sections of the central Alvand Kuh. Indeed, barren slopes devoid of any protective vegetation, erosion, and the accumulation of fertile soil in gullies and the vicinity of rivers could be seen everywhere.

In 1989 the government decided to close the high pastures of the Alvand Kuh to all kinds of animal husbandry for three years, and launched a seeding and planting programme in an attempt to reconcile man with his environment. The results of this desperate and belated endeavour seemed poor, and my nomadic friends thought so too. During this period they were forced to cut back the size of their flocks by almost 25% for lack of pasture and winter forage, furthermore nothing was done to offset the hardship which resulted from this. Their village has no school, mosque, hammam or shop and still lacks electricity. Only a few of the sixty-five children visit schools in Sahneh.

More than ever before Ahmad 'Ali, the Rahmati and the Torkashvand in general are constrained by the ecological situation and find themselves in increasing economic difficulty. It seems as if their struggle for survival as nomads is lost. The encroachment of agriculture on former fertile pastures and the desertification of the poorer grasslands appear irreversible.

Every spring I know that Ahmad 'Ali and his companions will be longing for the time when they can leave their winter quarters and set out for their ancestral homelands, the breezy green summer pastures of the Alvand Kuh. But with their home badly damaged if not destroyed, where can they go with their herds now?

Giving barley to the goats. Barley and straw are purchased or kept from preceding harvests and fed to animals, when pasture is scarce. Goats are given barley only if they are weak, thin or pregnant. Amala tribe, on the way to winter quarters south of Qir, autumn 1987.

THE QASHQA'I

Yassaman Amir-Moez

INTRODUCTION

The Qashqa'i (*Qashqay eli,* T.; *il-e* Qashqa'yi, P.)[1] consist of a number of tribes, including the Amala, Shesh Baylu,[2] Fars Madān, Darrashurlu, Buyug Kashkullu, Kuchuk Kashkullu, Qarachah'i, Safi Khānlu and a small ruling Jāni Khānlu clan.[3] The number and composition of the tribes have changed over time. Their number is estimated to be 400,000 if settled Qashqa'i are included.

A comprehensive history of this tribe has yet to be written. They speak a western Ghuz Turkic dialect close to Āzari Turkish, the language of the Oghuz Turks, who moved west from Central Asia in the ninth and tenth centuries in various groups and at various times. Their origins and the date of their presence in Fārs, an old subject of controversy, should not be interpreted as the origin of the Qashqa'i tribe. Many Qashqa'i still believe that their ancestors came to Iran from Central Asia at the time of Hulagu (1258) and Timur (1336–1405). A few trace descent from the Khalaj, one of the largest Turkic tribes moved by Timur from Asia Minor to central and eastern Iran at the end of the fourteenth century.[4] These Turkic bands were rugged and ferocious warriors and in south Iran they soon took over territories occupied by the indigenous nomadic and settled groups they subjugated.

Jān Mohammad Khān (Jāni Aqa),[5] the founder of the Qashqa'i tribe, integrated into his domain Turks, Lurs, Persians, Kurds and Laks to form one of the largest tribes in Iran in the eighteenth century. In 1818–19, the title of *ilkhāni* (paramount tribal leader) was bestowed by the Qajar Shah on the leader of the Qashqa'i tribe. 'Up to that year, nobody in Fārs, had been called by the title "Ilkhani"' (Fasa'i, quoted by Busse 1972: 160). The Qashqa'i leaders have all belonged to the Jāni Khānlu clan and trace direct descent from Jāni Aqa. The *ilkhāni* (*buyug khan*, T.) maintained law and order in south-west Iran and he was also responsible for army conscription, leadership in the Qashqa'i tribe and the collection and payment of taxes to the government. He assessed the tax on each of the component tribes (*tāyefa*) and held the leaders of these tribes (*kalāntar*) and the headmen (*kadkhodā*) of their subtribes (*tira*) responsible for its delivery in cash and animals.

Changed political and economic conditions in the twentieth century, the abolition of the title of *ilkhāni* and its rights (1955–7), the removal of paramount tribal leaders, government control of land use and migration and loss of tribal territory and pasture land following national land reform (1963) have not cut off the Qashqa'i from their traditional way of life. The account that follows is an attempt to describe the Qashqa'i in their daily life.

NOMADISM AND THE MIGRATION

In spring and autumn the Qashqa'i migrate between their summer and winter quarters, which are separated by a considerable distance. The spring migration is from the lowlands south and west of the Zāgros range to the northern highlands of these mountains, and in autumn they return to the lowlands. Almost all the Qashqa'i migrate, following definite routes and timetables on each journey. The name for their summer quarters is *sarhad* and for their winter quarters *garmsir. Miānband* is the term used for the area between.

The southern and western limits of garmsir run parallel to the towns of Bandar 'Abbās and Bandar Gonāveh, which are on the Persian Gulf coast, and its northern limit is Shirāz, the main urban centre in south-west Iran. Sarhad is between Shahrezā, Ābādeh and Mount Dinā. Miānband lies in a triangle formed by Firuzābād, Kāzerun and Shirāz.

The migration routes and timetables are well-established, and the organisation is regulated by time-tested customs. Each section of each sub-tribe (*tira*) within each tribe (*tāyefa*) departs from the seasonal pastures at the same time and occupies a given portion of the migratory route for a

Flock owners and shepherds need to keep a close watch on their animals and will often walk along with them during the entire journey. Gallehzan Amala on migration, 1988.

limited period to allow the groups following them to use the route. The starting point, the final destination and the bottlenecks along the way are all clearly defined. Traditionally the purpose of this regulation was to ensure water and pasture were available to each tribe until it reached its destination. The terms *Turk yolu* (path) or *oba yolu* (*oba*, nomad family or camp; *yol*, path) are used for the migration route.

The tribal leaders assign to each group rights over its migratory route. These include exploitation of water and natural vegetation as well as passage through uncultivated and cultivated areas after the harvest. The rights are temporary because each route is used by a succession of tribal groups.

When migrating 'downwards' from sarhad, the nomads follow two main routes and converge in miānband. There the migration divides into two groups again. The first group, the Amala, Shesh Baylu and Kuchuk Kashkullu travel south towards Firuzābād, Hangam and Qir-va-Kārzin to Lār and Khonj, and the Qarachah'i move westwards. The Fars Madan remain in the area of Lake Parishān (Fāmur). The second group, the Buyug Kashkullu and Darrashurlu, pass by Kāzerun to the west of Shirāz and then migrate west and north-west towards Gonāveh, Milātun and Gachsārān. The Buyug Kashkullu and Darrashurlu have winter pastures to the north-west of Shirāz. Because the passage through the mountains is difficult, especially for camels, and the area is populated by Lurs who often oppose the Qashqa'i passage, they are forced to skirt the region on their journeys.

When migrating 'upwards', the pattern is reversed.

Since the 1960s government interference has significantly affected the Qashqa'i way of life. In the 1950s the paramount leader, assisted by tribal leaders, headmen and elders, controlled the migrations. The spring migration began on or around 21 March and arrived in sarhad two months later, when the grass there had reached its full growth. But from the mid-1960s until 1975 the central government controlled the timing of migrations through military force. The government officials ignored ecological and economic factors when they decided migratory schedules, and the schedules varied from year to year. The Qashqa'i pastoral economy suffered accordingly. The central government ceased to control migrations in 1975 but the pre-1960s pattern has not been re-established.

Some even leave garmsir in February and early March and reach sarhad as early as the beginning of April because they worry about other people expropriating their pastures. They arrive before the grass has sprouted and their herds trample the new growth into the mud that is formed as the snow melts. This leads to soil erosion later in the year. Others leave garmsir early because they fear there will be no grazing along the migratory route.

Until the 1960s use of the summer and winter pastures was decided by the Qashqa'i themselves according to historical and political precedents, taking into account economic and ecological factors. Following national land reform and the nationalisation of pastures, the government prohibited the nomads from deciding for themselves and they were forced to remain on the parcels of land they were assigned by government officials. Nomads with no land or inadequate amounts of land are forced to rent pastures or to settle. Before the 1960s nomads could change and expand their pasture areas with little restriction or limitation, but afterwards they were forced to settle or at best to remain with their groups on inadequate pastures. Rights to pasture set by new laws after the 1960s influenced the composition of residential groups and made familiar, more flexible patterns of co-residence nearly impossible.

Military control of the Qashqa'i changed hands after the revolution of 1979. Although the late Shah's gendarmerie continues to operate, a special unit of Revolutionary Guards called the Tribal Revolutionary Guards (*Sepah-e Pāsdārān-e 'Ashāyer*) supervises tribal affairs. Migratory patterns are largely unaffected by the Islamic regime, and most Qashqa'i , who are still armed, continue to pursue many of their customary forms of migration and subsistence. Because the Qashqa'i society is a dispersed one, it has proved impossible for the central government to dominate it completely or radically alter it.

Excited discussion begins as early as February, but the migration does not actually begin until late March, when the summer pastures are still covered with ice and snow. The Qashqa'i are forced out of their winter pastures by the increasing heat, scarcity of water, growing number of insects and the desire to save some vegetation for their return to the area the next autumn. With spring's arrival, they will leave behind the inconveniences and dangers that winter posed to them and their animals, and during the month between the abandonment of winter camps and their departure there is a feeling of joy, gaiety and restless anticipation in the air.

The migration in the spring and autumn is one of the few times when the nomads meet with other tribal groups and with members of non-Qashqa'i society. The women wear their best, most colourful clothing and jewellery. Animals, especially camels, are decorated with bells, beads and tassels and are covered with fine weavings, which are indications of family wealth.

The customary date of departure from garmsir is 21 March, the first day of spring (the spring equinox). Environmental and climatic conditions often determine an earlier or, less frequently, a later departure. Shortly before the 21st, the tribal leaders co-ordinate the migration and meet with their respective headmen to draw up the migratory schedule, and they in turn meet with elders to impart instructions. The schedule includes the timing and organisation of movement as well as the sequence in which tribal segments leave.

On the day, the encampment members anxiously and respectfully wait for the group's elder to dismantle his tent, which is the signal for the commencement of the migration. Then each household takes down their own tent, each competing with the others to be the first to finish packing and be ready to move. The entire group then moves a short distance. This is done to gauge the proper pace of travel and to allow everyone to make sure that everything is in order and that nothing has been left behind. The following day the migration begins in earnest. Although they do not move every day, when they do the move is begun as early in the morning as possible, partly in order to secure good camping sites later in the day before other migrating groups occupy them. Later, as the weather becomes warmer, the nomads avoid the heat of the day by leaving before sunrise. Herds move out of camp first and always start earlier than people and pack animals.

Moving the herds entails considerable problems. Their number at this time of the year is large, and a close watch has to be kept to prevent animals straying or being stolen. The pace of travel has to be regulated to prevent them from becoming overly tired or engorged with grass. Animals have to be prevented from damaging crops when the route passes through rural areas, especially when and where the balance of power in these areas rests with the sedentary society. If possible, year-old

above
Shesh Baylu (Shesh Boluki) on migration near Firuzābād. The men move first with the herds. Women, children and old men walk or ride on donkeys and mules already loaded with belongings. October 1984.

right
In spring the Qashqa'i move from the lowlands to the highlands of the Zāgros mountains. The 21st of March, the first day of spring, is the customary date of departure for the migration, an eagerly awaited event. March 1985.

male lambs and kids are fattened on the journey because most of them are sold shortly after the nomads' arrival in sarhad. Luckily natural pasture is abundant at this time of year.

The protection of the people and their possessions, including animals, requires the vigilance, support and co-operation of the entire migratory group. Therefore members of tribal sections usually migrate closely together so that they can quickly converge and respond collectively to emergencies. They travel only a few hours a day. One or two men on horseback ride ahead of the rest of the group in order to locate a suitable, safe camping area with adequate water and vegetation nearby. They choose camp sites away from sources of water in order to prevent herds from becoming mixed and to avoid disturbing or confronting other nomads. The amount of time spent camping varies from a few hours to a number of days depending largely on the availability of water and pasture and the distance from the final destination. The headmen usually decide the duration of each stop, but individual families hold the right to decide for themselves whether to stay or to move. During short stops, the pack animals are unloaded and the tent cloth is used for a temporary shelter that can serve for an overnight stay as well. Tents are pitched for a stay of two or more nights. Another reason for staying in one place is for a woman to give birth. Her family postpones the day's migration until after the birth, and then resumes migrating right after if the mother and baby are well. During the migration, infants and newborn lambs and kids are carried in the arms of women and young girls. An infant is carried on its mother's back wrapped in a cloth folded into a triangle, with the ends passing over the shoulders, crossing over the chest, under the arms and tied at the back. Small children who cannot walk long distances are attached two by two and ride donkeys or mules.

The Qashqa'i also periodically stay long enough in one place to convert milk into yoghurt, butter and clarified butter, part of which they sell or trade in markets and villages. However, most of the milk is saved for the young animals, who arrive in sarhad fattened on mother's milk and fresh green grass.

Several rivers have to be crossed on the journey. Where they exist, the nomads use main roads and bridges to cross rivers and streams, but with difficulty because of traffic congestion and because many motorists do not exercise caution with the nomads' herds. Otherwise, they cross at shallow places and on the backs of horses and pack animals. On rare occasions they float across rivers by inflating the goat skin bags normally used for storing water. When crossing a shallow

A Shesh Baylu (Shesh Boluki) family on migration. The women travel in all their finery and make a magnificent spectacle. The fullness of their skirts is accentuated by a band of organza ruffles sewn along the lower edge. October 1984.

river some of the men form a chain to help the women, children and animals to cross, and others stand downstream to retrieve animals and other possessions that might be swept away. The camels, horses, mules and donkeys cross first. Goats are pulled by their horns and used to induce the rest of the herds to follow.

The climate in miānband at the time of the spring migration is mild. The area has become heavily cultivated since the 1960s land reform and excellent pastures are now few. Miānband is a cross road and meeting place for Qashqa'i of different tribal sections. It has also served as a place of refuge for outlaws because of its mountainous terrain and dense savannah-type vegetation, and is the favoured place for women to gather herbs and other wild plants.

Qashqa'i migrate through Borun Dameh. Borun Dameh means 'mountain protruding into the plain', and the mountain is Kuh-e Barfi near Shirāz. A cement factory constructed along this mountain in the 1940s serves as a landmark. The suburbs of Shirāz have grown so dramatically since the mid-1960s that they block passage through Borun Dameh and force the nomads to cross the Kuh-e Barfi by passes or to traverse its slopes. On the route there are a number of very important archeological and historic sites, which include Bishapur, the Sassanid capital, the monumental rock reliefs at Naqsh-e Rostam, the ceremonial palace of the Achaemenids at Persepolis (fifth century BC) and the Sassanid rock relief carved on the cliffs above Tang-Āb River near Firuzābād. Many Qashqa'i halt their migrations long enough to travel to Shirāz to purchase goods and services of various kinds. Until the 1950s usually only men made this trip. In the 1960s and 1970s women began to accompany them in greater numbers. At first women and children travelled to town only for medical care and to visit relatives settled there, but now, increasingly, they go to shop in the Shirāz bazaar.

The summer pastures are located in the high valleys and plateaux of the Zāgros Mountains, many of the peaks of which extend to 11,000 feet (3,600 metres), and the spectacular Mount Dinā to 14,465 feet (4,409 metres). The valleys begin at altitudes of 6,500–8,000 feet (2,000–2,500 metres. (An altitude of 8,000 feet [2,500 metres] marks the limit for year-round habitation.) Because the best spring and summer pastures are located at the higher altitudes, pastoral productivity increases with altitude up to a height of 10,000 feet (3,000 metres). Most Qashqa'i nomadic pastoralists are found at an altitude of 6,500 feet (2,000 metres) in the summer.

Most precipitation in sarhad is in the form of snow, which begins to melt with the coming of spring and the slow rise in temperature. This precipitation provides the land of sarhad with a reservoir of moisture, and, aided by cool weather which persists throughout summer, produces luxuriant vegetation of a steppe variety. The cold period begins with rainfall in the autumn that is followed by snowfall throughout winter. Thus the period of active vegetation growth is limited to the spring and summer seasons, the time of the utilisation of pastoral resources in this mountainous area. The stay in sarhad is only a few months because of the early onset of wind, cold and snow, and because the quantities of grazing and natural fuel are limited. There used to be a dense forest in sarhad (Garrod 1946a: 35–6) but the area is now deforested and the nomads have to burn dried camel dung, shrubs and bushes.

Contacts with sedentary society in sarhad are more frequent than in garmsir, largely because of the intensity of economic activity in late spring and early summer. Since the national land reforms of the 1960s, Qashqa'i pastoralists have lost much of their summer grazing land and have gradually become a minority in an area now legally and spatially controlled by sedentary, mostly non-Qashqa'i, farmers. Most valleys, as well as most land near sources of water, are cultivated, with the result that the pastures available to nomads have become progressively smaller and further apart. Since the late 1960s, agriculturalists in the area have taken to raising sheep and goats themselves, and these people and herds, along with thousands of herds belonging to commercial city-based herd owners, come to exploit most of the free pastures. Qashqa'i pastoralists are forced to arrive at sarhad early in the spring in order to locate and protect pastures, since the good grass is usually gone by May. Nomads are increasingly obliged to use supplementary feed for their animals, a costly and complicated undertaking. Kuchuk Kashkullu do not spend more than two months in summer pastures under these new conditions. Some Qashqa'i cultivate cereals in sarhad and a few have established orchards of fruit trees. Some have settled in sarhad and lessened their reliance on pastoralism in favour of agriculture.

In sarhad the nomads pitch their tents, the 'summer yurt'[6] (*tawsān yurdu*), in a central site close to water at the bottom of hills. The roof of the tent is flat, and one long side is kept open to facilitate the passage of air in hot weather. The front of the tent is decorated with colourful ropes and tassels. Although they remain in the same general area, the position of the tents is shifted several times for hygienic purposes and to be closer to new grass. Summer encampments are sometimes larger than those of winter, and tents are within view of one another.

Women spend part of the summer processing the abundance of milk, and they take advantage of the quality and quantity of water to dye yarn for weaving projects planned for the summer and the following autumn and winter. Summer is the time for festive wedding ceremonies because of the good weather and the cash available from animal sales. As soon as cold winds begin to blow and grazing disappears, preparations are made for the return to garmsir. The customary time of departure is September. Some Qashqa'i usually start migrating earlier, towards the end of August, while Darrashurlu and Buyug Kashkullu can only migrate two or three weeks later, in the middle of September, because of the limitations of their winter pastures.

The organisation and formation of camps during the autumn migration differ from those of spring, and show a dramatic contrast to them. In the spring the aim is to disperse as much as possible to exploit the abundant vegetation, but during the autumn, when natural grazing is lacking, larger groups are formed which closely follow the paths of those ahead of them. In the spring the nomads are pressured by cultivators to keep their herds out of cultivated fields, while in the autumn the herds are free to move through the valleys where fields have long been harvested. In order to supervise the flocks, the spring camps are set high up on slopes, where water is plentiful, away from cultivated areas, but the autumn camps are set up in flat valley bottoms to be near wells and to supervise flocks dispersed in harvested fields. The springs found during the spring migration are usually dry by the time of the nomads' autumn passage.

The autumn migration is thus a time of scarcity, both of water and vegetation. Although the herds are now small it is still difficult to feed them. The paucity of vegetation forces the goats to eat thorny bushes, and the other animals are fed hay, straw and clover. The nomads camp where they

Camels carry the heaviest loads on the migration, including the tent and tent poles, and are only ever ridden by women. The Qashqa'i do not give their camels names nor are they branded. They are recognized by their appearance and individual behaviour. Shesh Baylu (Shesh Boluki) travelling towards their summer pastures west of Ābādeh, 1984.

find water and usually they migrate no longer than two or three hours a day. When crossing over mountains, however, they travel as many as ten hours a day in order to avoid camping in locations that fall on the route of other migrating groups. As in the spring, women and children gather wild foods such as nuts and fruits, and men trade pastoral produce for the products of local villagers.

Despite the difficulties the Qashqa'i are in no hurry to arrive early at garmsir, where water and vegetation are scarce as well, and during years when autumn conditions in garmsir are dry and hot, they exploit all available resources, including grass, stubble in fields and tree leaves, in order to try to extend the migration. Garmsir covers a vast, sprawling area through which pass major communication routes. A road goes from Shirāz to Firuzābād, the Qashqa'i 'capital city', and another links Shirāz with Bandar 'Abbās through the towns of Jahrom, Qir, Evaz and Lār.

Garmsir starts at the narrow coastal plain along the Persian Gulf and rises up into 'tangled hills' which are deeply dissected by storm-water channels and small streams that dry up in summer. Meagre springs offer brackish sulphurous water (Garrod 1946: 32). The height of the hills ranges from 1,000 to 2,300 feet above sea level (300 to 700 metres). Valleys start at 330 feet (100 metres)

and have an average altitude of 1,000–1,300 feet (300–400 metres). The hill slopes are steep and the valleys are narrow.

Until the 1950s and early 1960s, parts of garmsir contained thick forests of jujube trees (*konār*), but now only a few scattered pockets of these trees remain. Wild almond trees no taller than bushes are still plentiful. Because of the low levels of precipitation the vegetation is far from luxuriant and drinking water is in short supply, especially before the onset of the winter rains. During a rainy winter, the pastures flourish and vegetation reaches its optimal growth before the beginning of spring. The new grass appears after the first rains. With spring's arrival, the rain ceases, temperatures begin to rise and all plants except thorny ones wilt and die. After a good autumn and winter, the grass grows as much as a metre and covers large areas. There are more years of poor rainfall than good.

Land in garmsir is fertile (except in most areas of the territories of the Darrashurlu and Buyug Kashkullu), specially when precipitation is high. In garmsir it is the Qashqa'i practice to cultivate cereals and a few grow citrus fruits and date palms. However, the heat and humidity, particularly in summer, inhibit the development of year-round settled life, so that the agricultural settlements in the area are usually small and poor. The valleys and plains at lower altitudes than those used by the nomads would have been settled centuries ago by farming peoples if sufficient water had been available. The Qashqa'i camp in the hills, which are unsuitable for crops, and follow a pattern of pasture utilisation that maximises the exploitation and conservation of vegetal resources. When they arrive in the autumn, they set up camps on sites they call the 'autumn yurt' (*fayez yurdu*) on those parts of the plains where there is still some dried vegetation to be found. After the first rainfalls and a drop in temperature, the camps are moved into the mountains where there is protection against thunderstorms and heavy winter rains and winds. This camp site is termed the 'winter yurt' (*qesh yurdu; qeshlaq*) and the nomads stay there until the spring. The shallow pools (*goro*) that have been constructed in previous years close to their encampments for the collection of rain water for their animals are quickly repaired and improved. For their personal use the nomads prefer the rain water that accumulates in pools in crevices (*qaqlugh*).

With the approach of spring around the forty-fifth day of winter, or shortly thereafter, when the temperature over the mountains begins to rise and pastures become depleted of vegetation, the nomads move their camps down to sites in the plains they call the 'spring yurt' (*yaz yurdu*), which is a different site to that used in autumn.

In winter camps the tents are pitched close to one another, but the camps themselves are scattered over a wide pasture area in order to take advantage of sites naturally protected by hills and gorges. Because they are in close proximity in a single camp, people can provide immediate support and assistance to one another during the most difficult period of the year. Towards spring, people assemble in larger camps prior to the spring migration.

The semi-annual migrations, called by Barth (1961: 153) 'the central rite of nomadic society', bring together family members who at other times of the year see little of each other. Usually members of single sub-tribes migrate more or less together, perhaps a few days apart, using similar schedules and routes. When these groups are not migrating, they split into various units and are often separated by wide distances. The groups are tightly organised to protect people, animals and belongings as they pass through potentially hostile territory. The number of families travelling together within a migratory unit is a sign of strength and an indication of the loyalty and political affiliation of group members. Nevertheless, families are constantly being lost from the group on the journey, for a variety of reasons. Families may remain behind to help a woman in childbirth or when animals are lost, or just move faster than the general pace of travel. Some, particularly the poorest, who own few pack animals, may inevitably fall behind. Some families may move faster in order to reach sarhad early and others slow down to allow men who have remained in garmsir to catch up with them. Each family makes its own decisions concerning these issues, independently of the headman.

The migration provides Qashqa'i families opportunities to engage in large-scale social interactions. They affirm their relationships with headmen and elders by camping and migrating with them. Those who have married outside their groups are able to visit relatives. Women renew and expand their social ties by visiting their natal families and more distant relatives they are not able see at other times of the year. Men and some women make trips to cities during the migration.

The problems of traversing potentially hostile territory bring Qashqa'i families close to one

A young camel being trained to carry loads. During the training session it is hobbled and the burden, initially very light, is increased by degrees over a period of time.

another and temporarily enable them to be free of the competition over access to and exploitation of seasonal pastures. It is a time for the reinforcement of a distinct socio-cultural and tribal identity, an opportunity for those Qashqa'i whose lives revolve around members of small family groups during the rest of the year to sharpen their awareness of being members of a large, complex society.

Qashqa'i use Turkish and Persian terms, Turk and Tajik, to describe themselves and others in the region. Turk and Tajik look down on one another's principal mode of subsistence. They compete for access to and exploitation of land. When a Qashqa'i abandons nomadism for village life, he loses his status in the eyes of Turks for becoming integrated into Tajik society (*tat oldi*). For Qashqa'i being Tajik is synonymous with being weak and desiring only material possessions. The Qashqa'i poet Mazun (1857–1925) says: 'Too long have I stayed in Paskohak, where I have turned yellow, weak, impotent and taken on the nature of Tajiks'.

TRANSPORTATION

Pack animals are the basic means of transportation during migrations and are highly regarded. The Qashqa'i use camels, mules, donkeys and horses as pack animals. Camels and mules carry the heaviest loads, camels transporting tent cloths, tent poles and heavy woven bags. Camels, mules and donkeys transport the women and children. Horses of lesser quality are used for transporting loads and for agriculture, those of better quality being reserved for riding. On occasion individual Qashqa'i will carry loads themselves. Pack animals are not ordinarily protected from thunderstorms or cold weather.

The wealth of a family is indicated by the number and quality of their animals. The wealthiest have camels, mules and horses, those less wealthy mules and donkeys, and the poorest only donkeys. For the Qashqa'i it is a matter of prestige to own and ride good horses, especially thoroughbreds. Most of the Qashqa'i's Arab horses were introduced by members of the Darrashurlu tribe, which has winter quarters close to the Arabs of Khuzestān. The main breeds are Khersan, Sharak, Saglaveh, Vaznah and Obaida. The saddle (*hagar*) they use, which they buy in town from a saddle-maker, is a faithful reproduction of a type used by European cavalry at the end of the nineteenth century. At the age of one year horses are branded on the hindquarter. These brands are sometimes passed from father to son. The mane and tail are also cut at this time. Unlike the other pack animals, horses are protected in inclement weather by shelters (*kamer*, *kapar*) consisting of a stone wall roofed with branches and reeds. In normal weather a circle of thorny bushes is used at night.

Camels are thought of as sensitive, noble and faithful animals. They are pampered, petted and spoken to with affection and respect and are not marked or branded. Only women ride them, never men. The Qashqa'i breed only the one-humped Arabian camel (*Camelus dromedarius*) and do not cross-breed them with the two-humped Bactrian camel to raise hybrids. Newborn camels are wrapped up and strapped to their mother's back on migration. They begin carrying light training loads when still quite young. When older, on migration, they are used for the large baggage and heavy goods, and to carry women. Swift camels are not heavily laden. Old and troublesome camels are sold. The camel saddle (*jahaz*) has a single pad over the hump and resembles the north Arabian saddle, but differs from it in having horizontal sticks on each side that are about 8 inches (20 cm) longer than the width of the saddle. If the load to be transported is not heavy the saddle is supported only by a simple stomach-band.

The national land reforms in the 1960s led to an increase in the amount of land under cultivation and so the Qashqa'i had to keep a close watch on their camels' grazing habits. Some hired drovers, but others sold their camels, preferring to use donkeys and mules or even rented trucks and vans. However, since the 1980s the number of camels has increased dramatically due to the fact that a demand for camel meat has developed.

Jeeps and trucks were introduced after the Second World War by wealthy leaders who purchased them in Tehran, and as road building continued most wealthy Qashqa'i also bought them. Since the 1960s many Qashqa'i have rented trucks and vans in order to transport their heavy belongings, and sometimes people (young children, elderly men and some women), between seasonal pastures. Some families have bought four-wheel drives, vans or pickup trucks and use them for transportation between garmsir and sarhad.

A man of the Amala tribe near Kāzerun at the beginning of the migration to their summer quarters. It is a matter of pride and prestige to own fine riding-horses, which receive special attention and are protected from inclement weather. Horses, unlike camels, are branded and given individual names.

Smoke rising from the winter tent of a Darrashurlu family. The goat hair tent cloth has an open weave which allows smoke to pass through. When wet, the cloth shrinks and it becomes fairly waterproof. The ability of the cloth to resist rain diminishes as it becomes worn. The winter tent is better suited to harsh weather. It differs from the summer tent in having a ridge along its length which helps the rain to run off. The ridge is formed by several narrow wooden planks supported on poles. Newborn lambs and kids are often brought inside the winter tent for protection. Near Bushehr, 1988.

THE TENT

The black goat hair tent used by the Qashqa'i is rectangular in plan and well-suited to their mobile lifestyle. It is light, easily transported and can be pitched and dismantled relatively quickly. The term *qara chador* (black tent) is used for it.

The size of a tent tends to indicate the social status and wealth of the family that own it, as do the quality of the tent cloth (as indicated by the regularity and uniformity of the weave) and the kind of wood used for the poles. However families of widely differing means can have tents looking very much alike, for there are no rules governing what size and shape a tent may be, and in practice there is considerable variation.

Every family makes its own tent. The tent cloth, woven by women, consists of narrow strips of plain-woven goat hair 12–20 inches (30–50 cm) wide and 20–50 feet (6–15 metres) long which are sewn together by men into large panels. The roof panel and side panels are joined to each other with wooden pins (*chelal*) carved from wild pistachio wood, and the whole structure is supported by poles. The material woven for the roof of the tent has a tighter weave than that used for the sides. It has the remarkable property of being sufficiently open to allow smoke to escape, yet in the rain the hair, impregnated with natural lanolin, contracts to form a virtually waterproof surface.

When the tent is erected the roof panel is supported by two parallel rows of poles, one along the back of the tent and one along the front. A small tent has poles 6–7 feet (180–210 cm) long whereas a rich man's tent can have poles twice that length. The roof is kept tightly stretched by guy ropes fastened to pieces of carved wood (*dom sukh*) attached to its edge by loops of goat hair rope at the points where the poles are placed. The guy ropes are tied to stakes hammered into the ground. Side panels are attached to the roof panel by wooden pins.

The external form of the tent varies according to the time of year and to the conditions on migration. In summer the tent is closed on one long side (the back) and on the two short sides. The other long side (the front) remains completely open. The roof panel is flat and the three side panels hang to within a few inches of the ground to allow air to circulate in the hot weather. To make more shade, a narrow, woven goat hair band is sometimes attached to the edge of the roof panel at the front of the tent and laid across the guy ropes. A reed mat or screen of special construction extends beyond and in line with the short sides of the tent to act as a screen and windbreak. It is held in place by short poles hammered into the ground. Brightly coloured ropes and tassels are also a feature of the summer tent.

The summer tent is used on migration but is only pitched when a stop longer than one day is planned or when the weather is poor. If rain threatens, the roof is raised into a ridge to allow run-off. Improvised temporary shelters are also used to give protection from wind and perhaps light rain. Typically a single tent panel is laid over four poles or across a tripod.

The winter form of tent is actually used in late autumn and winter. It is closed on all four sides and only a small opening for entrance and exit is left in one shorter side. On very cold days this opening is closed by a reed mat. The tent cloth comes down very close to the ground but does not touch it. Reed mats, because they are cheaper than tent cloth, are used at the bottom to seal the tent against the weather. The roof is given a central ridge along its full length to allow water to run off easily. The ridge is formed by a line of narrow planks supported by poles which makes the ridge about 3 feet (1 metre) higher than the walls. The guy ropes are often tied to forked branches held on the ground by heavy stones, which gives stability in rainy, muddy and windy conditions.

The work of pitching and striking a tent is done in a fixed order to simplify the task, and it takes two hours to put up a tent and less to take it down. The heavy work, such as carrying the tent poles and lifting the large roof panel, is done by men, while women and older children assist by pinning on the side panels and fastening the ropes. If there is an elder son to help his father then the women and older children do not do any of the heavy work. If there is no older son a woman helps her husband wrap and unwrap the tent, place the poles under it, attach the guy ropes to stakes and hammer them.

The site of an encampment as well as the individual spot where the tent is pitched are both described by a single term—*yurd*. In garmsir, where rain can be expected, a sloping spot is usually chosen and a level platform of packed earth (*saku*) constructed. In sarhad, as there is no rain during summer, a flat spot is chosen. The sites are mostly the same each year. Most Qashqa'i families return year after year to camp sites where they, their parents, and often their grandparents, have pitched their tents before.

above
Shesh Baylu (Shesh Boluki) women weaving outside their summer tent. The summer tent, which is open at the front, is made with strips of woven goat hair sewn and pinned together and erected on rows of poles along the length of the tent. The roof is flat and stretched tight. Near Ābādeh, 1984.

left
The sides of the summer tent are kept several centimeters from the ground and are attached to the roof with small wooden pins.

opposite above
A tent erected in its cool weather form with a ridged roof. The cane or reed screen here extends beyond the sides of the tent to serve as a wind break. Darrashurlu, 1984.

opposite below
A tent has been pitched during the migration. It usually takes the form of a summer tent and may only be pitched when nomads plan a stop longer than a day or when weather conditions are poor. If rain threatens, the roof is raised to a peak to allow run-off. When no tent is erected, temporary shelter from wind and light rain can be obtained by putting a strip of tent cloth over four poles or draping it over a tripod. Darrashurlu, spring 1986. (See p. 222)

A large tent belonging to Ahangar Rostami, seen here with his wife. He, as headman of the Ahangar section of the Shesh Baylu (Shesh Boluki) tribe, is wealthier than the average headman and has a tent of corresponding size. The piled rug in the foreground has a traditional Shesh Boluki design called *kaleh asbi*. 1989

The tents within each encampment are usually erected to face in the same direction, preferably to the north-east to take advantage of the warmth of the rising sun in the morning and to avoid the hot sun of the afternoon. This ensures that no tent faces the entrance of any other and gives privacy to families living close by one another. Life in and around the tent is directed towards the front and visitors always approach from there so that they can be observed, even if it means making a large circle to do so. It is actually an unnecessary precaution in view of the fact that dogs guard each tent, making surprise appearances unlikely.

The layout inside the tent is always the same. A protective row of stones is arranged along the back wall of the tent to raise goods off the ground. Three to four courses of stones are used in garmsir, where winter rains can make the ground wet and muddy. The structure (*uk dashu*, *yurd dashu*) is a symbol of the home and family. The large bags and storage sacks that contain most of the family's household goods are placed on the stones to keep them off the ground. Bedding and woven items, all neatly folded, are put on top of the sacks in an orderly pile and the pile is then covered with a *gelim* or *jajim*. In some tents the pillows are covered with white cloth and a wide band of brightly coloured fabric. The whole baggage and bedding pile is called *uk*, *aiy* and *ikimas*. The pile may extend along the left wall (facing out from inside). Along the right wall women usually store food and stack up their cooking equipment, sometimes throwing an old felt rug over them.

For longer stays small stones and gravel are spread on the ground inside the tent, and outside in front as well. The floor of the tent is usually covered with felt rugs (*namad*) or cotton rugs (*zilu*), both made in towns and villages. If a family has pile rugs they will be spread out to receive guests, though wealthy families may have them on the floor all the time.

The organisation of the space within the tent is regulated by time-honoured customs. Though there is no physical barrier, an invisible boundary exists between the men's and women's areas. The women carry on their work on the right (facing out from inside), baking bread, cooking and preparing milk products. Water containers hang from the pole to the back on the right side and firewood is stored along the adjacent wall, and nearby is kept a woven bag containing bread-making equipment. If there is a baby its hammock (*nane*) will be slung in the women's area. Women control many of the objects and activities in and around the tent, though they cannot be said to own it, for the tent is not part of the dowry they bring with them on marriage. When men are in the tent they sit by the fire on the left side (facing out from inside). It is here that a host prepares tea for himself and his guests. There is another division within the tent, an upper part, the place of honour, and a lower part near the entrance. The tent is the centre of the daily activities of both men and women.

The hearth (*ojaq*, *qazma*) is the symbolic centre of the tent and family. When a tent has been pitched, a man digs a fire pit some 8 inches (20 cm) deep and lines it with three or more flat stones to prevent the sides crumbling. The hearth in summer is at the entrance to the tent towards the left, and in winter it occupies a central position inside. Most tents have a second cooking hearth constructed by the women, though the small tent of a poor family may have only one. It is the fire of the main hearth which warms the tent at night in winter. On a cold night family members take turns to attend the fire, uncover live coals from the ashes with tongs and spread them out to provide more heat.

During the hours of darkness the tent is lit with kerosene lanterns, either the simple type with a wick or the more expensive pressurised type. Since the late 1970s bottled gas has come into use and a few wealthy families have acquired electrical generators At bedtime, a few hours after sunset, women and girls lay out bedding on the ground in front of the baggage pile where everyone will sleep in a row, side by side. Blankets are layered on top of the sleepers, in effect making a single bed. Husband and wife may sleep in the middle surrounded by their children (girls on the right and boys on the left) in ascending order of age, eldest on the outside, or they sleep at the ends with the young children huddled in the middle so that they can attend to their chores without waking them. The family rises at dawn or just before.

When a newly married son and his bride are with the family they sleep either behind the baggage pile on the far left or behind a temporary curtain hung on a rope for the night. It is here on the left that a bride usually stores her dowry goods and the possessions she is accumulating for her future independent household.

SHELTERS, HUTS AND HOUSES

In winter some protection is needed for the animals against rain, wind, snow and predators, so shelters are built out of stones and covered with branches and reeds. Special protection for new-born, sick and weak animals is also given in the form of a tent or other temporary shelter. A few families build single-room stone huts for storage.

Until the 1920s permanent structures were rare in Qashqa'i territory, but the remains of some early buildings belonging to paramount leaders still exist. A fortified settlement with thick mud walls and massive rounded towers called the Parian Fortress can be seen at Qir-va-Kārzin. There is also the Jāniābād fortress near Farrāshband, built for Hajji Nasrollah Khān (?–1896) by non-Qashqa'i workers. It includes a fortified stone tower that was plastered on the outside, a majestic house and a large bath-house. During his rule (1918–33) Ismā'il Khān Soulat ad-Douleh built a splendid residence (Bāgh-e Hezāreh) near Firuzābād, now ruined. He also built a twenty-room guest-house and a stable at Chāh Kāzemeh in garmsir.

In the early 1930s Rezā Shah Pahlavi tried to force all the nomads in Iran to settle. Military forces banned seasonal migrations and the Qashqa'i were made to stay wherever they happened to be. When Rezā Shah abdicated in 1941, the great majority destroyed the houses they had been forced to occupy and resumed their nomadic life. The Qashqa'i , who despise permanent dwellings, call these terrible years 'the time of the wood doors' (*takhta-qapu*). Since then the Qashqa'i have become subject to new pressures which have caused them to settle in both sarhad and garmsir where they build houses of the type typically found in rural Iran. The poorer families have houses of beaten

A Shesh Baylu (Shesh Boluki) woman inside a rudimentary mud-walled hut covered with tent cloth. She belongs to a group of families which move very little. The interior is organised in the same way as a tent. Both men and women smoke tobacco, but only women of advanced years will smoke in public. Near Ābādeh, summer 1984.

earth or sun-dried brick consisting of a single room, often arranged like the inside of a tent. Sometimes they add a length of tent cloth pitched on poles along the front to give shade. At the other extreme, wealthy families own brick houses, usually in garmsir, with many rooms, running water and even electricity.

LIVESTOCK HUSBANDRY

The pastoral economy of the Qashqa'i is based on the periodic sale and exchange of animals and animal products in village and city markets. The market value of sheep is twice that of goats and they are looked after with greater care. The sheep are of the fat-tailed variety (hairy, black-faced, horned and with lop-ears). With excellent pasture they are highly productive. On the other hand goats are more hardy than sheep and can survive when conditions are poor and pasture scanty. Families with access only to poor pastures keep goats with a few sheep, or goats alone, and those families which do not migrate and stay all year in the summer pastures raise only goats.

No reliable information is available on the number of animals owned by the Qashqa'i at any given time. According to available figures, in the early 1940s they owned approximately 660,000 sheep and goats, 22,000 horses, 58,000 donkeys and 18,000 camels (Razmara 1944: 115). If we take these approximate figures and assume that they tripled in the prosperous years following the Second World War, then by the late 1950s the Qashqa'i could have owned 2 million sheep and goats. More recent sources (National Centre of Statistics of Iran, 1980) estimate that in 1978 there were 874,000 sheep and 976,000 goats in Fārs province, and the Nomad Census of 1987 has figures of 1.3 million sheep, 1.6 million goats, 9,000 cattle, 1,800 camels and 47,000 donkeys and mules, but there is no way of knowing how accurate these figures are.

The erratic climate and lack of effective disease control make the pastoral economy a fragile, 'high-risk' one (Loeffler 1977: 270). Bad years occur more often than good ones and every eight to ten years south Iran is hit by a severe drought. After a drought in 1961 and a decline in the market for sheep skins, attempts were made to find means of reducing the impact of the unpredictable climate. Inoculation was introduced for the prevention of disease, greater use made of supplementary fodder, and rams were no longer chosen for the colour of their fleece in an attempt to find strains more resistant to drought conditions and extremes of temperature. Another drought in 1971 made it a catastrophic year and affected the Buyug Kashkullu and Darrashurlu tribes worst of all. The winter of 1980–1 was also considered bad because the first rain of the winter season did not fall until January 1981, two to three months later than usual, and then there was little of it.

By tradition, rights to pasture are held by individuals and passed from father to son, or may be granted by tribal leaders to those politically affiliated to them. Since the national land reform of 1963 pasture rights have been granted by the government. Those holding pasture rights work by themselves and do not combine their flocks with others or form family or camp co-operatives as a mean of solving labour problems. Mutual assistance is only given when animals are lost or stolen or are being sheared or branded.

The size of a flock (*bor* P., *suru* T.) depends on the quality of the pasture available. In fact the flock size remains fairly constant and is in effect the maximum number of animals which can be kept on the available pasture when it is grazed one section at a time in sequence, a method which involves movement within a general area both in sarhad and garmsir in addition to the main seasonal migration. The flock is led by a male goat chosen for his height, length of hair and the beauty of his horns. At three he is castrated, becomes calm and obedient and learns to obey the orders of the shepherd who makes a specific sound for each movement required. He is treated with care, his hair allowed to grow long and he wears a large bell on a strap round his neck. For a mixed flock of 400 sheep and goats, three or four such animals are needed. Protection of the flock is provided by shepherd dogs which are kept in addition to the camp dogs. They are not used to direct or assemble the animals, but to deter predators and thieves. Dogs and horses are the only animals given personal names.

Shearing takes place once a year, soon after arrival in sarhad. The sheep are first washed in a river or stream to clean their wool and then, after a few days of drying, are shorn by means of *dokar* (shears with two metal blades) made by gypsies. One man holds the animal while another shears it and they take turns throughout the day in order to maintain the pace. Alternatively the legs may be tied. Branding is done a few days before the spring migration, a time when the animals come into close contact with other animals and are most at risk of being lost. Wooden-handled cast-iron branding irons are used and are made to order by gypsies.

Sick and injured animals are treated both by modern methods, available in veterinary centres, and by traditional methods, or a combination of the two. A fractured shoulder is treated by wrapping the animals in an old felt rug with four holes for the limbs and sewing the edges together. A mid-leg fracture is stabilised with two sticks wrapped around with cloth and tied with yarn. Other fractures are treated with a cast made out of gum tragacanth, flour and water. It stays in place for a month.

Animals are rarely killed and eaten by the nomads themselves, contrary to popular belief, except on special occasions such as weddings, funerals and the arrival of special guests. Animals products too are consumed sparingly because of their economic importance. For example, raw milk is made into yoghurt and cheese, never sold. Fresh yoghurt is not sold either but processed into such products as butter, yoghurt paste (*masopus*), dried curds (*kashk*) and dehydrated paste (*qaraqurut*); these are discussed in the section on food. Qashqa'i prefer to transform their butter into clarified butter (*yagh*) because it keeps longer and is more profitable to sell or barter. Many families trade clarified butter for rice as the Qashqa'i migrate northwards in the spring through rice-producing areas around Shirāz. They take the rice with them, make the clarified butter during their residence in sarhad and give the amount they owe when they pass through the area again during their autumn migration. Families with only a few animals sell all the clarified butter they produce, those

Morning milking during the migration, north of Shirāz. Milking is done by one or two women who squat on the ground with a receptacle between their legs. Sheep are milked before goats but Qashqa'i women mix the milk of both together. Spring 1988.

with numerous animals their surplus, and those families with a man having an important political or social role involving the frequent entertainment of guests may even buy from others.

Goat hair and sheep's wool are of special importance in the nomadic economy and are both sold (or traded) and converted into more valuable woven goods. Some goats produce a fine underwool (*kork*) which is obtained by combing them with a large wooden comb made by gypsies. This is sold to make felt, mohair (*termeh*) and other fine fabrics. Other animal products include fleeces and goat, kid and lamb skins, which are made into bags and sacks, and horns, which are used for knife handles and sticks. The children collect sheep's knucklebones for games.

The time for selling animals is between late spring and the end of summer, especially after arrival in sarhad. Formerly animals were only sold to non-Qashqa'i animal buyers (*chubdar*) who visited the encampments but since the 1970s animals have also been driven to highways, transported to cities in rented vans or trucks and sold directly to buyers at caravanserais or government slaughterhouses. At the slaughterhouse, workers form the animals into pairs and select one pair at random. The weight of this pair is used as the basis for calculating the overall price, on which the seller must pay a government tax.

Nomads who have difficulty surviving as independent pastoralists can continue their nomadic livelihood and make a profit by entering into a contract (*nimsud*) with a merchant. The most common arrangement is for a merchant to entrust a number of animals to the care of a nomad for a stated period of time. Contracts run from six months to six years and during this time the shepherd cares for all the needs of the animals. At the end of the period the animals are sold and the profit divided equally between the two parties.

Cash has become essential in Qashqa'i society and with it the money-lender. In both garmsir and sarhad, merchants, whose role has increasingly become that of money-lender, create long-term relationships which sometimes stretch back to the previous generation. The nomads always need wheat flour, sugar and tea, and from time to time they buy rice, salt, animal feed, cloth, clothing, metalwork and leather goods. However they rarely have the necessary cash because they only have a cash income once a year so they borrow it from the retailers or their relatives who act as money-lenders. Goods are given to the nomads on credit with a promise that they will pay when their animals are sold. The interest charged is from 30 to 50 per cent per year. In practice the full sum may not be repaid so the trading relationship continues.

AGRICULTURE

Although the practice of agriculture enables the Qashqa'i to reduce their dependence on the sedentary population, they face a number of severe problems in this area. The best land does not belong to them any more but to absentee, often urban-based, non-Qashqa'i and to non-Qashqa'i villagers. Their cultivated lands are subject to encroachment and they often leave guards on them while they migrate and reside in other seasonal pastures. Because generally they are still far from roads they have difficulty in bringing harvesters to their crops, and because they lack storage space they are often obliged to sell their grain cheaply and to buy it back later at higher prices. Lastly, few Qashqa'i are able to acquire loans from banks or agricultural credit associations and they are therefore forced to borrow money at high interest rates from money-lenders.

The land is extremely fertile and if conditions are right the nomads can grow up to three crops a year, one in garmsir and two in sarhad. As the harvests in garmsir can be twice as large as in sarhad, most Qashqa'i prefer to cultivate there. In garmsir cereals ripen in five months. However, if rain only falls in winter, the crop will have insufficient water for its growth and maturity.

Wheat and barley are grown in garmsir, sarhad and miānband, often side by side. Bread made from wheat flour is the Qashqa'i staple food. Barley is used as animal feed except by those who are poor. Fruit trees are also grown and this will be described later in the section.

Dry farming is the most popular form of farming, but there is some irrigated farming in both garmsir and sarhad. Those landowners who dig wells and install motorised pumps find themselves compensated by rising land values. The ploughing is done with draft animals after the first rain has moistened the land. Different plough types are used for garmsir and sarhad. In garmsir a light-weight, two-handled plough is used that the nomads make themselves. In sarhad, because the soil is hard and heavy, they use a strong one-handled plough that they buy in town. Tractors

Cooking the evening meal during a short stop on the downward migration. Amala tribe, autum 1987.

have been in limited use since the 1960s, Qashqa'i contracting their sedentary neighbours who own them to do the ploughing.

The seed that is used is saved from a previous harvest or is bought in town. It is stored in a white cloth bag sewn by women from purchased cloth. The fields are surrounded with barriers of rock or thorny branches to protect them, particularly from grazing herds and wild pigs. Pillars of stone are constructed to frighten away birds and animals and are the only kind of scarecrow the nomads use.

Harvesting (*bichmag*) is done by hand with a sickle. In garmsir the reapers start work before sunrise and stop in the early morning and then work again from the late afternoon through the night. This is in order to avoid the harsh sun and high temperatures of that time of year. As the cereals, mainly wheat, are not ripe in garmsir at the time the nomads need to migrate to sarhad, some men stay behind or return from the migration in order to harvest. Their families, herds and belongings are left in the care of others (see Curzon 1892: 112). The harvested crops in garmsir are immediately moved to a secure area and covered with thorny bushes to protect them, while in sarhad they are transported to the threshing ground on braided mats pulled by donkeys.

The threshing ground is usually located near the fields and has a post in the middle of it. The harvested sheaves are spread around the post and the threshing is done by mules and donkeys connected to it by a cord and metal ring. They circle the post trampling the stalks with their hooves and breaking the seeds from them as they go. A man holds the animals' harnesses and urges them on. When this process is complete the threshed grain is winnowed by throwing it into the air with a fork. The wind blows the chaff away and the grain falls to the ground. The grain is collected, sieved and then piled on a cloth to be weighed.

The planting of fruit trees was a form of land exploitation encouraged by the government in the early 1960s, and agricultural co-operatives and banks offered loans at low interest rates. Many Darrashurlu particularly have benefited. They began planting apple trees in their sarhad in the mid-1960s and their orchards now provide them with an income more important than that derived from herding and the cultivation of cereals. Qaisar Aqa, headman of the Nari'i subtribe of the Darrashurlu, recounts the story of how orchard production in the Darrashurlu sarhad began:

"In the early 1960s, the government wanted to sedentarise the nomadic Turks and encourage them to do agriculture. The government announced that loans would be given to any Qashqa'i who would make gardens. The two important Darrashurlu leaders (*kalāntar*), Ziād Khān and Ayāz Khān, were the first ones to get credit in 1964–5. Then, as government money was involved, they were obliged to make orchards. Ayāz Khān received 80,000 tomans in credit, and he began with 800 trees which he bought from an agricultural co-operative in Karaj near Tehran. A few years later, when he became sick, he borrowed 10,000 tomans from a money-lender, Hajji Mozaffar, in order to go to Germany for hospital care. On his return, he did not know how to pay back his debts. It was the first year that his orchard was productive, and he planned to rent out the harvest. [Renting an orchard entails finding another person to hire workers to harvest and to sell the fruit at a high enough price to cover the rent paid, workers' salaries and transportation costs for the fruit, and still make a profit.] Mashhadi Hajji Hoseyn, another money-lender and a merchant from Shahrezā, asked Ayāz Khān 'for permission' to rent his orchard. He offered 16,000 tomans, and when he saw that Ayāz Khān was silent and amazed he said, 'A few tomans more or less. Please understand that I have expenses too.' Ayāz Khān was actually speechless because he could not believe that such an income was possible from agriculture. He rented the orchard immediately. In the following days, this incredible story circulated among the Darrashurlu. Even those who were not in socioeconomic positions similar to Ayāz Khān were encouraged." (Personal communication, Gachsārān, 1981)

The Darrashurlu begin their orchards by buying small apple trees from the Ministry of Agriculture in Isfahān. Sometimes clover or alfalfa are planted at the base of the trees in order to fertilise the soil and cushion the apples when they fall. The successful Darrashurlu venture in apple cultivation is unmatched anywhere in Qashqa'i territory. Citrus fruits (green lemon, orange, mandarin and tangerine) and dates, traditional crops in southern Iran, are cultivated in some Qashqa'i areas.

FOOD

It is commonly assumed that nomadic pastoralists consume as many animal products as they wish. This is not true. Their animals are their capital, their investment, and are raised to be sold. The Qashqa'i, along with many other pastoralists, rarely consume meat or milk, though they do like drinking plain milk (*sud*) and enjoy both the rich thick milk from the first milking (*aqoz*) and that from the second (*bulama*). They eat milk products in small quantities and for limited periods of the year.

Milk products are made from a mixture of sheep and goat milk. To begin with, the milk is mixed in a pot and then filtered through a cloth before being boiled in a large pot (*qazan*) placed on a supporting frame over a fire. The milk is constantly stirred until it boils, then the pot is placed on the ground and allowed to cool. The next stage is the making of yoghurt (*yoghort*, *qateq*), which is itself a stage in the production of butter and its derivatives. To do this, a woman adds yoghurt starter (*maya*) to the measure of a thirtieth of the volume of the milk, adding an acidic element such as lime or pomegranate juice or wild pistachios (*ban*). The pot is covered and placed near a source of heat to allow the yoghurt to form. The yoghurt-making process is usually begun in the early morning to take advantage of the heat of the day. The yoghurt is then ready by the afternoon.

Yoghurt is eaten plain, sweetened or salted, with bread, with vegetables and as an ingredient of meat dishes and soups, though most of it is not eaten but converted into butter. Milk and yoghurt are never sold. Some Qashqa'i make a dehydrated paste (*masopus*) from it by putting the yoghurt in a suspended goat skin bag and allowing the liquid to drain off. This tasty paste has the advantages of not being either bulky or heavy and it keeps for a long time.

Butter (*kara*) is made by churning yoghurt in a goat skin bag suspended from a bar attached to a wooden tripod. It takes two to three hours of hard, exhausting, monotonous pushing and pulling of the bag by one woman or two. Chunks of butter rise to the surface of the liquid in the bag and are periodically scooped out by hand until no more rise. The butter is then pressed in a cloth to remove excess water and salt added to preserve it.

Clarified butter (*yagh*) is produced by boiling fresh butter in a very clean pan. The froth that appears on the surface is removed with a spoon and the oil that is left allowed to cool and transferred to a small goat skin bag. After it is poured into the bag, the residue (*yaqlichina*, *darti*) at the bottom of the pan is re-heated, mixed with flour and sour milk and eaten with dates and bread, principally during the autumn migration. Clarified butter is the principal substance used for cooking. It is also a marketable product that brings in more money than butter.

Sour milk (*ayran*) is the liquid left after the butter has been churned. Several products are made from it. It is much appreciated as a nourishing and refreshing drink, either plain, or salted and flavoured with dried herbs. It is also processed into *kashk* (dried curds). First most of the liquid is boiled off and then the residue is hung over a pan to allow the rest of the liquid to drain off. The resulting paste is salted, rolled into small balls and left to dry hard in the open air either on a woven mat suspended between tripods or on the flat roof of the tent. The balls will keep for years, and they are also sold. Dried curds are ground with a pestle and mortar, diluted with water and then drunk, cooked with vegetables, converted into soup or used as yeast for making bread.

Three kinds of dehydrated pastes are made from sour milk, *masana*, *chokalug* and *qaraqurut*. Sour milk is boiled until a heavy substance (*masana*) forms, left to cool and then drained in a bag. *Chokalug* results if the milk is boiled longer and then drained as before. Sometimes orange peel, wild herbs, turmeric and salt are added to *masana* and *chokalug*, which are eaten with vegetables and bread. The liquid from *chokalug* is used as a starter to make cheese. *Qaraqurut* is prepared from the liquid that remains after all other milk products have been made. This liquid is filtered and boiled for many hours to obtain a sharp-tasting, deep brown paste that is used as a condiment, an ingredient for meat sauces and as a yeast for making bread. Children are given small pieces as a treat. Like the other pastes it keeps for a long time and is sold or exchanged.

Cheese (*paner*) is the last of the milk products, and is made at the time of year when animals are producing 'white milk', a term used for low fat milk. They do this at the end of the period of lactation when feeding on dry grass. As usual a mixture of sheep and goat milk is used, although a few nomads use only goat. The liquid (*kaserma*, *pichak*) that derives from the production of *chokalug* is mixed with some milk, salted and added to the pot of milk as a starter. In an hour, the mixture begins to thicken. It is placed in a bag for the excess liquid to drain out and the cheese is ready to eat after a few hours. It is eaten fresh and is also salted for storage for use over several months. A small amount of cheese is also sold.

The meat from domesticated and wild animals is prepared in many different ways, first use being made of the offal. The head is boiled, the flesh removed and stuffed into a caul (the membrane covering the intestines of a sheep), which is then wrapped with the cleaned intestines, grilled over a fire on a skewer and eaten with bread and yoghurt. The head is also cooked with water, *qaraqurut*, salt, and onions and tomatoes, if available. Sometimes it is buried in warm coals and ashes overnight and then served for breakfast with bread and salt.

The stomach and intestines are cleaned, cooked directly on the open fire, salted and eaten. Stomachs are also cleaned and boiled. Sometimes the cleaned intestines are wrapped round skewered liver, kidneys and lung and grilled until crisp and tasty. Lamb or kid stomach is stuffed with the breast meat, liver and kidney of the animal, wrapped with cleaned intestines and grilled (*pardajigar*).

Liver (*dudma jigar*) is cooked directly on the fire. It is also crushed with a stone, mixed with wild oregano and placed in a caul which is then cooked over a fire on a skewer. When the caul burns, the liver mixture (*pijigar*) is cooked. A paste (*dumbajigar*) from the liver and head meat of a sheep is made by boiling, salting and rolling the mixture in a caul. *Masafa* is a Qashqa'i speciality made

One of the first tasks in the morning is churning the whole-milk yoghurt, which has been forming over night. The goat-skin churn is suspended from a tripod which is often set up over a smoldering fire. Warmth can speed up the process of butter formation from some three hours to around two. From time to time the butter is scooped out until no more appears. Here she is emptying out the residual liquid which will then be processed further. Amala tribe, south of Qir on their upward migration, 1986.

with sheep liver and kidneys that are stewed with wild herbs and yoghurt. One variation of the stew contains chopped liver, rice, chick-peas, sour milk, onions and other vegetables. Feet are boiled, and the skin, marrow and whatever meat there is eaten. Testicles (*dombalan*) are grilled directly on top of hot coals. The sheep's tail (*quyruq*) is used by poor Qashqa'i to make clarified fat for cooking. Some choose to sell their butter and clarified butter and purchase the much cheaper vegetable oil. Others use only their own supplies of clarified butter. The Qashqa'i still dislike the taste of vegetable oil and claim it causes various ailments.

To prepare meat and organs, they are cut into square pieces, placed on wooden-handled metal skewers (*sikh*) and cooked over coals. To make *saj kebab*, a speciality, women fry small strips of salted meat with diced onion in melted butter in a metal pan (*saj*). When the meat is cooked, some *qaraqurut* diluted with water is added and the dish is served covered with bread fried in the same pan. To make *qorma* and *boz qorma*, small pieces of goat meat are fried in the *saj* with onions, *qaraqurut*,

A Shesh Baylu (Shesh Boluki) woman making bread early in the morning. The Qashqa'i diet is based on bread made with wheat flour. Usually two women help one another to bake the bread (*chorag*) over an open fire, one rolling the dough and the other baking it on the metal griddle. During migration bread is baked every three to four days, whereas in camp baking usually takes place daily in the afternoon. Wealthy families who have many guests hire a woman to make bread both morning and afternoon because the bread loses its freshness after a day despite attempts to keep it wrapped and moist. September 1984.

right
Having erected a simple wind-break using a strip of tent cloth and a tripod, this Shesh Baylu (Shesh Boluki) woman prepares a meal, adding salt from her specially woven salt bag. Spring 1988.

Darrashurlu men having tea on their way to the winter camp. Tea is served very hot in small glasses with saucers. The tea may be poured into the saucer to cool it and then drunk from the saucer through lumps of sugar held in the teeth

salt and pepper. It can be eaten immediately, sometimes with boiled eggs and fresh onions, or stored in a sack made out of the goat's stomach and kept for months. Meatballs are made by wrapping hard-boiled eggs in chopped meat and frying them or cooking them in water and sugar. The balls are served with rice (*chelo masala*). Meat is also cooked with onions and then added to partially cooked rice and steamed. A meat stew (*awgush*) is made from diced meat, bones, fat, onions, chick-peas and *qaraqurut* and eaten with quantities of bread dipped in the juice. In most cases the *awgush* contains more fat and bones than meat. Another stew based on wheat (*buqda shurbası*) is made, sometimes using goat meat. Melted clarified butter is poured on top and some sugar sprinkled on.

Chickens, game birds (particularly partridges) and eggs are eaten. Chickens are cut into pieces and grilled, and sometimes the meat is marinated in oil, lemon juice and chopped onions for several hours before being barbecued. Birds stuffed with pomegranate seeds or juniper berries are fried in a metal pan. A tasty dish is made with year-old capons (*khasi*). Small partridges and other young birds are fried with aubergines and onions and then cooked with sour grapes. Eggs from chickens and wild birds are fried and boiled.

The staple food of the Qashqa'i is actually wheat bread. The necessary flour is obtained by a Qashqa'i man taking his grain and that of several other households to the mill at the nearest settlement. The man pays five to ten percent of the grain milled for the service. Poor Qashqa'i grind small quantities of wheat with a hand mill consisting of two stone wheels, the top one being turned with a wooden handle (see Wulff 1969: 277).

For sweetening their tea, the Qashqa'i like hard chunks of sugar chipped from a large sugar cone with this special metal tool, a cross between pliers and scissors. The sugar cone and cutter are kept in a woven bag with a drawstring. The teapot, glasses, saucers, and sometimes spoons are kept in a purpose-made wooden box called a 'thousand things' (*hezar pisha*) which has compartments lined with red or purple velvet for each item. These boxes are made in Shiraz and Yazd. Darrashurlu, 1988.

Women cook the bread (*chorag*) that is eaten every day. A woman and her older daughter will often work together, one rolling the dough and the other baking the bread. The bread-making is usually begun in the late morning. The flour is sifted, cleaned and mixed with water and salt in a metal pan. The dough is worked for half an hour until it reaches the desired condition, then the pan is covered and the dough left to rest. In the early afternoon a square of camel hair cloth is laid out near the fire and dusted with flour. The soft cloth provides a good, non-adhering surface for rolling out the dough. The baker flours her hands, tears off some dough (5–6 oz/150 g) and forms it into a ball. She puts the ball on the cloth and rolls it flat with the aid of a thin stick (*okhlu*). The rolled dough is then cooked on a convex metal pan (*saj*) with a raised rim about 24 inches (60 cm) in diameter. This is balanced on three rocks or a supporting tripod over an open fire.

When the bread is done on one side it is flipped over with the stick to cook on the other. The breads are not cooked singly, however. Each fresh piece of rolled dough is placed on top of the one before, and the pile is flipped over to place the new piece directly on the pan. When seven or eight breads have accumulated, the pile is removed from the pan and a new one begun. When all the dough has been made into bread, each piece is sprinkled with water to moisten it and then all the breads are wrapped in a large cloth.

Other breads are occasionally made by the same process. *Tapu* is a thick round leavened bread 8 inches (20 cm) in diameter made from wheat flour, water, salt and yeast. *Shirin chorag* is a sweet bread made from wheat flour, milk sugar and yeast. *Ranginak* is a special sweet made from flour, butter, nuts and cooked dates. *Halva* is made from wheat flour, butter, sugar and water and a moister variation (*bereshtuk*) of it is made for women after childbirth.

Rice (*düğü*) is bought and stored carefully in bags. When it is used, the women first pound it in a wooden mortar to separate the husks from the kernels. Special rice dishes are prepared in spring, with wild artichokes, camomile and herbs.

Fresh vegetables are occasionally acquired from itinerant pedlars who bring them on mules or in vans from nearby towns. The Qashqa'i buy them with cash or on credit, or exchange their milk products. Mushrooms are gathered in the spring on migration and are salted and cooked upside down with the stems removed either directly on the coals or fried. They are also salted, grilled and preserved by drying in the sun.

Oranges, lemons, jujubes, dates in garmsir, apples in sarhad as well as other wild fruit are occasionally eaten. Fruit is also purchased from or exchanged with villagers and itinerant merchants. Grapes are gathered or bought to eat or to make a grape syrup. Pomegranates (*nar*) are bought in miānband. They are eaten fresh or the juice is boiled to make a syrup (*nar roba*), which, like the other syrups made, will keep for several months in special skin bags. A few Qashqa'i own date palms but most buy dates in garmsir to eat with bread, rice and tea. Pitted dates are cooked, reduced to jam and mixed with lemon juice to make a syrup (*limu roba*). Pitted dates are also reduced, mixed with sesame seeds and formed into balls that make a compact, rich, high energy food (*konjed-khorma*).

The Qashqa'i drink tea, and both men and women prepare it. Water is boiled in a metal kettle sitting directly on the hot coals or resting on a small metal frame, and the tea is made in a ceramic teapot. It is served as hot as possible in a small glass on a saucer with lumps of sugar on it. The tea is cooled down by pouring it from the glass into the saucer and the lumps of sugar are held in the teeth as the tea is sipped. Tea is always offered to guests regardless of the time of day. It is served by the men, or, in the tents of the tribal leaders, by servants. Guests are served in order of status, men before women. When guests are more numerous than tea glasses, the glasses are rinsed with boiling water after a guest has finished drinking, filled with tea and served to other guests. Tribal leaders often own Russian-style silver tea-glass holders with handles, as well as silver trays and spoons. The sugar lumps come from a large sugar cone. Chunks are knocked off it with a metal chopper and reduced to bite-sized lumps with a metal cutter. The sugar cone, and often the chopper and cutter, are kept in a special woven bag, or a cloth one. The teapot, glasses and saucers are stored in a specially made wooden box with well-padded compartments for each item. The inside is covered with a soft fabric, most often a red-purple velvet. These boxes, which are called 'a thousand things' (*hezar pisha*), are made in cities, particularly Shirāz and Yazd.

Cigarettes and tobacco are smoked by some Qashqa'i. Tobacco is stored in a sheep skin pouch and smoked with a water pipe that is sometimes used collectively, being passed from person to person.

On important occasions and during ceremonies, Qashqa'i eat around a large rectangular cloth spread on rugs. They are served trays of food and help themselves from the piles of flat bread placed along the cloth. Servants stand close to guests to fill water glasses and bring additional bread and dishes. They also help guests to wash by pouring water over their hand or fingers from a pitcher into a bowl and handing them a towel. The Qashqa'i eat with their right hand by picking up food with the thumb and first two fingers, often with the help of a chunk of bread, though wealthy Qashqa'i use individual plates and spoons.

GATHERING

By means of gathering the Qashqa'i make great use of many of the natural products in their environment. These products are consumed, exchanged, given as gifts or sold for much-needed cash, and generally form a supplement to other economic activities. But for some Qashqa'i they are not just a supplement but important sources of nutrition. Gathering helps those who are poor, those who lack sufficient numbers of animals for subsistence and those who lack access to pastures to continue nomadism and avoid sedentarisation.

Gathering is done by women and children, mainly during migration. Some is done by children in a casual way when they are free from other chores, but it is the women who do most of it, going frequently throughout the year on gathering trips with their daughters to seek out special substances. Thus they provision their households with gathered products, many of which they store in small cloth packets in a special woven bag.

It is worth mentioning here the question of drinking water. The nomads camp near water sources on the migrations and choose their winter and summer camp sites on the basis of its proximity. In garmsir, until the rains fall, only a few sources of water are found, but thereafter it is available in natural pools found in gorges and in small man-made ponds that are built near encampments. In sarhad, water sources are numerous. Some Qashqa'i use well-water in or near their pastures.

Men are involved in the gathering of salt and wood. Salt is much in demand by pastoralists for their animals and men collect it from surface or subsurface deposits and transport it back on mules or camels. In the case of wood, men and boys gather the heavy wood and women and girls the brushwood. Sometimes the men do this in groups and share the results among their households.

Wood is used as a fuel in the form of firewood and charcoal, and for tools and equipment. They make charcoal by burning wood without oxygen in underground pits for twenty-four hours. Firewood and charcoal are also sold, being transported in bags by donkeys to camps and towns for this purpose. Selling charcoal is more lucrative than selling firewood. The Qashqa'i are beginning to have to face the necessity of finding alternatives to wood and its products. The deforestation in their territory has been severe in the twentieth century and it is estimated that 90 per cent of the forests of the Zāgros Mountains have been destroyed since 1945 (Firouz 1974: 11). This is the result of human and animal population increases, the transformation of forests into agricultural land, the introduction of tractors and the rise in the prices that can be got for wood and charcoal.

An insect secretion (*angaza*) is gathered from the leaves of chestnut trees in the early morning hours of June and July, at altitudes where forests are found. The secretion is sold and it is exported and used for pharmaceutical purposes. Men gather honey (*bal*) by making large fires to drive away the bees from their nests. Cochineal-type insects are gathered by women at the end of winter in garmsir and boiled to produce a bright red dye. Bird's eggs are collected and children often go on egg finding expeditions, carrying with them some raw wool to cushion the eggs during the trip back to camp.

Acorns (*balut*) are collected for sale and to roast with salt. The poorest Qashqa'i use them to make bread. The skin inside the shell is used for tanning goat skin bags. Oak trees are found mainly in miānband at altitudes above 6,500 feet (2,000 metres). The leaves, when combined with other substances, produce a deep purple dye. Walnuts are both eaten and sold, and the peel is used to dye wool light brown. The Qashqa'i claim that walnut trees (*qoz aqaj*) grow where the crows have seeded them. Gathered nuts, walnuts, almonds, pistachios and acorns, are shelled and roasted with salt over a fire in a pan or on a stone pillar. Almond oil is utilised in medicine, and some women use it as a moisturiser for their skin and hair. The sap (*zudu*) of the tree is gathered and sold for export to pharmaceutical companies. A tree resin (*saqez*) is chewed by children.

Gum tragacanth (*katira*) is a source of income for poor Qashqa'i who are able to sell it in town

Preparing food gathered in the wild for cooking. Gathering is an important factor in Qashqa'i economy and especially for those who are poor. Throughout the year, women provision their households with items they have gathered which they dry and store in small cloth packets. Shesh Baylu (Shesh Boluki), spring 1988.

because Iran exports the substance to western countries. Barberries (*zereshk*) are collected and sold, principally by Darrashurlu and Buyug Kashkullu women during the migration. Some berries are kept for use in cooking. A shrub that produces a small acid fruit (*faraj*) resembling capers grows wild in the vicinity of Kāzerun. Its fruit is gathered primarily by Fars Madan and Buyug Kashkullu women for sale in Firuzābād where a sour relish (*torshi*) is made with them.

One of the most commercialised gathered products is *gaz*, which is the powdered extract of a sugar produced by the leaves of tamarisk bushes. It is sold in Isfahān primarily for the production of a distinctive Iranian sweet, a nougat filled with pistachios or almonds. Women collect *gaz* by laying cloths on the ground under the small bush and hitting it with sticks

Pomegranate, fig, apple, quince, pear and cherry trees grow wild in sarhad, as do grape vines. Olive trees became scarce by the 1970s. Jujube (*konar*) forests used to be abundant in garmsir but by the 1980s they were becoming scarce and were of a small size. The fruits, produced twice a year (spring and autumn), are delicious and have reddish orang pits. Some Qashqa'i sell the fruits which are collected with difficulty because the trees are thorny. The leaves are fed to all animals except sheep and also dried and made into a powder (*sedr*) used by women for their skin and hair.

The goat has a fractured leg. The aim is to immobolize it either by binding two sticks around it or by fashioning a cast out of flour paste mixed with gum arabic.
Shesh Baylu (Shesh Boluki), 1988.

Much use is made of plants, roots and herbs, of course. Of the plants, reeds (*qamesh*) are made into the screens (*chiq*) used in most tents, and are sold in villages and towns. The reeds are gathered at the edges of salty marshes in garmsir. Wild rhubarb (*eshqen*) is found in spring in miānband and gathered during the migration. A variety of fennel (*badian*) is collected in spring. Spinach (*tola*) grows in garmsir, in mountainous areas protected from the wind. Roots are dug out of the ground with sticks. Wild artichoke (*kangar*) is dug up, washed, cut up and then cooked and eaten either plain or mixed with yoghurt, or is cooked with rice. Onions and garlic are gathered in sarhad.

Herbs are pulled by hand or cut with a small sickle (*ronjak*). Many are believed to have medicinal qualities, and others are of course used for culinary purposes being mixed with milk products, stews, meat sauces and rice. Mint and watercress are cut near springs and streams. Camomile flourishes at the beginning of spring in garmsir, and its flowers are gathered for culinary use. Marjoram is used for cooking and as a medicine. Many others could be mentioned, but some herbs have disappeared from the natural environment for the reasons already mentioned in connection with wood. Herbs are also used as a supplementary feed for animals.

The Qashqa'i collect, eat, store and sell several kinds of mushrooms (*dombalaq*). One variety (*qar dombalaq*) grows at an altitude of 6,500 feet (2,000 metres) and on slopes where snow has just melted. Truffles (*qizil dombalaq*) are sought out with the aid of a special stick. The Qashqa'i believe that mushrooms proliferate in years when thunderstorms are frequent.

Lastly, flowers; women gather them for pleasure and to give as gifts, and some are used for dyeing wool. Delphiniums are used for cooking and as a medicine.

HUNTING AND WEAPONRY

Hunting is the favourite sport of Qashqa'i nomads and they respect and admire good hunters and marksmen. It is an exclusively male sport and a vital part of the tribal cultural identity. In addition it is an important factor in the economy, because of the meat it provides. The hunters distribute the meat of game animals and birds within camps and kinship groups. The legs and head of large game animals are often given to political leaders, and these political leaders themselves distribute the game they have shot to loyal followers.

The pursuit and catching of animals is begun by boys at an early age. Boys and girls learn how to use a gun at around six or seven. Children are feverishly eager to go on hunting trips and when a boy or young man brings home his first game he is warmly received by his parents and neighbours. The women of his encampment bless him by pouring wheat flour over his head as a prayer for future abundance and prosperity in his life. The Qashqa'i could hunt anywhere in the tribal territory until the 1960s and they did so in both garmsir and sarhad, and on migration. Since then two areas have been denied them, Bamu and Dasht-e Arzhan. Bamu, situated north of Shirāz and famous for game, became a national game preserve under government control. Most Qashqa'i migrate through it twice a year. Dasht-e Arzhan, also famous for game, has been turned into a national park covering 750 square miles (1,900 square km), and it includes Lake Parishān (Fāmur). (See Appendix 2: GAME BIRDS AND ANIMALS, p. 251)

Game is scarce at present, both birds and animals, and not just because of the effects of hunting. A complex of ecological factors also influences the game population. But in previous times game was plentiful, particularly in the 1940s and early 1950s. The forced disarmament and settlement of the Qashqa'i by Rezā Shah in the 1930s led to a severe reduction in the size of their herds and ultimately had the effect of turning part of south Iran into a national park where there was no hunting, almost no grazing and very little agriculture. When the Qashqa'i resumed migrations in 1941 following Rezā Shah's abdication they found that game was plentiful. Garrod (1946: 33) reported that abundant game, including wild pigs, leopards, ibex and gazelle, was found in the mountains and valleys of Qashqa'i territory. From 1965 to 1978 the Qashqa'i were again disarmed, and only those who were influential in government circles were able to acquire gun permits. In 1978–9 there was a large influx of guns and ammunition into south Iran due to the lack of government control during the revolutionary period, and as a result game has become scarce. The Qashqa'i are not solely responsible for this. Nomadic hunters cannot easily over-hunt any given area because they only spend a certain time in each location. Nevertheless, because non-Qashqa'i men hunt without restraint in the nomads' territory, the Qashqa'i often say that if they do not shoot game the non-Qashqa'i will. Qashqa'i hunters, despite their concern at the disappearance of game, feel that any attempts by them to control hunting are fruitless.

As mentioned earlier, a complex of ecological factors affects the amount of game found in Qashqa'i territory. Population growth, deforestation, expansion of cultivated land and overgrazing are equally if not more important than hunting in determining the availability of game. The population of Iran at the turn of the twentieth century was estimated at 8–10 million. The seven to eight-fold increase in size since then has left little space for wildlife anywhere in Iran. Indeed, the present-day situation of the wildlife in Qashqa'i territory is little different from that of the wildlife in other parts of Iran where nomads are not found.

A variety of hunting techniques are employed. Trapping, especially by boys, is one. They most often use the deadfall trap, which involves the fall of a large flat stone supported by a stick. A small hole is dug in the ground under the stone and bait placed in it. The prey dislodges the stick when it enters the hole. Such traps are placed close to trees frequented by birds, whose habits are closely watched. Another technique is stalking (*barag*). When individuals or groups of hunters locate game at a distance they approach it cautiously, trying to get near enough to shoot it. In beating and flushing (*shekar surmag*) some hunters hide while beaters (*daq suran*) drive the game towards them. Gazelles may be driven by beaters towards obstacles or into gorges where they have to reverse direction, thereby passing close to the hunters and giving them a good shot. Horses are also used in hunting gazelles and are trained from an early age to be accustomed to the noise of gunfire. Hunting in mountains is a speciality because of the climbing involved. When hunters (*kamaro*) reach a den or lair where game is located, they attach a bell to a rope they suspend from the cliff in front of the mouth of the prey's den (*shekaf*) and ring it loudly to surprise and frighten the animal. The idea is that the animal runs away and becomes an easy victim for the hunter hidden below the cliff.

The technique for hunting partridges in the mountains is perhaps unique to the Qashqa'i. Men gather at the bottom of a mountain or hill slope and travel silently in a group up the slope. On reaching a certain level, one man stops and waits while the others continue. After they have climbed another 150 feet (50 metres) or so (the effective range of a shotgun), a second hunter stops and waits, and so on until there is a perpendicular line of hunters at 150 feet (50 metre) intervals from the base to the top of the slope. The man at the top begins the hunt by marching horizontally along the slope. The hunter below him does the same at his own level but lags a few paces behind the leader. Each hunter below follows this pattern. This technique is adapted to the habits of partridges, which fly downhill when approached from the top of a slope. Birds forced into flight by this technique fly away from the hunters and have no chance to hide. Their flights become shorter and shorter and finally the hunters can shoot them down relatively easily.

In rain, most birds fly near the ground, become quickly exhausted and hence are easier to hunt. Sometimes, especially when the hunters lack guns or cartridges, such birds are followed on the run or on horseback and captured by hand. Another technique involves the camel. The great bustard is cautious and able to disappear quickly, and the only animal it does not fear is the camel. Thus the hunter conceals himself behind a camel and drives it in progressively smaller circles around the bird until he is close enough to shoot it. Hunting with raptors has been completely supplanted by guns. The paramount leader Ismā'il Khān Soulat ad-Dowleh was the last known hunter to have used falcons for gazelle hunting. Birds of prey are broken in by being deprived of sleep and food for several days. They are then trained to obey orders and tested before being released. They are fed from their master's hand or from the horns of a dead gazelle with chunks of meat washed free of blood in warm water.

The weapons used for hunting, raiding, warfare and defence by the Qashqa'i in former times—axes, sabres, swords, knives, bows and arrows—fell out of use with the introductions of firearms. In the middle of the nineteenth century they were using percussion cap guns and fuse-guns (*hasan musa*). These massive and heavy guns had to be propped up on special tripods and could be fired only from the ground. They were replaced successively by wick guns that had shorter barrels, by wheel or sheave guns and by flintlock guns (*sarporeh chakhmaqi*), some of which were double-barrelled. Toward the end of the century Martin and Rogers rifles were introduced to Iran. They had a unique cartridge and a range of 1,600–2,000 feet (500–600 metres). During World War I the rifles used by European cavalry were introduced to the Qashqa'i. They included the French three-shot rifle (*seh tir*), the English .303 Lee Enfield Major and the rifle used by the German army, known by the name of the German who introduced it, Wilhelm Wassmuss. By the very early part of the twentieth century it was rare to see anyone with an outdated gun (Demorgny 1913: 97–9).

In 1930 the famous Czechoslovakian 7.92 mm Brno rifle, named after the city where they were made, arrived in Iran. This was the standard rifle of the German army during World War II and Rezā Shah bought them for the Iranian army. It came in three models of the same calibre. Since the 1940s the Brno has been the favourite gun of Qashqa'i men due to its accuracy over long distances and because the barrel does not become too hot after continuous firing. The German 7.92 mm rifle is also used. Shotguns, two-barrelled 12-, 16-, and 20-gauge, are also used for hunting, but are considered of limited use in war other than ambush because their range is no more than 160 feet (50 metres).

The Qashqa'i acquired their arms from local dealers from the end of the nineteenth century on, particularly from the Shirāz bazaar, where they stopped during the migrations. They also bought arms from smugglers and gun runners who brought them by way of the ports of the Persian Gulf. The Qashqa'i met these smugglers and runners in their territory and in such towns as Khonj, Jahrom and Lār. All arms buying and trading took place in garmsir. The buying of guns took on a more clandestine character in the 1930s with the beginning of serious government efforts to collect customs duties on imported arms and ammunition. A subsequent black market developed and flourished whenever the government attempted to prohibit or control the supply of arms and ammunition, and smuggling increased. Raiding and warfare have been sources of arms both before and during the twentieth century. The weapons were usually taken from captured soldiers from the Iranian army and gendarmerie and from the British military forces in south Iran.

In 1931–2 the Qashqa'i were completely and systematically disarmed and only in 1941 did they

Large bedding bags and saddle bags woven by Darrashurlu women packed and ready for loading in the early morning before setting off to the summer pastures. Near Dogonbadān, spring 1988.

become armed again. That year, a Qashqa'i lieutenant from Amala returned to Qashqa'i territory with sixteen Brno rifles and it was quickly adopted.

Besides firearms, elementary weapons such as wooden sticks, clubs (*chomaq*) and slings are used. Among the clubs one is called 'six wings' (*sheshpar*) because it has six sharp ridges or spokes on its head and another is called 'cowtail' (*dom gohu*) because it has a head covered in leather. Another (*tokhmag*) has a broad, flattish end for holding and a fat, rounded head and ordinarily is used for pounding in tent stakes.

WEAVING

There is no myth about the origin of weaving among the Qashqa'i, but they do have a number of beliefs and customs in connection with it: a weaving can be begun only on auspicious days; no weaving is done during mourning or death rites; weaving is resumed on the fortieth day of mourning and immediately after childbirth. Amulets, charms and talismans are attached to the weavings and special prayers said for protection.

Women have sole charge of all the tasks connected with weaving once the sheep are shorn and the wool stored. Women of every age participate in weaving, each age having duties appropriate to

Both women are using drop spindles to produce heavy-duty yarn. The woman on the right is spinning goat hair, probably for weaving into tent cloth. Behind the women and on the ground are multi-purpose screens (*chiq*) made from reeds, canes or wands. Mostly they are used to form part of the tent wall. In summer they reduce heat glare and permit ventilation while excluding animals, and in winter act as a vital wind break.
Shesh Baylu (Shesh Boluki), 1989.

it, and they start learning their craft in childhood. Very young girls learn all the processes involved by watching and helping their mothers, and they actively participate in different tasks from the age of six or seven, but their real work starts when they begin to prepare their dowry. Old women supervise the dyeing, spinning and weaving when they cannot work any more, and remain in charge as long as they live. A woman's weaving skills are respected and her woven items are the pride of her family. Her skill can substantially raise the level of her family's prosperity. Most Qashqa'i families supply their own functional necessities, so a woman has to be capable of supplying her family's demands for woven materials. This work is in addition to the long hours she spends in the other domains of family economic life. Therefore, despite the difficulties, she always makes the time to weave when the stops are long enough. The women pay visits to one another when they are weaving, and it is altogether a very social activity. They sit with one another and weave when the men are away from the encampment, which happens mainly in the afternoons.

Weaving a flat-woven *jajim* requires the labour of two women for five to seven days, if they have no other work, but it takes them four to six weeks when they are busy and have to fit the work into their other tasks. A tapestry-woven *gelim* takes two women six to eight weeks. A proficient weaver making a knotted pile carpet can tie some thirty knots per minute, 6,000–7,000 knots a day if she works for four hours. Depending on the width of the carpet, this amounts to about ten rows. Salzer (1974: 104) reports: 'Among the Kashkulli Kuchik, a three meter long qali [knotted pile carpet] took three women about three months of actual weaving to complete. One qali, two and a half meters long, woven by two women, took eight months to finish even though only three months of actual weaving were necessary'.

Although what she makes is primarily either for functional use, for dowries and ceremonial gifts to important people, it also represents a form of wealth. The more woven items a family owns, the wealthier it is. Woven items are displayed in the back of the tent folded one on top of another, or spread out on the ground. Weavings can be sold when extra cash is needed, or sold to cover a debt. Men do the selling. Not all women weave regularly, however. Very poor Qashqa'i only weave occasionally, because usually they own few animals and do not have enough wool or hair, or the necessary equipment. Those Qashqa'i who have only goats or goats and a few sheep use hair or combine it with a limited amount of wool. Wealthy Qashqa'i women too are rarely regular weavers as they do not have to provide the necessities of their households. Their work is nevertheless generally excellent because they learn the art at a very young age from skilled women who work at it continuously or from servants or retainers who, among their other tasks, are contracted to weave, spin a certain amount of yarn and dye it. Men perform only those jobs in weaving that require strength, like shearing and loom-making, or the use of sharp tools. Women do not handle any metal tool bigger or sharper than large scissors or a carpet comb. Weaving is not thought to be a prestigious or valued activity for men or boys, so they never do it.

Since the 1950s the weavers have adapted their output to the demands of the market and make more pile rugs and bags because a pile rug brings in more money than a flatweave of the same size and quality. The initial cost of the quality wool and dyes needed for a pile carpet is high, and pile work takes longer than flatweave. The actual time depends on the dimensions, the quality and complexity of the motifs, the number of hours the weaver can spend on it and how fast and well she works. Many Qashqa'i women do not make more than a few pile rugs in their lives unless they weave for the market or for wealthy leaders. It has become a sign of status to own and display pile rugs.

The loom the Qashqa'i use is the horizontal ground loom, which is constructed by men from simple local materials and is easily assembled, dismantled and transported. It consists of a warp beam and a breast beam, pegs that are hammered into the ground, a heddle rod usually supported by a tripod, a shed stick and cords. The beams are made from two straight wild pistachio branches.

Warping the loom requires precision and stamina. It is very hard work and can take a whole day. The warp and breast beams are set some distance apart on stones and held firm with wooden pegs. To form the warp two women sit at opposite ends of the loom and pass a ball of yarn to and fro between them in such a way as to pass round both beams. A child often runs back and forth with the ball of yarn. Each time a weaver breaks down her loom she loses the warp tension, and as a result her piece can become lop-sided, uneven or curved, or may develop convergent selvedges. For this reason a weaver is careful to take into account when deciding the size of a piece of work the frequency with which she is changing camp sites and the time she has available to work on it. When she is moving camps fairly often the weaving width is kept small, no more than a metre, for the reason that it is easily rolled up and transported. Large widths are only woven at fixed seasonal encampments, in a permanent settlement or when several weavers can work together to finish a piece rapidly.

When the warping is completed, a rod, the shed stick, is inserted across the warp, passing over and under alternate strands. A tripod is set up over the warp threads with two legs towards the weaver to support a heddle bar. Alternate warps are lifted by loops of string that pass round it. The shed and counter shed are formed by moving the shed stick towards or away from the heddles. Alternatively, for certain flatweaves, the bar can serve as a support for four rockers which are attached by twisted woollen cords to two pairs of heddle rods. In this case the shed and counter shed are formed by raising and lowering the heddle rods through the action of the rockers. The tripod and heddle rods are moved along the length of the loom as the weaving progresses.

Weaving is done in the open air with the loom at the right side of the tent looking out. When space is lacking or shade is necessary, a tent cloth is extended on two tent poles to protect the weaver. Sometimes the loom is placed in nearby shade. Heavy rain and windy days make weaving impossible. Most weaving is done in the winter in garmsir. Early morning is best, when the humidity helps the warp keep well stretched.

Markers are an important feature of weavings done by more than one woman. When women decide to weave together, they agree beforehand on the kind of item to be made, its structure, dimensions and colours, and the amount of work each will do, and then, as they weave, each makes a small coloured tuft at the end of each row she completes by passing a thread two or three times through the woven edge. In this way each one knows which sections she has worked

A woman from the Kheiratlu sub-tribe of the Darrashurlu weaving a *gelim*. Weaving is done on the horizontal ground loom constructed by Qashqa'i men from simple local materials. The loom is similar to that used by many Middle Eastern nomads. It consists of two straight branches of strong wild pistachio tree used for the warp beam (*oyanki ağajı*) and breast beam (*ilarki ağajı*) held in place by four pegs (*mikh*), a tripod (*chadma bağı*) supporting the heddle apparatus, a heddle-rod (*kuju*), a shed-stick (*tabku*) (here a metal bar), plus ropes and cords. Large widths are only woven at fixed seasonal encamptments, in permanent settlements, or when several weavers help each other to finish a piece.

on and how much she has done. The markers are not obvious, but weavers and others attentive to such details can point them out. It is safe to assume that different hands have been at work when variations occur on each side of a well-known design. The distance between the marker tufts in a rug woven at a fixed encampment, is much greater than on the rugs woven in busier andless settled circumstances.

MATERIALS

Shearing is done in sarhad soon after the nomads arrive, when the weather is warm. The sheep are washed in the springs there and allowed to dry under the sun for a day before the men shear them. After shearing, the wool from each animal is sorted into the following categories and stored by men and women in large rectangular bags (*awkash*): neck, shoulder and back wool—short, used for pile weaves; side wool—long and even, used for flatwoven covers and bags; tail and leg wool—coarse, used for ropes. Ram's wool is sold; ewe's wool is used for coarser pile weavings; and lamb's wool for fine pile rugs. Goat and camel hair are not washed or sorted. Goat hair is dry, slippery and difficult to spin. Camel hair is soft, rare and expensive.

Finer threads are spun from wool with a long staple. Piles of raw wool are beaten with a thin stick which at the same time both separates the wool fibres and rearranges them in a manner suitable for spinning. Bit by bit as it is beaten, the wool is delicately drawn into a compact ribbon or rove that is wrapped around itself to form a bundle. Hair is also beaten with a thin stick but then combed with a long wooden comb that consists of a handle and a bar with two parallel rows of metal teeth.

The spinning of the raw wool or hair is done as soon as the fibres are ready. A bundle of wool is placed under the arm or over the head and the rove wound round the left forearm with the end held in the hand. A sliver of wool consisting of a few strands from the end of the rove is then attached to a spindle which is twirled with the right hand. The spin is always clockwise (z). The fingers of both hands work together to draw out the rove into an even strand which is formed into a thread by the rotation of the spindle. When the spindle reaches the ground the spun thread is wound round it, the next length of rove drawn out and the twirling and drawing actions repeated. Having spun since childhood the women do it with ease and precision. The yarn is removed from the spindles, wound into balls and sorted according to the type of weaving for which each is best suited. Pile yarn is called *qalılık*.

The spindle (*kerman*) consists of two curved lengths of horn arranged in the form of a concave cross that is pierced in the centre by a steel or wooden shaft. The metal shafts are bought from gypsy tinkers. When a strong yarn is needed, two strands are plied together using a pair of spindles suspended from a horizontal bar. These spindles each consist of a thin metal shaft set into the centre of a wooden disc. Goat hair yarn is used for weaving tent cloths, and for ropes and bags when mixed with wool. Camel hair yarn is used for bread cloth, Koran covers or in specific areas of ceremonial rugs.

The use of ready spun and dyed industrial woollen yarn is increasing, and many Qashqa'i sell all their own wool to buy it. The yarn, made from Australian and New Zealand wool, is commercially processed and dyed. It lacks the quality of Qashqa'i wool but having ready-to-use yarn of uniform diameter and standard length saves the Qashqa'i weavers time and trouble, lessens their dependence on the yields of their flocks, and is especially convenient for those who make carpets for sale.

Cotton has been used in Qashqa'i weavings since the beginning of the twentieth century, and increasingly since the 1930s and 1940s. It was introduced because the Iranian and international markets demanded tightly woven rugs with dense pile and the only way to achieve this was to use cotton for the foundation. With a cotton warp and weft the weaving loses its blanket-like nature and becomes a semi-rigid floor covering. Silk has always been used in Qashqa'i weavings, but only in a limited amount. A proficient weaver would put one strand of silk in a flatweave or a couple of knots in a pile rug as a signature. Silk as a foundation has only been used since the 1960s and now some *gelims* and rugs are completely woven in it.

DYEING

Dyeing is usually done in sarhad where there is plenty of pure, fresh spring water. Yarn dyed in garmsir and in towns is believed not to have the same fine lustre and quality. Some wool is not dyed, but used in its natural colours—white, ivory, grey, brown and black. Hair is never dyed.

Qashqa'i women do not readily divulge the details of their dyeing methods and always keep some details secret. For example, a woman will not stipulate the quantities of substances mixed together to produce particular colours, certain details of operations will be unclear in her explanations and substances will be added or unexplained actions taken when she thinks she is unobserved. Girls and young women take many years to learn to dye, which they do by helping the oldest able-bodied woman of a household with her dyeing operations.

Yarn to be dyed red or yellow is immersed in a large pot of boiling water and mordanted with alum (*zaj*) over a charcoal fire after it has been washed with a vegetal soap (*choğan*) gathered in sarhad. The yarn is then dried in the open air over tent ropes or rocks or on the branches of the few trees before being dyed, for which it is again put into a pot of boiling water. The dyes (both natural and chemical are used), which are mixed with water, are added and everything is boiled for at least an hour over a slow fire. During the whole process, the yarn is stirred with a stick to separate the threads and allow the dye to penetrate evenly. The yarn is dried in the same way as after mordanting. It is then rinsed thoroughly several times, pounded with the fists to squeeze off the dye, given

Women weaving striped cloth to make into sacks for grain and flour. Shesh Baylu (Shesh Boluki), at their summer camp near Khosrow Shirin, 1984.

another rinse, and then dried again. Finally, the yarn is wound into loose balls (*khora*) and stored in bags. Dyeing lasts one full day. Women try to accumulate enough yarn in the needed colours before beginning a weaving project.

Red (*qızıl*) is primarily made from madder roots (*boyaq*) gathered in sarhad or miānband, or purchased in towns. Another deep red is made from cochineal-like insects collected in garmsir. Shesh Baylu women made a red from a barley-like herb (*golkez*) they gather in sarhad. A blue-red is obtained from a mixture of madder and cochineal. To obtain orange (*naranji*), yarn dyed with madder is dipped into a decoction of crushed pomegranate skins or willow leaves. A deep coral (*dughi*) is made from a mixture of madder and sour milk. The colour is difficult to obtain and is only made in the summer, when the large amounts of sour milk (*ayran*, T., *dugh*, P.) it needs are available. Qashqa'i women create many yellows (*sarı*) from the weld plant (*morder-aqajı*), which grows wild primarily in sarhad, and from two herbs (*naz*, *gandal*) that grow wild in the miānband wheat fields in spring. A deep straw yellow is made from a mixture of weld and *gandal*. Willow

(*söğüt*), wild pistachio and grape leaves make three different deep yellows. Pomegranate skins yield an apricot yellow, and a mustard yellow when mixed with *gandal* or weld. A yellow orange is produced from a mixture of *naz* and turmeric, which is bought in town.

Light brown (*boz*) is made with acorn cups. For a deep brown, acorn cups and pomegranate skins are mixed. A brick brown is obtained from mixing acorn cups and madder. A yellow brown comes from mixing acorn cups with weld. To produce green (*göy*), blue-dyed yarn is dipped into a boiling solution of weld. For a light hazel green, turmeric is added. Blue (*göy, al*) is obtained with indigo (*nil*). Violet (*banowsh*)is obtained by dyeing blue yarn with madder. Purple is made by boiling the ashes of tree leaves (*ban*) with pomegranate skins or madder remnants.

Synthetic dyes were introduced to Iran in the 1870s. The use of synthetic dyes purchased in towns is increasing because dye plants are becoming scarce in the seasonal pastures and along the migratory routes. This is due to the expansion of cultivation and the increasing number of herds. Furthermore women who no longer follow the nomadic way of life have no opportunity to gather them.

ITEMS WOVEN WITHOUT PILE

Tent cloths are woven in a warp-faced plain weave, undyed black goat hair being used for both warp and weft. Although this cloth is woven in the simplest weave it is never made by beginners because it requires strong hands and must be very regular. Two types of tent cloth are made: a loose weave for the walls and a more compacted one for the tent roof. Men sew the pieces of cloth together with a big needle and black goat hair thread. The tent, the family dwelling, is the biggest and most important woven item. Traditionally, a woman only starts weaving a tent after she has married, has had children and spent some time living with her in-laws.

Gelims are woven for use as blankets. They are usually 6 to 10 feet (2–3 metres) long and 3 to 5 feet (1.0–1.7 metres) wide and are weft-faced plain weaves worked in slit or dovetail tapestry. Multiple lively colours are traditionally used for the weft and undyed ivory or brown to dark brown wool for the warp. Silk and cotton yarns have made their appearance in them since the 1960s.

One special and important *gelim* is made to cover the stack of belongings arranged along the back wall of the tent. The long *gelim* is a distinctive feature of Qashqa'i tents. Its function is to protect the belongings from the evil eye, that is from the effects of the gaze of strangers, neighbours and kin. The owner's subtribe or tribe can be identified by the designs and colours in it and it provides visible evidence of the ability of the women living in the tent. Also woven is a simple rectangular cloth approximately 31 by 35 inches (80 by 90 cm) using camel hair in a slit tapestry structure with a wool border of reciprocal triangles.

Jajims are used as blankets or to cover the stacks of possessions. Most are made with vertical stripes (*konara*) in twill weave. Many have a plain central field with a simple checkered border (*masurkash*), and some a diamond or checkerboard design. They are woven very rapidly in one, two or four pieces that are sewn together by men using big needles and yarn. Horse blankets (*chul*) are made to keep them warm and to protect their backs. They are 40 by 60 inches (100 by 150 cm) and consist of two rectangles of cloth sewn together along one long side, with two small flaps at one short end of the enlarged rectangle, each continuing the line of a longer side. Some are patterned with weft wrapping or weft float brocading on a plain-woven ground of undyed dark wool, others with warp-faced plain weave and weft-faced complementary weave. Elaborate horse blankets with up to twelve colours are made for use only on special occasions and at ceremonies.

Bags are much used by nomads for storing and transporting grain, salt, bedding and a variety of other things, and some of the different sorts will now be described.

A *mafrash* is a box-like bag that consists of two end panels, a bottom panel and two long side panels with top flaps for closure. *Mafrash* are always used in pairs and can be crushed to a flat rectangle when empty. Every family traditionally owns at least one pair because a bride brings the bedding and clothing part of her dowry in them to her husband's home. In some tents pairs of *mafrash* are aligned beside the grain and straw bags at the back of the tent and covered with a *gelim* under the folded blankets and rugs. Many Qashqa'i families cannot afford them. Leather bindings, buckles and straps are sometimes added by urban leather artisans specialised in saddlery. When the Qashqa'i men sew the pieces together they use big needles and spun woollen thread, and they add braided ropes, tasselled cords and fastenings at the bag's opening.

A *baladan* is used to transport the equipment used for baking bread. This is a long, narrow, rectangular bag adorned with tassels. It has a long braid by which it can be hung from a tent pole or from a camel during migration.

Grain and straw bags (*chual*) are large, approximately 47–51 inches (120–130 cm) long and 28–32 inches (70–80) wide, and consist of two pieces sewn together. Men sew the bags shut along the selvedges by cross-wrapping with red and green thread. The opening is sewn completely shut when the bag is full and re-sewn each time it is opened. The *duz torba* (salt bag) is used to store and transport salt and has a uniquely shaped top which serves as a closing flap. A system of slits and loops fastens the bag at the top of its narrow neck. A decorative rectangular bag is made to protect the water pipe. This often hangs from a tent pole in the rear of the tent.

The *chanta* is a small bag approximately a foot (30 cm) square that women use for their small personal items. It has a braided cord sewn on to it and long heavy tassels hanging from the bottom. In camp they are slung from a tent pole and during migration from the back of a pack animal.

Double saddle-bags are used by the nomads to carry necessities when travelling on horseback. Leather backs are sometimes added by urban artisans. The bags are closed by pulling goat hair loops on the body of the bag through vertical slits in the front flap and passing each one through its neighbour.

Narrow bands are tablet-woven in ivory and dark blue or red and black wool and serve a variety of purposes. In sarhad, these bands are used to decorate tents. Wealthy Qashqa'i have them the length of their large tents. They are also used for camel and horse trappings, for securing the loads of pack animals, as girths for the pack saddle and as tethers. The chest and head bands of camels and horses are ornamented with tassels.

KNOTTED PILE WEAVINGS

According to a legend, the Qashqa'i learnt how to weave pile rugs and bags from Bollu women of the Amala tribe. Pile weaves are produced more in some tribal groups than in others and some groups are admired for specific weavings. The finest pile rugs are woven by women of the Kuchuk Kashkullu and the Bollu subtribe of the Amala, the finest flatweaves (*gelim* and *jajim*) by women of the Buyug Kashkullu and Darrashurlu, and the finest *gabbas* by women of the Darrashurlu and Shesh Baylu. Many nomadic Qashqa'i women do not weave pile rugs and many families do not use them.

According to Qashqa'i women the quality of a pile weaving depends on the regularity and fineness of the yarn used. The thinner the yarn the finer the weaving. Qashqa'i pile rugs generally have two ground wefts between each row of knots. The weft is passed by hand through the shed and counter shed without using any special implement and is beaten in after every pick with a comb beater (*karket*) which has steel blades attached to a heavy handle. Knots are first cut with scissors (*dokar*) and then evened with a knife blade (*siq*). Pile rugs are begun and finished with a dozen rows of weft-faced plain weave or weft-faced brocade (*suf*). The warp ends (*sarabi*) may be braided or left loose.

Qashqa'i women do not use cartoons or sketches as do the rural and urban weavers. Instead, they weave from memory or copy the design directly from another rug. They also copy from a type of small rug with samples of various designs woven into it.

The Qashqa'i have never been an isolated people. In the course of time many groups have joined the tribe bringing with them their own characteristic designs and structures that have been incorporated into Qashqa'i weaving. According to Garrod (1946b), 'The Kashkuli designs have been influenced by their incorporation, more than a century ago, of a section of the Borcharqchi [Buchaqchi] tribe [of Kermān].' This Kermani subtribe probably learnt the art of weaving in sedentary workshops for they reproduced designs they shared with other weavers in Iran and elsewhere. Garrod goes on to say: 'The sections most noted for their rugs are the Kashkuli, the Shishbuluki, and the Bullu. Of these only the Shishbuluki show much Turkman influence in their designs, in the form of a large and formalised tarantula which dominates the four corners of the field' (pp. 301–2). In the case of designs considered to have been borrowed from sedentary workshop productions, the Qashqa'i weavers continue to reproduce them with little alteration despite the rich design tradition around them.

One of the finest Qashqa'i pile weave designs is the *nazem*, which is a speciality of the women of the Kermani subtribe. *Nazem* is identified by rug dealers and specialists as being inspired by the Mughal Indian Mille Fleurs prayer rugs. A widespread design is *kaleh asbi*. It is considered by the

Shesh Baylu (Shesh Boluki) women weaving a knotted-pile carpet near Shirin Cheshmeh. Summer, 1989. When women weave together, they agree beforehand on the structure, colours, dimensions of the item and the amount of work to be done by each. They attach small coloured tufts at the end of the rows they have woven which are almost invisible. Variations in the design can indicate that different pairs of hands have been at work. Weaving is a social activity and women make it an occasion to visit each other and help with the work.

Qashqa'i almost as a tribal emblem and is shared by the Shesh Baylu, Fars Madan and Amala tribes. The centre field is composed of three stepped diamond medallions each enclosing a diamond with hooked projections and rosettes. Elaborate rugs are produced with fields covered with smaller and larger birds, vegetable and geometric designs. Other designs include versions of the *boteh* pattern derived ultimately from Indian textiles, and the Herati pattern which originated two or three centuries ago and is now widely used in Iran, Turkestan and the Caucasus.

Piled horse blankets show a variety of patterns such as rows of confronted peacocks, stylised birds, trees, plant ornaments, rosettes, gazelles or geometric motifs. *Chantas* (small square bags for personal items) are woven with a pile face with traditional motifs of hooked diamond medallions with a field filled with gazelles, rosettes, angular *boteh* and rosettes. Pile saddle-bags are woven with designs similar to pile rugs. Two designs are exclusively used for saddle-bags: *shah neshin*, a hooked diamond medallion balanced symmetrically by four smaller ones, and *qızıl qaychi* or 'red scissors', a lattice containing hooked motifs.

There are two other types of piled rug which should be mentioned, the *gabba* and the *khersak*. The *gabba* is the most widespread type of pile rug among relatively wealthy nomadic families. *Gabbas* are spread out on felt rugs to cover the floor of the tent when guests are present. They are also used on very cold nights as heavy blankets. Average quality wool is used and the rug is characterised by a high pile covering the numerous wefts. The number of wefts varies from four to eight

Qashqa'i women wear a full-length, sleeved tunic (*keynak*) slit up both sides to the hip. A variation has a cut in the front for women who are breast-feeding. The two sides are closed with a pin . A short waist-length jacket (*arkhalıq*) can be worn over the tunic. It has long sleeves that cover the hands to protect them from the sun, wind and cold. The jacket opens in front and usually has no fasteners. Women who live and work as nomadic pastoralists wear two or three full skirts, with sometimes the remnants of one or two additional ones underneath. A lightweight, often transparent scarf (*charqat*) is worn on a daily basis. Head-scarf colours reflect age and status. The colours used are white, pale blue, green, yellow, and finally black and brown. A long, colourful, silk head-band (*yaylıq*) is often worn over the head-scarf, wrapped around the head and then knotted loosely at the nape of the neck. The ends are allowed to trail down the back. A number of details of dress including the way the headdress is worn can distinguish Qashqa'i women of different groups from each other and from other women in the area who dress in a similar manner. Amala, on upward migration near Kāzerun, 1986.

shoots between each row of knots. The knots are symmetrical and the knotting coarse. Traditional geometric designs are used. Many Qashqa'i, and especially Darrashurlu, weave *gabbas* with a field covered with one or several lions with or without a sun and sword (Tanavoli 1977). The Shesh Baylu, and especially its Qarayarlu subtribe, weave *gabbas* with designs inspired by the bas-reliefs and ruins of Persepolis. The *khersak* is coarser than the *gabba,* has a higher pile, and six to ten shoots of weft are passed between each row of knots. It is woven from mediocre quality undyed wool yarns using symmetrical knotting. (For WOVEN STRUCTURES see Appendix, p.320).

CLOTHING AND PERSONAL ADORNMENT

The Qashqa'i wear a fixed set of clothes in a well-developed style that distinguishes them from non-Qashqa'i people and symbolises their identity. The style has, however, changed over time due to both internal and external influences. The women do not weave items of apparel, so they adapt the materials they buy in markets to their clothing needs, and are dependent on what the market provides. Their clothes are based on industrial products and fabrics, and their sewing notions are learnt from markets and itinerant merchants. Several items of apparel (felt cloak, hat and shoes) are made by non-Qashqa'i specialists.

MEN'S CLOTHING

The nature of men's clothing before the twentieth century can be seen in paintings, drawings and photographs of prominent Qashqa'i leaders from that time, who often frequented cities (Oberling 1974, Fraser 1825: 93; Goldsmid 1874a and b: 576). Photographs and descriptions of nomadic Qashqa'i clothes have continued to appear since the turn of the twentieth century (see Demorgny

1913a: 93; Duncan 1946, 1982; Douglas 1951; Shor 1952; Edwards 1953: 385; Ullens de Schooten 1956), so there is no shortage of information on the changes that have taken place.

Before 1928, men used to wear white tunics (*keynak*) made from a single length of cloth folded in half, with no shoulder seams, and holes for the head and arms. The sleeves were sewn to the straight edge of the body piece. More elaborate tunics were made by professional tailors and used by the wealthy.

A tunic (*arkhalıq*) was worn, open and overlapped in front and secured with a cummerbund, surplus cloth often being allowed to blouse above the band. The tunic reached to mid-leg and flared at the bottom, and the sides were slit. It had long sleeves that finished in pointed ends covering the hands. A fine fabric (*termeh*) was used, a special cotton (*mahut-e fastuni*), but it could be an inexpensive one (*chit*) in up to seven lively colours, either solid or with diverse patterns. The lining was a different fabric, usually in another colour or colours, sometimes with a floral design, and a felt or cardboard stiffener to hold the neck firm. The wide cloth cummerbund (*shal-o arkhalıq*) was always worn with the cloak. This was 10 or 13 feet (3 or 4 metres) long and 1 foot 8 inches to 8 feet (0.5–2.5 metres) wide and made either from a single piece of cotton fabric or two pieces sewn together. White or brown was used, or various lively colours and designs.

The wide-legged trousers (*tuman*) the men wore were made of two lengths of fabric sewn together, most often a thick, satiny, black cotton. A cord gathered the trousers at the waist.

As in so many other areas of Qashqa'i life, from 1929 to 1941 Rezā Shah imposed clothing reforms in order to create a more homogeneous modern society in Iran. Men were required to wear European-style trousers and suit jackets and a distinctive hat (*kolah Pahlavi*, P.; *shapka Pahlavi*, T.) reminiscent of that worn by French gendarmes (see Bayat 1986: 145–52; Oberling 1974: 152). Even after Rezā Shah's abdication in 1941 and the formal ending of clothing restrictions, men continued to wear European-style shirts, jackets and trousers. They sometimes wear traditional clothes during wedding ceremonies.

A thin cloak (*choqqa*) is sometimes worn over other apparel, and its use was probably adopted from Lur neighbours and the non-Qashqa'i inhabitants of garmsir. Six pieces of cloth are sewn together with the seams inside, and it is either secured and closed by two cords with brightly coloured tassels at the ends or worn loosely as a coat. The cost of a *choqqa* depends on the quality of wool or cloth used and the type of weaving. The best quality ones are brought from Mecca, Kuwait and other areas across the Persian Gulf. In the nineteenth and twentieth centuries the Qashqa'i men used the *choqqa* as a ceremonial dress and wore it during marriage ceremonies and mourning rituals, during war and upon the visit of a prominent leader. It represented Qashqa'i tribal identity. The German spy Schulze-Holthus (1954: 227, 232) mentions Qashqa'i warriors wearing it in battle in 1943: 'And then it happened. From the tall grass sprang wild figures with fluttering white tschogas [*choqqas*] yelling and waving their rifles. The effect was magnificent.' After the Islamic revolution in 1979 and the return of the paramount leaders from exile, the *choqqa* re-emerged as an important item of apparel. Worn over the regular shirt and trousers, it showed that the wearer honoured the paramount khāns and was at their service as a warrior and guard. The *choqqa* symbolised tribal affiliation to the leaders, who had been away for almost twenty-five years.

The only outer garment not worn by all nomadic Qashqa'i men is the felt cloak (*kapanak*) usually worn by shepherds. This is a heavy, ankle-length coat with long sleeves, made of thick brown, beige or grey felt. These are purchased ready-made from specialised felt-makers in towns and villages.

Loose-fitting trousers tied with a drawstring at the waist are worn by many men. These striped trousers are worn when sleeping or relaxing in the tent, and some men wear them as everyday trousers as they conduct their various pastoral chores in and around the encampment. They wear their European-style trousers on top of them when guests are present and when they go to town or travel away from the encampment. The striped trousers are often sewn by Qashqa'i women from purchased cloth, although they can also be purchased ready-made in markets.

Both men and women wear the same sort of hand-made shoes (*kalash*), called *giva*. Constructed by specialists (*givakash*) they have an upper crocheted from cotton thread and a thick sole made of compressed layers of cloth laid vertically, sometimes accordion pleated, and sewn through with gut. The sole and heel are reinforced with animal horn and skin, and the seams between the sole and upper are trimmed with leather strips. A wide leather strip protects the heel.

On migration women like to wear their best clothes. Up to 20 metres (65 feet) of cloth are used to make each of these very full skirts. Many women wear three to four skirts at a time and some women wear up to twelve or even fifteen skirts, one over the other. Gallehzan Amala, April 1988.

More than one style of hat has been used by Qashqa'i men over time and the present distinctive and unique head-dress is a very recent development. A portrait of the *ilkhāni* Jāni Aqa from the beginning of the nineteenth century shows him with a high-crowned dark hat (Oberling 1974: 242), while other later portraits of Qashqa'i *ilkhānis* show them wearing tall conical hats (pp. 244–8). Demorgny (1913a: 93) describes the Qashqa'i as wearing flared hats made of black felt. Photographs from the 1930s show the last Qashqa'i paramount leaders (Oberling 1974: 249–50) wearing short conical black felt hats that are also described by Goldsmid (1874b: 578). In Bayat (1986: 149) there is an important photograph of a leader of the Kashkullu tribe that shows a different type of tall conical black hat, one that is wider on the top.

The present-day style of felt hat, rounded on top and with two side flaps (*dogush*), dates from the 1940s and was introduced by Nāser Khān (*ilkhāni* from 1920 to 1928 and again from 1941 to 1954). 'I needed a hat with flaps to protect my face and ears from the sun, wind and cold. I commissioned a hat with two flaps in Shirāz and had no intention of changing the Qashqa'i traditional headwear' (Nāser Khān, personal communication, Moreh Lupeh, October 1980). This hat was not created on the basis of earlier models, although it resembles the high pointed hats with flaps over the ears (*kopak*) worn by the Central Asian Sakas depicted on the famous bas-reliefs in the Achaemenid palace at Persepolis, and 'a little skullcap, slit on each side, called dogoosheh' (Morier 1816: 155; see also Fraser 1825: 93) worn by peasants near Ābādeh. Nāser Khān's new hat was admired by Qashqa'i men and they gradually, and then *en masse*, adopted it in symbolic recognition of their tribal affiliation to the paramount leader. The 5-inch (13-cm) tall tan or grey felt *dogush* has become the most prominent symbol of Qashqa'i identity. Qashqa'i children's clothes, especially boys', resemble those of adults.

When a bride is prepared for marriage, the hair in two sections by her ears is cut to a level just below her ear lobes, and the hair growing above the forehead is cut in bangs to just above the eyebrows. This hair-style is distinctive of a new bride, and a newly married woman keeps these sections of hair short until she gives birth to her first child or until she has been married for some years. Once the hair is allowed to grow out it is twisted and then wrapped around the cords holding the cap in place that are tied under the chin. Sometimes these twisted sections are tucked into the head-scarf.

top
A newly married Qashqa'i woman who identifies herself Qara Quni. Near Firuzābād, 1985.

centre
A Kheiratlu Darrashurlu woman. Winter camp near Bushehr, 1988.

bottom
An elderly Kheiratlu Darrashurlu woman. Winter camp near Bushehr, 1988.

WOMEN'S CLOTHES

The style of women's clothes is of course different from the men's. They mostly wear the same type and cannot usually be distinguished socially from one another except by the quality of materials used and the number of garments owned. Many women own only one set of clothes, the set they wear, with possibly another new skirt and tunic, which they save for ceremonial occasions, such as weddings. They also wear them during the migrations, when they are on display to others.

The cloth for women's clothes is usually bought for them by men from the markets in towns, although since the 1960s the women have begun to purchase cloth themselves. The cloth is given when it is necessary to make new clothes for ceremonies and migrations. Cloth is the gift men give most often to their married sisters, around the time of the New Year. Women also give gifts of cloth to female relatives; some pieces are passed from woman to woman several times before they are finally made into items of apparel. Women sew their own clothes, usually by hand. Women from wealthier families own hand-turned sewing machines, but they also have some of their clothes sewn by other Qashqa'i women, by professional Qashqa'i tailors and urban tailors. Women also buy ready-made clothes from the Shirāz bazaar.

Colours are important to the Qashqa'i and women tend to wear the most lively, vivid ones. Richness of fabric, ornament in clothing and the number of garments worn mark social rank, while colour demonstrates aesthetic notions and conveys information about age and status.

All Qashqa'i women wear the same style of clothes, whatever their age or the event. What varies is the colour of the fabric from which the costume is sewn, and it does so according to the age of the wearer and nature of the occasion. Thus dress for ceremonial occasions is not marked by variation in style; instead, colour and a fixed combination of garments identify the costume's function.

A child's (*ushaq*) clothes are usually made with remnants of cloth from her mother's and older sister's clothes. A young girl (*qız*) wears very bright and lively colours, as does a young woman of marriageable age. Only a bride (*galin*) wears vivid red colours but is not supposed to dress so as to attract undue attention, for fear of the evil eye (which would jeopardise her life, her potential fertility and a pregnancy). Women of other status avoid red or at least avoid wearing much of it. A young wife and mother (*arvat, ana*) mixes bright and less bright colours in the fabrics she wears. Patterned fabric that contains red along with other colours is acceptable for such women. Elderly women wear greys and blacks.

Qashqa'i women wear a knee-length sleeved tunic (*keynak*) slit up both sides to the hip. This traditional garment is a closed one without shoulder seams made from a single length of cloth folded in half, with holes for the head and arms. Diverse kinds of fabric, patterns and colours are used. A variation is made for women who breast-feed: the tunic has a cut in the front and the two sides are closed with a pin. A more complicated version with shoulder seams, and the sleeves, sides and back all cut out separately, often along curved lines, is made by tailors and women who know how to cut and sew garments. The length of the tunic has changed over time. After the 1950s some women made their tunics longer, to reach their calves and almost the hems of their skirts, and some women made the neck opening larger.

A short, waist-length jacket (*arkhalıq*) is worn over the tunic. It has long sleeves, often styled to end in a point, that cover the hands to protect them from the sun, wind and cold. These long sleeves are tucked back to leave the hands free in daily work. Some women wear square or rectangular silver arm-plates on the outside of their upper arms and tuck the sleeve ends under them. The jacket opens in front and usually has no fasteners, and the sides are sometimes slit to permit greater freedom of movement. The material is usually velvet in a single colour, lined with patterned cotton. The hems and edges often have decorative trim purchased in markets. Women either sew their own jackets, have them made by Qashqa'i tailors or buy them ready-made in the Shirāz bazaar.

Another type of jacket was worn over the *arkhalıq* by paramount leaders' wives and daughters. It was flared at the hip and the bottom part covered the upper legs. The long *arkhalıq* was made in velvet and embroidered.

The skirt (*tuman*) is probably the most prominent item of apparel. It contains up to 50–65 feet (15–20 metres) long of cloth and is gathered at the waist with a cord threaded through a narrow hem and knotted in front with the ends tucked inside. The voluminous gathers are distributed about the waist with fewer in the front than at the sides. Various fabrics are used, plain cottons, synthetics,

above
Shesh Baylu (Shesh Boluki) women belonging to the groom's family at a wedding. Shirin Cheshmeh, 1989.

right
Qashqa'i women in every-day dress spinning goat hair and wool. Autumn 1987.

shiny gold- or silver-threaded, in single colours, stripes or patterns. The skirt is worn low on the hips.

Women want their skirts to look as full as possible so most wear more than one at a time, many three or four and some twelve to fifteen. When many skirts are worn, they are layered from just above the waist to the hip, to avoid bunching too many pleats on top of one another. Those women who live and work as nomadic pastoralists wear two or three complete skirts, with sometimes the remnants of one or two additional ones underneath. Those who can afford many skirts carefully assess their height and physique to ascertain how many skirts look best on them.

Pleated organza ruffles are sewn on the bottom of the skirts to increase the fullness. Some are a third of the length of the skirt and reach to just below the knees. The length of the fabric used is twice that of the skirt to which it is sewn. The bottom of the skirt is therefore very full. One to four rows of ribbons, rick-rack braid and other kinds of trim in different colours are often sewn on the seam connecting the skirt proper with the pleated ruffles, and on the ruffle itself. With the different kinds and colours of cloth used for the skirt body and the pleated ruffle, and the various trims in assorted designs and colours, skirts made in this fashion are a festival of fabrics and colours. Women seek out metallic fabrics, gold- and silver-threaded cloth, and trim with metallic highlights, all of which create a sparkling display, especially at night by firelight and in the sun during the day. Because many skirts are layered, additional designs and colours show themselves as the women move and sit. Some women make the top skirt out of transparent fabric, sometimes shot with gold or silver threads, so that the patterns and colours of the second skirt show through. Innovations in clothing complement and maintain earlier styles of clothes and add elegance to women's attire.

Skirts are subjected to considerable wear and tear. They become worn from the rough terrain, ripped and tattered from often being caught on rocks and thorny shrubs and bushes, and burned from their frequent proximity to fires. The innermost skirts are often short because of this kind of damage, and also because they have been the source of scraps of cloth for household tasks and to bandage injuries. Skirts are worn in order of their age and degree of wear, the newest on top, the oldest next to the skin, often serving as underwear. Wealthy women with servants keep keys to various locked containers (mostly holding food supplies) in a pocket sewn on to an inner skirt.

When a woman acquires a new skirt, the one she has only occasionally worn becomes the skirt she wears every day. The new one is only worn on ceremonial occasions, as when visitors call, and during the migration. Otherwise it is rolled up, tied with its own waist cord and kept in the household baggage, or hung from a rope stretched between two tent poles. Women can be seen slipping on a new skirt when an unexpected guest approaches the tent.

For headgear, women wear scarves, headbands and sometimes caps. The scarf (*charqat*) is a lightweight one, sometimes in a transparent fabric, and is worn on a daily basis. A square or rectangular piece of fabric about 6 feet (2 metres) square in size is folded into a triangle and cut. The cut piece is divided in two, and each piece is sewn to a side of the open cloth. To wear the head-scarf, the rounded edge, which is formed in the centre of the long side, is placed high on the forehead near the hairline and the two hemmed edges joined under the chin with an ornamental pin or metal fastener (*asmalıq*, *chapa*). Some Qashqa'i women, particularly those of wealthy families, sew patterns of sequins in single or multiple colours on their head-scarves, and on their tunics. Head-scarf colours also reflect age and status. The colours used are white, pale blue, green, yellow, and finally black and brown.

A long colourful headband (*yaylıq*) is often worn over the head-scarf. Fabric 6 feet (2 metres) square is folded several times lengthwise, wrapped around the head and then knotted loosely at the nape of the neck. The ends are allowed to trail down the back. The headband does not hide the head-scarf. Bold, colourful, resist-dyed silks imported from Turkestan and bought in the Shirāz bazaar are used. In the 1920s, the less expensive headbands were industrial products, and since the 1930s synthetic fabrics have been the most commonly used. The headband is added when the woman wants to be well dressed on ceremonial and other special occasions, including the migration. However, the long loose ends often interfere with a woman's work and so the headband is slipped off.

Caps (*kolaqcha*) made out of two pieces of cloth sewn together, often velvet or shiny material, are worn by some women. The cap covers the top of the back of the head and reaches the ears, and is often held in place by two narrow braided cords tied under the chin. The cap helps to hold the thin material of the head-scarf in place, and to keep the scarf clean.

Many women in south Iran, particularly tribal women, dress in a similar fashion to Qashqa'i women. The distinction between Qashqa'i and non-Qashqa'i and between women of different Qashqa'i tribes is made by differences in the ways clothes are worn. Tribal affiliations used to be recognisable from different styles of wearing head-scarves and headbands. Shesh Baylu women did not close the head-scarf under the chin but rather passed it around the neck. Some Darrashurlu brought the left side of the head-scarf to the right side and fastened it above the ear. Buyug Kashkullu women knotted the headband on the side rather than behind the head, following the custom of their Kurdish ancestors.

The non-Qashqa'i tunic side openings end lower down than the Qashqa'i, which end on the hip, where the skirt begins. The head-scarf of non-Qashqa'i women does not have the rounded edge on the forehead, and is fastened right under the chin, whereas the Qashqa'i head-scarf is fastened further down, on the throat. The non-Qashqa'i headband is folded to form a wider band than the Qashqa'i. It hides the head-scarf more completely on the top and sides of the head, is set further back on the head and has a large knot. The Qashqa'i headband does not hide the head-scarf and its rounded edge is placed up on the head-scarf and not flattened on the head. The knot is down over the nape of the neck and is small and loose.

Qashqa'i women do not wear quantities of jewellery. The most common piece is the neck pin (*asmalıq*, *chapa*), which fastens the two sides of the head-scarf under the chin and is either a simple metal pin (even a safety pin), a pin with some artificial or semi-precious stones such as turquoise, or a gold pin. Gold pins, often with some ornaments hanging from them, such as coins, fish or crescents, are purchased in Shirāz and Lār. Some wear a brooch (*bashdehasa*) on the headband that is sometimes fish-shaped (an ancient symbol of fertility in Asia).

Necklaces are also worn. Brides receive one to three necklaces during their wedding ceremony. One is made of cloves (*mikhak*), another of dyed wild pistachios and a third of cloves and pistachios. These necklaces are supposed to be worn until death. Women attach various antique and new gold, silver and alloy coins to their necklaces as well as amulets shaped like coins with writing and numbers on them. Another necklace called *sineriz* is popular and contains numerous fish-shaped pieces, crescents and coin-sized discs. The necklace is made in gold, silver and alloys. Some women own necklaces of coral beads and gold or silver coins (*fatalishahi*, *ashrafi*). Earrings, bracelets and armbands are worn by some women. Gold jewellery is preferred to silver. The favourite precious and semi-precious stones are ruby, turquoise and coral.

Amulets and talismans are worn by women, children and occasionally men. Fabric packets of velvet and mohair (*termeh*) containing some substance or a special item like a tiny Koran are pinned to the arm or worn close to the body. Some have cowrie shells or pieces of coral sewn on the outside. Small cylinders of gold or silver or other metals are worn with such items as written prayers inside. Mothers attach small pieces of alum, along with other stones, cowries, pearls, coins, chunks of salt and blue beads, to their children's caps or the backs of their shirts or undershirts.

Qashqa'i women are proud of their long hair, which they wear in many braids down their back. Many women never cut their hair, and some women's hair reaches their calves. Both girls and women part their hair in the middle and braid the two parts into dozens of small braids from the level of the ears. Unmarried girls make a small section of hair in front of each ear into one braid. When they are prepared for marriage, the hair in these two sections is cut to just below the ear lobes and the hair above the forehead in bangs to just above the eyebrows. A newly-married woman keeps these sections of hair short. Later the hair is allowed to grow out and is twisted and wrapped around the cords that hold the cap in place. Sometimes these twisted sections are tucked into the head-scarf. Nomadic Qashqa'i women wash their hair more often than any other part of themselves. They use a mud purchased in sarhad or powdered jujube leaves (*sedr*). Some apply henna and rinse their hair with sour milk. After washing they add clarified butter or chicken-breast fat, or oil from wild almonds as a conditioner.

As for make-up, some women apply kohl (*surma*) around their eyes, which they make in total darkness from burnt wild almonds during the first night of the moon in a clear, cloudless sky. They keep the powder in a small cloth bag and apply it with a stick men make from animal horn. Mothers surround the eyes of newborn babies with kohl in an attempt to avert the evil eye, and apply it to children having eye problems. Men also use it when they have eye trouble.

Tattooing on the face, hands and body is used as an adornment and for medical reasons. Facial tattoos, especially on the lower lip, are considered marks of beauty, while others are considered good for arthritis and other joint pains. Ritual specialists (*usta*) and itinerant gypsies make the tattoos using pins and dyes to mark the skin.

The Qashqa'i wash rather than bath, and only certain parts of their bodies with any regularity, the face, neck, arms, hands and feet. Girls are washed from head to toe and shampooed the night before they are married and this may be the only such time in their lives. Sometimes, in order to wash, women erect a small shelter by putting a tent cloth over a tripod, or use the lamb pen inside the winter tent if they know that all men and older boys are absent. Mothers wash young children with a cloth dipped into a pan of warm water. Wealthy women use a small tent for washing whose floor is covered with a reed mat. In garmsir it is placed near a well and a small fire or brazier of coals helps to keep the inside warm. In sarhad it is placed near a spring. A pan of hot water is put just inside the tent opening and a servant repeatedly refills it. Another servant often helps with scrubbing the body and washing the hair.

BELIEFS AND CUSTOMS

The Qashqa'i are Shi'a Muslims, but neither mosques nor madrasas exist in their territory, there are no communal religious gatherings and no religiously trained individual or practitioner is attached to the tribe or performs mediation or other religious tasks. Those who pray regularly or on special occasions always do it individually. The most respected Shi'a saint is 'Abbas. Men and women swear oaths by him, which they usually keep for they fear him. They pile up a few stones, swear the oath and then scatter the pile.

Pilgrimages are not generally undertaken by the Qashqa'i. When in Shirāz they visit the Vakil Mosque and the tomb of Shah-e Cheragh, a ninth-century martyr, the principal pilgrimage site of Fārs province. On migrations they visit the dwellings, cupolas, shrines, graves, rocks and wells they pass that are associated with holy men, and they pay their respects to the seyyeds and dervishes that live at such places. Few of these sites have religious significance for them. The solitary trees they pass are believed to have grown where a holy man planted a stick and are sacred. Women tie ribbons to the branches and ask for a wish to be granted.

As to calendrical festivals, these are celebrated within the framework of two separate systems, the Islamic year and the Iranian solar year, the vestige of a Zoroastrian and animistic religious past (first millennium BC). These calendars are certainly important to the Qashqa'i but they tend to regulate events in terms of their twice-yearly migrations. Thus the advent of the Iranian New Year on 20–21 March, the spring equinox, the first day of spring, is overshadowed by the beginning of the spring migration. The nomads are preoccupied with the move and celebrate the New Year without much ceremony, although they certainly honour it with new clothes, visits to elders and family members, the baking of sweets and the exchange of gifts and good wishes for the coming year.

Some Qashqa'i celebrate the New Year by looking at mares, since it is believed this will bring them a happy year. This may be an echo of the chief festival of the nomadic Mongols, Tartars, Kazakhs, Kirghiz and Tuvinians of ancient times. This was a spring festival (*isiakh*) and took place when they began to milk the mares. A form of *isiakh* is still celebrated at the appearance of the first green shoots and is connected to the cult of the horse among the Qashqa'i but has lost its former religious significance under the influence of Islam and Persianate culture.

On the forty-fifth day of winter, pastoralists put spots of dye in lively colours on their sheep as a sign of victory over the high risk winter season, and as a sign of celebration of approaching spring. On the night before the last Wednesday of the year, the families of the encampment gather big piles of dried thorny bushes and light them as the sun sets. Women sprinkle on the fires some wild rue seeds which explode and jump. The herds are driven between two big fires to ensure the animals will remain healthy in the coming year; then young boys rhythmically beat pots and pans unless there is a musician present while everybody, men and women, young and old, jumps over the flames one at a time chanting verses of purification for the expulsion of evil: 'My yellowness to you, and your redness to me'. 'The colour yellow, symbolic of age, sickness and the paleness of winter is ritually traded for the colour red, symbolic of life, new blood and earth' (Amir-Moez 1991: 7–8).

Sweets, nuts and fruit are eaten and people play music, sing and dance. When the fires have died

The occasion is a wedding between a Shesh Baylu (Shesh Boluki) man and a Darrashurlu woman. The festivities take place over two days. It is time to make bread and guests go to different tents and do whatever they can to help. Shesh Baylu camp, 1989.

down to ashes, young women gather them in a pan and carry them to a remote place and throw them away, along, it is believed, with all the diseases and misfortunes of the previous year.

Wolves are the subject of many beliefs and legends among the Qashqa'i. For example, brides receive wolf paws (*qurd ali*) on their wedding day; women will touch a pregnant woman's stomach and say with a satisfying smile, 'It is a wolf'; mothers like to call their newborn 'wolf', and sometimes cry out loud, 'This is a baby wolf'. Active, sharp, smart children are called 'wolf's child' (*qurd ushaghı*). This is considered very high praise.[7]

The hearth (*ojaq, qazma*) is the symbolic centre of the tent. They are round, square, rectangular or oval. Each tribal group has its own particular shape, and each family its own variation of it. Digging the hearth is a strictly masculine task, performed by the most senior man. The hearth is respected and no one will walk over it or throw anything into it. When a bride leaves home, she performs a ritual of respect and gratitude to her father's hearth. When a person dies their hearth is kept alight for seven days and hearths are also kept alight beside gravestones. The hearths of the camp sites of the paramount tribal leaders are held to be sacred. People believe they can make misery and misfortune befall those who act against the leaders. Oaths are sworn 'by the ashes of Jāni Khān's hearth'.

The power to call forth rain and thus ensure the fertile growth of grass and crops is ascribed to a legendary spiritual, wise, elderly man, Kosah Galin. A young man impersonates him in a ceremony that is meant to ensure adequate rainfall. Nowadays he is dressed in the long felt coat worn by shepherds, and two small metal pendants are attached to his back, symbolising the sun and the moon. He wears a crown-like cap surmounted by two antlers, an indication of his connection with the upper world, the deer being considered to be connected with the heavenly sphere. His face is whitened with wheat flour, he wears a white wool or goat hair beard and carries a drum, most often a cooking pan, and drumstick. The members of the encampment gather round Kosah Galin and they all march in procession from one tent to another chanting to the drumming of pots and pans, 'I am Kosah Galin, I bring wind, I prick the sky with antlers, I bring rain'. Women sprinkle flour or water over his head and people welcome him with small gifts and pray for prosperity and rain. Afterwards there is music, singing and celebration till midnight.

Kosah Galin does not lapse into that ecstatic state which symbolises a voyage to other worlds but he is undoubtedly a shamanistic figure whose task is to communicate with the heavenly sphere and summon his helping spirit to provide rain by singing incantations to music.

The evil eye, a wicked and dangerous power present in the gaze of others, is strongly believed in by the Qashqa'i as it is everywhere else in Iran (Donaldson 1963; Watson 1979: 233–4), and they have many beliefs about it. For example, the gaze of strangers is feared because of it; they do not socialise when an important product such as clarified butter is made for fear that the evil eye will adversely affect its quality and quantity; and any food out of the ordinary they have acquired is shared with the other families of the encampment because they believe that if they do not the evil eye will cause them some illness and misfortune. A wide range of charms against bewitchment and other dangerous forces are worn, especially by women and children. Women wear necklaces of beads, salt crystal and coins, and tiger teeth are pinned to their caps. Amulets in the form of small cloth packets containing special items or a magic substance are sewn or pinned to the arms, and powerful words written by a dervish on a piece of paper are worn wrapped in fabric or in a prayer case.

Children are protected by having strings of beads mixed with coins, rags, small metal bells, buttons, amulets, capon feathers and other objects tied or sewn to their caps, jackets or clothes, and talismans made from owl, eagle and falcon feathers. A peculiar way of protecting a child from the evil eye is to wet the finger with saliva and apply it to the potential victim.

Animals are protected by the same sort of strings as children, these being tied to their necks or legs. Men carve pieces of wood and hang them from the necks of their most valued animals, particularly rams and camels. Like the children, they are protected by the application of saliva to a certain part of their body. Bags containing grain, salt and water, and horse blankets, are protected by beads, coins and amulets.

There is belief in evil spirits. Male (*jin*) and female (*peri*) are believed to appear at sunset and bring bad luck to people crossing ruins and rivers, or transporting salt, fire or milk products. To be safe, people carry a metal item to ward them off. There are Qashqa'i who believe that evil spirits cause animal illness and that they can cure them by passing them through a passage they dig under the ground. The most wicked evil spirit is considered to be Al, an invisible, hideous, witch-like creature that particularly appears at a childbirth and is likely to seize the mother's liver to kill her and the child. The ritual midwives perform to scare Al away is a dramatic one, perhaps the most dramatic the Qashqa'i have.

According to legend Al inhabits water and fears horses, metal and the colour black. The midwives remove all water in the vicinity of a woman in labour. Men gallop horses close by the tent chanting, '*Qach qara qach, ged o'qara'*. (The galloping sound and neigh of mares are considered to help a newborn infant stay alive.) Braids of black horse hair are knotted around the mother's ankles and wrists and black lines are drawn on her face and body with a powder made of indigo, gunpowder or charcoal. A pair of blackened old shoes are attached together and hung over her head as antlers and she is surrounded by blackened metal objects, pans, chains and swords. A big fire is made in which all the women who have gathered to help, burn wild rue and pray.

If the woman in labour begins haemorrhaging and is in real danger it is an indication that Al is already in her. If she faints or loses consciousness, Al is about to carry her to the other world. To dislodge the invisible spirit, the midwives beat the mother on her hands, fingers, face. Symbolically she undergoes torture, her limbs are cut off, she is killed and hacked apart and then, if she is lucky, reconstituted, brought back to life freed of illness and of the spirit Al.

Weddings are important festive occasions among the Qashqa'i and are usually celebrated in the good weather of sarhad after the yearly sale of animals. With the help and contributions of their kin, and of those who are invited to attend, most Qashqa'i families are capable of celebrating elaborate weddings on a relatively large scale. The groom's family borrows tents as well as various items for cooking and feeding the guests, and all those who are invited, close and distant kin, friends and neighbours, give whatever they can, be it money, animals or gifts. Invitations are circulated verbally. Tents are pitched in a circle in a fresh area close to a spring. Musicians arrive first and the continuous piercing sound of a kind of reed shawm (*sorna*) and the steady beat of a large drum (*naqareh*) signal the people for miles around that a wedding is taking place. Guests arrive dressed in their best clothes bringing with them gifts of animals and other things. Close kin help to gather firewood, cook and serve the meals and entertain the guests during the three- to seven-day celebration. The groom's family has purchased from town all the goods necessary for the party.

During the celebrations women and sometimes men perform a three-stepped slow dance (*aqorhali*) holding colourful handkerchiefs, and a faster dance (*ashrafimagana*). Men do their stick dance (*ho*) to the rhythm of a drum and sometimes sing solo love songs to a three-stringed bowed instrument (*setar*). Women produce at weddings the ululation (*kill*) they also produce at times of conflict and war.

A bride sees no part of her wedding. She is kept in her father's tent during the celebrations to make preparations and to complete her dowry, which has been prepared for her for years. The dowry, which includes a number of woven items, animals, horses and jewellery matches in importance and value the bride-price paid by the groom's father to the bride's family, and is relative to the family's status. During this time new clothes are sewn for the bride and women from her family gather to help, each of them bringing a gift.

Finally, the bride is washed completely and her hair, hands and feet are dyed with henna. Her long hair is made into many plaits and an older woman cuts her bangs and forelocks. A tunic for her is finished at the last minute and the neckline is cut open by her older brother as a sign of consent to her marriage. She is dressed in new clothes of reddish colour and wears wedding necklaces and all the jewellery she owns or has received as wedding gifts. She laments because she is being torn away from those she loves, and she cries and refuses to speak or co-operate with anybody.

Once she is dressed and adorned, the bride is taken to the family hearth by her older brother. She steps round it three times and kneels to press her forehead to it in farewell. She puts her fingers in the ashes and places them in her mouth. Her mother tucks wheat flour, salt and some money in a cloth she ties around her daughter's waist. A large party from the wedding encampment then attacks the bride's tent, shooting in the air, and ritually kidnaps her. The wedding contract, previously written by an elderly literate Qashqa'i, is signed by the fathers of the bride and groom and witnessed.

The bride is placed on a white horse adorned with weavings and tassels and her dowry on another. These horses are given to her by her father. A small boy rides behind her so that she will arrive in her new encampment with a male child. As she leaves, family and friends sing and dance to a very sad and nostalgic song (*ana-am-hay*). The bride's wails can be heard as she rides away. She is kept covered by special weavings and should not show her face.

As the procession passes an encampment a ram, symbol of fertility, is led in her path. When she arrives at the bridal tent, made of flatweaves over three tent poles and pitched near the groom's father's tent, she is received by her mother-in-law who welcomes her with a gift. The groom, who has been in hiding up to this point, is taken by relatives back to his father who offers him his hand to kiss as consent to the marriage. The groom then joins the bride in the bridal tent to consummate the marriage. On the seventh day after the marriage, the bride is invited by her father-in-law to his tent and he welcomes her with the gift of an animal.

NON-PASTORAL LIVELIHOODS

Most Qashqa'i gain their livelihood by livestock husbandry combined with some agriculture. The remainder rely on other means to support themselves, and they have an important role in Qashqa'i society. In former times those employed by other Qashqa'i would receive the goods necessary to sustain their families (*jira*), including rice, wheat, sugar, tea, milk products and clothes. Their salaries and terms of employment were not made explicit and cash payments were rare. Some of these non-pastoral livelihoods have a long history, while others have appeared since the 1960s.

There are, or at least were, roughly four categories of livelihood that the non-pastoralist Qashqa'i can follow. First, in the past they could serve the khāns or other leaders. Second, they can serve other pastoralists by caring for their animals, performing agricultural labour, hunting, music, tinkering, medicine, and so on. This category provides employment for Qashqa'i and for those non-Qashqa'i groups who live in Qashqa'i territory. Third, they can sell to non-Qashqa'i the products of weaving and gathering, or provide services such as harvesting or acting as armed escorts to trade caravans. Fourth, there was thievery and brigandage.

SERVING THE KHĀN

The paramount leader's retainers were drawn from the Amala (worker) tribe. This tribe was formed from people of other Qashqa'i groups, and tribes in south Iran, who left for political and economic reasons to seek sanctuary with the buyug Khān. The majority of the Amala practised nomadic pastoralism but the rest were at the service of the paramount leader in various ways.

The more important, the paramount leader, the more numerous and complex the hierarchy of individuals that served him. Many retainers inherited their positions from their parents while others, attracted by his power, were drawn to abandon their groups of origin for his personal service. Those not of the Amala tribal affiliation joined it when they entered his service. The paramount leader migrated seasonally between garmsir and sarhad like the other Qashqa'i. He occupied the choicest and best pasture lands and Amala tribespeople surrounded him. The number of tents in his encampment indicated his power and popularity.

When the paramount leader wanted to reward a family for some special service he would give them pastoral and agricultural land, and occasionally territory in garmsir and sarhad. Within the Amala the Mokhtar Khānlu and Bahmanbeglu subtribes were created in this way. On the other hand, a tribal section could lose rights and privileges when it fell into disfavour. Three important tribes or tribal sections disappeared or were reduced in size and importance for this reason. The Rahimlu and Ard Kapān, once powerful tribes, were subjugated and their members eventually absorbed into other tribes, and the Safi Khānlu, also an important tribe, was reduced to insignificance.

The khān's retinue can be roughly divided into four categories: household, administrative, overseers of animals and lands, and military. Various posts within this schema were always filled by people from particular Amala subtribes.

His household retainers tended to the personal needs of the khān, his family, guests and visitors. Butlers (*noukar*) and maids (*kolfat*) served them directly. *Mirzās* were tutors to each of the paramount leader's children. Cooks (*āshpaz*) worked in and around the cooking tent (*ābdār khāneh*). *Nāzem* were responsible for the household budget and for shopping. *Farrāsh* pitched and dismantled tents and served tea during audiences. *Gharāvol* served as guards and messengers.

Skilled weavers and tailors resided permanently in the leader's camp and worked for him and his family. Most of the weavers were Bollu Amala and of the Kermanlu subtribe of the Kuchuk Kashkullu. There were also musicians (*'ashıq*, *changi*) resident in the camp.

The *Mirzās* served as advisers, scribes, accountants and tax recorders. They advised the khān when important decisions were to be taken and accompanied him on trips. They liaised between the khān and his contacts in rural and urban sedentary groups and wrote out contracts (*bonchaq*) allotting rights to pastures and other lands.

Tax collecting employed a fair-sized body of men. The paramount leader periodically collected an animal tax from all Qashqa'i and he had representatives in the tribes who negotiated with the tribal leaders (*kalāntar*) concerning this payment, and they also had tax collectors (*nāyeb*) who negotiated with headmen. The tax (*gallehbegireh*, 'taking herds') was usually calculated as 3 per cent (*sad-o-seh*) of the value of the herds owned by tribal members. The kalāntars considered their share of the tax as payment for the services they performed for tribal members during the preceding year. The khān also paid government taxes from his share.

Various overseers were in charge of the khān's animals and lands. The chief shepherd (*mokhtābād*) and shepherds who looked after the flocks all came from the Chubonkara subtribe. The head groom (*mirākhor*) and grooms (*mehtar*) that looked after the horses (*rameh*) and stables

Unloading camels for a short stop on the downward migration. The Qashqa'i use only single-humped Arabian camels and do not cross-breed them with the two-humped Bactrian camel. Camels are an important asset, they are respected, petted and spoken to with affection, and the nomads like to decorate them with various bands, tassels and protective talismans. Amala on their downward migration, south of Qir, 1986.

all came from the Mehtar Khānlu. Another set of men cared for the camels. Overseers (*nāyeb*) were responsible for the khān's pastures, agricultural lands and villages.

A team of skilled hunters led by a chief (*mir shekār*) accompanied the khān on hunts. They were experts on the terrain, the game and the techniques of hunting. The *mir shekār* also served as head beater when game was flushed. Lastly, falconers (*qushchi*) raised and cared for the paramount leader's falcons.

The last category were military. The paramount leader needed protection against state agents and military forces, and against neighbouring tribal groups during periods of conflict. Within his encampment Amala families served as his bodyguards and around it lived men proven in battle skills who were personally loyal to him. These gunmen (*tofangchi*) and armed cavalry (*atlı*) were his personal army. In times of conflict they could number as many as 10,000 (Bayat 1986: 61). The khān could also summon gunmen from the component groups of the Qashqa'i tribe by issuing oral or written orders to the tribal leaders and headmen, who sent their bravest and most outstanding warriors.

Another group of men (*yasāvol*) always accompanied the khān on his travels. They stayed at the leader's right side, walking or riding slightly to his rear, and carried a metal-headed club (*chomaq*), symbol of the khān's authority, with which they threatened to hit anyone who went ahead of him. They belonged to the Damir Chomaqlu subtribe of the Amala.

Wealthy members of the paramount leader's family and the major tribal leaders also had supporting bodies of servants and assistants, but to a less elaborated degree than the paramount leader's. Even when tribal leaders were wealthy none of them assembled a staff equivalent to the khān's. A small Amala subtribe served the principal leader and other chiefs in each tribe. Today, the main Amala tribe contains possibly 8,000 families and its subtribes a few hundred families each. With the exile of the paramount leader and members of his family in the 1950s, the positions described mostly disappeared. Only wealthy leaders still maintain their staffs of servants and assistants.

A melée of laden mules and donkeys stop at a water source north of Shirāz on their way to their summer quarters at Āsupās. Gallehzan Amala, April 1988.

SERVING OTHER PASTORALISTS

The second category of employment generally includes those who work for others and is divided into Qashqa'i and non-Qashqa'i employments.

Those Qashqa'i who own too few animals for subsistence, and who often lack access to adequate pasture lands, seek employment as shepherds (*chubon*). Such shepherds do not form a group, caste or clan, nor do they have social cohesion. They move around the tribal territory to find work because herd owners prefer not to hire shepherds who are their kin, even if distant, or who are from their tribal section. A contract between a shepherd and a flock or herd owner is often written down and witnessed. This process continues the customs of the past, when poor people joined the Qashqa'i tribe by placing themselves under the protection of the leaders, and often became their shepherds or the shepherds of others.

Shepherds are mostly young unmarried men and adolescent boys and they live in their employer's tent. Those with independent households bring their families and tents with them during their employment. They camp next to their employer and follow his pattern of migration. These families are considered alien to the encampment and are not usually well integrated into it because of the lack of kin ties and their low socio-economic status. A shepherd's salary depends on his age and circumstances, whether married and with a family, or unmarried, and the herd owner's tribal affiliation. Salaries vary throughout the Qashqa'i tribes. The owner is obliged to provide food, clothes and shoes, and sometimes shelter. He is responsible for all costs, such as supplementary feed and veterinary expenses, related to the care of his own animals and those of the shepherd.

Shepherds wear a long felt cloak with sleeves (*kapanak*) that they purchase from professional non-Qashqa'i felt-makers in villages and towns. This is the only clothing peculiar to them. They carry a stick (*cheqen*) 5 feet (1.5 metres) long, one end of which is sometimes thicker than the other. The thinner end may be forked or crooked to enable the shepherd to catch hold of animals by their legs. They often own dogs.

Agricultural labour, for cash or a portion of the harvest, has become an important source of income for some since the 1960s. Landowners, Qashqa'i and non-Qashqa'i, hire men and older boys as seasonal agricultural labourers to do all or part of the tasks of cultivation. When land, water, seed, tools and draft animals are provided, the workers receive for their work a fourth or fifth of the harvest. The 'five-fifths' contract is common in Iranian agriculture and is generally applied and accepted in Qashqa'i territory.

Some Qashqa'i are skilled in recognising human and animal footprints and in tracking them to their origin or place of rest (*pay surmush uzuna*). When a Qashqa'i is the victim of an animal thief, he asks the help of such trackers. If the animals are located, the thief is obligated by tribal custom to return them, and the animal's owner to give the tracker a payment to compensate him for his efforts and for the 'wear and tear' on his shoes. When Qashqa'i steal animals they aim for the herds belonging to non-kin and especially non-Qashqa'i.

Medicine is another area of employment. There are specialists in traditional medicine, the setting of broken human and animal bones (*shekasteh-band*) and midwifery. Ritual specialists treat mental diseases. Literate men (*Mirzā*) read passages from the Koran at funerals, and write marriage contracts and prayers to ward off the evil eye. They also read government documents or write letters on behalf of nomads. Soothsayers make money by divination and reading omens through a set of forty-two garbonzo beans (*fāl-e nokhod*).

The attached groups living in Qashqa'i territory and providing essential services to them, the camel drivers, gypsy iron workers, musicians and ritual specialists, do not have common origins; nor are they economically and socio-politically affiliated. Their only point in common is that their specialised skills are their capital. The movement of such groups is because of the needs of trade rather than the need to find food for their animals (Berland 1982).

Camel drivers (*darqa*) are found in all Qashqa'i tribes. They belong to a clan they claim is descended from the Quraysh (Karosh) tribe of Arabia, the tribe of the prophet Mohammad. Darqa are dark-skinned and have their own language, but also speak Turkic. Both the men and women are talented singers and reed flute players and they have their own special songs. They gather once a year in garmsir and an elder assigns work in a particular Qashqa'i group to each one there. His assignment is apparently irrevocable. They are hired by Qashqa'i families unable to take care of their camels, and sometimes a family will hire a driver in partnership with other families. Their work is concentrated in garmsir because camels are set free in sarhad. Camels require special care and feeding and they tend to roam widely if not carefully supervised.

Camels drivers are the poorest members of nomadic society and have to supplement their camel driving income by collecting and selling, or transporting, such natural resources as gum tragacanth, tree saps, firewood, charcoal and reeds. Some camel drivers herd buffalo in garmsir and do not migrate. Since the 1960s, with land reform and the expansion of cultivation into Qashqa'i pastures and along the migratory routes, the difficulties of tending camels have greatly increased.

The gypsy tinkers (*ghorbat*) in their territory are despised by the Qashqa'i. These *ghorbat* have their own language but many also speak Turkic. They are an endogamous group and can only socialise with and marry each other. They are not allowed to wear Qashqa'i dress so their appearance is drastically different from that of their hosts. Their tents are shabby and show signs of poverty and dirt. They are of low social status, often very poor, and are not welcome in Qashqa'i camps, whether for begging, carrying news or selling their goods. Their presence in Qashqa'i territory is tolerated only because the men produce and repair iron tools. Their women produce woven reed mats (*chiq*), woven baskets and brooms, and these ready-made objects are sold for cash or traded for animal products and grain. *Ghorbats* traditionally did not have access to land.

The musicians and singers in Qashqa'i territory come from special castes or groups called *'ashıq changian*. Originally from the Caucasus and Shirvan, they have been scattered in Iran, Afghanistan and Turkey for a hundred years at least. Although they are extremely respected, they are not allowed to marry Qashqa'i women. They perform at Qashqa'i wedding ceremonies and rites of passage and are paid in cash or in animals. They also supply other specialised services such as dentistry and barbering.

GOODS AND SERVICES SOLD TO NON-QASHQA'I

Those who sell products or services to non-Qashqa'i include weavers. Before the 1960s most weaving was done to fulfil domestic needs, and woven goods were sold and traded in urban markets only when cash and goods were needed. Since the 1960s weaving has become an income-producing activity for many families. Private weaving workshops were set up in Firuzābād and Shahrezā, and in Shirāz a government weaving workshop was opened and a weaving school was set up in which the skills of the Qashqa'i and Lur weavers were combined. The Firuzābād workshop employs weavers of the Kermanlu subtribe of the Kuchuk Kashkullu tribe, who weave pile rugs and flatweaves. The workshop in Shahrezā specialises in weaving goat hair strips for tents. With the increasing commercialisation of weaving, many individual weavers receive from urban merchants and moneylenders advances in the form of cash or goods on credit on woven goods not yet begun or completed. These contracts are not to the economic advantage of the weavers, other than to provide their families with a small amount of cash or credit, but their family's desperate economic circumstances force them into such arrangements.

Some poor Qashqa'i, as already mentioned, survive as nomads through collecting and selling products derived from the natural environments in which they live and migrate. Families in great economic difficulties, as a last resort, send sons to work in towns and cities. This often does not have the hoped-for result because most of their income is used to pay for rent, food, clothes and transportation in their new urban surroundings.

Before the development of motorised transport and paved or improved roads, some Qashqa'i worked for sedentary agriculturalists, transporting harvested crops from fields to villages.

Until the 1960s, some Qashqa'i provided armed escorts in south Iran for merchants and their trade goods. These merchants carried rice, sugar and other items in large sacks on camels between cities, towns, smaller settlements and ports on the Persian Gulf. The escorts were paid in cash for this work (*qafele kashi*).

THIEVERY AND BRIGANDAGE

One of the small Qashqa'i groups, the Gallehzan (those who steal herds) is famous for thievery. A boy has to become a herd thief in order to be considered a real man in Gallehzan society. If he has not raided a herd or stolen animals, no father will give him a daughter to marry and he is rejected and humiliated by everybody. Much cultivation is found in Gallehzan territory and the sedentary agriculturalists, who do not dare to confront them, bribe them by hiring them as guards to protect their fields from Gallehzan flocks. These guards are said to earn their money by 'watching the plains' (*dash-e buni*).

Thieves and highway robbers (*dozd-e sar-e gardaneh*, 'thieves at passes and bottlenecks') used to frequent the trade routes from the Persian Gulf ports to Shirāz. Qashqa'i leaders at different levels occasionally received a third of the goods stolen in tribute, and the remaining two-thirds were divided among those who had participated in the robbery. Until the 1950s, the general insecurity along the trade routes in south Iran was such that few non-Qashqa'i city dwellers wanted to travel through Qashqa'i territory, for fear of theft. A traveller needed to solicit the favour of a tribal chief in order to travel in security.

Sherzad Beg Duzu Kurdi was a famous brigand at the beginning of the twentieth century who attacked roads leading to Kermān, Isfahān, Kāshān and Yazd. Another legendary brigand was Mohammad Nowruz of the Amala tribe, who became an outlaw following the years of drought in the early 1960s. The authorities failed to capture Nowruz, even with parachuted troops, and he resumed an ordinary nomadic life after the revolution in 1979.

RECENT DEVELOPMENTS

Since the 1960s, new and changed forms of livelihoods have emerged. The development of the Office of Tribal Education in Shirāz and the provision of elementary education to many children provided opportunities for a number of Qashqa'i to become teachers and to acquire bureaucratic positions connected with the Office. Many teachers moved on to other kinds of professional and white-collar jobs in cities and towns in the area, particularly in government offices.

Because many customary non-pastoral livelihoods have disappeared from Qashqa'i territory, many who have relied on them have been forced to change radically their life-styles and modes of survival. The predominant pattern for those who are unable to continue as nomads is for them to settle in small villages in garmsir or sarhad and become agricultural labourers on land owned by others. Many become part of the poorly paid, often unemployed, and usually under-employed, urban proletariat. They often live in shanty towns on the edges of cities and towns in the region.

For wealthy Qashqa'i, particularly members of the families of the leaders, a host of other occupations and specialisations has become possible. They, along with other members of the aristocracy and upper middle classes, of which they are a part, have taken advantage of the rapidly changing economic circumstances in Iran in the 1960s, 1970s, and in the post-revolutionary period of the 1980s. In the past forty years a number of families have sent their sons (and daughters) to university, sometimes in western countries, and many have entered professional careers.

THE NOMADS OF KERMĀN: ON THE ECONOMY OF NOMADISM

Georg Stöber

A woman belonging to a nomadic Afshār family from the Kermān region which had moved to Khorāsān in search of better pasture. December 1987.

The province of Kermān, situated between Fārs to the west and Baluchistān to the east, is largely covered by chains of high mountains, with low-lying areas in between. In addition to a village population, the region is inhabited by nomads who spend the summer in the mountains and the winter in the lowlands. The nomads return to the same pastures and camp sites year after year. In their winter quarters (*garmsir, qeshlaq*) they have stone walls over which they pitch their tents, and in their summer quarters (*sarhad, yaylaq*) some families have trees, fields, and even simple houses.

The nomads begin their spring migration between the end of March and the beginning of May, and return in September, October or November. In those cases where the seasonal pastures are 150 or 200 kilometres apart the journey can take up to two and a half months particularly in spring time, when the flocks have to be milked and the milk processed. In autumn, on the other hand, the families are able to make the journey more quickly because shepherds often go ahead with the animals leaving them with only their baggage to take care of. Nowadays some even make the journey by truck. Nomadic groups in one of the mountain chains such as the Kuh-e Khabr, intermediate between the low-lying areas in the south and the high mountains in the centre of the province, migrate over far shorter distances. For some it can be a matter of several kilometres, with the migration taking just a few hours. Whether the migrations are long or short, the way of life is a form of mobile pastoralism.

There are numerous 'tribes' of differing origin in the province of Kermān. Most of them are very small, consisting of perhaps ten families. They include the Baluch who are said to have migrated into adjacent Baluchistān via Kermān, Persian-speaking groups and others speaking a Turkic dialect. The largest 'tribal' group is the Turkic-speaking Afshār, who are estimated at one or two thousand families and divided into several independent subtribes.

The Afshār came to the Iranian plateau and Asia Minor in the eleventh century as part of the Oghuz, and in the second half of the thirteenth under the Mongols. The Afshār who joined the Safavid forces at the beginning of the sixteenth century as one of the Qizilbash tribes were recruited from their descendants. Later when various Afshār groups or their leaders became involved in administrative and military duties in different parts of the country, the Afshār were dispersed all over Iran and separated into independent 'tribes'. The Afshār of Kermān may descend from an Afshār group which came to Kermān under Safavid rule. Others may have joined them later. The Bochaqchi, on the other hand, separated and are today an independent tribe. Even among the tribesmen there is no agreement as to which group may be labelled 'Afshār', especially since the former tribal leadership was abolished in 1962 and a politically united Afshār tribe no longer exists.

The principal livelihood of the Kermān nomads is animal husbandry. Supplementary income is derived from several other sources, the most important of which are agriculture, carpet weaving and, today, casual labour. Their flocks consist of sheep and goats in widely varying proportions. Most households keep poultry to enrich the menu from time to time. For transport purposes some groups, especially Baluch, keep (one-humped) Arabian camels, but the universal pack animal of the Kermān nomads is the donkey. If necessary oxen, which are mostly kept by families involved in agriculture, can substitute for donkeys.

The shepherds mentioned earlier pasture the herds away from the camps of their owners, particularly during summer and autumn. This division of labour keeps the animals out of the fields and enables the owners to concentrate on agriculture. The shepherds are paid for their work predominantly in cash, but also in kind. So they may receive cash, or kids and lambs—for example one for

top
A tent belonging to one of the many Afshār tribes in the Kermān region, here pitched in their winter quarters near Jiroft.

centre
A large tent belonging to a family of the Rāyeni tribe at their winter quarters north of Hājiābād, January 1988.

bottom
A family calling themselves Afshār making *kashk* balls (salted milk protein) which are dried and stored for the winter when they will be reconstituted with water and eaten with bread. Near Bardsir, 1988.

A family belonging to the Amiri tribe in their winter quarters at Golāshkerd near Kahnuj. In spring they will travel 100 miles (160 km) north-east to the slopes of mount Lālezār north-east of Darmazār. 1988.

every fifteen animals in the flock—and in addition some grain, wool and clothing. The job appeals mainly to poor or young fellow-tribesmen whose flocks are too small to provide them a living. During the last decades economic changes in Iran have upset this system. Needy tribesmen now find it more profitable to become unskilled labourers, as we see later. The resulting shortage of shepherds puts the burden of work on the herd owners who either do it individually or cooperate by delegating it in turn to one of their families for a year at a time.

The sheep and goats provide the nomads with milk, wool, meat and skins. The females are in milk for about five months after giving birth to a lamb or kid in winter. Their yield is not high; in a good year a sheep gives 0.3 to 0.5 litres per day and a good goat 0.7. Though a goat gives more milk, the taste of sheep's milk is preferred. For the first two or three months the milk is needed for the young animals, after which the nomad women process it into yoghurt (*māst*), butter and clarified butter (*rowghan*), *kashk* (a dried product from buttermilk), and dried cheese. Apart from the yoghurt, these products can be stored for the milkless part of the year. Most of the milk products are consumed by the owners, but if the herd is large enough to produce one, the surplus may be sold.

The female offspring serve to replace the mothers too old to bear, and to enlarge the flock. Only a few of the male offspring need to be kept for this purpose as a small number of rams and bucks can serve the whole flock. The rest are slaughtered or sold. Generally the nomads prefer cash as they eat little meat but have need of money for a variety of expenses. If possible the lambs and kids are kept until the age of two or three when they fetch the best price. Whether or not this is feasible depends on the amount of cash needed and the number of kids and lambs available for sale. When winter pasture is scarce and the nomads have to feed the animals with barley, and sometimes pay for watering them too, they may find it more economical to sell animals when young rather than keep them till they are older.

Once a year, in April, the sheep are shorn for their wool which, among other things, is used to make carpets. Goat hair is used for making tent cloth, ropes, etc., and the fine under-wool, *kork*, is processed into felt and in former times was used by urban weavers to make expensive shawls.

A Turkic-speaking Afshār woman north of Hajiābād, January 1988. On the floor are various machine-made textiles. She sits on a knotted-pile carpet of typical Afshār workmanship. The processing of wool into carpets is an important source of income for these nomads.

The nomads keep some of these products for their own use, but sell some wool and the *kork*. Market demand, especially for *kork*, has sometimes influenced the composition of the herds (Bradburd 1979: 57).

The carpets of the nomads are woven on portable horizontal looms in small sizes. In contrast, the well-known Kermāni carpets are produced on vertical looms by specialised settled weavers in the city of Kermān and its surrounding villages. Many rugs are called 'Afshāris' whether or not they are woven by real Afshār women. Even pieces made by settled villagers with patterns influenced by the carpets of Kermān are included in this category. Perhaps because of intermarriage particular patterns do not appear to be woven by one group alone, and not all groups weave carpets. Nevertheless some groups or regions have typical designs and colours. The Afshār groups I visited often wove a design with one or two vertical rows of white conjoined rhombs (*gol*) on a figured dark blue ground which is surrounded by a red field and enclosed by a frame with three points at each end (*kalleh*). Oral tradition has it that long ago the *gol* pattern was borrowed from the Qashqa'i tribe. Neighbouring groups used patterns which are said to imitate the designs of urban shawls of the nineteenth century. These are just preliminary remarks; a study of nomadic carpet production in the province of Kermān has yet to be made.

It is worth mentioning that cash can be earned from gathering gum tragacanth, the resin of a bush growing in the mountains. Iran is an exporter of this gum.

The staple diet of the Iranian nomads is bread, so many of them try to grow at least some grain for themselves. Those who possess fields in their summer quarters, and the rights to use water for irrigation, plough the land and sow the wheat crop before they leave in the autumn. The harvest takes place the following July. In addition to wheat, barley, potatoes, legumes and other vegetables may be grown. All these are sown in springtime and harvested in the autumn. However, only some nomads do this because most of them are on migration at the time. Others get peasants to cultivate the soil, sometimes settled, impoverished tribesmen. Before the Iranian land reform of the 1960s

A family of Persian-speaking nomads north of Kermān, summer 1984.

this practice was more widespread and generally the peasants were not connected with the tribe. During the 'White Revolution' such lands were expropriated and some nomads lost their agricultural resources. On the other hand others intensified their farming activities to secure their claim to the land.

Even though the nomads produce a major part of their food and equipment themselves, Iranian nomadism is not a subsistence economy. The tribesmen are more or less obliged to purchase sugar, tea, cloth, consumer goods, and at least part of their grain. In return they have to sell their own products, principally livestock and to a lesser extent milk products (clarified butter and *kashk*), wool and carpets. The dominant markets for their products are in the towns, especially Kermān, the provincial capital. The way commercial transactions are organised is highly variable. Nomads may travel to the town with their goods or animals on the hoof, sell them to butchers in the livestock market or to traders in the bazaar, and use the proceeds to buy what they need. Alternatively they may sell to livestock dealers who visit the camp and pay for their purchases in cash. Likewise itinerant traders come to *sarhad* or *garmsir* to sell their wares and take the products of the nomads in return. Transactions with these pedlars are very unfavourable because they get lower prices for their goods than on the urban market and have to pay higher prices. As a result this type of exchange has diminished. Instead everyday items are available in villages near the camps where shops and co-operative societies (of which a land-owning nomad may be a member) have grown up. For bigger purchases they find it better to go to one of the larger cities. Grain is available in the villages from landowners with large stocks, for which the nomads have to pay in cash.

The quantity of goods a nomad needs to sell depends, of course, not only on the amount he needs to buy, but also on the price he receives for his products and the price he has to pay for his purchases (the internal terms of trade). These values are always changing so it is impossible to anticipate exactly how many animals a nomadic family will need. Tribesmen with too few animals to make ends meet must find a supplementary source of income, intensify the weaving of carpets for sale, or restrict their consumption of milk products so as to have more to sell.

A Soleymani family at their winter quarters near Kahnuj. Shearing takes place once a year in April. The steel shears have blades which can be separated for sharpening; they have no spring and both hands are needed to use them. The Soleymani spend the Summer at Rābor near Bāft. 1988.

In former times caravan traffic, between Bandar ʿAbbās and Yazd for example, provided opportunities for extra income through brigandage. The Bochaqchi in particular were notorious robbers, as were the Baluch intruding from Baluchistān. Banditry came to an end with the intensification of state control during the second half of the twentieth century. New opportunities arose as a result of economic developments, particularly in the 1960s and 70s, and many jobs became available which could be taken up by uneducated migrant labourers, for example in the mines or in the building sector. The earnings from these occupations often became more important than those from husbandry.

Economic developments of this type give rise to changes in the pattern of nomadism, but to discuss them we must look further into the past. In the 1920s and 30s it was the policy of the central government under Rezā Shah to settle all the tribes in Iran in order to control them better. This was mainly achieved by force, with high loss of life. In the province of Kermān this policy was perhaps pursued with less vigour than in some other provinces, but nevertheless several groups had to abandon their migration and settle. After the abdication of Rezā Shah in 1941 the majority of tribesmen in Iran returned to nomadism wherever possible, but in Kermān province things were never the same as before. Those groups with a mixed economy, such as the Afshār of Deh Bakri in the Jebāl Bārez mountains (south-east of Bam), who had changed their main activities from animal husbandry to agriculture, remained settled. Only a small number of poor landless families returned to nomadism. Other groups took up short-distance migrations in the vicinity of their place of settlement. These changes may have contributed to the confusing picture of nomadism in Kermān today.

The land reform of the 1960s led the former leadership to modernise their agricultural activities as a means of avoiding expropriation, or to establish themselves in one of the larger towns. The nomads who were dispossessed lost their agricultural income and became increasingly vulnerable to economic stress. If the number of their animals became too small then casual labour became their main or only source of income. Sometimes they stuck to a form of migration, but the general tendency was to settle. This often meant that former nomads lived in tents but did not

In former times the fine under-wool of goats (*kork*) was woven into luxurious shawls and used to make the most expensive carpets. What is called *kork* in the carpet trade today is usually fine quality sheep's wool. The nomads sell the *kork* from their goats which is traded in the west as 'Cashmere'. Rāyeni tribe, January 1988.

move them for several years at a time. On the other hand tribesmen who possessed land in their summer quarters sometimes erected a house there and, especially if they had only a few animals, stayed there throughout the year. Agriculture, and sometimes trade, then became their most important source of income. Generally cultivation increased in *sarhad* and tribesmen who remained nomadic participated in this.

Before the revolution the increase in cultivation in the winter quarters, garmsir, was even greater than in sarhad. This was brought about not by nomads but by agro-entrepreneurs, often townsmen. Wells were drilled for pump irrigation and the ground cleared for large-scale mechanised agriculture, a process which seems to some extent to have come to a halt since the Iranian revolution in 1979. Nomads who had their winter camps on this land were obliged to look for new pastures and camping grounds. Shortage of grazing for the nomads has been further exacerbated in both *garmsir* and *sarhad* by growing numbers of flocks belonging to city-based livestock owners. This pressure increases the vulnerability of the nomads' livestock to natural stresses, such as drought, and obliges them to spend more on supplementary fodder.

Since the 1960s the picture seems to be one of general deterioration in the position of the nomads. Large social and political units have broken up, their members dispersed and the territory divided. Economic inequality and diversity of activities have increased, yet even if the group as a whole has not done better than before, at least some of its members have. For several years in the 1970s some groups were hardly affected by the various restrictions and prices moved in a favourable direction. Richer nomads in particular found themselves quite well off and some of them chose to settle. Thus the tendency for nomads to settle is not only a consequence of poverty. It can also result from growing wealth, a change in economic orientation and a desire for a more comfortable life. Whether or not a core of tribesmen will continue their nomadic way of life is not solely a matter of their choice; it depends also on government politics, the general economic climate, and the possibilities and openings offered by the wider Iranian society to which they belong.

Sunset on the main peaks of Mount Savalan, across the top of an *alachıgh*. Summer 1987

SHAHSEVAN NOMADS OF MOGHĀN

Richard Tapper

INTRODUCTION

Shahsevan is the name of a variety of tribal groups whose remnants, numbering perhaps 300,000 people, live in various parts of Iran. They are Shi'ite Muslims and speak dialects of Āzarbāijāni Turkish. Most Shahsevan are now settled villagers or townspeople and preserve little of their former tribal organisation or pastoral nomadic economy and culture, but nearly 50,000 of them, in nearly 6,000 families, still live a nomadic or semi-nomadic life in the province of Ardabil, close to the former Soviet frontier. Most of these nomads winter near sea level on the Moghān steppe, and spend the summer 100 miles or so to the south at between 7,000 and 12,000 feet up in the high pastures of Mount Savalan (nearly 16,000 feet), Qosha, Bāghrow and Bozgush ranges, in the districts of Ardabil, Meshkin, Tabriz and Sarāb. Another 30,000 or so Qaradāghi nomads, whose culture and way of life is similar to that of the Shahsevan, inhabit the valleys and mountains of Qaradāgh, north of Tabriz and Ahar, some of them migrating to summer in the high plateaux of Mount Sahand, south of Tabriz.

HISTORY

Some of the Shahsevan tribes are probably of Kurdish origins, but most are descended from the Turkish Oghuz or Ghuzz peoples who came to Iran from Central Asia a millennium ago. Many of these groups can be traced back to the great Shāmlu and Afshār tribes of the Qizilbash confederacy that brought the Safavid dynasty to power in Iran around AD 1500.

'Shahsevan' literally means 'those who love the Shah'. In most recent accounts, the Shahsevan are said to have originated as a special composite tribe created by the Safavid Shah 'Abbās I in about 1600. There is no historical evidence to support this story, however, and it is unlikely that there was a single unified tribal group of this name until a century later.

Since the early eighteenth century the Shahsevan have figured prominently in the history of Āzarbāijān and the south-eastern Caucasus, an area which has often been a battleground between Iran and her neighbours. In the 1720s the Safavid dynasty collapsed. Invading from the south-east, Mahmud Ghiljai the Afghan captured the Safavid capital Isfahān, while Ottoman armies occupied Āzarbāijān and partitioned the eastern Transcaucasus with Russia, whose forces had invaded the south-western shores of the Caspian. Tribal warriors of the Shahsevan were active, along with other local groups such as the Shaqāqi, in resisting the Ottomans in the Ardabil-Moghān region; some of them eventually surrendered in Moghān in early 1729, others managed to escape across the Aras river to take refuge in Russian territory.

When he recovered the area for Iran shortly afterwards, Tahmāsp Qoli Khān Afshār (later to become Nāder Shah) moved those tribes of Moghān and Ardabil who had surrendered to the Ottomans to other parts of Iran, particularly to his home province of Khorāsān. He unified the remaining tribes of Moghān, which had taken Russian protection, as a confederacy under a paramount chief, Badr Khān Sarikhānbeglu Afshār. These Shahsevan were the ancestors of the present-day Ardabil and Moghān tribes, and Badr Khān's family ruled them for the next hundred years or so. Meanwhile, after Nāder Shah's death in 1747, the groups exiled to Khorāsān began to return; the Shaqāqi to Sarāb and Miāneh, south of their original homes in Meshkin, and important tribes which later became known as the Shahsevan Afshār, Qotbeglu, Afshār Dovairan and Shahsevan Inanlu to the country between Miāneh, Zanjān, Qom, Sāveh and Tehran.

Some time before 1800, Badr Khān Sarikhānbeglu's family split in two, dividing the Moghān Shahsevan into two branches, one associated with the city and district of Ardabil, the other with

Two girths (*bastırıkh*) used to stabilise the tent struts (*chubukh*) inside the tent.

the neighbouring district of Meshkin, which had no town of any size. The khans and most of the tribes of the Ardabil branch soon settled and dispersed in and around the city, but also in other parts of Iran. In the mid-nineteenth century the ruling family of the Meshkin branch became settled too. At this time the numbers of Shahsevan nomads in the region fluctuated between 6,000 and 12,000 families.

Early in the nineteenth century, after two wars with Iran, Russia conquered the southern Caucasus and established the present Āzarbāijān frontier of Iran. This deprived the Shahsevan nomads of the greater part of their traditional winter quarters in the Moghān steppe. Although they were for many years permitted to cross the frontier in winter to camp in their old pastures, this was increasingly restricted by the Russian authorities, who were attempting to develop the steppe, bringing in outsiders to settle and cultivate the best lands. As a result the tribes became increasingly lawless, disrupting trade and settlement far into both Russia and Iran. Their raids caused friction between the two countries, and each government regularly exaggerated the extent of the damage and sought to blame it on the other: the Russians accused the Iranians of failing to curb the raids, the Iranians suspected the Russians of instigating them in order to justify their own military intervention, which eventually came in the early twentieth century.

In 1884 the Russian frontier was finally closed to the Shahsevan nomads. By this time the Shahsevan were no longer a centralised confederacy controlled by the former paramount chiefs. Six or seven of the larger and more powerful tribes, under their own chiefs, each attracted a following of weaker tribes. The tribes of the region, including not only the Meshkin and Ardabil Shahsevan but groups from neighbouring regions such as the Hajji ʿAlilu and Chalabianlu of Qaradāgh and the Dalikanlu and the Shatranlu of Khalkhāl, were organised into a shifting series of rival alliances and coalitions. The more powerful chiefs controlled the whole region politically, exploited all the pastures and owned much of the farmland. Between 1884 and 1922 central government control was intermittent and weak; the period is remembered as that of the outlaws (*ashrarlıkh*) or the khans (*khankhanlıkh*).

Between 1905 and 1911 Iran was in the throes of its Constitutional Revolution. A Constitution was granted in summer 1906 by Mozaffaroddin Shah, but thrown out in 1908 by his son and successor Mohammad ʿAli Shah, who was however deposed a year later. Although many Shahsevan initially supported the Constitutionalists, in late 1909, with secret Russian encouragement, most Shahsevan chiefs and their followers joined the tribes of Qaradāgh and Khalkhāl to form a Tribal Union under the leadership of Rahim Khān Chalabianlu of Qaradāgh. The tribal warriors sacked the city of Ardabil and threatened to march on Tehran in the name of Islam to restore Mohammad ʿAli Shah. Over the following months government forces from Tehran defeated Rahim Khān and most of his allies and took numerous captured Shahsevan chiefs in chains to Tehran. They were soon back, however, and resumed their resistance against both Russian occupation forces and the Iranian government. A further sustained offensive against them in 1912, this time by Russian Cossacks, was inconclusive, and they maintained independence of the Iranian government for another decade. Old men interviewed in the 1960s preserved vivid memories of those times, of their victories over the Cossacks, and of their raiding expeditions (called *anjini* in mocking reference to the *anjoman* local cells of the Constitutional movement) into Russia and inside Iran.

The Shahsevan were among the first of the major tribal groups to come under the control of Rezā Khān (later to become Rezā Shah Pahlavi). In 1922–3 his army managed to defeat or win over the Shahsevan chiefs, and several of the more recalcitrant were executed. Under the Pahlavis (1925–78) the influence of the remaining chiefs of individual tribes was very much weakened, and they lost the arbitrary power over their followers they had once enjoyed. In conformity with their name, the Shahsevan remained loyal to the rulers, and provided useful support for Tehran government forces at the time of the Soviet occupation of Āzarbāijān of 1941–6 and the short-lived Democrat regime of 1946.

Rezā Shah's enforced settlement in the 1930s brought great hardship to the Shahsevan, like other nomads in Iran. The settlement programme failed, having been undertaken without proper planning or provision of facilities: the nomads were not turned into farmers. At the end of Rezā Shah's reign many Shahsevan resumed their nomadic life even without any flocks to tend. The period was remembered with such loathing that until the 1960s even the building of a mud hut by a nomad in his pasture lands was regarded as a betrayal by other nomads.

An *alachıgh* half-erected in a new camping spot. The stones for the *yük* have been laid out, and the housewife is busy arranging the furniture. The men still have to arrange the struts and the girths and insert the pegs and the central stake, before putting on the felt coverings. Spring 1983, at the foot of Mount Savalan near Meshkin-Shahr.

During the 1960s and 1970s massive government-backed irrigation schemes were put into effect in Iranian Moghān, latterly involving co-operation with the Soviets in exploitation of the waters of the Aras river. Much of the remaining winter pastures were removed from the Shahsevan nomads and many more of them were forced to settle, though increasingly they saw advantages in doing so, particularly where they were able to find good land. Other government policies made life very difficult for the remaining pastoralists.

The culture and social structure of the Shahsevan tribes have been strongly marked by their location on this sensitive frontier, and by the history of their involvement in conflicts there, not only between Iran and the Ottomans and Russians but also between the Shahsevan and neighbouring tribal groups. Out of this history, one particular feature of Shahsevan life has emerged as distinctive and closely associated with Shahsevan identity: the *alachıgh* tent.

THE SHAHSEVAN ALACHIGH

This is a round, felt-covered tent or hut of the Central Asian type commonly known as yurt or kibitka. The spider-like wooden framework consists of a heavy central wooden roof ring (*chambara*) and a number (usually 24, 26 or 28) of curved struts (*chubukh*) which are slotted into it and radiate out and down to the ground. The roof ring itself is anchored to the ground in the centre of the tent by thick ropes normally attached to a massive stake (*chöski*), though in hard ground it may be necessary to use iron pegs or boulders to hold the roof ring down. The struts are bound firmly by two long girths (*bastırıkh*) of decoratively woven webbing, whose ends are attached to wooden pegs in the ground outside the framework; this prevents the structure from twisting, and the whole arrangement is sufficient to hold the tent in place even under the worst weather conditions. Outside the struts and resting horizontally on the ground are long strips of flexible canework matting, as a windbreak and to keep small animals from slipping into the tent.

left above
At a campsite halfway along the migration route, the men of a family throw up one of the felt covers, while one of the women, seated on top, waits to fasten it down. Geyiklu tribe, near Salavat, May 1966.

left below
Geyiklu camps at Peynli, at the end of the spring migration, May 1966. Camps wait here for a few weeks until their spring and summer grazing is ready for them.

The structure so formed is from 18 to 24 feet (5.5 to 7.5 metres) in diameter and nearly 10 feet (3 metres) in height. One of the 3 foot (1 metre) gaps between the struts is left open as a doorway (*qapı*).

The tent cover comprises three large felt mats (*kecha*). Two mats are strapped on opposite sides of the structure, leaving a gap for the doorway in front; the larger gap at the back is covered by the third mat, which also overlaps with the other two. Shahsevan men make the felt mats from the wool of their own sheep, with the aid of village-based specialist carders (*hallaj*), who tour the camps in teams of two during the summer months. The *hallaj*, working inside a tent, tease and card the wool, lay it out on a cloth, dampen it and then wrap it around a wooden pole. The bundle is then taken outside the tent to a ground that has been specially prepared, where a party of three to five men of the camp roll it up and down with their feet for half an hour or so, stamping rhythmically on it. The bundle is then opened, the strip of felt removed and then rolled up next to the pole. A fresh lot of wool is added to the cloth which is then rolled around the felt and the pole; in effect each bundle contains two strips, one already rolled once, the other fresh.

After enough strips have been made for the new tent (this takes two to three days), another party is formed to cut them to shape and stitch them into mats. Each mat is made up of numerous strips stitched together, in an upper and a lower section, each section being arc-shaped to fit the tent frame. The edges of the two upper sections adjacent to the door are extended over the doorway but arranged so that they can be flipped back and secured open to make a smoke hole (*atanakh*). The door (*qapılıkh*) is a single strip of felt, specially made to size, with coloured wool designs laid on to it during the fulling, and reinforced on the inside by a strip of canework matting; it is loose, but attached by ropes to the roof ring so that it can be rolled up over the doorway. There is nothing to mark the threshold of the tent, but the top of the doorway is formed where one of the girths joins the two door struts, with possibly some tassels hanging from it. The roof ring is covered by a specially shaped circular top mat strapped down from inside and surmounted by a decorative topknot (*qotaz* or *ponchakh*).

The framework is bought from carpenters in Ardabil. It should last up to twenty years, while the felt mats need replacing every three years.

Such a tent is heavier and sturdier than most other types of nomad tent. It is expensive to maintain, and only two out of three Shahsevan families can afford one: poorer families use the barrel-vaulted *küma*, a smaller, simpler and cheaper construction. A very few wealthy Shahsevan, mostly from the families of chiefs, have a canvas ridge tent for guests. Dairy merchants visiting the Shahsevan camps in spring to buy milk use large canvas marquees as cheese factories. The Shahsevan know that the Kurds and other nomad tribes of the Zāgros use rectangular goat hair tents, but locally these are used only by the gypsies they occasionally see. Most Shahsevan are not familiar with any other form of tent: by definition, to be a pastoral nomad in this region is both to be Shahsevan and to live in an *alachıgh* (or *küma*).

The *alachıgh* has a uniform structure among the Shahsevan, with only minor variations in size and degree of decoration. Apart from being an ordinary family dwelling (*av*), however, it can serve many specialised purposes. By the re-arrangement of objects and space inside, it can be converted into a workshop (*kar-khana*) for men who are making felt or shearing, or for women who are processing milk or weaving; a reception tent (*mehman-khana*) for a rich man, into which no women may come; a mosque (*masjed*) for devotions, sermons or orations at major religious celebrations, which only men use; a kitchen (*ashpaz-khana*) for women catering for major feasts; or a reception tent at feasts, for the exclusive use of either men or women.

Inside the ordinary family dwelling the most important feature is the hearth (*ojagh*), which lies between the door and the central stake. The rest of the floor is normally bare or covered with rough kelims, rugs or carpets being laid down only for guests or on special occasions. The arrangement of household equipment and furniture is regular. Storage packs—*farmash* for bedding and *chuwal* for food and other supplies—are ranged around the back perimeter furthest from the door. These are known collectively as the 'load' (*yük*). Tea-making and cooking utensils, as well as the spinning wheel and other equipment, are kept closer to the door. The area near the door is 'down' (*ashaghı*); the housewife carries out her main activities there, either side of the hearth, commonly (but not always) food preparation on the right (looking out), weaving, spinning and other craft work on the left. In winter, or cold weather, a fire is kept burning in the hearth and family

Men stitch the cut felt strips together to form part of one of the three main covering felts for a new tent. Western slopes of Mount Savalan, near Moil village, 1987.

right top
A wool-dresser or bow-carder (*hallaj*) with his bow and mallet prepares raw wool for felt making by teasing it apart with the vibrating string of the bow which is plucked with the mallet. These *hallaj* would come from the local villages and towns to tour the camps in July and August in teams of two. But since about 1990 they have set up workshops in Meshkin-Shahr, so the nomads must now bring their wool to town.

right
The carded wool is moistened, rolled up around a pole, then taken out to a prepared piece of ground, where men of the camp stamp it up and down for half and hour or so. 1987.

Women gathered outside an *alachıgh*, while one of them makes bread on a griddle over an open fire. Three of the women have head-dresses indicating they are established married women; the other two are younger, probably unmarried girls. Near Meshkin-Shahr, at the foot of Mount Savalan, summer 1983.

and guests gather round it, though not on the door side. The back of the tent is 'up' (*yokharı*); this is the main entertainment area for visitors, who have to pass either side of the hearth to reach it from the door. The back is also the family sleeping area: if there is a new bride, she and her husband will sleep behind a curtain (*parda*) to the left for the first year or so. This is the only partition in the home; it will be replaced by a hammock (*yürük*), slung between one of the struts and the central tackle, as a cradle for a new baby.

In each family tent lives a household of seven or eight people on average, but sometimes as few as two or as many as nineteen or twenty. The Shahsevan prefer larger households, and often brothers and their wives and children, or an old couple and their married sons, stay together. The family dwelling is the domain of women, who are inconvenienced when their husbands bring guests, space having to be made and rugs laid down at the back or, worse, near the hearth. Within the home, however, there is no rigid division of space associated with sex or seniority. Ideally a household has two tents: a newer and finer looking one as reception room, with the best rugs, where the men of the household may sit or sleep even when there are no guests; the other as 'kitchen' for women and their guests. In practice very few other than members of the families of chiefs have a permanent reception tent, or more than one, always ready for visitors. Among ordinary nomads, the few men with more than one wife will almost always have a tent for each, the better of which, usually that of the senior wife, can be quickly converted into a reception tent if important visitors arrive. The wife is expected to join in the catering arrangements in her co-wife's tent.

At various festivities, the tents set aside for entertainment and reception are often specially decorated, for example with coloured tassels. The hearths may be removed to accommodate more guests and the tents emptied of furniture except for a few bedding packs, the whole floor being laid with the best carpets and rugs available in the camp, or borrowed even from neighbouring camps. The author has been one of seventy-five guests feeding inside an ordinary *alachıgh*, and one of twenty sleeping there. During the religious ceremonies of Moharram and Ramadan, wealthy men (chiefs and elders) set aside a tent as a mosque in which men perform individual prayers and

participate in communal services led by mullahs invited for the occasion. Such mosques are specially adorned: the hearth is removed, the whole floor is covered in carpets, and the stake, the roof ring and the walls are hung with cloths embroidered or printed with religious texts and symbols.

When a tent is used as a men's reception tent, or as a mosque, the most honoured place is 'up' at the back, opposite the door, and the most humble 'down' by the door, on either side. On such occasions no women are present, though during some religious ceremonies they may gather around the outside of the tent towards the back, participating invisibly but not inaudibly. If the tent is in use as both kitchen and women's reception tent at a wedding, for example, the older women sit at the back and the younger sit by the stake, leaving the hearth free for cooking.

The hearth is the focus of family life as the source of both food and warmth and in a family dwelling it is of great ritual and symbolic importance to the Shahsevan as it is among other peoples of Turkic origins. It is otherwise in a reception tent, where the hearth is covered up or ignored and food is brought in from a kitchen tent. The domestic hearth represents the values of the united joint family. *Ojagh* also means 'house' in the sense of descendants, and a well known proverb states, 'A hearth without issue has neither warmth nor blessing' (*Sonsuz ojaghın na istisi na barakati olar*). Certain rituals take place at the hearth: for example, at a bride's departure from home on her wedding day, her father takes her three times anti-clockwise round it as he prays for children for her. The most important woven items in a bride's trousseau are one or more 'hearth rugs' (*ojagh-qıraghı*), woven to a particular format, which are never used or displayed. Finally, the space between the stake and the hearth is known mockingly as the 'brother-in-law or son-in-law's place'. Smoke gets in one's eyes if one sits there.

THE PASTORAL ECONOMY

Shahsevan nomads herd flocks of sheep and goats, known collectively as *davar*. Sheep are raised for milk and milk products, wool and meat; goats are kept only in small numbers, mainly as flock leaders. Most families raise chickens for eggs and meat, and a few keep cows for milk.

Both one humped dromedaries (male: *lök*, female: *arvana*) and two-humped Bactrian camels (male: *bughur*, female: *hacha-maya*) are raised, the latter mainly for breeding hybrids (male: *nar*, female: *maya*), huge beasts capable of carrying a complete tent weighing nearly half a ton. Camels are the main means of transport, particularly for carrying tents and chattels on migration, with donkeys in a subsidiary role. Horses have always been valued as personal transport, but are something of a prestigious luxury.

Every family has several fierce dogs for guarding the home and the animals against thieves and wolves. Though they treat them very harshly, and regard them as religiously unclean (*mundar*), the nomads are often very attached to their dogs. Only dogs and horses are given personal names, on the grounds that they are the only animals which are intelligent enough to respond if called.

Some nomads have relatives in villages, with whom they co-operate in a dual economy, sharing or exchanging pastoral for agricultural produce. Most, however, must sell milk, wool and surplus animals to tradesmen in order to obtain wheat flour and other supplies, bread being the staple food of the nomads. Male lambs are usually castrated and fattened as wethers (*erkek toghlu*) until a year or more old before being sold, directly or through traders, on to the national meat market. Female lambs are all kept for replacing the breeding ewes (*dishi davar*), the core of every family's flock.

There is a range from ordinary and less well-off nomads, whose pastoral activities are aimed first at producing enough to trade for daily necessities and for the occasional major expenses such as weddings, to the wealthy, who produce for profit and investment. The wealthiest nomads raise flocks of sheep commercially and own shares in village lands as absentee landlords.

Poorer men, without the pastoral resources to support their families independently, often work as hired shepherds (*choban*) and are paid a proportion of the animals they tend, 5 per cent for every six month contract period. Others go to towns and villages seasonally for casual wage labour. Each camp is visited almost every day by itinerant pedlars (*charchi*), but householders go on major shopping expeditions to town at least twice a year, for example as they pass by during the migrations. Most purchases are made on credit, to be paid off from the next season's milk or wool sales.

Herding, milking, shearing and the marketing of produce are the work of men. With the lambs being born between November and February, the milking season lasts roughly six months, from

Outside a barrel-vaulted *küma* at the foot of Mount Savalan two woman talk while food is being prepared. Summer 1987.

January to July. Shearing is carried out twice a year: in spring, when the clips are mostly sold, and in summer, for making felt. Men also see to the erection and maintenance of the tents. The household head is rarely at home during the day unless he has guests. Younger men and boys help with the herding and fetch fuel. Hunting of gazelle, wild goats and sheep was once a valued male activity, but there is now little game left in either Moghān or the mountains, other than game birds, and few men other than idle members of chiefly families indulge in it.

Women and girls may help with herding and milking in the absence of men, and they may also go out to fetch water or gather wild greens or fuel, but they normally stay in camp to run the household. They bake piles of flat (but leavened) bread on a curved iron griddle (*saj*) over the hearth at least once a day, and they are also responsible for cooking both regular and ceremonial meals, for weaving and for keeping the inside of the tent clean. They turn milk into cheese, yoghourt and butter for home consumption. Every housewife has a churn (*tulugh*) she suspends from the ubiquitous tripod (*chatma*). The churn is traditionally made from a goat skin or (in the case of a large family) a calf skin, but nowadays some families buy a wooden churn from the bazaar.

Shahsevan women produce a variety of colourful and intricate textiles. They have two types of loom (*hanna*). One is the ground loom, stretched out between pegs on the ground, with the heddle rod suspended beneath the tripod. On this they weave such items as girths for the tent frame, as well as long strips of cloth, sometimes in highly decorative patterns, which may then be cut and sewn together to make blankets for both people and the larger animals. Most families also own one or two upright looms, which are much more substantial and may have to be stored in a nearby village; these are used for the more complex flat weaving, brocading and occasionally knotting of carpets, rugs and storage bags. All these items are for domestic use and figure prominently in girls' trousseaux on marriage. Since about 1970, however, these textiles, which used to be known variously as 'Kurdish' or 'Caucasian', have been recognised and valued by the international oriental

A housewife outside her *alachıgh*, rolls dough to make the standard flat (but leavened) bread (*apak*); on the right are the finished pieces and on the left a piece is cooking on the convex griddle over the open fire. Near Qotur Su, spring 1984.

carpet trade as Shahsevan products, and hard times and escalating prices have forced many nomads to sell items never intended for the market.

CAMPS AND MIGRATIONS

Shahsevan nomads commonly join forces in co-operative herding and camping groups (*oba*) of two to six households, with a combined flock of 200–250 milking ewes and, depending on the time of year, a similar number of yearling lambs or wethers. In the camp site (*yurt*), the tents of a herding group will be pitched up to 50 yards apart, usually oriented downhill or downwind, where possible leaving a central space where the animals will sleep. Such a herding unit usually camps on its own in the mountain pastures between June and early September, though other such camps may be close by. Each camp has its recognised elder or 'grey beard' (*aq-saqal*).

During the period from November to April, two or more herding camps join to form winter camps, more compact 'villages' of 10–15 tents and numerous fixed corrals and stables, often underground. Winter camps too are called *oba* and are led by a senior elder. Two or more such winter camps (25–50 tents) comprise a basic nomadic community, which moves and camps as a unit during the migrations between winter and summer quarters, and gathers together on ceremonial occasions.

An English observer in 1820 wrote of Moghān, 'During the winter and spring months, this immense tract ... becomes abundant in fertility and the richest pasturage, feeding thousands of flocks belonging to the Eelauts [tribespeople] from the mountains of Azerbijan ... From the peculiar luxuriance of the pastures, it has always been a favourite place of encampment with conquering armies, as well as with peaceable tribes.' Another observer reported around the same time: 'The Persians say, that the grass is sufficiently high to cover a man and his horse, and hide an army from view, when encamped.' This was only a slight exaggeration, to judge from the present author's experience of conditions in Moghān in spring 1966.

On arrival in Moghān in November, the camps usually spend a few weeks in their 'autumn quarters' (*güzak*) while they repair the stabling and other structures in their winter camp sites, before occupying their winter quarters (*qıshlagh*) proper. During the main lambing season (November to February) the new lambs must be carefully reared and protected from the weather. From February the camps are visited by town-based dairy companies who erect large canvas tents nearby as 'factories', buy up the surplus milk and make cheese for transport to the cities.

The Iranian New Year (21 March) marks the beginning of spring, the most pleasant season in Moghān. After the shepherds renew their contracts, the winter camps break up to scatter in herding camps over the rolling hills, now blanketed by tall grass and flowers, but the season is brief, and by the beginning of May the sun is scorching the steppe (*chöl*) into semi-desert. A few feverish days are spent mowing and stacking hay in preparation for next winter, before the nomads start the migration southwards and upwards. Within ten days of the first departure, Moghān is empty of nomads.

The tents are dismantled the evening before a move is planned. Each move begins well before dawn, so long as the sky is clear, and lasts about four hours. An average household has three or four camels strung together nose to tail. The first is preferably a hybrid, carrying a complete tent. The others carry bedding, carpets and supplies, with women and small children perched on top. Some men and boys accompany the flocks, which move slowly and graze on the way. Others lead the camels on foot or astride donkeys. Elders and other men wealthy enough to have horses ride ahead to inspect possible stopping places (*düshalga*). Although the migration routes (*elyolu*) are well established, there is no certainty that traditional stopping places will be available; they may already be occupied by an earlier nomad camp, or they are liable to have been cultivated by villagers. Camp leaders often have friends in villages along the route, and possibly even own land there, which allows them to camp nearby, and usually leads to exchanges of visits and often produce. Pedlars often visit the camps, and sometimes set up shop along the migration route. Also along the route are a variety of small shrines, ranging from votive trees (*pir*) to small buildings (*ojagh*) housing mendicants renowned for specific abilities such as curing snake bite. However, few nomads, men or women, visit these shrines, which appear to be patronised more by local villagers.

On arrival at camp, the camels are unloaded and the men set about erecting the tents, which normally takes up to an hour, but can be done in 15 minutes if it is raining. Women arrange the furniture and prepare a simple breakfast of bread, cheese and tea before setting about their usual chores. Men, unless tending the animals, spend the rest of the day dozing, discussing whether or where to move the next night, and visiting friends in nearby villages or camps. Information is eagerly sought about conditions on the road ahead, particularly at bottlenecks such as passes and river crossings, and about the state of the grazing at higher altitudes. Towards nightfall the men, and often the senior women, of the camp will gather on neutral ground to have a final discussion of plans for the next few days.

The spring migration in May to June is quick, lasting from two to four weeks, and the nomads hurry to leave the growing heat of the plains and get the best of the new grazing in the foothills of the mountains as the snows melt. For about a month (June to July) individual herding camps move every few days progressively higher through their 'spring pastures' (*yazlagh*) before reaching the summer quarters (*yaylagh*). The summer months are busy: the women draw the last of the ewes' milk before the lambs are weaned, make butter, spin and weave; the men do the summer shearing and make felt and new tent covers with the help of village-based wool carders (*hallaj*). Weddings are often held towards the end of summer.

The autumn migration between September and November is a leisurely affair, lasting up to two months. When damp and clinging mists herald the end of summer, the camps descend to the foothills, leaving the flocks with the shepherds a few weeks longer in the high pastures. The nomads delay their return to Moghān until adequate autumn rains have fallen there; when they too come down to the foothills, the animals make do with grazing the stubble in the harvested fields. Apart from the lack of fodder, there are no great hazards on the autumn trek, the rivers being low and camp sites plentiful. Meanwhile the ewes are pregnant and ready to throw their lambs soon after the nomads arrive in Moghān for the winter.

Since the mid-1960s, with the improvement of the roads and other facilities, the Shahsevan, like

Spring migration, Bozgush, south of Sarāb, spring 1983. The two leading camels are being ridden by women. In the background to the right the poles of a *küma* are visible.

nomads elsewhere in the Middle East, have gradually abandoned camels and donkeys in favour of trucks for transporting both household goods and flocks between summer and winter quarters. The advantage is that the expense of keeping camels is saved and the rigours of the migration are avoided. However, early experiments with truck transport were not always successful: apart from the expense involved in hiring the truck, flock owners often found they had arrived too early, in spring before the last frosts or before the snow had properly melted from the mountain pastures, or in autumn before the rains had brought up new grass in Moghān.

ECONOMIC, SOCIAL AND POLITICAL ORGANISATION

The pasture lands are legally owned by the state, but the traditional Shahsevan system of grazing rights is highly distinctive. Not only does each tribe have a recognised 'territory', but each community has traditional rights to defined areas in summer and winter quarters, and each full member usually has rights to a specific share in these pastures, rights he may, with the consent of fellow members, either rent or sell for cash. Similarly, nomads who have sold or lost their grazing rights, as well as outsiders from the villages or towns, may rent grazing for their animals from owners with a surplus to dispose of. They may join the camp of the owner as a 'client' member of the community or set up a separate camp of their own.

The male householders of a herding camp are usually a 'core' of brothers or paternal cousins, but may include hired shepherds and clients, often related to 'core' members by marriage. Men of a community most often form a lineage or 'navel' (*göbak*), tracing descent in the paternal line from an ancestor some four generations back, whose name they usually bear.

About four marriages in ten involve couples from the same community, but unlike many Muslims Shahsevan rarely marry their first paternal cousins. A more common link is between a man and his mother's brother's daughter. Most often marriages are made between distant relatives

A household on the move consisting of four camels, three donkeys and several dogs. The housewife is driving one of the loaded donkeys, her husband leading the camel train; the first camel, a hybrid (*nar*), carries the complete *alachıgh*. Geyiklu tribe, Moghan, spring 1966.

right top
A family just arrived at a campsite along the route; the work of unloading the camels and erecting the tent now begins. Geyiklu tribe, spring 1966.

right bottom
A wedding procession begins: two camels covered with fine local carpets leave the camp of the groom loaded with the last instalment of gifts of clothing for the bride and her family. On the first rides a hired musician, playing the shawm; on the second ride a sister and an aunt of the groom. They will be followed by a delegation of important men and women, who hope to persuade the bride's family to allow her to be brought back the following day to her new home. Geyiklu tribe, October 1966.

from the same community, or from neighbouring communities. Many boys and girls are able to choose their own partners, and say they marry for love. A woman married out of the community never loses her original lineage identity, though her interests and loyalties are expected to become those of the community of her husband and children. There is virtually no divorce or separation. Perhaps three men in a community have second wives, who are usually widows in their second marriage.

Livestock and other movable property are usually inherited by men only. Shahsevan follow Islamic law in recognising that a daughter has the right to inherit half a son's share in pastures or farmland, though in practice she almost always transfers her inheritance to one or all of her brothers. Women do own certain items of household property, however, and may be able to accumulate cash and valuables, the existence of which is often kept secret until their death, when they pass to their children.

Where men now all wear European-style shirt, trousers and jacket, with a brimmed hat or peaked cap, women continue to wear the traditional clothing of multiple skirts under an overshirt, with a decorated waistcoat jacket on top. This style of clothing has changed little, though fashions in materials vary constantly. The age and status of women are evident in their style of head covering. They do not wear veils, but cover the lower part of the face in the presence of unrelated men. This rule is strictly observed by engaged girls and newly married women, but young girls and older women are more casual.

A father participates indulgently in the bringing up of daughters and young sons, often leaving normal discipline to their mother, but as a boy approaches the age when he can help with the herding, he becomes liable to severe discipline by his father. Boys are taught the qualities of bravery and stamina associated with their warrior tradition, as well as moderation, respect for elders and jealousy

Inside an *alachıgh*, a woman works alone at her upright loom (*göy-hannasi*) weaving a *khorjun* saddle-bag. Geyiklu tribe, summer 1966.

of community honour. Girls should be modest, but also responsible, strong and hardy. Many stories are told of Shahsevan nomad women giving birth during the migration, managing households on their own, or berating warriors who returned home defeated and forcing them to return to face and overcome their enemies. In the past there was at least one woman who was chief of a major Shahsevan tribe and commanded a powerful force of warriors.

The Shahsevan are said to be organised politically into thirty-two tribes (*tayfa*). Although every Shahsevan knows which tribe he belongs to, nobody can agree on an exact list of the thirty-two. Many tribes have no more than a vague idea of common origins. Only a few consider they are descendants of a common ancestor, after whom they are named, such as the former 'noble' tribes, those tracing common descent with Badr Khān's family. Other tribes bear the names of old Turkish tribes (Begdilu, Ajirlu, Inanlu, Takila), from whom they are presumably descended. Yet others preserve the name of an occupation or duty: Sarvanlar were reputedly camel drivers (*sarvan*) of the chiefs; Jelowdarlu were their grooms (*jelowdar*); Yurtchi found their camp sites (*yurt*); Damirchilu may have been blacksmiths, Zargar goldsmiths.

Little trace is now left of the original organisation of the Moghān Shahsevan as a centralised tribal confederacy (*el*) of some 10,000 families under a single paramount chief (*elbey*). From the late nineteenth until the middle of the twentieth century the tribes have been nominally autonomous political groups, each with a compact territory and a chief (*bey*). Although they lost their power under the Pahlavi regime, several chiefs and their families remained a privileged class. Like the family of the paramount chief before them, most of the chiefs lost touch with ordinary nomad society, and by the 1970s the tribes they had led lost much of their cohesion as political groups, though their social identity persists.

The tribes divide administratively into sections or sub-tribes (*tira*), which usually coincide with the most important social groups, the nomadic communities. The thirty-odd Shahsevan nomad tribes today vary in size from fifty families in two or three sections to nearly 1,000 families in twenty-five or more sections. There are few contacts, and less than one marriage in ten, between tribes, each of which feels itself different in subtle ways from the others.

As we have seen, the communities usually do claim to be lineages (*göbak*), with members sharing a collective obligation to defend each other's honour and to consult each other in matters such as marriage which touch on that honour. Between tribes, and often between communities (sections), there is recognised competition, and sometimes conflict, in terms of honour and status, but within the communities there is expected to be solidarity and unanimity of opinion.

Each community, like each camp, has a recognised male elder (*aq-saqal*). With the abolition of the official role of the chiefs, the authorities now deal directly with these community elders. An elder has a difficult job as official leader responsible for all dealings with the authorities, and he is also expected to direct community activities. He or his son should be literate. Members of the community look to his life-style as a source and symbol of their honour, and he should be wealthy enough not only to entertain important visitors but also to provide lavish entertainment at feasts. There are commonly wide differences of wealth in a nomadic community. An elder may own several hundred sheep, 5–10 camels and some donkeys and horses, while a poor kinsman may have only 15 sheep and 2 camels and have to supplement his income by working as a shepherd or by casual labour or petty trading. If a family falls on particularly hard times, the elder will ensure that all members contribute to their welfare. Despite these economic inequalities, there is a strong sense of social egalitarianism within the community, and the elder rarely attempts to exercise his authority openly, for fear of challenge by rivals for leadership. Instead, with most of the community, he must use skilful persuasion.

Shahsevan women too have their leaders, who play an important part in the community, not only by regulating relations among women but also by making decisions and forming opinion on matters concerning men. Once past childbearing age, women often reach positions of considerable respect, and a few become influential leaders or 'grey hairs' (*aq-birchak*) who are comparable to male elders but perform their role somewhat differently. Women leaders are consulted privately by the male elders, but among the women they exercise their influence in public, at feasts attended by guests from a wide range of communities. Men and women are formally segregated in most situations, but especially at feasts. While the men are enjoying music and other entertainment, in the women's tent the leaders are likely to discuss matters of importance to both men and women, such as marriage arrangements, disputes, irregular behaviour among community members, or broader subjects bearing on economic and political affairs. Opinions are formed and decisions made which are then spread as the women return home and tell their men folk and friends. This unusual information network among the women serves a most important function for the society as a whole.

Shahsevan people are on the whole inward looking and community oriented, holding strongly that any expression of hostility among kinsfolk is shameful and should be kept secret from outsiders. Disputes, especially where women are involved, are not discussed openly but are resolved if possible by private communications between elders and participants. They draw strong boundaries around the household, the camp and the community, groups whose composition is clearly defined in terms of the rights and duties of membership. In this they contrast strongly with some other nomadic peoples known to the author, such as the Durrani Pashtuns of Afghanistan, for whom internal groupings such as households and camps are not sharply bounded and the crucial social boundary is that distinguishing Durranis as a whole from the many neighbouring groups of different language or cultural background.

A woman weaving a *jejim* at her ground-loom (*yer-hannasi*). On the southern slopes of Mount Savalan, summer 1987.

RELIGIOUS AND CEREMONIAL ORGANISATION

As with other Shiʿites, Shahsevan religious beliefs focus on death and the afterlife: the major annual religious occasion is the first ten days of the month of Moharram, commemorating the martyrdom of Imam Hoseyn in AD 680. Ceremonies in Moharram and during Ramadan, the month of fasting, are community affairs directed by the elder, but with everybody contributing to the expenses of feasting and the hire of a mullah, who is invited from a nearby village or town to officiate in the nomad camp. Every family observes the Feast of Sacrifice, which coincides with the annual pilgrimage to Mecca. Great respect is paid to those who have made pilgrimages to Mecca and to the Shiʿite shrines at Karbalā and Najaf in Iraq and at Mashhad in north-eastern Iran. The departure and return of Mecca pilgrims are occasions for their families to hold large parties for friends and relatives. Concepts of the nature of paradise and hell are based on standard Koranic and Islamic traditions, and are little elaborated. Funerals are simple affairs: immediately after death the body is washed and buried in a nearby village graveyard, the rite being supervised by a mullah. Commemorative feasts follow on the third, seventh and fortieth days and the anniversary.

Ceremonies associated with marriage are the most elaborate and colourful occasions among the Shahsevan. Several years of visits, exchanges and large feasts culminate in the wedding (*toy*), a week or more of festivities leading to the fetching of the bride to join her husband's family. Circumcision for boys is seen as a religious duty, but religion plays little part in the ceremony, which resembles a wedding.

Guests at major life cycle ceremonies (weddings, circumcisions, pilgrimage departures, funeral feasts) are from the sponsor's circle of *kheir-ü-sharr* (literally 'good-and-bad': those whose feasts he or she attends and who attend his or hers). They contribute money towards the expenses of the feasting and often loan food or equipment. There is a lively tradition among both men and women of story telling and of tribal songs and dances; however, most music at festivities today is performed by hired musicians from the villages and cities. Favourites are the minstrels (*ashıgh*) who travel throughout the region to perform at wedding and circumcision feasts.

In both summer and winter quarters the nomads are within a day or so's travel from towns and cities with modern medical facilities. These are, however, often basic and can be costly, and are only resorted to in severe emergencies. Shahsevan women, and some men, believe in the malicious power of spirits of various kinds to harm the weak, especially child bearing women, children and animals. Beliefs in the evil eye are also common, but vague. Such beliefs are only invoked on the occasion of some malignant or unexpected illness or sudden death, or on the failure of modern medicine. Each community has at least one man and one woman 'doctor' (*hakim*) with a knowledge of charms and counter-measures against evil forces, and of traditional herbal and magico-religious remedies for common ailments. In addition, camp visitors include itinerant Seyyeds and specialist prayer writers (*dua-yazan*) whose services may be called on. More powerful experts in traditional medicine are to be found in the towns and villages.

SETTLEMENT, IDENTITY AND CHANGE

Shahsevan nomads are fewer than one quarter of the rural population of this region. They share their Turki language and Shiʿite religion with the settled people, and they are in close economic and administrative contact with the market towns and with the villagers, who practise extensive irrigated and rain-fed cultivation.

Shahsevan call all the villagers and townspeople 'Tat'. Although this term literally means 'Persian speakers', that is the dominant majority in the country rather than the region, the Shahsevan use it for settled people, whatever their ethnic or linguistic affiliations. There is some ill feeling and prejudice between nomad Shahsevan and settled Tat, reflecting partly competition for the marginal lands which form the shifting boundary between pasture and cultivation, but mainly the history of Shahsevan tribal dominance, as expressed in the following verses by a Meshkin villager:

The Tat said: 'O Shahsevan, come, cease your migrations,
Settle down, take your ease, drink that filthy water no more;
Death cannot trouble you, you have so many troubles now!'
The Shahsevan replied: 'O Tat, why do I need houses or walls?
Tell me of wealth, booty, mares, the fat of sheep and goats!
Come, winter or summer, see what tulip gardens I have!'

above
Male guests eating lunch inside a crowded guest tent. As is the custom, they are eating in pairs, the photographer being the pair of the man on the bottom right; this is the 'lower' part of the tent, around the hearth, where tea is brewing. The brimmed hats of those in the picture indicate senior men, and off the picture to the right, in the 'upper' part of the tent, there are others, probably higher status. Near Moil village, western slopes of Mount Savalan, summer 1987.

below
Men seated at the back of an *alachıgh*; three new *chuwal* storage sacks on top of stones are part of the *yük*. Near At Güli, northern slopes of Mount Savalan, summer 1987.

Three women and their small children seated on felts in the back of an *alachıgh*. On the hearth a kettle is boiling, while the teapot warms in the ashes. This is clearly a stony site: in place of the heavy central stake holding down the roof-ring, smaller pegs have been reinforced with heavy rocks. South of Tabriz, at the foot of Sahand, spring 1984.

The only partition inside the tent is a curtain (*parda*). A new bride and her husband will sleep behind the *parda* during their first year of marriage or until their first child is born, when it will be replaced by a hammock for the new baby.

A century ago, Shahsevan identity in this region implied membership of one of the recognised tribes (*tayfa*) through political allegiance to its chief. Most tribespeople were pastoral nomads, but large numbers were settled farmers. Where nomads settled in their tribal communities (as they did in much of the region), the abandonment of migratory movements and nomad tents did not lead immediately to loss of Shahsevan identity.

The balance has since shifted in favour of settled society. After decades of government suppression of the political structure of chiefs and tribes, 'Shahsevan' has come to signify tent-dwelling pastoral nomads. The Shahsevan now attach a great deal of importance to both their nomadic movements and their dwellings, the main features in their culture that distinguish them from non-nomadic Tats. The migrations and in particular the *alachıgh* are now central symbols of Shahsevan identity.

Now most nomads who settle soon lose their tribal identity and become Tat. To be Shahsevan today is less a matter of descent or political or cultural affiliation than of demonstrated commitment to nomadism. Nevertheless, the conflict and antipathy between nomad and settled do not prevent intermarriage, friendship and other social relations between Shahsevan and Tat.

Tent dwelling and a nomadic way of life are basic to the Shahsevan identity. Their annual cycle of movement gives them a different view of time and space from that of settled people; for example, winter and summer are spoken of as places as well as seasons of the year. In the past, all the nomads knew of the mountains in winter was that they were deep under snow, while they reckoned Moghān to be impossibly hot and infested with snakes during the summer. But as more and more Shahsevan settle, and cultivation spreads throughout the region at the expense of pasture land, so they are adopting a more sedentary view of the world.

Having suffered economic and social discrimination under the Pahlavis, like other pastoral nomads in Iran, life has improved under the Islamic Republic. Soon after the 1978–9 Revolution the Shahsevan had their name, with its royalist connotation, officially changed to 'Elsevan', literally 'those who love the people (or tribe)'. The new name was never used among the ordinary nomads, and by 1992 was no longer widely used officially. The Organisation for the Nomadic Peoples of Iran within the Ministry of Rural Reconstruction has made enlightened efforts to promote viable development for the pastoral nomads without enforced settlement. One sign of this success is that, according to official figures, Shahsevan nomads in 1990 numbered as many as they did a quarter of a century earlier.

As a final note it should be said that, although the description of Shahsevan economic and social organisation given here is based on the author's field study in the 1960s, brief return visits in 1993 and 1995 indicate that it is still largely valid.

Warming up the horses before the beginning of a race at Dashtak-e Olya on the northern bank of the Atrek River, 1987.

FROM NOMADS TO FARMERS: THE TURKMEN OF IRAN

Jon Thompson

THE SUBJUGATION OF THE TURKMEN

In 1837 and 1848, Bode, a Russian Baron, visited the Turkmen tribes of Iran, known then throughout the English-speaking world as Persia. At the time the Turkmen were under attack from two directions at the same time—from the south by the army of the Shah, and from the north by the Uzbek forces of the Khan of Khiva. To reach the Yomut and Göklen tribes, Bode travelled through Iran, then ruled by the Qājār dynasty, and when he describes the Turkmen as 'more inhuman than the other wandering barbarous tribes', 'slave dealers', 'callous to the suffering of [their] fellow-creatures' with 'very few redeeming qualities to palliate the evil propensities of their nature', it is evident that he regarded them from an Iranian point of view (de Bode 1848).

The reasons for the almost organic hostility of Iranians at this time towards the Turkmen are embedded in history. Their relationship was one of continuous conflict, like two mutually hostile species in nature which coexist in a state of constant competition (Barthold 1962). The instinct of the Qājār government was to regulate and control; the wish of the Turkmen nomads was to live independently according to the ancient and traditional norms of their society. The Turkmen had their own system of customary law (*töre*) which was based on justice, equality and compassion, and gave independence and equality to every member of Turkmen society. They also wished to avoid paying taxes to a power they did not acknowledge, and to prevent their young men from being drafted for military service.

The Qājār authorities were repeatedly annoyed by the unruly Turkmen tribes along their border; they would raid them, punish them, often with extreme severity, take their livestock, kill them, force them to flee, and demand tribute, taxes and reparations, but they could never eliminate them, nor, it seems, could they come to an agreeable coexistence. In the face of extreme danger the principal means of survival for the Turkmen was flight northwards into the desert. Those who fled recovered gradually; the population grew, their herds multiplied, and they lived to fight again. To speed up their recovery and at the same time take revenge for their losses they would raid villages in Khorāsān, plunder its inhabitants, take their livestock and sell the inhabitants into slavery. The cruelty and indifference to human misery that characterised these conflicts was, in the opinion of more impartial observers such as Charles Marvin, manifested by the Iranians and the Turkmen in equal degree (Marvin 1881).

In the days before firearms the two sides were fairly evenly matched. Even when the Iranian army did begin to use firearms in the sixteenth century the highly mobile Turkmen who knew the terrain would seek to draw the Iranian forces into the desert where they would be at risk from shortage of food and water. The policy of Shah ʿAbbās towards the Turkmen in the seventeenth century was one of containment rather than conquest, whereas in the eighteenth century Nāder Shah, who was of Turkic Qizilbash origin, set out to defeat the Turkmen and having conquered them he treated them with such severity that hatred of Qizilbash (their term for Iranian) rule became the subject of popular poetry and song and remains embedded in the folk memory of the Turkmen to this day.[1]

The real superiority of advancing military technology over the traditional Turkmen tactics of mobility, surprise and flight, became fully evident for the first time when Russian artillery and rockets were directed against them in 1870. From then on, the combination of deceitful political manipulation and the force of the Russian army quickly put an end to Turkmen independence. The major part of Turkmen territory came under Russian rule, while the remaining part was divided between Afghanistan, then within the British sphere of influence, and Iran.

A young unmarried woman of the Gökleñ tribe at Garkaz north of Bojnurd, close to the border with Turkmenistan, 1986.

The seeds of this state of affairs were sown in 1801 when leaders of a segment of the Abdal tribe in conflict with the Khan of Khiva appealed to the Russian authorities to become Russian subjects. This event focussed Russian interest on the possibility of extending their influence in Central Asia.

The possibility of progress in this direction was given impetus when the Russian army, after several years of skirmishes and intrigue in the Caucasus, finally routed the Iranian army and drove them out of the northern part of Tālesh and part of Moghān. The treaty of Golestān in 1813 established these parts of the Caucasus, formerly considered to be Iranian, as Russian territory and Iran was forbidden to have any naval power in the Caspian sea. With this prohibition in place the Russians felt free to make use of their advantage to extend their influence. With a view to finding a suitable place to build a fort, an agent, Major Ponomarev, was sent laden with gifts to soften up the Turkmen and at the same time to reconnoitre the eastern coast of the Caspian sea.

The Iranian government, eager to regain its lost territories in the Caucasus, went to war again with Russia in 1826 with considerable initial successes. The campaign, however, ended in disaster and under threat of losing the whole of the rich province of Āzarbāijān, including the city of Tabriz, the Shah was obliged to make a humiliating settlement and pay a large indemnity, the terms of which were set down in the treaty of Torkmanchai. This treaty, signed in 1828, fixed the border almost as it stands today.

Sore over the loss of the Caucasian territories, the Shah and his military leaders were encouraged to turn their attention towards Central Asia and Afghanistan. They began by asserting their authority over the Yomut in the valley of the Gorgān river around Asterābād in order to raise money for their eastern campaigns which were intended to extend Iranian sovereignty into

above
A Yomut Shepherd inside his *götikme*. Near Incheh Borun, 1986.

below
A Göklan woman at Garkaz close to the border with Turkmenistan, north of Bojnurd, 1986.

Afghanistan. The coastal Yomut, however, who had been flourishing in the absence of an Iranian naval presence, had extended their fishing activities in the Caspian and were now trading along its shores. They did not consider themselves to be subjects of the Shah and were not in a mood to submit.

At the same time the Khan of Khiva, in a series of campaigns, was pressing the Turkmen from the north. So in 1834, when the Russians decided, on the basis of Ponomarev's recommendations, to build a fort on the Mangyshlak peninsula, the Turkmen put up no resistance because there was a perception among them that the presence of a friendly foreign power might not be such a bad thing. They were carefully supported in this belief by Russian reassurances to the effect that their intention was solely to promote trade in the region. By the time the Turkmen discovered that they had been deceived it was too late to prevent the inexorable extension of Russian power into central Asia, conducted all too often, even by the standards of those times, with the most distressing, extreme and wanton cruelty.

In an ironical twist Russian influence in the region was increased when the Iranians, eager to control the fishing activities of the coastal Turkmen, asked permission to have a small naval presence in the south-eastern Caspian. The Russians refused and undertook to maintain order themselves. In 1841 a Russian naval base was established at Āshurādeh, a few miles from the mouth of the Gorgān river on a narrow spit of land which is now joined to the Iranian mainland, though at the time it was an island. By this move the Russians were able to control both trade and fishing, and at the same time exert their influence over the Turkmen by the now familiar technique of sending them to prison or exile if they failed to submit to orders.

Between the early 1840s and 1860s the Turkmen were so hard pressed by both the Khivans and the Iranians that the leaders of the Salor, Saryk and Tekke tribes met and concluded that it would be wise to forget ancient rivalries and unite against the common threat. When, in 1860, a large Iranian army set out to conquer Merv, the Turkmen tribes, depleted and exhausted by years of warfare, were in a weak position and the fall of Merv seemed inevitable. However, complacency on the part of the commander of the Iranian army led to its defeat and gave the Turkmen a temporary respite.

So severe was the antipathy of the Yomut to the Tekke that they could not be persuaded to join the tribal union, and after their humiliating defeat at Merv the Iranian authorities turned to the now isolated Yomut and made demands for the payment of taxes. When these were refused the Iranian army devastated the region of Asterābād (now Gorgān) and the Gorgān valley south of the Atrak wreaking terrible destruction on the people, their property and livestock. The devastation was repeated five years later in 1867. By this means Iranian forces were able to gain control of the region and the Yomut had no option but to submit.

Plans to build a second fort on the eastern shore of the Caspian, this time further south at Kizil Su (Krasnovodsk in Russian), were approved by the Tsar in 1865. This was a fateful decision for the Turkmen. The fort was built in 1869 to the alarm of the Iranian authorities, and with good reason. From this firm base the Russians were able to conduct effective military operations in what was soon to become their Transcaspian Province. In 1873 Khiva was attacked and its army defeated, the only worthwhile defence being provided by the northern branch of the Yomut Turkmen who were prepared to fight for their independence in spite of years of oppression by the Khan of Khiva. For their pains the Yomut were treated with shameful severity by the Russian commander, General Kaufman. The following year it was the turn of the Mangyshlak and Atrak Yomuts to meet the force of Russian arms. Ten years later, with the defeat of the Tekke at Gök Tepe in 1881 and the fall of Merv in 1884, it was all over for the Turkmen. Throughout this period the Iranian authorities had been placated and effectively neutralised by Russian assurances that they acknowledged Iranian rule up to the river Atrak though not beyond. The lower course of this river from its junction with the Sumbar remains the boundary today.[2]

THE TURKMEN OBSERVED

In Bode's account of his visit to the Turkmen, published in 1848, he observed two principal modes of subsistence. To the north were the *charva*. This word derives from Persian *chārpādār*, meaning those who own and hire out the four-footed (i.e. beasts of burden). These are the pastoral nomads who keep cattle, sheep, horses and camels in large numbers and live mainly on the products of their animals. To the south he came across the primarily agricultural *chomur*, an ancient Turkic word

A Göklan family inside their tent (*öy*) near Gokjeh village near Kalāleh, 1987.

which refers to their mud-built houses. They too keep livestock, though in much smaller numbers and their animals travel only short distances in search of pasture. He makes two other interesting observations. The first is that although the land available to the nomadic *charva* is of inferior quality, they do plant some crops. The second is that in Turkmen society the more settled agricultural *chomur* have a lower status than the *charva*. He says that when one of the settled *chomur* becomes enriched he will acquire livestock and the necessary equipment, quit the fertile Gorgān valley and join his more independent brethren in the arid region to the north. Likewise when one of the nomadic *charva* becomes impoverished he will take up the sedentary life of the *chomur*.

James Fraser who was travelling in the region some years earlier describes the Gorgān valley as 'a country which for beauty and richness I have seldom seen equalled' and he indicates that it is a region eminently suited to agriculture (Fraser 1825). Another description of the region is provided by General Petrusevich who was briefly Governor General of the newly formed Russian province of Transcaspia before being killed at the battle of Gök Tepe in January 1881. He had travelled extensively in Khorāsān and in Turkmen territory making numerous observations. He describes the land occupied by the Göklans as 'almost the most beautiful corner of the whole of northern Persia . . . one of the most favoured spots in the world.'[3]

By the time de Morgan visited the region in 1890, also from the Iranian side, the boundaries had been drawn and the Turkmen tribes remaining under Iranian rule were mainly *chomur*, those engaged in agriculture. Like Bode he takes a disparaging and patronising view of the Turkmen, describing them as bandits and plunderers, coarse-mannered and far from intelligent (de Morgan 1894, 1: 83-112). The tribes he names in the Gorgān valley include the Ugurjali along the coast, next to them the Jafarbai and Atabai Yomuts, and furthest to the east the Göklan. He did not visit the nomadic *charva* in the north.

Since the time of those nineteenth-century travellers, whose accounts include descriptions of large Turkmen encampments with thousands of animals, there has been a tendency for the *charva* to settle. At the same time the trend has been for the *chomur* to increase the area of land under cultivation and to reduce the number of their livestock. This process accelerated in the second half of the twentieth century to the point that today the Turkmen of Iran are mostly settled in villages and there may no longer be any *charva* who live all the year round in tents.

This process of course has been a gradual one. At the time of de Morgan's visit most *chomur* families would organise some division of labour during the rainy season to take their livestock a

A Yomut shepherd and his family outside their *götikme*, a lightweight tent with no wall trellis. Near Incheh Borun, 1986.

short distance to the hills in the south where they established temporary tented encampments. In the course of time, as the size of their flocks diminished, families would agree to combine their flocks and divide up the work of taking the animals for winter grazing, or alternatively would share the cost of hiring a shepherd. In this way the existing remnants of a former nomadic lifestyle were reduced still further. The pattern here could be seen as a gradual adaptation by a formerly nomadic community to a mode of subsistence better adapted to the local climatic conditions, however Irons argues convincingly that the change from nomadism to farming can be better explained as an adaptation to the surrounding political realities (Irons 1974, 1975).

To the north of the Gorgān valley, where there is less rainfall, the terrain is poorly suited to agriculture. Here the vegetation is sparse except in the rainy season and the fundamental principle of the pastoral nomadic way of life—that of optimising the yield of sustenance by moving between sets of marginal terrain according to the availability of vegetation—comes naturally into effect. Here too, especially in the region of Gokcha Dagh and Khoor Dagh, the traditional *charva* way of life has survived longest and many families still own a tent which may be used for part of the year. However, changes in the wider world—the pressure for both girls and boys to go to school, the availability of motor vehicles and the convenience of manufactured goods—have all had their effect in altering the outlook, aspirations and life style of Iran's former nomads in the direction of promoting settlement in permanent dwellings. While the northern *charva* can be seen to have followed a similar pattern of settlement to their southern neighbours, their settling appears to be an adaptation to altered sets of constraints, both political and economic. Greater integration into the cash economy, the availability of supplies that can be bought, greater ease of transport and the need for children's education have all served to diminish dependence on a single mode of subsistence in favour of closer integration into a settled village-based life.

MATERIAL CULTURE

In the closing decades of the twentieth century some aspects of the material culture of the Turkmen became quite well known in Europe and America. This has been brought about by greatly increased opportunities for travel, a growing interest in 'alternative' ways of life and by the sudden appearance of Turkmen artefacts of all kinds in the market place, an event which signals the disappearance of their traditional way of life.

The distinctive felt-covered trellis tent of the northern nomads has been the subject of scholarly

Yomut women weaving a knotted-pile carpet inside their tent. Hottan village near Morāveh Tappeh, 1986.

study (Andrews 1973, 1980, 1997), and is increasingly becoming a focus of popular interest. Oregon state parks currently have 150 'yurts' for the use of visitors all the year round and they are now spreading to parks in North County, California, while enthusiasts for alternative living in Britain can have canvas-covered trellis tents made to order by a craftsman living in Wales. The traditional felt tent of the Turkmen (*öy*) can still be found among the inhabitants of the Turkmen plain in Iran, though it is used mainly as a sort of out-house or storage area adjacent to a permanent dwelling. In the Gokcha Dagh shepherds still use their felt tents, often in a reduced form called *götikme* which lacks the folding trellis sections (*ganāt*). Having no vertical wall, the curved roof struts rest directly on the ground in the same manner as the *alachıgh* of the Shahsevan. Although the head-room is much reduced it has the advantage of being lighter and easier to transport than the öy, from which it differs in having a shorter cane screen and differently curved roof struts to accommodate the door.

In the last quarter of the nineteenth century rapid impoverishment of the Turkmen under Russian rule caused them to sell their weavings and embroideries which were much admired in both Russia and Europe and soon became items of international trade. One event in particular is known to have caused the sale of carpets and other textiles in great quantity; that was the defeat of the nothern Yomuts in 1873 who were fighting both for the defence of Khiva and for the preservation of their independence from Russian rule. Their shameful treatment at the hands of General Kaufman has already been mentioned. Those of the Yomut who were left alive after a merciless massacre of all the men, women and children his troops could find, were obliged to pay an indemnity of some 300,000 roubles, a sum which General Kaufman knew very well was so large as to be impossible for them to pay. In their attempt to raise the money the Yomuts sold everything they possessed. Their most valuable assets were livestock, carpets and jewellery. The silver in their jewellery will have been recycled, whereas the carpets entered the marketplace at a time when the fashion for 'oriental' carpets in Europe was growing fast. Herbert Coxon, a carpet dealer from Newcastle, England, visited Baku looking for carpets ten years after this event and noted that carpets sold to pay off the indemnity had been bought by Russian officers and were also to be found for sale in the bazaars of Karshi and Bukhara (Coxon 1883: 61). The carpets of the defeated Tekke were soon to follow, and to promote their sale they were romantically described by merchants as 'Royal Bukhara' and 'Princess Bukhara' carpets. In that brief period towards the close of the nineteenth century great quantities of carpets which had been made by the Turkmen and used by them for both ritual and practical purposes were sold to the west. These carpets are the few documents we have of this aspect of their material culture prior to their enforced settlement. Within Turkmen society the function of woven objects extended far beyond their practical utility. They were indicators of a woman's skill, hence her 'value' as a wife, and they played an important role in socially significant ritual practices—weddings, the reception of guests etc. Since each tribe used a distinctive set of patterns and had its own colour style, weavings also served to reinforce a sense of tribal identity. However, when the Tekke, Saryk, Chaudur and northern Yomut were forcibly settled they were obliged to join the cash economy and it was a small step for them to direct their weaving skills towards increasing the family income. The combination of a changing life style, the need to earn money and the perceived demands of the market place brought about rapid changes in both the form and decoration of their weavings. In this new situation the value of a woman's weaving skills was enhanced, but the purely commercial nature of her work meant that the social significance of the weavings themselves was lost. Among the Turkmen of Iran where settlement has been more gradual, some of the traditional types of weavings suitable for a mud house are still being made, whereas items specific to the tent, such as girths and wall bags are not. Weavers are also adapting to the needs of the market in ways similar to those observed after the Russian conquest (Irons 1990).

In the 1970s economic necessity forced many Turkmen women to sell their silver jewellery, which for them was a traditional form of adornment and at the same time a means for storing wealth. Pieces of every kind were brought for sale and in great quantity. Much of it found its way to the West where it has become fairly well known. Many of the items sold at that time had been handed down as heirlooms and some of them may be quite old. However, conservatism in both taste and craftsmanship makes them extremely hard to date. As with their weavings the jewellery of each tribe can be recognised by its distinctive style (Firouz 1978, Schletzer & Schletzer 1983).

In spite of the progressive transformation of the Turkmen from nomads to farmers there is one heritage from their remote past which they have preserved with extraordinary diligence—the blood line of their horses. There are two principal breeds, the Akhal Tekke and the Yomut; a third, the Cheneran, is a cavalry horse developed in the eighteenth century from a cross between the Turkmen and the horse used by the nomads of Fars. The Akhal Tekke horse appears to be a descendant of the ancient 'hot-blooded' horse of the steppes known to the ancient Greeks as the Nisean horse and there is evidence to indicate that the coveted 'Arab' thoroughbred of the western world is genetically related to the Turkmen horse. The pure bred Akhal Tekke is a beautiful creature with a long, thin neck, long legs, a long face with a straight profile and a fine silky coat. It is noted for its speed, powers of endurance and intelligence. The Yomut is similar but slightly smaller and heavier, it having more of the Arab and Fars strains in it. The importance of the Turkmen horse as breeding stock is being increasingly recognised world-wide. Although horses are highly valued and their owners lavish immense care on them, it is of some interest that the Turkmen, whose language preserves archaic features and who exhibit notable conservatism in their customs and dress, do not drink fermented mare's milk (*kymys*) and have no tradition of horse sacrifice, customs characteristic of the Altaic nomads. Instead they drink fermented camel's milk and the wool of the camel they regard as sacred.

Today the Turkmen are moving ever closer to the urban agricultural way of life and the material evidence of their nomadic past is fast disappearing, nevertheless they retain a sense of tribal identity and the memory of pastoral life in the desert-steppe remains very much alive.

A Tālesh family inside their hemicylindrical hut in Gilān, west of Asālem. Summer 1987.

THE TĀLESH PASTORALISTS IN NORTH-WESTERN ALBORZ

Marcel Bazin

THE LAND AND THE PEOPLE

The word Tālesh is used as the name of both the region and its inhabitants. The Tālesh region is the north-western end of the Alborz mountain chain, or more exactly its north-eastern humid side, between the deep-cut Sefidrud river and the Araxes valley. It forms part of the Caspian fringe of Iran where extensive forests give an unusual environment to pastoral life when compared with the deserts and steppes of interior Iran.

The Tālesh people speak Tāleshi, a language of the north-western Iranian group. It is closely related to Tāti, the Iranian language spoken in Āzarbāijān before its Turkicisation and still surviving in several isolated spots, but is quite different from Gilāki, the language of the central plain of Gilān. Every Tāleshi valley or group of adjacent valleys has its own dialect. As for their religious affiliation, the Tālesh were Sunni Muslims, but the spread of Shiʿism from central Gilān and Āzarbāijān has gradually reduced the Sunni area to the central districts of Tālesh Dulāb, Asālem and Kargānrud. In northern Tālesh, conversion to Shiʿism has more or less paralleled the spread of Āzeri Turkish (Torki), which is the language of trade whereas Persian is the language of administration. But these changes have not affected the fierce pride the Tālesh take in their identity. Even a Turkish-speaking Shiʿite Tālesh will proclaim himself a Tālesh before anything else. His ethnic consciousness is deeply rooted in the mountainous environment and the practice of pastoral migrations along the Tālesh valleys.

The majority of Tālesh are now rice-growing peasants living in the narrow coastal plain or in the piedmont, while the rest are specialised husbandmen in the mountain areas. The two are not separate, however. The plain-dwellers take their cattle and flocks to summer pastures every year where they meet the members of the other group. The Tālesh themselves distinguish among the husbandmen the *gālesh* and the *chupān*. The *gālesh* raise cattle and sheep and may grow some cereals, and the *chupān* are shepherds who have only sheep and goats. The 'basic Tālesh' are the mountaineers, who expanded downstream and conquered the fringe of the alluvial plain.

THE FOUR ECOLOGICAL LEVELS OF TĀLESH

The Tālesh country can be divided into four levels of ecological conditions and land use. The Tālesh people migrate between these levels for various pastoral (or sometimes agro-pastoral) purposes. Various types of permanent and temporary dwellings are used, each appropriate to a particular level.

The lowest level is the agricultural plain, which starts as a narrow alluvial ribbon between Āstārā and Rezvānshahr in the northern part of Iranian Tālesh and widens into the central Gilān plain. The Tālesh populate a very narrow fringe of the plain that extends approximately from the foothills to the canal of Fumanāt, which brings irrigation water from the Sefidrud. Most of the original Hyrcanian forest has been cleared, but some remains on coarse alluvial fans. Most of the densely populated plain is covered by irrigated paddy-fields interspersed with loose hamlets (*mahalleh*), orchards and mulberry groves or small tobacco and tea plantations.

The traditional houses on the plain have wooden frameworks stuffed with clay—now, alas, being rapidly replaced by cement block houses—and comprise several specialised buildings including stables. Every family owns one or two horses as pack animals, one ox for ploughing the paddy-fields (when it hasn't been replaced by a Japanese-made motorised tiller) and several milch-cows with their calves. As there is little grazing available in the plain (the limited remains of forests, small sandy patches covered with thorny shrubs and *Gleditschia caspica* trees bearing edible pods) animals mainly graze rice-stubble on the fields in autumn, are fed with rice-straw in the stable during winter and are moved to the mountains in summer.

The second level is the foothills up to 2,600 feet (800 metres) above sea level and is very sparsely populated all along the chain. The winter quarters (*qeshlaq*) of the husbandmen are scattered all over this level.

This level is agro-pastoral in the north between Shānderman and the former Soviet border and purely pastoral in the southern valleys. The *gālesh* in the northern part grow tiny patches of corn, wheat and tobacco and live in wooden-framed houses covered with shingle-boards. In the south the bulk of the area consists of forest pasture land divided by elementary fences into extensive individual plots where cattle and sheep graze freely, unless an exceptionally thick snow cover compels their shelter. In order to provide for this necessity, the *gālesh* living in the southernmost valleys build an original type of house called *vuna-sarā*. This compact building made with billets generally has three storeys, the first for cattle and horses, the second for human beings and the third under the roof as 'emergency shelter' for sheep and goats. But the most usual type of shelter in the south is a simple oval or hemi-cylindrical hut called *pargā* or *poru*, made up of a bound framework of branches set into the ground and covered with goat hair fabric. When the husbandmen migrate they remove the fabric and leave the framework on the spot, where it remains as a token of their winter stay.

Permanent Tālesh settlements west of Fuman. The densely populated plain is covered with irrigated rice fields interspersed with orchards, mulberry groves and small tea and tobacco plantations.

The third level is the intermediate part of the mountain between 2,600 and 4,600 feet (800 and 1,400 metres) above sea level. On this level are the permanent settlements of cereal growers, the stopping places of the husbandmen on their way to the summer grazing lands, called *miyānkuh* (middle of the mountain) or *nesferudkhān* (half of the river), and the lowest summer resorts of the peasants from the plain. In the northern part of the chain, the lofty beech forests have been extensively cleared into wheat and barley fields around relatively compact villages of clustered houses. There is a dense network of pastoral routes in the remaining forests, which are often degraded into glades around the clusters of huts temporarily occupied in spring and autumn by shepherds, or for longer in summer by a few families from the rice growing hamlets of the plain.

The fourth level is that part of the mountain from 4,600 to 8,800 feet (1,400 to 2,700 metres) above sea level. Here are the true summer resorts, the *yaylaq* (a Turkish word extensively used in Iran) or *giriya* ('mountain' in Tāleshi). It includes the higher (sub-alpine) level of the forest, in which oaks and hornbeam take the place of beeches, and the alpine meadows. The forest has been gradually reduced, and its altitudinal limit lowered, by the action of pastoralists. People coming from the plain or the lower mountain levels spend the summer there, in seasonal settlements ranging in size from a few families to several hundred. The location of summer resorts is bound to the availability of good pasture land and drinking water, while fuel has often to be brought from lower-lying forest areas. Formerly, the traditional huts (*pargā*) were the predominant form of dwelling all over Tālesh summer resorts. Some of them are strengthened with bark, boards or low stone walls, but others have been replaced by wooden chalets (*ka*, i.e. simply 'house' in Tāleshi) built with planks or billets and covered with shingles, or various intermediate forms such as huts entirely made up of branches (*kumeh*) or houses covered with removable goat hair fabrics (*guāl*).

MIGRATION PATTERNS

The Tālesh migrations between these four levels have various forms which can be classified according to their spatio-temporal organisation and their degree of mobility. None of the Tālesh can be considered true nomads, since they do not carry the framework of their huts with them but leave it on the spot until they come back (or until somebody else takes the branches and uses them as fuel!). Since most of them have one or more fixed dwellings, they should be classified as semi-nomads, though some shepherds who live throughout the year under very simple *pargās* and stay in six or seven different grazing spots are not so far from being true nomads.

The simplest form of migration, but which involves the biggest number of people, is the migration of peasants from the plain. Since rice cultivation needs much work, they cannot stay a long time away from their *mahalleh*. They leave their permanent home in June, when the weeding of

below left
A shepherd and his sheep on a summer pasture at Māsāl, July 1976.

below right
A newly-built summer hut in Subātān, its wooden framework has not yet been covered with mud plaster. August 1972.

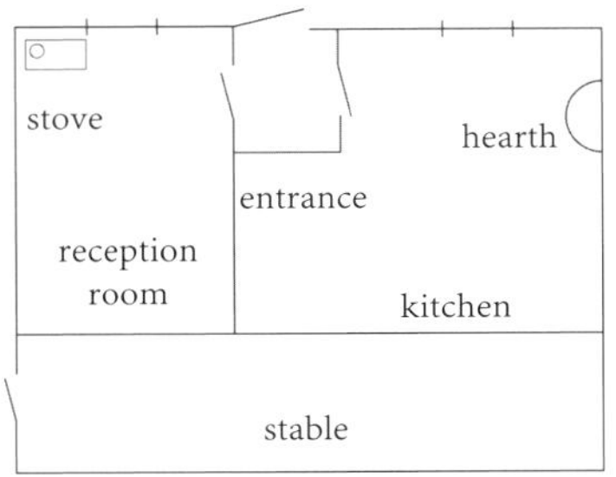

Plan of a wooden chalet in Subātān (Lisār valley).

the paddy-fields is over, go directly to their summer camp, spend six to eight weeks there and come back to the plain in August for harvest-time. Actually, as described, this form of migration is very rare, because the peasants wish to get the animals off the plain earlier than June in order for them to profit from a longer stay on the lush grasslands of the mountain. Therefore most families separate into two parts in May and some men take the cattle to the summer pasture and stay there alone for one month, while the women go on weeding the paddy-fields, the children attend school and the father, in some valleys, breeds silkworms. Everybody gathers together in the *yaylaq* in June. In August the labour force needed for harvest goes back to the plain (with the horses) while other members of the family stay in the mountains with the cattle until September.

Though some specialised husbandmen in the mountain use only two pastoral levels, their most usual migratory patterns are based upon three levels. Thus the herders leave their *qeshlaq* in spring, stop two or three weeks in the *miyānkuh* on their way to the summer resort, and a bit longer in autumn on their way back to the winter quarters. People having both cattle and sheep may take the latter to the upper levels earlier in spring and bring them back to the *qeshlaq* later in autumn. Others use different pasture land for cattle and flocks, especially in summer when sheep and goats can climb higher up the mountain. The most intricate migration forms are to be found in the northern half of Tālesh where agricultural activities in one or more levels interfere with

The traditional rectangular hemi-cylindrical hut (*pargā*) has a frame of bent wooden poles covered with three or four sheets made from strips of goat hair cloth. Between Asālem and Khalkhāl, summer 1987.

pastoral movements. Thus some members of the family go in advance (in early spring) to one of the summer camps in order to sow barley, and get down again to the *miyānkuh* village for harvesting wheat in July or to the *qeshlaq* hamlet for gathering corn in September.

THE ECONOMIC AND SOCIAL DYNAMICS OF PASTORALISM IN TĀLESH

Is this apparently archaic and severe way of life doomed to extinction? Certainly several factors seem to be pushing it in this direction:

1. The continuing development of agriculture in the plain and on the lower foothills, which is reducing the areas available for stock raising, and demanding more and more labour time.
2. Severe limitations to grazing rights in the mountains imposed by the forestry administration in order to protect the environment and to develop wood production, especially around the big sawmill of Asālem and the paper factory in Punel.
3. Migration to the towns by landless husbandmen who were impoverished when they were excluded from the land reforms of the 1960s.
4. More generally, the strong attraction of the 'modern' urban way of life.

But contrary factors operate against this trend towards decline:

1. The economic function of stock raising remains very important in Iran, and especially in the central Gilān plain, where animal husbandry is fairly insufficient. The main products of Tālesh husbandry are butter made from cow's milk in large pottery churns, cheese made from sheep and goat milk, raw wool and meat. The latter is the most important. The local or Gilāni stock-traders (*chubdār*) send a continuous stream of live animals to the towns of central and eastern Gilān. Textile crafts are limited to domestic weaving of goat hair fabric for covering the huts, of very plain *palaz* and *jajim* for the houses, and of partially felted *shal* for masculine costumes.
2. The opening of roads through the Tālesh chain, the first one in the early 1970s between Asālem and Khalkhāl, favoured the development of summer resorts along them that are now accessible by minibus to vacationers from Tehrān.
3. The Tālesh people are deeply attached to pastoral life. For them, attending summer pastures

A summer camp west of Asālem showing new-style wooden chalets (*ka*) roofed with shingles. The hemi-cylindrical huts (*pargā*) are now without their covering of goat hair cloth and branches, or more recently polythene sheeting, the owners having returned to the plains to harvest their rice fields. Between Asālem and Khalkhāl, summer 1985.

means not only fulfilling a technical task but also having much-appreciated holidays and proclaiming their Tālesh identity.

At the end of the 1970s, pastoral life was still quite lively in Tālesh, with 25 to 55 per cent of the population in the different districts taking part in pastoral migrations and in attending very lively summer bazaars in the mountains. There is, however, insufficient recent information to show in which direction the balance has since moved between the two above-mentioned antagonistic tendencies.

bedding and clothes
cradle
reception space
implements and food provisions
kitchen
hearth
stove
entrance

Plan of a hemicylindric hut in Larz Deh (Asālem valley).

The tent of Baluch nomads at Hāmun-e Tagur east of Khāsh, summer 1985.

THE BALUCH

Jon Thompson

The history of the Baluch has proved difficult to unravel. There are no historical records to indicate where they came from, though scanty literary references suggest that they arrived in their present location some 900 years ago after traversing Iran in a south-easterly direction (Frye 1960). Some information on the Baluch past has been obtained from the study of the Baluchi language which belongs to the north-western group of Iranian languages, that is to say it is related to modern Kurdish, Tati and Taleshi, though not descended from them. Baluchi is also related to Parthian and the connection between these two languages has led to the suggestion that prior to the Arab conquest the ancestral Baluch occupied a territory in physical proximity to the Parthians, 'south-east of the Caspian sea'. This region is currently occupied by the Turkmen and it is tempting to speculate, following the general drift of central Asian history, that the displacement of those Baluch ancestors was a result of the inward migration of Turkic nomads who in turn had been shunted westwards by major population movements originating far to the east—an event similar to the displacement of the Sakas by the westward movement of the Yüeh Chih centuries earlier (Elfenbein 1992).

Field studies have brought to light the difficulty of defining the term Baluch. Not all who call themselves Baluch—that includes both nomads and settled cultivators—were born such. It is evident that from time to time non-Baluch elements have adopted in varying degrees the Baluch way of life, language and cultural values and have thus become assimilated into Baluch society (Spooner 1975).

In physical appearance the Baluch resemble their Persian-speaking neighbours. A long, bony face, prominent, aquiline nose and a tall, lean body habitus are features frequently encountered. By tradition men wear their wavy hair long and sport a full beard, though they often trim or shave the moustache. Their principal garments are voluminous cotton trousers, narrow at the ankle; a long-sleeved tunic buttoned at the front and a white turban with the free end of the cloth hanging down the back. However the clothing of both men and women is slowly changing as locally made garments give way to bought, factory-made items. As in other societies the women are more conservative in their dress than the men. They have a liking for bright plain colours or bold floral prints which they tailor into a long-sleeved dress reaching to mid-calf. The vertical front opening is long enough for breast-feeding and kept closed with a pin or brooch. The bodice they decorate with embroidered panels which are sewn on. The sleeves of the dress and the bottoms of the trousers worn beneath the dress are enlivened with embroidered panels too. The head is covered with a long light-weight veil which can be used to cover the mouth and lower face in the presence of strangers.

The Baluch nomads of Iran are dispersed over a wide area. In the south the greatest numbers can be found in the rugged Makrān coastal mountain range in the province of Sistān and Baluchistān. They extend eastwards and north-east into the neighbouring Hormozgān and Kermān provinces and northwards in a narrow band sandwiched between the great salt desert of Lut to the west and the stony desert and salt wastes to the east in Pakistan and Afghanistan. This strip of Baluch territory extends northwards along Iran's eastern border to include Zāhedān and Zābol and further into the province of Khorāsān where smaller numbers can be found in the mountains north of Asadābād, north and south of Torbat-e Jām, and even in Turkmen territory south of Gonbad-e Kāvus. In the north their neighbours are black-tent nomads of the Persian-speaking Timuri tribe and Kurds, with whom there is some intermarriage. Around Zābol they share territory with the

The horizontal ground loom set up for weaving panels for the black tent using goat hair. Near Kāshi, not far from the south coast, winter 1988.

right
Baluch woman spinning goat hair for making tent cloth. On Kuh-e Taftān, near Sangān.

opposite above
A group of barrel-vaulted huts (*luk*) covered with rush matting north of Irān Shahr, 1985.

opposite below
The interior of a *luk* showing the bedding stack at the far end.

Gawdārān. Here and further south they mingle with the Brahui who speak a Dravidian language. Opinion differs as to whether the Brahui, who share the same life-style and values as the Baluch, are migrants from south India or the remains of an early indigenous people present in the area before the arrival of Indo-Europeans.

The mode of subsistence of the tent-dwelling pastoral nomads is in many respects similar to that of the other nomadic peoples of Iran. The small communities in Khorāsān follow the same pattern of migration as their Kurdish neighbours who migrate to the mountains in summer and return to the lowlands in winter. In contrast the majority of nomads in the south have no well-defined spring and autumn migration. Their movements tend to be more conditioned by the availability of pasture and water. This in turn depends on the rainfall which is notoriously capricious in this region. In some years there is no rainfall at all and the annual average taken over a number of years is unlikely to exceed 25 cm.

The classic Baluch tent has a woven, black, goat hair canopy supported by several poles of differing height and stabilised by ropes attached to its edge which are fastened to the ground at some distance from the tent. Its form varies from summer to winter and it may be only partially erected when travelling. In the south some nomads use what has been termed a 'barrel-vaulted hut' (*luk*). It has a frame consisting of two sets of flexible wooden hoops, their ends buried in the ground, each of which forms roughly a half circle. The hoops are of graduated diameter, the larger in the centre and the smaller at the periphery. Each set has all its hoops parallel and the first set is placed at right angles to the second. Where they cross, the main hoops are securely lashed together and secondary, thinner hoops are used to fill in the spaces between them. The result is a domed frame which is then covered with large sheets of plaited rush matting. The matting may extend all the way to the ground or a gap may be left for ventilation according to the season. The shape of the hut depends on how many hoops are used to form the each set. If the first has more than the second, then the hut becomes elongated into a 'tunnel' shape; if the numbers are more or less equal the hut is a rectangular dome with rounded corners.[1]

The economy of the nomadic pastoralists is based on the goat and to a lesser degree the sheep and the cow. Donkeys and camels are used for transport, and wealthier nomads keep good riding

above left
A Baluch man near Zāhedān, winter 1985.

above right
Two girls wearing miniature versions of the floral and embroidered garments worn by older women. Near Zāhedān, winter 1985

right
A Baluch woman near Sabzvārān (Jiroft) in winter 1985. The summer quarters for her family are on Kuh-e Jebal Bārez, territory shared with Turkic-speaking nomads of the Kermān region.

horses. Goats, though less valuable than sheep, are better adapted to the harsh and often extremely dry conditions. Where possible, small irrigated plots of land are cultivated. In recent years the construction of dams to trap sediment and moisture, an ancient technique for cultivation, has become increasingly important. The work is organised on a communal basis but the yield may not match the energy spent on them. For additional food the nomads barter with the settled population. Grain and dates are obtained in exchange for animal products, particularly clarified butter. Dates, a high-energy food, form an important part of the diet and the date harvest is a major event in their annual cycle. When the dates are ripe the nomads move to the settlements to assist the settled agricultural population with their harvest in return for a share of the crop.

The settled cultivators (*shahri*) also call themselves Baluch. Their principal settlements bear names which can be traced back to pre-Baluch times and they may descend from an earlier population already present in the area prior to the incursion of the nomads. The settled Baluch form a major stratum of a wider society in which two other elements can be identified: a ruling class and a class of ex-slaves. Today these latter classes are less in evidence than they used to be. The present administration in Iran has managed to extend its authority into the remotest corners of the country and the local ruling families have progressively lost their influence, though their high status in society, for example in terms of 'marrying up' or 'marrying down', is still recognised. Most of the ex-slaves—excluding slaves of African origin who are not readily accepted—have succeeded in becoming integrated into Baluch society (Spooner 1975: 176–8).

Baluch society is traditionally hierarchic and highly segmented into tribes and clans. While submission and allegiance to the authority of the chief was the basis of tribal solidarity, relationships between ordinary tribesman were based on equality. The local hereditary chief would reside in a fort, collect tithes and taxes from the settled population and rely on the allegiance and fighting skills of the nomads to maintain his power base. When times were hard the nomads, who possessed the best camels and horses and who were known for their warrior mentality and fighting prowess, were always ready to take the opportunity to profit from military campaigns and engage in raiding.

The Baluch are predominantly Sunni Muslims of the Hanafi School. Their literacy rate is rather low and their social norms are informed as much by tribal values as those of their better-educated religious brethren. Where these conflict, tribal values are likely to take precedence. Their religious allegiance sets them apart from their Shi'ite neighbours the Sistanis and from central government, which they perceive as dominated by Shi'ite clerics with a coercive religious agenda. Their sense of isolation has been further increased by the success of central government in controlling raiding activities and suppressing the chiefs and their private militias. Furthermore, while better education, advances in technology and regional aid programmes for agriculture have brought perceptible benefits to the settled population, little has been received by the nomads who are turning to smuggling instead of raiding as an alternative source of income.[2]

Fast changing events seem to be placing the nomads at an increasing disadvantage. The political implications of any move by the central government towards integration are not lost on the tribal chiefs who stand to lose any remaining authority they may have. A deep-rooted sense of tribal loyalty and fidelity to traditional virtues—hospitality, honour, bravery, equality, independence, forbearance—favour the status quo. Adherence to tradition thus tends to resist any developments likely to hasten the encroachment of outside influences, particularly those of central government—and that includes the building of roads in Baluch territory.

In the past the sense of allegiance to tribe may have served as an effective instrument for maintaining tribal integrity and the continuity of established traditions, but it has also been an unending source of faction and dissent (Spooner 1969). No chief has ever managed to establish his rule over all the tribes for any length of time, and no external pressure has succeeded in generating a feeling of Baluch nationhood. In the prevailing circumstances it seems unlikely that the nomads will be able to resist the forces of change. We have only to remember how the Bakhtiāri remained powerful and independent through centuries of coercion and oppression, only to succumb rapidly to change in the face of economic inducements. Prospects of economic and material benefits have the power to influence the aspirations of even the most traditionally-minded individuals.

Atypical hut of the type used by the *gāvdārān* made from clay and reeds.

THE CATTLE BREEDERS OF SISTĀN

Georg Stöber

The Persian-speaking cattle breeders (*gāvdārān,* pronounced gowdārān) of Sistān stand out in several ways from the other nomadic groups described in this book. They pasture cattle as opposed to sheep and goats, and live not on the mountain slopes but on a clay plain among swamps on the margins of semi-permanent lakes on the border between Iran and Afghanistan. The swampy, seasonally inundated reed beds seem out of place in the deserts of eastern Iran with their very low rainfall. Indeed the water in the lakes comes not from local rains but from precipitation in the mountains of the Hindukush in central Afghanistan. The river Helmand brings this water to the deserts of Sistān where, finding no outlet to the sea, it gathers in lakes before evaporating. The water level of the Helmand river is low in winter because most of the precipitation falls as snow. It rises in spring as the snow melts, then drops during the summer to its lowest level in the autumn. The volume of water discharged by the river varies greatly from year to year.

When the flood-water level is at its highest, considerable parts of the flat inland delta of the Helmand river are inundated. The highest parts of the area are submerged for some days only and, when the water recedes, herbs and grasses grow there. The deeper parts, called *neyzār*, are covered with water for a longer period and become swamps. The shoots of the reeds and bulrushes (*Phragmites communis, Typha angustifolia*) that grow there begin to sprout at the end of February or the beginning of March. By April or May the reeds stand up to five metres high, and the bulrushes three metres. In late summer they dry up and provide both food for cattle and raw material for various products including huts and reed boats (*tutans*).

The seasonal course of the inundation determines where pasture is to be found and where the *gāvdārān,* the mobile cattle breeders, stay. They spend late winter and spring at fixed places at the edge of the inundated area which are more or less safe from flood. Here they live in dwellings of clay and reed, both abundant building materials in this delta region. These constructions provide them with some shelter from the cold weather. When the floods are not too high the animals may be able to find some grazing, otherwise they have to be kept in these settlements and fed with reeds cut the previous year. Old, dry reed beds are often cleared by setting fire to them in late winter before they are covered by the rising water level. This makes it easier for the cattle to find young reed shoots in spring. If there is insufficient food and water available in the vicinity of the settlement, a male member of the household may take the animals some distance away to find pasture.

When the water recedes in late spring, the *gāvdārān* move their grazing animals and their camp sites little by little from the edge to the centre of the *neyzār*. On the higher spots they set up rows of tents with arches made from tamarisk branches covered by reed mats (*hasir*), and begin collecting fodder for the period during autumn, early winter and the time of the high flood when the animals have to be fed in the settlements. For this purpose reeds are cut in the *neyzār* and stored in a safe place during late spring and early summer. Some areas which were grazed on the way into the *neyzār* are burned so that the reeds will shoot again as the water is rising. This provides pasture for the move back to the winter and spring settlements after the winter solstice.

In addition to the *gāvdārān*, who move with the seasons, there are sedentary cattle breeders who live in places at the edge of the inundated area where their cattle can graze unaccompanied nearby. Their grazing is quite restricted compared to that available to their mobile brethren, so the amount of fodder they have to cut is even greater. On the other hand (governmental) services, such as schools, are more accessible to them, and some agriculture may be possible. Thus a settlement process has set in which can be compared to changes of a similar nature taking place in other nomadic groups.

Daily activities, spinning and preparing reeds for further use in a *gāvdārān* settlement at Kuh-e Khajeh south of Zābol.

The cattle breeders, who are organised into separate tribes (*tayfeh*, pl. *tavā'ef*), share their environment, the *neyzār*, with specialised fishermen and bird hunters (*sayād)*. In the delta the dry parts which can be irrigated are cultivated by farmers. The margins of the inundated areas are also seasonally grazed by nomadic flock owners, mainly Baluch, who also pasture their flocks on the mountains around Birjand, Qā'en, and further south in Baluchistān. These specialised occupational groups do not run a subsistence economy and are not self-sufficient. Rather they can be understood as elements of a single regional economic system, in that they exchange goods and labour with one another and have become mutually dependent. Their production is influenced by the demands of the 'market' even if exchange takes the form of barter, as in former times. As we shall see, the economy of the cattle breeders is affected by this market in several ways.

In general the aims of the cattle breeders are to produce milk and milk products, animals for slaughter, and in former times animal labour in the form of plough oxen. The milk is processed mainly into yoghurt (*māst*) and then into clarified butter (*rowghan*), and the buttermilk into the dried products, *kashk* and *qorut*. Most of the milk products are used by the cattle breeders themselves. A family herd is not very large and during a year only some of the cows have a calf and give milk for two to three months (some 2–3 litres a day for each cow). The small surplus can be sold but the fresh products, milk and yoghurt, are difficult to transport to market, the main one being Zābol, the district centre.

On average every cow gives birth to five or six calves during its lifetime. A female calf has to replace its mother. The others are slaughtered or used as draught animals and then slaughtered. As a general rule the cattle breeders do not slaughter for their own consumption. Instead two or three animals per year are sold by each family, not as calves but as three-year-olds on the hoof. In former times cattle dealers from Mashhad came to the camps of the *gāvdārān* to buy cattle which they transported to Khorāsān. Dealers from Sistān were also engaged in this trade, sending cattle as far afield as Esfahān and Shirāz. At the turn of the century 500 to 1000 head of cattle were being sold each year. The trade continues today. Dealers visit the settlements of the *gāvdārān* in the winter months and

top
Reed boats (*tutan*) made by the *gāvdārān* are used to travel on a channel leading from the village at the margin of the swamps (*neyzār*) to the deeper parts and to bring fodder consisting of cut reeds to the settlement. Hamunak village, 1978.

centre
Thick clouds of smoke darken the sky as the dry reed beds are burned to make it easier for the cattle to forage on the green shoots in the early spring. Walls made from chunks of mud and reeds give some protection from the cold wind. Hashemi settlement, February 1978.

bottom
Cattle on the dry bed of the *hāmun* during the summer drought of 1978.

opposite top
Inside a reed and clay hut, Kuh-e Khājeh, 1984.

opposite below left
A man from Kuh-e Khājeh, 1984

opposite below right
A girl from one of the neighbouring Sistāni-speaking nomad groups which camp at the edge of the swamps. Near Zābol Summer 1985.

below
Baluch nomads camp seasonally at the fringes of the flooded area where, after a short inundation, the vegetation provides good pasture for sheep. May 1978.

engage owners to drive cattle which have been purchased to Zābol or some other collecting place. From here they are either sent further afield or sold to local butchers. Today increasing numbers of animals are consumed within the region and the town of Zābol has become a growing market.

The preparation of milk products is more or less subsistence orientated, whereas the sale of animals for slaughter maintains relations with the external market. The hiring out of plough oxen, on the other hand, links cattle breeding to other economic sectors within Sistān, especially farming. In former times bulls were castrated and the stronger animals trained as plough oxen. As few farmers owned draught animals they had to hire them for ploughing and threshing from the *gāvdārān* who obtained agricultural products, especially wheat, in return. This enabled them, more or less, to avoid the grain market and its fluctuating prices. In the 1960s, however, land reform and the mechanisation of agriculture brought this important source of income virtually to an end.

In some cases, particularly among those *gāvdārān* who took up a sedentary way of life, it was possible for them to balance the loss with some agriculture of their own. In other cases girls learned carpet weaving from nomadic families pasturing their sheep nearby, or the men took up the weaving for sale of the reed mats which usually cover their dwellings. However, the possibilities for earning money other than by cattle herding are very limited. If we add the frequent stress of droughts or high floods, their economic position, which was one of relative prominence in the past, especially when compared with the bad situation of the farming population (which we cannot discuss here), is characterised today by the loss of important links with the economy of the region and by the lack of possibilities for making a good living as migrant pastoralists. This is why *gāvdārān* settle and why this singular form of Iranian pastoralism may not survive in times to come.

above top
Salt bag. Shesh Baylu (Shesh Boluki), 1988.

above
A saddle bag showing its closure system of loops passed through slits, with the end loop secured by a small padlock. In this case the main decoration of the face (not the border) is worked in weft float brocade. Shesh Baylu, 1989.

opposite above left
Mafrash or bedding bag. Darrashurlu, 1988.

opposite above right
Saddle bags. Darrashurlu, 1988.

opposite below
The wife of the headman of the Qara Yarlu branch of the Shesh Baylu (Shesh Boluki), a skilled weaver in her well-appointed tent. 1984.

below
Baladan used for carrying pipes. Kashkullu, 1986.

APPENDIX 1: QASHQA'I WOVEN STRUCTURES

The following summarises the weaving structures of the items described in the weaving section. The terminology is that of Emery (1966) and Rowe (1977). For the application of this terminology to Qashqa'i weaving see Wertime (1979: 33–54).

Baladan (small, narrow bag): patterned with weft-float brocading or a complementary weft-weave based on diamond twill. Both dyed and undyed wool yarns are used. They have fields divided into horizontal panels.

Bands: made using the technique of tablet or card weaving.

Chanta (small bag for personal items): made in slit tapestry weave and knotted pile.

Flour or grain bags: woven in weft-float brocade or a complementary weft weave based on diamond twill. The warp is often ivory or brown wool and the weft wool dyed in red, mustard yellow, brown and black.

Horse blankets and saddle-bags: formerly woven in *oyu*, a warp-faced complementary warp pattern weave using two colours, red and green for the borders, ivory and blue for the field. The technique has not been used at least since the 1930s because Qashqa'i women do not know how to set up the loom for it. The *oyu* structure was also woven by the Shesh Baylu, Darrashurlu and Amala tribes.

Mafrash (bedding bag): for the bottom panel complementary weft-weave based on herringbone twill (*charkh*) is used to create an extremely solid weave; for the side panels this is combined with weft-float brocading (*rend*) in multiple colours. Undyed ivory or brown wool is used for the warp.

Saddle bags: woven in a complementary weft-weave based on herringbone twill (*charkh*). The slit panels are twill with chevron or zigzag patterns in either red and green, dark blue and white or dark blue and red. The backs are slit tapestry in red or green or plain weave.

Salt bags: usually a weft-faced complementary weft-weave. It is made as a single piece which is folded and the sides are stitched together by men.

Straw bags: made in warp-faced plain weave with wide stripes using undyed ivory or brown wool, and sometimes hair.

ITEM	WEAVING STRUCTURE
Baladan	Weft-float brocade or complementary weft-weave based on diamond twill
Bands	Tablet-woven
Chanta	Slit tapestry and knotted pile
Flour or grain bags	Weft-float brocade
Horse blankets	Weft float brocade or weft wrapping or warp-faced plain weave and weft-faced complementary weave.
Mafrash	Bottom: Complementary weft-weave based on herringbone twill Sides: Weft-float brocade
Saddle-bags	Face: Complementary weft-weave based on herringbone twill Panel: Herringbone twill and slit tapestry Back: Plain weave
Salt bags	Weft-face complementary weft-weave
Straw bags	Warp-faced plain weave

right
Horse blanket used on special occasions. South of Qir, autumn 1987.

APPENDIX 2: GAME BIRDS AND ANIMALS HUNTED BY THE QASHQA'I

The Qashqa'i hunt both land and water birds. The following are the most commonly hunted land birds: the red-legged partridge (*kähl̈ik*, T.; *kabk*, P.), which is found in garmsir and sarhad and is the favourite of the game birds; the Caspian snow cock (*qar kähliği*), which is the size of a small turkey, lives in sarhad in mountainous areas at altitudes above 8,200 feet (2,500 metres) and does not migrate; a type of quail (*gar kähliği*) that resembles the Australian quail and crosses Iran on its migration from Africa to Russia (quails are hunted in spring in the wheat fields); the see-see partridge (*tuhu*), which lives in saline and dry areas, is not found above 650–1,000 feet (200–300 metres) and does not migrate; the black partridge (*doraj*), which lives close to fields and water in garmsir and is hunted in forests in winter; the sand-grouse (*qara baqorlaq*), which lives in the hills of south Iran; the great bustard (*hubara*), a sand-coloured and cautious bird that spends a few months in garmsir; the brownish-grey lark (*sercheh*), which flies in flocks and makes short-range migrations; and the *alabakhtak*, a pigeon (*guarchin*).

Among the water birds hunted are the wild goose (*qızıl qaz*) which is distinguished by its pinkish colour; a small grey type of snipe (*su qushu*) that lives in sarhad; and ducks, which are abundant, the most common one being the green-necked (*yashıl bash*). Various aquatic birds are found at Lake Parishān in Fars Madān territory in the Arzhan Plain west of Kāzerun, and once 255 species of birds were recorded there. Two lakes there hosted white pelicans, spoonbills, glossy ibises, flamingos, white-headed ducks, marbled teals, ruffs and cranes. In 1973 70,000 wild fowl were seen on the Arzhan marsh and 180,000 on Lake Parishān (Firouz 1974: 47).

Many game birds have disappeared from Qashqa'i territory due to over-hunting, the collection of eggs for eating, the clearing of trees and forests and the expansion of herds and grazing.

The game animals hunted include: wolves (*qurd*), jackals (*chaqal*) and foxes (*tilki*), which are tracked down because of the danger they pose to herds; striped hyenas (*kaftar*) and brown bears (*ayı*), whose parts are used in traditional medicines; wild pigs (*domqoz*), hunted by men in groups; the small jebeer gazelle of garmsir (*ahu bozi*) and the Persian gazelle of sarhad (*safidak jeyran*) with a white spot under its tail (both particular favourites and which have progressively disappeared from Qashqa'i territory); ibexes (*pazan*); and wild goats (*gacha*), which live in the high mountains perfectly at ease on rocky outcroppings and steep slopes. The most treasured game are wild rams (*quch*) and wild sheep (*qoyin*) whose meat is preferred to that of wild goats. Rabbits (*dushan*) used to be numerous, especially in miānband. A few panthers (*palang*) still exist and are hunted. The Persian deer (*gavazn*), the lion (*shir*) and the Asian cheetah (*quz*) disappeared from Qashqa'i territory by World War I.

NUMBERS OF HOUSEHOLDS AND ANIMALS OWNED AMONG *IL* AND *TAYFEH* LARGER THAN 2,000 HOUSEHOLDS; THE 1987 CENSUS

NAME OF GROUP (LOCATION)	HOUSEHOLDS	ANIMALS	ANIMALS PER HOUSEHOLD
IL:			
Bakhtiāri (ChahārMahāl, Khuzestān)	27,960	2,452,092	88
Qashqa'i (Fārs)	16,891	3,707,506	219
Mamivand (Lor)	6,768	1,036,384	153
Boyer Ahmad Soflā (Kohgilu etc.)	6,230	446,290	72
Ilsevan (= Shahsevan; Āzarbāijān)	5,897	855,415	145
Khamseh (Fārs)	4,768	2,310,909	485
Qaradāgh/Arasbārān	4,676	409,482	88
Mamasani (Fārs)	3,356	401,868	120
Bahme'i (Kohgilu)	3,041	389,355	128
Boyer Ahmad 'Olyā	2,970	362,999	122
Tayyebi (Kohgilu etc)	2,693	275,052	102
Jabāl-e Bārezi (Kermān and Coast)	2,475	568,446	230
Zelqeh (Lorestān, Khuzistān, Hamadān)	2,272	101,788	45
Jalāli (Western Āzarbāijān)	2,238	312,781	140
Baluch	2,236	167,242	75
Afshār (Kermān, Coast)	2,074	239,702	116
Kurd (Darreh-Shahr)	2,559		
Total	99,104		
Others	81,119		
TOTAL	180,223		

Table based on preliminary results of the 1987 census, see Qanbari (1989), and table at end of Shahbāzi (1990).

NOTES

PAGES 10-39 INTRODUCTION: THE NOMADS OF IRAN
Richard Tapper

1 See Lambton (1971a); Towfiq (1987); Cribb (1991); Planhol (1968); Khazanov (1984).
2 Lees and Bates (1974); Hole (1978). Khazanov (1984) argues for considerably later origins.
3 See Ibn Khaldun (1967) and the huge literature devoted to his theories.
4 See, e.g., Tapper (1983b) and (1991a).
5 A point made by Thomas Stauffer (1965); see also Abbott, below.
6 In some remoter areas this was not true: Daniel Bradburd (1990) reports of the nomads of Kerman that they actually prospered in the new economic conditions.
7 Beck (1991: 186–7) (1982).
8 Shahshahani (1986: 75–6).
9 Naficy (1979: 223).
10 Lois Beck (1980a).
11 Statistical Centre of Iran (Plan and Budget Organization) and Iran's Tribal Affairs Organization (Ministry of Jahad-e-Sazandegi), *Socio-Economic Census of Nomadic Tribes, 1987*, Country, Vol. 6: *Tribal Atlas* (in Persian), p. i.
12 See Towfiq (1987) for earlier censuses. 'Transhumance' refers to seasonal movements of animals and people between summer and winter quarters, with settlements and fixed dwellings in one or both of these; for Digard (this volume) and others, however, in transhumance the animals are accompanied only by shepherds, not the families of the owners.
14 Cribb (1991: 17).
15 Bradburd (1990).
16 This was the case with nomads in a neighbouring country, Afghanistan, where these issues were (until the recent years of turmoil) even more distinct: tribalism, as a political issue for the country, especially among the Pashtuns, was quite separate from pastoralism and nomadism. Most Pashtun tribespeople have long been settled village or town-dwellers. Pastoralism shaded between long-range nomadism and village transhumance and was rather more explicitly an economic issue. Many Afghan nomads pursued long-distance trade, and most, whether traders or pastoralists, were Pashtuns, as were the rulers of the country. In most situations they would likely give their tribal and ethno-linguistic identity equal weight with their pastoralism, and far more than the contingent element of nomadism. On Afghan nomadism and settlement, see Tapper (1974) and (1991b).
17 Fredrik Barth writes of 'the pervasive conviction among urban Iranians to whom I spoke [in 1958] that all tribesmen in Iran—the land of Kurds and Lurs and Baluchis—should be nomads' (1992: 177).
18 Lambton (1971a: 1095–6); Towfiq (1987: 707). The singulars have much more specific references in contemporary Iranian tribal societies.
19 But cf. Nāder Afshār-Nāderi's attempt to establish the reverse in the 1970s (1983: 331).
20 By 1993, in a further shift, some members of the Organization were using a slightly more accurate translation: Organization for Nomadic Affairs.
21 Statistical Centre of Iran, *Socio-economic Census of Nomadic Tribes*, Vol. 2–2: Ilsevan (Shahsevan), p. vi; also in *Zakhāyer-e Enqelāb* 11, summer 1990, pp. 77–81; *Zakhāyer-e Enqelāb* 19, summer 1992, pp. 17ff.
22 Morier (1837: 239–41).
23 Barth (1961). Earlier studies in Persian by Bavar and Bahmanbegi are interesting but not very specific on socio-economic detail.
24 E.g., among many others, Sahlins (1966), but also Barth himself (1961: 49). The above paragraphs are an idiosyncratic 'reading' of Barth's study, for the purposes of this article. On the problems of reading *Nomads of South Persia,* see below; others have recently 'misread' Barth's text as a study of segmentary lineage organization, see correspondence by Brian Street and Susan Wright in *Man* 1992.
25 E.g. Smith (1978); Lindner (1982) and (1983); Garthwaite (1983); Manz (1989); Foran (1993).
26 William Irons (various articles) many years ago made the same point about the specificity of the Basseri by comparing various aspects of Bāseri and Yomut Turkmen economy, politics and society. For a detailed comparison between Bāseri, Türkmen and Shahsevan nomadic social organization, see Tapper (1979a: 240 ff.).
27 Barth (1961: 123–33). A rather different 'typical' model is suggested by the remarkable similarities, e.g., between constituent groups of the fifteenth-century Aq Qoyunlu and the sixteenth-century Qizilbash, and nineteenth-century tribal confederacies such as the Boyer Ahmad and the Shahsevan; see Woods (1976), McChesney (1981), Loeffler (1978: 154 ff.), Tapper (1983b).
28 See Tapper (1970a: 252).
29 See also Bradburd (1990) on the Komachi of Kermān.
30 Irons (1975).
31 Salzman (1972).
32 Only horses and dogs have names (see Amir-Moez, Tapper).
33 See particularly Beck (1980b); Bradburd (1980) and (1990); Black-Michaud (1986).
34 See Nancy Tapper (1978), and other essays in Beck and Keddie (1978).
35 Crone (1986).
36 Lindner (1982) and (1983). For fuller comments on Crone and Lindner, see Tapper (1991a).
37 See Tapper (1991a) and (1991c).
38 Irons (1974); Glatzer (1983); Bradburd (1990).

39 Beck (1991: 204).
40 Lambton (1971a); Towfiq (1987); Kunke (1991).
41 Barfield (1991).
42 See Appendix 1, which lists these 17 'major' *il*. The listing of the remaining, smaller *il* poses further classification problems. In particular, while 'Kord' constitutes a major *il*, there are several separate Kurdish *il* listed. Apparently the smallest *il* had only 15 nomad households, while some 'independent *tāyfeh*' were represented by one nomad household each. This remains to be explained. It is also noteworthy that two thirds of the 'independent *tāyfeh*' were in the eastern parts of Iran: Kermān, Baluchistān, Sistān, Khorāsān.
43 Cf. Beck's classification of tribal groups by size and location in relation to frontiers (1991: 199).
44 Different historical patterns of tribal relations to the state have been explored by Digard (1973, 1987), Garthwaite (1983), Beck (1991), Kiavand (1989), Tapper (1983, 1991a, 1991c) and others.
45 Yapp (1983); Gellner (1983).
46 Bradburd (1990); he has other arguments to explain Komachi lack of political centralization. Cf. Glatzer (1983).
47 Cf. Barth's comments on such government aggregation in Fars (1961: 132).
48 See numerous recent monographs, and S. Wright (1992). It should also be noted that historians and ethnographers have, through their writings, been among the 'creators' of tribal ethnic identities; the Shahsevan (see Tapper) are just one among many well-documented cases in the Middle East.
49 See Street (1990), and comments by Barth (1992)
50 Cf. *qaum* in Afghanistan: Tapper and Tapper (1982); and cf. discussion of Kurdish terms by van Bruinessen (1992: 60 ff.).
51 Cf. van Bruinessen (1983) and Tapper (1979a).
52 See Tapper (1988) on different versions of Shahsevan origins, and S. Wright (1992) on Doshmanziari and others.
53 Nikitine (1929: 122–3), my translation.
54 Lancaster (1981). Cf. Ibn Khaldun (1967: 100), quoted in Cribb (1991: 53). See also Lindner (1983).
55 Tapper (1979b). In the more sparsely populated areas of the south and east, such as Kirmān, where large-scale organization is rare, the larger community, coinciding with a *tāyfeh* such as the Komachi, appears to be unstable in composition (Bradburd 1990). Cf. Anderson (1983).
56 Tapper (1979a); Bradburd (1990).
57 See Tapper (1984a), Peters (1984) and Tavakolian (1984).
58 Elsewhere I have shown the importance of shifts in identity in the case of the Shahsevan nomads, and variations as between different classes of Shahsevan society; and contrasted the case of the Durrani of northern Afghanistan. See Tapper (1988), (1989) and (1984b).
59 Public Record Office, Foreign Office Files 248/192 (Abbott to Alison no. 38 of 29.11.1860).
60 For a major recent compilation of materials in Persian, see Afshār-Sistāni (1987).
61 See Beck (1992). Descriptions in English of nomadic life under the Islamic Republic are still few; the above account derives from Beck, and from personal information, mainly second-hand, on other major groups such as Bakhtiāri, Shahsevan, and Lor.
62 For development of this and other points touched on in this Introduction, see Tapper (1994).
63 See also Bradburd (1990) for the Komachi.
64 The last section is based largely on visits to Iran in September 1992 and August–September 1993 which were made possible by grants from the British Institute for Persian Studies (1992 and 1993) and the Nuffield Foundation (1993). I am indebted to Ziba Mir-Hosseini for sharing her knowledge of the nomads with me. I am also grateful to numerous officials and private individuals in Iran who have been willing to discuss the present and future of the nomads.

PAGES 48-89 BAKHTIĀRI
Jean-Pierre Digard

1 Since writing this chapter, the author has revisited the Bakhtiari, see Digard (1998) [Eds].

PAGES 90-111 SACRED SPACES & POTENT PLACES IN THE BAKHTIARI MOUNTAINS *David Brooks*

1 The spring migration of the Bakhtiāri is the subject of two major documentary films. The classic *Grass* was filmed by Merian Cooper and Ernest Schoedsack in 1924 with the Baba Ahmad sub-tribe (*tāyfeh*). See also Cooper (1925). *People of the Wind*, a feature documentary filmed by Anthony Howarth in 1972 with the Bābādi *tāyfeh* on the Monar migration route, was an Academy Award and Golden Globe nominee. See also Brooks (1981). The author made the spring migration, also on the Monar route, with the Osiwand *tāyfeh* in 1964 and 1966. For an interesting literary account of the southern Bakhtiāri route through these mountains see Sackville-West (1928).
2 Garthwaite (1983: 74), quoting Sardar Zafar (1911–1914: 6).
3 See also Donaldson (1938: 59).
4 *When the lion shows his teeth do not think that the lion smiles!*
Even when he smiles don't be secure: he will be more bloodthirsty.
Rumi, *Mathnavi*, M13039; quoted by Schimmel (1978: 107).
5 Bishop (1891, 1: 343). There is an illustration of a stone lion gravestone in Bishop (1891, 2: 8). The original photograph is in I. L. Bird Bishop, Photographic Album (1890), Collection 94, in Special Collection Department, Research Library, University of California, Los Angeles.
6 Tanavoli (1978: 21), with photographs of the stone lions.
7 *All the lions seek moonlight. I am a Lion and the friend of the moonlight.*
Rumi, *Diwan* 919/9674, quoted in Schimmel (1978: 155).
8 Donaldson (1938: 59), on such sacred trees.
9 Sardar As'ad (1909: 531). Sardar As'ad states that this shrine is associated with the Shah Ne'matollahi school of dervishes.
10 Hoseyn Qoli Khan's diary (Kitābcheh), in Garthwaite (1983: 156).
11 '[The Imam Rezā is] also popularly known as "zāmen-e āhu", the protector of the gazelles' (Richard 1980: 17).

PAGES 134-143 THE WORLD OF THE PEOPLE OF DEH KOH
Reinhold Loeffler

1 The name Deh Koh was first used by Erika Friedl (1989). The following account refers to the period of around 1965–75, the culture of which appears to be closest to the situation depicted by the photographs of this volume. However, no claim is made that the description is also valid for other parts of Boyer Ahmad. The second and third sections refer primarily to the men of this village; women see their world in related though nevertheless significantly different ways. But even among men there exists great diversity in how they view the world. I have tried to lay down notions that appear to form a fairly common substratum. For a detailed account of individual world views see Loeffler (1988).
2 Though aware of the resulting ecological degradation, they feel they cannot concern themselves with it. 'This lies in the hands of God,' they say, 'for every door that closes, God opens five others'.

PAGES 144-159 KURDISH NOMADS OF WESTERN ĀZARBĀIJĀN
Lale Yalçın-Heckmann

1 My knowledge of Kurdish nomads is based on my anthropological study of Kurdish tribesmen and nomads in south-east Turkey, in the

province of Hakkāri (Yalçın-Heckmann 1991). I travelled extensively in Hakkāri, and partly in Van, during my anthropological fieldwork in 1980–2, and made further brief visits in 1985, 1987, 1991 and 1992. Hakkāri is bordered by Iran and Iraq and its inhabitants are ethnic Kurds with tribal and kinship ties stretching across the frontiers into both countries. I studied one particular tribal group in depth, but I also studied others to a lesser degree. In addition, in 1980, I was able to make some comparisons of the Kurdish culture of different countries by crossing into Iran with a few Hakkāri tribesmen. My impression was that this culture is fairly homogeneous despite the frontiers and I received the same impression of the cultures of neighbouring mountains and valleys. There are of course local differences which demarcate tribal and other social boundaries, differences of dress, sometimes in language or religious domination. Therefore, in writing about the Kurdish nomads in Hakkāri, which I know the best, I nevertheless hope to project an image of the general cultural features of their neighbours in Iran.

2 Bois, Minorsky and MacKenzie (1981).
3 Minorsky (1927).
4 Minorsky (1927: 1134).
5 Minorsky (1927 1139).
6 O'Ballance (1973); van Bruinessen (1978/1992) and (1983).
7 van Bruinessen (1978: 328).
8 Eagleton (1963: 6–7); and van Bruinessen (1978: 329).
9 Minorsky (1927: 1148).
10 van Bruinessen (1983).
11 Ghassemlou (1965: 109).
12 See van Bruinessen (1983: 393).
13 Beck (1986); Garthwaite (1983); and Tapper (1979a).
14 See Beck (1986: 139).

PAGES 160-173 THE KURDS OF KHORĀSĀN

Mohammad-Hossein Papoli-Yazdi

1 Eyewitness estimate.
2 The political power of some of the Kurdish *il khans* extended beyond the boundaries of the region in northern Khorāsān where they lived. As evidence of this see Alexander Chodzko, the Russian consular agent in Rasht in about 1830: 'The Kurds have been in Gilan since the time of Nader Shah; they all belong to the Kurdish family of Rishvand and their hereditary leader, who bears the title of *Il Khan*, resides in Quchan in the mountains of Khorāsān' (1850: 207).
3 According to Ghassemlou (1981: 159), 'there are 400,000 Kurds in the north of Khorāsān.' The author however gives no source.
4 In the fourteenth and fifteenth centuries the whole of the Turkmen steppe was a huge winter pasture for the nomads of northern Khorāsān (Aubin 1971).

PAGES 190-251 THE QASHQA'I

Yassaman Amir Moez

1 The Qashqa'i tribe has been called a 'confederacy' in recent anthropological studies. I define and explain the Qashqa'i tribe as a confederacy of tribal groups, but I use 'tribe' as a legitimate translation of the Persian term *il* [see 'Introduction'; Eds].
2 [The author uses the term 'Shesh Baylu' for the group referred to in other sources as Shesh Boluki; Eds]
3 Fifteen years of participant observation and study among the ruling members of the Qashqa'i tribe allow me to assert that these rulers call themselves, and are called by other Qashqa'i, Jāni Khānlu. The use of the name 'Shāhilu' for a ruling lineage or clan of the Qashqa'i is not accurate in spite of its use by some authors.
4 For historical speculations about the origin of the Qashqa'i and their previous locations and movement into south-west Iran, see Abbott (1857), Aubin (1955), Balayan (1960), Beck (1986), Cahen (1965), Curzon (1892), Demorgny (1913), Fasa'i (1895–96), Garrod (1946b), Minorsky (1939–42), Oberling (1974), Picot (1897), Sümer (1978).
5 The etymology of the name Qashqa'i has been discussed in many sources and commonly explained as 'Those of the Horses with the White Spots on their Foreheads' (*Qashqa Atlılar*) or 'Those who have fled' (Oberling 1974: 32–3). The name Qashqa'i is used as the name of the tribe but also as the family name of the members of the Jāni Khānlu clan. Other Qashqa'i use the name of their respective tribes (Shesh Baylu, Kashkullu, and so on). It appears that the name Qashqa'i was that of the founder of the tribe and might therefore have been of geographic origin connected with the Qashqa river area in Transoxiana, a region bounded by the two great rivers of Central Asia—the Amu Darya and the Syr Darya (Oxus and Jaxartes). It was then Persianised with the 'i'.
6 In a number of Turkic languages the word *yurt* means 'camp', 'place', 'country' or 'region'. It probably entered the Russian language via Tartar (Basilov 1989: 101). In Russian usage the word *yurt* is applied to the actual felt tent of the northern nomads, as opposed to the place where tents are pitched.
7 Legend has it that when the ancestors of the Turks were destroyed by enemies, a ten-year-old boy was rescued by a she-wolf and carried off into the mountains north of the Turfan depression. When the boy grew up, he took the she-wolf to wife. A she-wolf became the mythical Mongol queen Alanqoa, whose progeny allegedly included Chingiz Khan. Timur (AD 1336–1405) claimed he was descended from Alanqoa in order to establish the legitimacy of his rule (Lentz and Lowry 1989: 27).

PAGES 284-291 THE TURKMEN

Jon Thompson

1 The spirit of their suffering is vividly captured by the poems of Makhtumkuli who was a member of the Göklen tribe. He is described by Barthold, as 'the national poet of all the Turkmans' (1962, 3: 159); see Makhtumkuli (1995: 53, 78).
2 A detailed account of this period is given in Saray (1989).
3 Quoted in translation by Marvin (1881: 49–64).

PAGES 298-303 THE BALUCH

Jon Thompson

1 For Baluch dwellings, see Ferdinand (1959) and Andrews (1997).
2 For a valuable general essay on the Baluch see Spooner (1992); also Spooner (1984), Salzman (1972); Salzman's monograph (2000) unfortunately appeared too late to be taken into account .

BIBLIOGRAPHY

Abbott, Keith Edward

1857 'Notes Taken on a Journey Eastwards from Shiraz to Fessa and Darab, Thence Westwards by Jehrum to Kazerun, in 1850', *Journal of the Royal Geographical Society of London* 27, pp. 149-84.

Ādamiyat, Roknzādeh.

1964 *Delirān-e Tangestān*: *Fārs va Jang-e Beynolmelal* [The Brave Warriors of Tangestan: Fars and the World War], Tehran.

Afshār-Nāderi, Nāder

1983 'Eskān-e 'Ashāyer va Natāyej-e Ejtemā'i va Eqtesādi-ye ān' (translation of 1971 report, 'The Settlement of Nomads and its Social and Economic Effects), *Ilāt va 'Ashāyer,* Tehran, Kitāb-e Agāh.

Afshār-Sistāni, Iraj

1987 *Il-hā, Chādor-neshinān va Tavāyef-e 'Ashāyeri-ye Irān* [Tribes, tent-dwellers and Nomadic Clans of Iran], 2 Vols, Tehran, Homā.

Ajami, Ismā'il *et al.*

1974 *Tireh-ye 'Amaleh-ye Fārsi-Madān* [The Amaleh Subtribe of the Farsi-Madan], Shiraz University, Department of Human Sciences.

Ajami, Ismā'il, and David J. Marsden

1974 *Report on a Study of Pastoral Nomadism among the Farsi-Madan Section of the Qashqa'i,* Shiraz, Pahlavi University.

Allemagne, Henri-René d'

1911 *Du Khorâssân au pays des Backhtiaris. Trois mois de voyage en Perse,* 4 vols, Paris, Hachette.

Allgrove, Joan

1976 (ed.) *The Qashqa'i of Iran*, Manchester University, Whitworth Art Gallery.

1978 'The Qashqa'i', in A. Landreau (ed.), *Yoruk, the Nomadic Weaving Tradition of the Middle East*, Pittsburg, Carnegie Institute, Museum of Art.

1979 'Fars, the Land and Its People', in D. Black and C. Loveless (eds), *Woven Gardens*, London, David Black Oriental Carpets.

Amānollahi, Sekandar

1977 *Ilāt va 'Ashāyer-e Fārs* [The Tribes of Fārs], Shiraz University, Department of Demography.

Amir-Moez, Yassaman

1985 *Les Techniques des Pasteurs Nomades Qashqaye du Sud-Ouest de l'Iran,* thèse de doctorat de 3me cycle, Université de Paris, École des Hautes Études en Sciences Sociales.

1991 'The Magic of Noruz: Iranian New Year's Day Celebrations', *Folklife Center News* 13 (2, Spring).

Anderson, Benedict

1983 *Imagined Communities*, London, Verso.

Andrews, Peter Alford

1973 'The White House of Khurasan: the Felt Tents of the Iranian Yomut and Göklen', *Iran* 11, pp. 93-110.

1980 'The Türkmen Tent', in Louise W. Mackie and Jon Thompson (eds), *Turkmen Tribal Carpets and Traditions*, Washington DC, Textile Museum.

1997 *Nomad Tent Types in the Middle East*, part I, Wiesbaden, Dr Ludwig Reichert.

Arfa, *Gen.* Hassan

1965 *Under Five Shahs*, New York, William Morrow.

Āsaf, Mohammad Hāshem, Rostam al-Hokamā

1972 *Rostam al-tavārikh*, ed. Mohammad Moshiri, Tehran, Amir Kabir.

Aubin, Jean

1955 'Références pour Lar médiévale', *Journal Asiatique* 243, pp. 491-505.

1971 'Réseau pastoral et réseau caravanier. Les grand'routes du Khurâssân à l'époque Mongole', *Le Monde Iranien et l'Islam* 1, pp. 105-30.

Avery, Peter

1957 'By Car from Shiraz to Khuzistan', *Journal of the Royal Central Asian Society* 44 (July-October), pp. 187-92.

Bahmanbegi, Mohammad

1945-6 *'Orf va Ādat dar 'Ashāyer-e Fārs* [*Customs and Traditions of the Nomads of Fars*], Tehran, Azar Publishing.

1971 'Qashqai: Hardy Shepherds of Iran's Zagros Mountains Build a Future through Tent-School Education', in Melville Grosvenor (ed.), *Nomads of the World*, Washington DC, National Geographic Society.

1976 'Tārikhcheh-ye Mokhtasari az Fa'āliat-hā-ye Edāreh-ye Koll-e Āmuzesh-e 'Ashāyeri' [Short Summary of the Activities of the Office of Tribal Education], paper submitted at the Conference of Study and Analysis of Tribes in Iran, Kermanshāh.

1989 *Il-e Man Bokhārā-ye Man* [My Tribe, My Bokhara], Tehran, Agah.

Bala, Mirza

1953 'Kaşkay', *Islam Ansiklopedisi* 6, pp. 414-17.

Balayan, B. P.

1960 'K Voprosu ob Obshchnosti Etnogeneza Shakhseven i Kashkaytsev' [On the Question of the Common Origins of the Shahsevan and the Qashqai], *Vostokovedcheskiy Sbornik* (Yerevan) 1, pp. 331-77.

Ballard, *Lieut.* J. A.

1861 'The Persian War of 1856-1857', *Blackwood's Edinburgh Magazine* 15 (September), pp. 343-63.

Barfield, Thomas J.

1991 'Tribe and State Relations: the Inner Asian Perspective,' in Philip Khoury and Joseph Kostiner (eds), *Tribes and State Formation in the Middle East*, Berkeley, University of California Press.

Barker, Paul

1981 'Tent Schools of the Qashqa'i: a Paradox of Local Initiative and State Control', in Michael Bonine and Nikki Keddie (eds), *Modern Iran: The Dialectics of Continuity and Change*, Albany, State University of New York Press.

Barth, Frederick

1959 'The Land Use Pattern of Migratory Tribes of South Persia', *Norsk Geografisk Tidsskrift* 17, pp. 1-11.

1961 *Nomads of South Persia*: *The Basseri Tribe of the Khamseh Confederacy*, London, Allen and Unwin.

1973 'A General Perspective on Nomad-Sedentary Relations in the Middle East', in Cynthia Nelson (ed.), *The Desert and the Sown. Nomads in the Wider Society*, Berkeley, University of California.

1992 'Method in our Critique of Anthropology', *Man (N.S.)* 27, pp. 175-7.

Barthold, Wilhelm (Vasily Vladimirovich)

1927 'Kashka'i', *Encyclopedia of Islam* 2, p. 790.

1962 *Four Studies on the History of Central Asia*, Leiden, E. J. Brill, 3, pp. 121-70.

Bayāt, Kāveh

1986 *Shuresh-e 'Ashāyer-e Fārs, 1307-1309* [The Uprising of the Tribes of Fārs, 1928-1930], Tehran, Zarin.

Bazin, Marcel

1980 *Le Tâlech, une Région Ethnique au Nord de l'Iran* (Institut Français d'Iranologie de Téhéran, Bibliothèque Iranienne No. 23), 2 vols, Paris, Editions A. D. P. F.

Bazin, Marcel, and Christian Bromberger, in collaboration with A. Askari and A. Karimi

1982 *Gilân et Azarbâyjân Oriental. Cartes et Documents Ethnographiques* (Institut Français d'Iranologie de Téhéran, Bibliothèque Iranienne No. 24), Paris, Editions A. D. P. F.

Beazley, Elisabeth, and Michael Harverson
1982 *Working Buildings of the Iranian Plateau*, Warminster, Aris and Phillips.

Beck, Lois
1978 'Women among Qashqa'i Nomadic Pastoralists in Iran', in Lois Beck and Nikki Keddie (eds), *Women in the Muslim World*, Cambridge, Mass. and London, Harvard University Press.
1980a 'Revolutionary Iran and its Tribal Peoples', *MERIP Reports* 87, pp. 14-20.
1980b 'Herd Owners and Hired Shepherds: The Qashqa'i of Iran', *Ethnology* 19 (3), pp. 327-51.
1982 'Nomads and Urbanites, Involuntary Hosts and Uninvited Guests', *Middle Eastern Studies* 18 (4), pp. 426-44.
1986 *The Qashqa'i of Iran*, New Haven and London, Yale University Press.
1991 'Tribes and the State in Nineteenth and Twentieth Century Iran', in Philip Khoury and Joseph Kostiner (eds), *Tribes and State Formation in the Middle East*, Berkeley, University of California Press.
1992 'Qashqa'i Nomads and the Islamic Republic', *Middle East Report* 177 (July-August), pp. 36-41.

Beck, Lois, and Nikki R. Keddie
1981 *The Qashgai People of Southern Iran* (Pamphlet Series 14), Los Angeles, UCLA Museum of Cultural History.

Beck, Lois, and Nikki Keddie (eds)
1978 *Women in the Muslim World*, Cambridge, Mass. & London, Harvard University Press.

Behruz, J. (comp.)
1963 *Iran Almanac*, 3rd edition, Tehran.
1969 *Iran Almanac*, 8th edition, Tehran.

Bell, Mark S.
1885 *Military Report on South-West Persia, Including the Provinces of Khuzistan (Arabistan), Luristan, and Parts of Fars* (Simla, Government Central Branch Press), London, India Office Library L/MIL/17/15/9.
1889 'A Visit to the Karun River and Kum', *Blackwood's Edinburgh Magazine* 145.

Berland, Joseph C.
1982 *No Fingers are Alike: Cognitive Amplifiers in Social Context*, Cambridge, Mass. & London, Harvard University Press.

Betteridge, Anne
1981 'Specialists in Miraculous Action; Some Shrines in Shiraz', unpublished paper.

Binford, L. R.
1972a 'Archaeology and Anthropology', in L. R. Binford (ed.), *An Archaeological Perspective*, New York, Seminar Press.
1972b 'Methodological Considerations in the Archaeological Use of Ethnographic Data', in L. R. Binford (ed.), *An Archaeological Perspective*, New York, Seminar Press.
1983 *In Pursuit of the Past. Decoding the Archaeological Record*, London, Thames & Hudson.

Bishop, Isabella L. Bird
1891 *Journeys in Persia and Kurdistan*, 2 vols, London, John Murray.
1892 'The Upper Karun Region and the Bakhtiari Lurs', *Scottish Geographical Magazine* 8, pp. 1-14.

Black, David, and Clive Loveless (eds)
1971 *The Undiscovered Kilim*, London, David Black Oriental Carpets.
1979 *Woven Gardens*, London, David Black Oriental Carpets.

Black-Michaud, Jacob
1986 *Sheep and Land: the Economics of Power in a Tribal Society*, Cambridge, Cambridge University Press, and Paris, Maison des Sciences de l'Homme.

Bobek, Hans
1968 'Vegetation', in W. B. Fisher (ed.), *The Land of Iran*, Volume 1 of *The Cambridge History of Iran*, Cambridge, Cambridge University Press.

Bode, Baron Clement Augustus de
1845 *Travels in Luristan and Arabistan*, 2 vols, London, J. Madden.
1848 'On the Yamut and Goklen Tribes of Turkmenia', *Journal of the Ethnological Society* 1, reprinted in Robert Pinner and Michael Franses (eds), *Aspects of the Weaving and Decorative Arts of Central Asia* (Turkoman Studies 1), London, Oguz Press, 1980.

Bois, Th., V. Minorsky and D. N. MacKenzie
1981 'Kurds, Kurdistan', *Encyclopedia of Islam* (new edition) 5, pp. 438-86.

Bolour, Youssef
1981 'Knotted Persian Saddle Covers: A Pictorial Survey', *Halı* 3 (4), pp. 268-72.

Bosworth, C. E.
1968 'The Political and Dynastic History of the Iranian World (AD 1000-1217)', in J. A. Boyle (ed.), *The Saljuq and Mongol Periods*, Volume 5 of *The Cambridge History of Iran*, Cambridge, Cambridge University Press.
1973 'Barbarian Incursions: the Coming of the Turks', in D. Richards (ed.), *Islamic Civilisation 950-1150*, Oxford, Cassirer.

Bosworth, C. E. and G. Doerfer
1978 'Khaladj', *Encyclopedia of Islam* (new edition) 4, pp. 917-18.

Boyle, John Andrew
1976 'Introduction', in Joan Allgrove (ed.), *The Qashqa'i of Iran*, Manchester University, Whitworth Art Gallery.

Bradburd, Daniel
1979 *Kinship and Contract: The Social Organisation of the Komachi of Kerman, Iran*, Ann Arbor 1979 (University Microfilms, 79 13116).
1980 'Never Give a Shepherd an Even Break: Class and Labor among the Komachi of Kerman, Iran', *American Anthropologist* 76, pp. 603-20.
1990 *Ambiguous Relations: Kin, Class and Conflict among Komachi Pastoralists*, Washington DC, Smithsonian.

Bretschneider, E.
1888 *Mediaeval Researches from Eastern Asiatic Sources*, 2 vols (reprinted, London, Routledge and Kegan Paul, 1937).

Bromberger, Christian
1986 *Habitat, Architecture et Société Rurale dans la Plaine du Gilân (Iran Septentrional)*, Paris, UNESCO.

Brooks, David H. M.
1981 *People of the Wind*, manuscript, Durham.
1983 'The Enemy Within: Limitations on Leadership in the Bakhtiari', in Richard Tapper (ed.), *The Conflict of Tribe and State in Iran and Afghanistan*, London, Croom Helm.

Bruinessen, Martin van
1978 *Agha, Shaikh and State: On the Social and Political Organisation of Kurdistan*, PhD dissertation, University of Utrecht.
1983 'Kurdish Tribes and the State of Iran: the Case of Simko's Revolt', in Richard Tapper (ed.), *The Conflict of Tribe and State in Iran and Afghanistan*, London, Croom Helm.
1992 *Agha, Shaikh and State* (2nd edition), London, Zed.

Budge, E. A. Wallis
1978 *Amulets and Superstitions*, New York, Dover.

Bulliet, Richard W.
1975 *The Camel and the Wheel*, Cambridge, Mass., Harvard University Press.

Burnes, Alexander,
1834 *Travels into Bokhara*, 3 vols, London, John Murray.

Burujeni, Sh.
1970-1 'Moshakhkhasāt-e Ensāni-ye Il-e Qashqā'i' [Human Characteristics of the Qashqa'i Tribe], *Sepāh-e Dānesh* 3, pp. 31-3.

Busse, Heribert
1972 *History of Persia under Qajar Rule*, translation of Hajji Mirzā Hasan Fasā'i, *Fārsnāma-ye Nāseri*, New York, Columbia University Press.

Byron, Robert
1934 'Notes on the Qal'a-i-Dukhtar at Firuzabad', *Bulletin of the American Institute for Persian Art and Archaeology* 7 (December), pp. 3-7.

Cahen, Claude
1965 'Ghuzz', *Encyclopedia of Islam* (new edition) 2, pp. 1106-11.

Causse, M. M. N.
1962 *Sur les Traces des Derniers Nomades*, Paris, Hachette.

Chappel, M.
1976 *British Cavalry Equipment 1800-1941* (Man at Arms Series No. 138), London, Osprey Publishing.
Chick, Herbert George
1916 'Past History of the Qashqais and Their Khans', in Arnold Talbot Wilson, *Report on Fars*, Simla, Government Monotype Press.
Chodzko, Alexandre
1849-50 'Le Guilan ou les Marais Caspiens', *Nouvelles Annales des Voyages et des Sciences Géographiques* 1849 (4), pp. 257-71; 1850(1), pp. 193-215, 285-306; 1850 (2), pp. 61-76, 200-9; 1850 (3), pp. 68-93.
Christian, *Capt.* A. J.
1919 *A Report on the Tribes of Fars*, Simla, Government Monotype Press.
Gonzáles de Clavijo, Ruy
1928 *Narrative of the Spanish Embassy to the Court of Timur 1403-1406*, trans. Guy le Strange, London, Routledge.
Cleaves, Francis Woodman
1982 (trans.) *The Secret History of the Mongols*, Cambridge, Mass., Harvard University Press.
Coon, Carleton S.
1955 'The Nomads', in Sydney Fisher (ed.), *Social Forces in the Middle East*, Ithaca, NY, Cornell University Press.
Cooper, Merian C.
1925 *Grass*, London & New York, G. P. Putnam's Sons.
Coxon, Herbert
1883 *Oriental Carpets, How They Are Made and Conveyed to Europe, with a Narrative of a Journey to the East in Search of Them*, London, T. Fisher Unwin.
Cribb, Roger
1991 *Nomads in Archaeology*, Cambridge, Cambridge University Press.
Crone, Patricia
1986 'The Tribe and the State', in J. A. Hall (ed.) *States in History*, Oxford, Blackwell.
Cronin, Vincent
1957 *The Last Migration*, London, Rupert Hart-Davis.
Curzon, *Lord* George Nathaniel
1892 *Persia and the Persian Question*, 2 vols, London, Longmans Green (reprinted New York, Barnes & Noble, 1960).
Danesh-Pazhou, E. M. (Hakimi Larijani)
1967 *Le Khorâssân à la fin du 18e et au début du 19e siècle*, thèse de doctorat de 3me cycle, Université de Paris, Faculté de lettres.
Demorgny, Gustave
1913 'Les Réformes Administratives en Perse: les Tribus du Fars', *Revue du Monde Musulman* 22, pp. 85-100; 23, pp. 3-108.
1914 *Les Institutions de la Police en Perse*, Paris, E. Leroux.
Digard, Jean-Pierre
1971 'La Parure chez les Baxtyâri', *Objets et Mondes* 9 (1), pp. 117-32.
1973 'Histoire et Anthropologie des Sociétés Nomades: le Cas d'une Tribu d'Iran', *Annales: Economies, Sociétés, Civilisations* 28(6), pp. 1423-35.
1974 'Campements Baxtyâri. Observations d'un Ethnologue sur des Matériaux Intéressant l'Archéologue', *Studia Iranica* 4 (1), pp. 117-29.
1976 'Note sur Quelques Vêtements Baxtyâri', *Cahiers de la Délégation Archéologique Française en Iran* 6, pp. 117-28.
1980 'Chiens de Campement et Chiens de Troupeau chez les Nomades Bakhtyâri d'Iran', *Studia Iranica* 9 (1), pp. 131-9.
1981 *Techniques des Nomades Baxtyâri d'Iran*, Paris, Maison des Sciences de l'Homme, Cambridge, Cambridge University Press (Persian translation by Asghar Karimi, *Fonun-e kuchneshinān-e Bakhtiyāri d'Iran,* Āstān-e Qods-e Razavi, 1366/1987).
1987 'Jeux de Structures: Segmentarité et Pouvoir chez les Nomades Baxtyari d'Iran', *l'Homme* 27(2), pp. 12-53.
1998 'Les Baxtyâri vingt ans après' (avec Asqar Karimi, Mohammad-Hoseyn Papoli-Yazdi), *Studia Iranica* 27, pp. 109-44.
Digard, Jean-Pierre, and Asghar Karimi
1989 'Les Baxtyâri sous influence occidentale. Acculturation et déculturation', in Y. Richard (ed.), *Entre l'Iran et l'Occident. Adaptation et Assimilation des Idées et des Techniques Occidentales*, Paris, Maison des Sciences de l'Homme.
Donaldson, Bess A.
1938 *The Wild Rue*, London, Luzac.
Douglas, William O.
1951 *Strange Lands and Friendly People*, New York, Harper.
1952 'World's Most Amazing Horses', *Science Digest* 32 (October), pp. 17-21.
Duncan, David Douglas
1946 '*Life* Goes on a Migration with Persian Tribesmen', *Life*, 29 July, pp. 99-105.
1982 *The World of Allah*, Boston, Houghton Mifflin.
Dupré, Adrien
1819 *Voyage en Perse, Fait dans les Années 1807, 1808, 1819*, 2 vols, Paris, J. G. Dentu.
Durand, Ella Rebe
1902 *An Autumn Tour in Western Persia*, London, Archibald, Constable & Co.
1899 'Diary', unpublished manuscript.
Dyson-Hudson, Neville
1972 'The Study of Nomads', in William G. Irons and Neville Dyson-Hudson (eds), *Perspectives on Nomadism*, Leiden, Brill.
Eagleton, William, Jr.
1963 *The Kurdish Republic of 1946*, Oxford, Oxford University Press.
Eastwick, Edward B.
1864 *Journal of a Diplomat's Three Years' Residence in Persia,* 2 vols, London, Smith Elder & Co.
Edmonds, C. J.
1922 'Luristan: Pish Kuh and Bala Garivah', *Geographical Journal* 61 (5), pp. 335-56, and (6), pp. 437-53.
Edwards, A. Cecil
1953 *The Persian Carpet*, London, Duckworth.
Ehmann, Dieter
1975 'Bahtiyāren. Persische Bergnomaden im Wandel der Zeit' (Beihefte zum *Tübinger Atlas des Vorderen Orients*), Wiesbaden, Dr Ludwig Reichert.
Elfenbein, J.
1992 'Baluchi Language and Literature', *Encyclopaedia Iranica* 3, pp. 633-44.
Emery, Irene
1966 *The Primary Structure of Fabrics*, Washington, Textile Museum.
Evans, Kathy
1991 'Najaf', *The Observer*, London, 26 May.
Faegre, Torvald
1979 *Tents: Architecture of the Nomads*, New York, Anchor Press.
Fasā'i, Hāji Mirzā Hasan
1895-6 *Tārikh-e Fārsnāmeh-ye Nāseri*, 2 vols, (reprinted Tehran, c. 1965).
Feilberg, C. G.
1944 *La Tente Noire. Contribution Ethnographique à l'Histoire Culturelle des Nomades*, Copenhagen, Nordisk Forlag.
Ferdinand, Klaus
1959 'The Baluchistan Barrel-vaulted Tent and its Affinities', *Folk* 1, pp. 27-50.
Field, Henry
1939 *Contributions to the Anthropology of Iran* (Anthropological Series 29/1), Chicago, Field Museum of Natural History.
Firouz, E.
1974 *The Environment of Iran*, Tehran, National Society for the Conservation of Natural Resources and Human Environment.
Firouz, Iran Ala
1978 *Silver Ornaments of the Turkoman*, Tehran, The Hamdami Foundation.
Firouz, T. (see also Towfiq, F.)
1983 'Dar bāreh-ye Tarkib va Sāzmān-e Ilāt va 'Ashāyer-e Irān' [On the Organisation of the Tribes of Irān], in *Ilāt va 'Ashāyer*, Tehran, Ketāb-e Āgāh, pp. 7-63.
Fletcher, J. F.
1986 'The Mongols: Ecological and Social Perspectives', *Harvard Journal of Asiatic Studies* 46 (1), pp. 11-50.
Foran, John
1993 *Fragile Resistance: Social Transformation in Iran from 1500 to the Revolution*, Boulder, Westview Press.
Franchini, F., and M. Vercelloti
1977 'Qashqayi Pastori Nomadi dell' Iran', *Viaggiare* 3 .

Franchis, Amadeo de, and John T. Wertime
1976 *Lori and Bakhtiyari Flatweaves*, Tehran, Tehran Rug Society.

Francklin, *Capt.* William
1788 *Observations Made on a Tour from Bengal to Persia, 1786-7*, Calcutta.

Fraser, David
1910 *Persia and Turkey in Revolt*, Edinburgh & London, Blackwood.

Fraser, James Baillie
1825 *Narrative of a Journey into Khorasan in the Years 1821 and 1822*, London, Longman etc.

Friedl, Erika
1989 *Women of Deh Koh: Lives in an Iranian Village*, Washington DC, Smithsonian.

Frye, Richard N.
1960 'Baluçistān. A. Geography and History', *Encyclopaedia of Islam* (new edition) 1, pp. 1005-6.
1963 *The Heritage of Persia*, Cleveland & New York, World Publishing.

Galitzin, Emmanuel
1851 *Nouvelles annales des voyages et des sciences géographiques*, Paris .

Garrod, Oliver
1946a 'The Nomadic Tribes of Persia Today', *Journal of the Royal Central Asian Society* 33 (1), pp. 32-46.
1946b 'The Qashqai Tribe of Fars', *Journal of the Royal Central Asian Society* 33 (2), pp. 293-306.

Garthwaite, Gene R.
1983 *Khans and Shahs. A Documentary Analysis of the Bakhtiyari in Iran*, Cambridge, Cambridge University Press.

Gashgai, Abdollah
1954 'The Gashgai in Iran', *Land Reborn* 5, pp. 6-7.

Gazetteer of Persia,
1914/1918 vol. 3 (including Fars, Luristan, Arabistan, Khuzistan and Yazd), Simla, General Staff of British India.

Gellner, Ernest
1983 'Tribal Society and its Enemies', in Richard Tapper (ed.), *The Conflict of Tribe and State in Iran and Afghanistan*, London, Croom Helm.

Ghashghai, F. B.
1975 'Les Tribus Ghashghayi and leurs Problèmes de Sédentarization en Iran', thèse de doctorat de 3me cycle, Université de Paris.

Ghashghai, H. B.
1981 'The Question of the Settlement of the Nomads of Iran', PhD dissertation, United States International University, School of Human Behaviour.

Ghashgai, H. R.
1942 *Zanān-e Qashqā'i* [*Qashqa'i Women*], University of Tehran, Department of Sociology.
1947 *Il-e Qashqā'i* [*The Qashqa'i Tribe*], Tehran, Institute of Health Research.

Ghassemlou, A. R.
1965 *Kurdistan and the Kurds*, London, Collet's.
1981 'Le Kurdistan d'Iran', in Gerard Chaliand (ed.), *Les Kurdes et le Kurdistan* (Petite Collection 247), Paris, Maspero.

Gibb, H. A. R.
1958-71 *The Travels of Ibn Battuta*, 3 vols, Cambridge, Hakluyt Society.

Glatzer, Bernt
1983 'Pashtun Nomads and the State', in Richard Tapper (ed.), *The Conflict of Tribe and State in Iran and Afghanistan*, London, Croom Helm.

Gluck, Jay and Sumi Hiramoto Gluck (eds)
1977 *A Survey of Persian Handicraft* (Survey of Persian Art), Tehran, New York, Bank Melli Iran.

Goldsmid, *Major Gen. Sir* Frederick John
1874a 'Notes on Recent Persian Travel', *Journal of the Royal Geographic Society of London* 94, pp. 183-203.
1874b *Telegraph and Travel*, London, Macmillan.

Goldstein, Melvyn C., and Cynthia M. Beall
1989 *Nomads of Western Tibet*, London, Serindia Publications.

Great Britain, Parliament,
Sessional Papers, cds. 4581, 4733, 5120, 5656, 6104, 6105, 6264, 6807, 7280.

Hand, *Capt.* Robert P.
1963 'Survey of the Tribes of Iran', US Counter-Insurgency Department, Army Special Warfare School.

Hatiboğlu, V.
1984 'Anadolunun Küzeyindeki Gaslar', *Cumhuriyet*, October 3.

Hedayat, Rezā Qoli Khān
1960 *Rowzat as-Safā-ye Nāseri*, 10 vols, Tehran.

Hekmat, Ali Asghar (ed.)
1963-4 *Iranshahr: a Survey of Iran's Land, People, Culture, Government and Economy*, 2 vols, UNESCO / Tehran University Press.

Hendershot, Clarence
1964 *White Tents in the Mountains: A Report on the Tribal Schools of Fars Province*, Tehran, Communications Resource Branch.

Hesse, Fritz.
1932 *Persien: Entwicklung und Gegenwart*, Berlin, Zentral-Verlag.

Hole, F.
1978 'Pastoral Nomadism in Western Iran,' in R. A. Gould (ed.), *Explorations in Ethnoarchaeology*, Albuquerque, University of New Mexico Press.

Housego, Jenny
1978 *Tribal Rugs. An Introduction to the Weavings of the Tribes of Iran*, London, Scorpion Publications.
1979 'A Study of Design in Fars Rugs', in David Black and Clive Loveless (eds), *Woven Gardens*, London, David Black Oriental Carpets.
1989 'Carpets', in R. Ferrier (ed.), *The Arts of Persia*, New Haven & London, Yale University Press.

Houtum Schindler, A.
1879 'Reisen im südwestlichen Persien', *Zeitschrift der Gesellschaft für Erdkunde zu Berlin* 14, pp. 307 ff.

Hütteroth, W. D.
1973 'Zum Kenntnisstand über Verbreitung und Typen von Bergnomadismus und Halbnomadismus in den Gebirgs- und Plateaulandschaften Südwestasiens', in C. Rathjens, C. Troll and H. Uhlig (eds), *Vergleichende Kulturgeographie der Hochgebirge des südlichen Asien* (Erdwissenschaftliche Forschung V), Wiesbaden.

Ibn Battuta
1853-9 *Voyages d'Ibn Batoutah*, ed. and trans. C. Defrémery and B. R. Sanguinetti, 4 vols, Paris.
1982 *Voyages*: II. *De la Mecque aux steppes russe et à l'Inde*, Paris, F. Maspero.

Ibn Hawqal
1938-9 *Kitāb Surat al-Ard* (Bibliotheca Geographorum Arabicorum 2), ed. J. H. Kramers (2nd edition), 2 vols, Leiden, Brill.

Ibn Khaldun
1967 *The Muqaddimah: an Introduction to History*, tr. F. Rosenthal, London, Routledge and Kegan Paul.

Irons, William G.
1974 'Nomadism as a Political Adaptation: the Case of the Yomut Turkmen', *American Ethnologist* 1(4), pp. 635-58.
1975 *The Yomut Turkmen: a Study of Social Organization among a Central Asian Turkic-speaking Population*, Ann Arbor, University of Michigan, Museum of Anthropology.
1990 'Production and Use of Textiles by the Turkmen', in George O'Bannon et al. *Vanishing Jewels: Central Asian Tribal Weavings*, Rochester, Rochester Museum and Science Center.

Irons, William G., and Neville Dyson-Hudson (eds)
1972 *Perspectives on Nomadism*, Leiden, Brill.

Iskandar Beg Munshi [Turkman]
1350/1971 *Tārikh-e Ālam-Ārā-ye 'Abbāsi*, 2 vols, Tehran.
1978 *History of Shah 'Abbas the Great*, trans. R. M. Savory, 2 vols, Boulder, Westview.

al-Istakhri, Abu Ishāq Ibrāhim b. Muhammad al-Fārsi
1927 *Kitāb Masālik al-Mamālik* (Bibliotheca Geographorum Arabicorum 1), ed. M. J. de Goeje (2nd edition), Leiden, Brill.

Ivanov, Mikhail Sergeevich
1961 *Plemena Farsa: Kashkaiskie, Khamse, Kukhgiluye, Mamasani*, Moscow, Nauka.

Jāvidfar, Ja'far
1355/1976 *'Ashāyer va Tarhhā-ye 'Omrāni*, Tehran.

Jéquier, M. Gustave
1914 'Remarques sur un Tchîkh Kurde du Musée d'Ethnographie de Neuchâtel', *Revue Suisse d'Ethnographie et d'Art Comparé* 1 (1), pp. 1-10.

Karimi, Asghar
1368/1990 *Safar be Diyār-e Bakhtiyāri* [Journey into Bakhtiāri Country], Tehran, Farhang-sarā.

Khanikof, Nicolas de
1861 *Mémoire sur la Partie Méridionale de l'Asie Centrale*, Paris, Société de Géographie.

Khazanov, A. M.
1984 *Nomads and the Outside World*, Cambridge, Cambridge University Press.

Khoury, Philip, and Joseph Kostiner (eds)
1991 *Tribes and State Formation in the Middle East*, Berkeley, University of California Press.

Khurmuji, Hājji Mohammad Ja'far Khān
1859 *Fārs Nāmeh*, Tehran, litho.

Kiāvand, 'Aziz
1989 *Hokumat, Siāsat va 'Ashāyer* [Government, Politics and Tribes], Tehran, 'Ashāyer Publications.

Kortum, Gerhard
1975 'Siedlungsgenetische Untersuchungen in Fars', *Erdkunde: Archiv für wissenschaftliche Geographie* 29 (1), pp. 10-20.
1979a *Entwicklungsprobleme und -projekte im bäuerlich-nomadischen Lebensraum Südpersiens. Fragenkreise 23523*, Paderborn, Ferdinand Schöning.
1979b 'Zur Bildung und Entwicklung des Qaşqai-Stammes 'Amale im 20. Jahrhundert', in Günter Schweizer (ed.), *Interdisziplinäre Iran-Forschung: Beiträge aus Kulturgeographie, Ethnologie, Soziologie und neuerer Geschichte* (Tübinger Atlas des Vorderen Orients, series B, no. 40), Wiesbaden, Universität Tübingen.
1980 *Zagros (Iran) Bergnomadismus und Ansiedlung der Qasqai* (Tübinger Atlas des Vorderen Orients Map Ax 12.2), Wiesbaden, Universität Tübingen.
1982 'Entwicklungskonzepte für den nomadischen Lebensraum der Qashqai in Fars/Iran: Ein perspektivischer Rückblick', in L. Janzen and F. Scholz (eds), *Nomadismus: Ein Entwicklungsproblem?* (Abhandlungen des Geographischen Instituts, Anthropogeographie 33), Berlin.

Kunke, Marina
1991 *Nomadenstämme in Persien im 18. und 19. Jahrhundert*, Berlin, Schwarz.

Lambton, Ann K. S.
1953 *Landlord and Peasant in Persia: A Study of Land Tenure and Land Revenue Administration*, London, Oxford University Press.
1971a 'Ilāt', *Encyclopedia of Islam* (new edition) 3, pp. 1095-110.
1971b 'Imāmzāda', *Encyclopedia of Islam* (new edition) 3, pp. 1169-70
1969 *The Persian Land Reform 1962-1966*, Oxford, Clarendon Press.

Lancaster, William
1981 *The Rwala Bedouin Today*, Cambridge, Cambridge University Press.

Lane, D. Austin
1923 'Hajji Mirza Hasan-i-Shirazi on the Nomad Tribes of Fars in the Fars-Nameh-i-Nasiri', *Journal of the Royal Asiatic Society of Great Britain*, April, pp. 209-31.

Layard, *Sir* Austen Henry
1846 'A Description of the Province of Khuzistan', *Journal of the Royal Geographical Society* 16, pp. 1-105.
1887 *Early Adventures in Persia, Susiana and Babylonia, Including a Residence Among the Bakhtiyaris and Other Wild Tribes*, 2 vols, New York & London, John Murray (new edition, 1894; reprinted, Gregg Int., England, 1971).

Lees, Susan, and Daniel G. Bates
1974 'The Origins of Specialized Nomadic Populations; a Systemic Model', *American Antiquity* 39, pp. 187-93.

Lentz, Thomas W., and Glenn D. Lowry
1989 *Timur and the Princely Vision: Persian Art and Culture in the Fifteenth Century*, Los Angeles County Museum of Art, and Washington DC, Arthur M. Sackler Gallery.

Le Strange, Guy
1905 *The Lands of the Eastern Caliphate: Mesopotamia, Persia, and Central Asia from the Moslem Conquest to the Time of Timur*, London, Frank Cass.
1912 *Description of the Province of Fars in Persia at the Beginning of the Fourteenth Century A.D.* (From the *Fars Nameh* of Ibn al-Balkhi), London, Royal Asiatic Society.

Lindner, Rudi Paul
1982 'What was a nomadic tribe?' *Comparative Studies in Society and History* 24, pp. 689-711.
1983 *Nomads and Ottomans in Medieval Anatolia*, Bloomington, Indiana University Press.

Loeffler, Reinhold
1978 'Tribal Order and the State: the Political Organisation of Boir Ahmad', *Iranian Studies* 11, pp. 145-71.
1988 *Islam in Practice: Religious Beliefs in a Persian Village*, Albany, State University of New York Press.

Lombard, M.
1978 *Les Textiles dans le Monde Musulman du VIIe au XIIe siècle*, Paris, La Haye & New York, Mouton.

Lyushkevich, F. D.
1971 'The Term "Tat" as an Ethnonym in Central Asia, Iran and Transcaucasia' (English Summary), *Soviet Ethnography* 3, pp. 25-32.

Magee, *Lieut.* G. F.
1948 *The Tribes of Fars*, Simla, Government of India Press.

Mahamedi, Hamid
1979 'On the Verbal System in Three Iranian Dialects of Fars', *Studia Iranica* 8, pp. 277-97.

Makhtumkuli
1995 *Songs from the Steppes of Central Asia: the Collected Poems of Makhtumkuli, Eighteenth Century Poet-Hero of Turkmenistan*, trans. Youssef Azemoun, versified by Brian Aldiss, Reading, Society of Friends of Makhtumkuli.

Mansouri, A.
1956 'Les tribus du Fars', thèse complémentaire de Géographie humaine, Paris, Sorbonne.

Manz, Beatrice Forbes
1989 *The Rise and Rule of Tamerlane*, Cambridge, Cambridge University Press.

Mar'ashi Safavi, Mirzā Ahmad Khalil
1949-50 *Majma' al-Tavārikh dar Tārikh-e Enqerāz-e Safaviyeh va Vaqāye-ye Ba'd*, ed. 'Abbas Eqbal, Tehran.

Marsden, David
1978 'The Social Structure of the Amaleh Tribe' (unpublished script).

Marvin, Charles
1881 *Merv, the Queen of the World*, London, Allen.

McChesney, Robert D.
1981 'Comments on "The Qajar Uymaq in the Safavid Period 1500-1722" ', *Iranian Studies* 14 (1-2), pp. 87-105.

Menges, Karl H.
1951 'Research in the Turkic Dialects of Iran', *Oriens* 5, pp. 273-9.

Military Report on Persia,
1924 Volume 4, Part 2, *Fars, the Gulf Ports, Yazd and Laristan*, Simla.

Miller, B. V.
1916 'Kocheviia plemena Farsistana,' *Vostochnii Sbornik* 2, pp. 200-23.

Ministry of Education, Department of Tribal Education
1972 *Statistics on the Qashqa'i*, Tehran, mimeographed.

Minorsky, Vladimir
1927 'Kurdistan' and 'Kurds', *Encyclopedia of Islam* 2, pp. 1130-55.

1939-42 'The Turkic Dialect of the Khalaj', *Bulletin of the School of Oriental and African Studies* 20, pp. 417-36.
1978 'A Civil and Military Review in Fars in 881/1476', *The Turks, Iran, and the Caucasus in the Middle Ages*, London, Variorum Reprints.

Monteil, Vincent
1966 *Les Tribus du Fars et la Sédentarisation des Nomades*, Paris, La Haye, Mouton.

Moore, Arthur
1914 *The Orient Express*, London, Constable.

Moore, Benjamin Burges
1915 *From Moscow to the Persian Gulf, Being the Journal of a Disenchanted Traveller in Turkestan and Persia*, New York, London, G. P. Putnam's sons.

Moorey, P. R. S.
1973 *Ancient Bronzes from Luristan*, London, British Museum Publications.

Morgan, Jacques de
1894-1905 *Mission Scientifique en Perse*, Paris, E. Leroux.

Morier, James Justinian
1812 *A Journey through Persia, Armenia, and Asia Minor to Constantinople in the years 1808 and 1809*, London, Longman &c.
1818 *A Second Journey through Persia, Armenia, and Asia Minor*, London, Longman &c.
1837 'Some Account of the Îliyáts, or Wandering Tribes of Persia, Obtained in the Years 1814 and 1815', *Journal of the Royal Geographic Society* 7, pp. 230-42.

Mortensen, Inge Demant
1993 *Nomads of Luristan*, Copenhagen, The Carlsberg Foundation / Rhodos.

Mortensen, P.
1972 'Seasonal Camps and Early Villages in the Zagros', in P. J. Ucko, R. Tringham and G. Dimbleby (eds), *Man, Settlement and Urbanism*, London, Duckworth.

Moser, Henri
1895 *A Travers l'Asie Centrale et la Perse*, Paris, Plon.

Motabar, M. and M. Mohseni
1980 'Direct and Indirect Observation in the Fertility and Mortality of the Qashqa'i Tribe, Southern Iran', *International Journal of Contemporary Sociology* 17 (3-4), pp. 226-43.

Mounsey, Augustus Henry
1872 *A Journey through the Caucasus and the Interior of Persia*, London, Smith, Elder.

Naficy, Hamid
1979 'Nonfiction Fiction: Documentaries on Iran', *Iranian Studies* 12, pp. 217-38.

Napier, George C.
1876 'Extracts of a Diary of a Tour in Khorassan etc.', *Journal of the Royal Geographical Society* 46, pp. 62-171.

Napier, *Capt.* G. S. F.
1900 *Military Report on Southern Persia*, Simla, Government Central Printing Office.

Naval Intelligence Division (Great Britain)
1945 *Persia* (Geographical Handbook Series, BR 525), Oxford.

Nikitine, Basile
1929 'Les Afşārs d'Urumiyeh,' *Journal Asiatique* 214, pp. 67-123.

Nisāri, Sirus
1350/1971 *Koliyāt-e Joghrāfiyā-ye Iran*, Tehran.

O'Ballance, E.
1973 *The Kurdish Revolt: 1961-1970*, London, Faber & Faber.

Oberling, Pierre
1960 *The Turkic Peoples of South Iran*, PhD dissertation, Columbia University, History Department (Ann Arbor, University Microfilms).
1964 'The Turkic Tribes of Southwestern Persia', *Ural-Altaische Jahrbucher* 35 (Fasc. B), pp. 164-80.
1970 'British Tribal Policy in Southern Persia 1906-1911', *Journal of Asian History* 4 (1), pp. 50-79.
1974 *The Qashqa'i Nomads of Fars*, The Hague, Mouton.

O'Connor, *Sir* Frederick
1931 *On the Frontier and Beyond*, London, John Murray.

Orhonlu, Cengiz
1966 'The Kashgais', *Cultura Turcica* 3, pp. 89-94.

Ouseley, *Sir* William
1819-23 *Travels in Various Countries of the East: More Particularly Persia*, 3 vols, London.

Papoli-Yazdi, Mohammad-Hossein
1991 *Le Nomadisme dans le Nord du Khorâssân*, Paris / Tehran, Institut Français de Recherche en Iran.

Parham, Cyrus
1973 *Qāli-ye Bolvardi* [*The Bolvardi Carpet*], Tehran.
1990 'Traces of Prehistoric Motifs in Tribal Rugs', *Oriental Rug Review* 10 (3), pp. 16-18.

Pelliot, Paul
1949 *Notes sur l'histoire de la Horde d'Or*, Paris, Librairie d'Amérique et d'Orient.

Peymān, Habibollāh
1968 *Towseh'eh va Tahlili az Sākhtemān-e Eqtesādi Ejtemā'i va Farhangi-ye Il-e Qashqā'i* [A Description and Analysis of the Economic, Social, and Cultural Structure of the Qashqa'i Confederacy], Tehran University, Institute of Health.

Pelly, *Sir* Lewis
1865a 'Remarks on a Recent Journey from Bushire to Shirauz', *Transactions of the Bombay Geographical Society* 17, pp. 141-74.
1865b 'A Brief Account of the Province of Fars', *Transactions of the Bombay Geographical Society* 17, pp. 175-85.

Perry, J. R.
1975 'Forced Migration in Iran during the 17th and 18th Centuries', *Iranian Studies* 8, pp. 199-216.

Peters, Emrys
1984 'The Paucity of Ritual among Middle Eastern Pastoralists', in Akbar S. Ahmed and David M. Hart (eds), *Islam in Tribal Societies*, London, Routledge.

Petsopoulos, Yanni
1979 *Les Kilims*, Fribourg, Office du Livre.

Picot, *Lieut. Col.* H.
1897 *Persia, Biographical Notices of Members of the Royal Family, Notables, Merchants, and Clergy*, Tehran.

Planhol, Xavier de
1968 'Geography of Settlement', in W. B. Fisher (ed.), *The Land of Iran*, Volume 1 of *The C ambridge History of Iran*, Cambridge University Press.
1968 *Fondements Géographiques de l'Histoire de l'Islam*, Paris, Flammarion.

Pour-Fickoui, Ali, and Marcel Bazin
1978 *Élevage et Vie Pastorale dans le Guilân (Iran Septentrional)*, Paris, Department de Géographie de l'Université de Paris Sorbonne No. 7.

Pullar, J.
1977 'Early Cultivation in the Zagros' *Iran* 15, pp. 15-37.

Qanbari, ʿAli
1367/1989 'Bahreh-vari dar Nezām-e Dāmdāri-ye ʿAshāyeri; Bar-rasi-ye Vazʿ-e Mowjud-e Jamʿiyat, Dām va Marāteʿ-e ʿAshāyeri (part 2),' *Zakhāyer-e Enqelāb* 5 (winter), pp. 57–75.

Rabino di Borgomale, Hyacinthe L.
1916 *Les tribus du Louristan. Médailles des Qādjārs* (Collection de la Revue du Monde Musulman), Paris, Ernest Leroux.
1928 *Mazandaran and Astarabad* (Gibb Memorial, new series, 7), London, Luzac.

Rawlinson, *Major Sir* Henry C.
1839 'Notes on a March from Zohab at the Foot of the Zagros, Along the Mountains to Khuzistan (Susiana), and from then Through the Province to Kermanshah, in the Year 1836', *Journal of the Royal Geographical Society of London* 9, pp. 26-116.

Razmārā, *Gen.* H. A.
1944-5 *Joghrāfiyā-ye Nezāmi-ye Irān*, Tehran.
1951 *Farhang-e Joghrāfiyā-ye Iran*, Tehran.

Richard, Yann
1980 *Le Shiʿisme en Iran: Iman et Révolution*, Paris, Librairie d'Amérique et d'Orient.

Ritter, Carl
1839 'Kurdes du Khorâssân', *Die Erdkunde von Asien* 8, pp. 392-400.

Rivadneyra, A.
1880-1 *Viaje al interior de Persia*, 3 vols, Madrid.

Rodkin, Angela.
1942 *Unveiled Iran*, London, Hutchinson.
Romaskevich, A.
1925 'Pesni Kashkaytsev', *Sbornik Museya Antropologii i Etnografii pri Rossiiskoi Akademii Nauk* 5 (2), pp. 573-610.
Rosman, Abraham, and Paula Rubel
1976 'Nomad-Sedentary Interethnic Relations in Iran and Afghanistan', *International Journal of Middle East Studies* 7 (4), pp. 545-70.
Rouholamini, M.
1967 *Une Civilization Traditionnelle du Mouton: Problèmes de l'Elevage Ovin dans les Tribus Nomades du Fars Iranien*, thèse de doctorat de 3me cycle, Université de Paris, Faculté de Lettres et Sciences Humaines.
Rowe, Ann Pollard
1977 *Warp-Patterned Weaves of the Andes*, Washington, Textile Museum.
Rowshani, Qodratollāh
1347/1968 *Seh Safarnāmeh: Herāt, Marv, Mashhad* [Three Journeys ...], Tehran, Tus.
Sackville-West, Victoria
1928 *Twelve Days*, London, Hogarth Press.
Safiri, Floreeda
1976 *The South Persia Rifles*, PhD dissertation, Oxford University.
Sahlins, Marshall
1966 *Tribesmen*, Englewood Cliffs, Prentice Hall.
Salzer, Richard
1974 *Social Organization of a Nomadic Pastoral Nobility in Southern Iran: The Kashkuli Kuchek Tribes of the Qashqa'i*, PhD dissertation, Berkeley, University of California, Anthropology Department.
1976 'The Black Tent', *Museum Digest* (Lubbock, Texas Tech University, West Texas Museum Association), (September-December), pp. 9-11.
Salzman, Philip Carl
1972 'Multi-resource Nomadism in Iranian Baluchistan', in William G. Irons and Neville Dyson-Hudson (eds), *Perspectives on Nomadism*, Leiden, Brill.
2000 *Black Tents of Baluchistan*, Washington and London, Smithsonian.
Sani' ad-Dowleh (Mohammad Hasan Khan, E'temād as-Saltaneh)
1301-3/1884-5 *Matla' ash-Shams*, 3 vols, Tehran, litho.
Saray, Mehmet
1989 *The Turkmens in the Age of Imperialism*, Ankara, Turkish Historical Society.
Sardār As'ad, Hājji 'Ali Qoli Khān
1327/1909 *Tārikh-e Bakhtiyāri* [History of the Bakhtiāri], ed. 'Abd ol-Hoseyn Lisān as-Saltaneh Sepehr, Tehran, litho (also 1333/1914; and Tehran, Farhangsarā, 1361/1982).
Sardār Zafar, Hājji Khosrow Khān
1329–1333/1911–1914 *Tārikh Bakhtiyari*, MS.
Schimmel, Annemarie
1978 *The Triumphal Sun; a Study of the Works of Jalaloddin Rumi*, London, Fine Books, The Hague, East-West Publications.
Schletzer, Dieter and Reinhold Schletzer
1983 *Old Silver Jewellery of the Turkoman; an Essay on Symbols in the Culture of Inner Asian Nomads*, trans. Paul Knight, Berlin, Reimer.
Schulze-Holthus, Berthold
1954 *Daybreak in Iran: A Story of the German Intelligence Service*, trans. Mervyn Savill, London, Staples Press.
Sepehr Mirza, M. T.
1958 *Tārikh-e Kāmel-e Qashqa'i* [Complete History of the Qashqa'i], Tehran
Shahbāzi, 'Abdollāh
1990 *Moqaddameh'i bar Shenākht-e Ilāt va 'Ashāyer*, Tehran, Ney.
Shahshahani, Soheila
1986 'History of anthropology in Iran', *Iranian Studies* 19, pp. 75-6.
Sheil, *Lady* Mary Leonora
1856 *Glimpses of Life and Manners in Persia*, London, John Murray.
Shirvāni, Zeyn ol-'Abedin
1892-3 *Bostān al-Siyāhat*, Tehran.
Shor, Jean and Franc
1952 'We Dwelt in Kashgai Tents', *National Geographic Magazine* 101 (6, June), pp. 805-32.
Smith, J. Masson, Jr.
1978 'Turanian Nomadism and Iranian Politics', *Iranian Studies* 11, pp. 57-81.
Soraya, Mehdi
1969 'Ghashgai Social Structure', *Islamic Culture* 43 (2), pp. 125-42.
Spooner, Brian
1969 'Politics, Kinship and Ecology in Southeast Persia', *Ethnology* 8 (2), pp. 139-52.
1975 'Nomadism in Baluchistan', in L. S. Leshnik and G-D. Sontheimer (eds), *Pastoralists and Nomads in South Asia*, Wiesbaden, Otto Harrassowitz.
1984 'Who are the Baluch?' in Edmund Bosworth and Carole Hillenbrand (eds), *Qajar Iran: Political, Social and Cultural Change, 1800-1925*, Edinburgh, Edinburgh University Press.
1992 'Baluchistan i. Geography, History and Ethnography', *Encyclopaedia Iranica* 3, pp. 598-632.
Stack, Edward
1882 *Six Months in Persia*, 2 vols, New York, G. P. Putnam's Sons.
Stark, Freya
1934 *Valley of the Assassins*, London, John Murray.
Statistical Centre of Iran
1345/1966 *Sarshomāri-ye 'omumi-e nofus va maskan* [National Census of Population and Housing].
Stauffer, Thomas R.
1963 'The Qashqa'i Nomads: a Contemporary Appraisal', *Harvard Review* 1 (3), pp. 28-39.
1965 'The Economics of Nomadism in Iran', *Middle East Journal* 19, pp. 284-302.
Stein, Aurel
1938 'An Archaeological Journey in Western Iran', *Geographical Journal* 92, pp. 314-342.
1940 *Old Routes of Western Iran*, London, Macmillan.
Street, Brian
1990 'Orientalist Discourse in the Anthropology of Iran, Afghanistan and Pakistan', in Richard Fardon (ed.), *Localizing Strategies: Regional Traditions of Ethnographic Writing*, Edinburgh, Scottish Academic Press.
1992 'Method in our Critique of Anthropology', *Man* (N.S.) 27, pp. 177-9.
Sümer, Faruk
1978 'Kashkay', *Encyclopedia of Islam* (new edition) 4, pp. 705-6.
Sykes, Christopher
1936 *Wassmus, 'The German Lawrence'*, London, Longmans, Green.
Sykes, *Sir* Percy Molesworth
1902 *Ten Thousand Miles in Persia or Eight Years in Iran*, London, John Murray.
Taillardat. F.
1930 'La révolte du Khouzistan et du Fars', *L'Asie Français*, May, pp. 176-9.
Tanavoli, Parviz
1977 *Lion Rugs of Fars*, Tehran, Sanat Ruz Press.
1978 *Lion Rugs from Fars* (Catalogue, Shahbanu Farah Foundation Festival of Arts Organisation).
Tāheri, Abolqāsem
1348/1969 *Joghrāfiyā-ye Tārikhi-ye Khorāsān az Nazar-e Jahāngardān* [Historical Geography of Khorassan as Described by Travellers], Tehran, Jashn-e Shāhanshāhi.
Tapper, Nancy
1978 'The Women's Sub-society among the Shahsevan Nomads of Iran,' in Lois Beck and Nikki Keddie (eds), *Women in the Muslim World*, Cambridge, Mass., Harvard University Press.
Tapper, Nancy, and Richard Tapper
1982 'Marriage Preferences and Ethnic Relations', *Folk* 24, pp. 157-77.
Tapper, Richard
1974a 'Nomadism in Modern Afghanistan: Asset or Anachronism?' in Louis Dupree and Lynn Albert (eds), *Afghanistan in the 1970s*, New York, Praeger.

1974b 'Shahsevan in Safavid Persia', *Bulletin of the School of Oriental and African Studies* 37(2), pp. 321-354.

1979a *Pasture and Politics: Economics, Conflict and Ritual among Shahsevan Nomads of Northwestern Iran*, London, Academic Press.

1979a 'The Organization of Nomadic Communities in Pastoral Societies of the Middle East', in Equipe anthropologie et écologie des sociétés pastorales (eds), *Pastoral Production and Society*, Cambridge, Cambridge University Press and Paris, Maison des Sciences de l'Homme.

1983a (ed.) *The Conflict of Tribe and State in Iran and Afghanistan*, London, Croom Helm.

1983b 'Nomads and Commissars in the Moghan Steppe: the Shahsevan Tribes in the Great Game', in Richard Tapper (ed.), *The Conflict of Tribe and State in Iran and Afghanistan*, London, Croom Helm.

1984a 'Ethnicity and Class: Dimensions of Group Identity in Northern Afghanistan,' in M. Nazif Shahrani and Robert L Canfield (eds), *Revolutions and Rebellions in Afghanistan*, Berkeley, University of California Press.

1984b 'Holier Than Thou: Islam in Three Tribal Societies', in Akbar S. Ahmed and David M. Hart (eds), *Islam in Tribal Societies*, London, Routledge.

1988 'History and Identity Among the Shahsevan', *Iranian Studies* 21 (3-4), pp. 84-108.

1989 'Ethnic Identities and Social Categories in Iran and Afghanistan', in Maryon Macdonald et al. (eds), *History and Ethnicity*, London, Tavistock.

1991 'Anthropologists, Historians and Tribespeople on Tribe and State Formation in the Middle East', in Philip S. Khoury and Joseph Kostiner (eds), *Tribes and State Formation in the Middle East*, Berkeley, University of California Press.

1991 'Golden Tent-pegs: Nomad Settlement and Change in Afghan Turkestan', in Shirin Akiner (ed.), *Cultural Continuity and Change in Central Asia*, London, KPI.

1991 'The Tribes in Eighteenth and Nineteenth Century Iran', in Peter Avery, Gavin Hambly and Charles Melville (eds), *From Nadir Shah to the Islamic Republic*, Volume 7 of *The Cambridge History of Iran*, Cambridge University Press.

1994 'Change, Cognition and Control: the Reconstruction of Nomadism in Iran', in C. M. Hann (ed.), *When History Accelerates*, London, Athlone.

1997 *Frontier Nomads of Iran. A Political and Social History of the Shahsevan*, Cambridge University Press.

Tavakolian, Bahram

1984 'Religiosity, Values and Economic Change among Sheikhanzai Nomads', in Akbar S. Ahmed and David M. Hart (eds), *Islam in Tribal Societies*, London, Routledge.

Thrane, H.

1964 'Archaeological Investigations in Western Luristan', *Acta Archaeologica* 35, pp...

Towfiq, F.

1987 ''Ashāyer', *Encyclopaedia Iranica* 2, pp. 707-24.

Toynbee, Arnold J.

1947 *A Study of History*, London, Oxford University Press.

Tribal Development Office, Office of the Government of Fars

1967 Map of the Migratory Routes of the Tribes of Fars, Shiraz.

Trubetskoi, V. V.

1966 *Bakhtiari. Osedlokochevye Plemena Irana*, Moscow, Nauka.

Truilhier M.

1838-41 'Mémoire descriptif de la Route de Téhéran à Meched et de Meched à Iezd. Reconnue en 1807', *Bulletin de la Société de Géographie* (2nd series) 9 and 10, pp. 109-45, 249-82, 313-29.

Tumansky, A.

1896 'Ot Kapiiskogo Morya k Hormudskomu Prolivu i Obratno', *Sbornik Materialov po Azii* 65, pp. 76-81.

Ullens de Schooten, Marie Thérèse

1954 'Among the Kashkai: A Tribal Migration in Persia', *Geographical Magazine* 27 (2), pp. 68-78.

1956 *Lords of the Mountains: Southern Persia and the Kashkai Tribe*, London, Chatto & Windus.

Varjāvand, Parviz, et al.

1347/1968 *Bāmadi. Tāyfeh'i az Bakhtyāri* [Bāmadi. A sub-tribe of the Bakhtiāri], Tehran University Press.

Waring, Edward Scott

1807 *A Tour to Sheeraz by the Route of Kazroon and Feerozabad*, London, T. Cadell & W. Davies (reprint, New York, Arno Press, 1973).

Warne, William E.

1956 *Mission for Peace: Point 4 in Iran*, Indianapolis, Bobbs-Merrill.

Warner, W. L.

1937 *A Black Civilisation*, New York, Harpers.

Watson, Patty Jo

1979 *Archaeological Ethnography in Western Iran* (Viking Fund Publications in Anthropology 57), Tucson, University of Arizona Press.

Wertime, John T.

1979 'Flat-Woven Structures Found in Nomadic and Village Weavings from the Near East and Central Asia', *Textile Museum Journal* 18, pp. 33–54

Wilber, Donald N.

1975 *Riza Shah Pahlavi : the Resurrection and Reconstruction of Iran*, Hicksville, NY, Exposition.

Wilson, *Sir* Arnold Talbot

1912 *Military Report on South-West Persia*, Volume 5, *Luristan*, Simla.

1916 *Report on Fars*, Simla, Government Monotype Press.

1932 *Persia*, London, Ernest Benn.

1942 *S.W. Persia: A Political Officer's Diary, 1907-1914*, London, New York, Oxford University Press.

Woods, John E.

1976 *The Aqquyunlu: Clan, Confederation, Empire*, Minneapolis and Chicago, Bibliotheca Islamica.

Wright, Denis

1977 *The English amongst the Persian during the Qajar Period, 1787-1921*, London, Heinemann.

Wright, H. (ed.)

1979 *Archaeological investigations in Northeastern Khuzestān, 1976* (Technical Reports 10, Contribution 5), Ann Arbor, University of Michigan, Museum of Anthropology.

Wright, Susan

1992 'Method in our critique of anthropology: a further comment', *Man* (N.S.) 27, pp. 642-4.

Wulff, Hans E.

1966 *The Traditional Crafts of Persia*, Cambridge, Mass. and London, M.I.T. Press.

Yalçın-Heckmann, L.

1991 *Tribe and Kinship Among the Kurds*, Frankfurt, Peter Lang.

Yapp, Malcolm

1983 'Tribes and States in the Khyber 1838–1842', in Richard Tapper (ed.), *The Conflict of Tribe and State in Iran and Afghanistan*, London, Croom Helm.

Yate, Charles Edward

1900 *Khurasan and Sistan*, Edinburgh and London, W. Blackwood.

Youssefizadeh, Mohammad Ali

1975 *Esquisse d'une Sociologie Tribale de l'Iran: la Structure Sociale et Economique des Tribus Shah Savan*, thèse de doctorat de 3me cycle, Université de Paris.

Zagarell, A.

1975 'Nomad and Settled in the Bakhtiari Mountains', *Sociologus* (NF) 25, pp. 127-38.

1982 'The Prehistory of the Northeast Bakhtiyari Mountains, Iran. The Rise of a Highland Way of Life' (Beihefte zum *Tübinger Atlas des Vorderen Orients* Series B, No. 42), Wiesbaden, Dr. Ludwig Reichert.

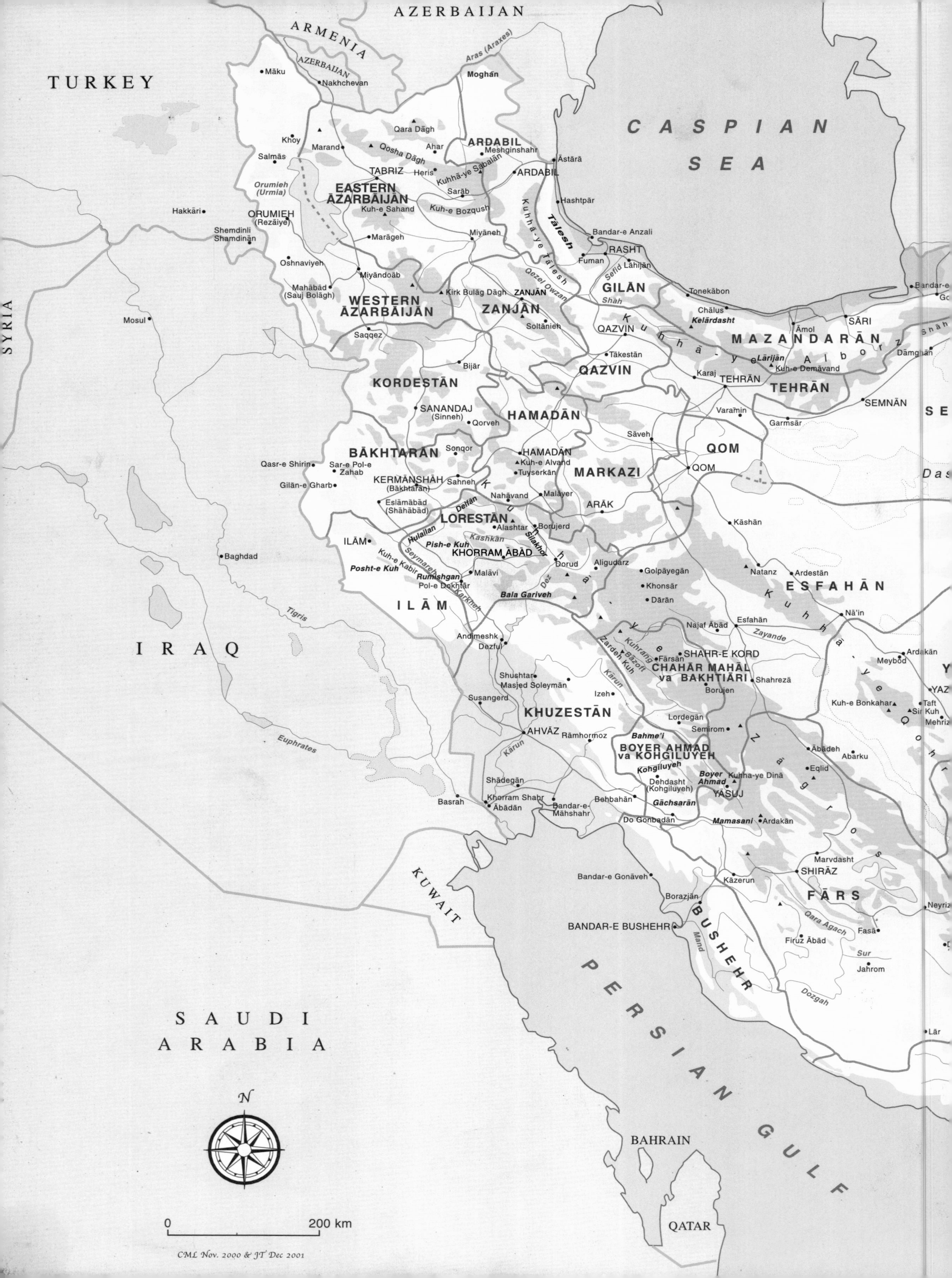
AZERBAIJAN
ARMENIA
AZERBAIJAN
TURKEY
CASPIAN SEA
SYRIA
IRAQ
KUWAIT
SAUDI ARABIA
BAHRAIN
QATAR
PERSIAN GULF
Aras (Araxes)
Moghān
Māku
Nakhchevan
Khoy
Salmās
Marand
Qara Dāgh
Ahar
Qosha Dāgh
ARDABIL
Meshginshahr
Āstārā
TABRIZ
Heris
Kuhhā-ye Sabalān
ARDABIL
EASTERN ĀZARBĀIJĀN
Sarāb
Kuh-e Sahand
Kuh-e Bozqush
Hashtpär
Orumieh (Urmia)
Hakkāri
ORUMIEH (Rezāiye)
Shemdinli Shamdinān
Marāgeh
Miyāneh
Tālesh
Kuhhā-ye Tālesh
Bandar-e Anzali
RASHT
Fuman
Lāhijān
Oshnaviyeh
Miyāndoāb
Qezel Owzan
Sefid
GILĀN
Tonekābon
Mahābād (Sauj Bolāgh)
Kirk Bulāg Dāgh
ZANJĀN
Shāh
Chālus
Kelārdasht
WESTERN ĀZARBĀIJĀN
ZANJĀN
Āmol
SĀRI
Mosul
Saqqez
Soltānieh
QAZVIN
MAZANDARĀN
Kuhhā-ye Alborz
Lārijān
Kuh-e Demāvand
Dāmghān
Tākestān
Bijār
QAZVIN
Karaj
TEHRĀN
TEHRĀN
KORDESTĀN
SEMNĀN
SANANDAJ (Sinneh)
HAMADĀN
Varāmin
Qorveh
Garmsār
Sāveh
BĀKHTARĀN
Sonqor
HAMADĀN
QOM
Qasr-e Shirin
Sar-e Pol-e Zahab
Kuh-e Alvand
QOM
KERMĀNSHĀH (Bākhtarān)
Sahneh
Tuyserkān
MARKAZI
Gilān-e Gharb
Nahāvand
Malāyer
Eslāmābād (Shāhābād)
Delfān
ARĀK
LORESTĀN
Kāshān
Alashtar
Borujerd
ILĀM
Hulailan
Kashkān
Pish-e Kuh
Silakhor
KHORRAM ĀBĀD
Baghdad
Seymareh
Kuh-e Kabir
Dorud
Aligudarz
Golpāyegān
Posht-e Kuh
Rumishgan
Malāvi
Natanz
Ardestān
Pol-e Dokhtar
Khonsār
Karkheh
Dez
ESFAHĀN
Bala Gariveh
Dārān
ILĀM
Nā'in
Tigris
Najaf Ābād
Esfahān
Zayande
Andimeshk
Dezful
Kuhrang
Bāzoft
Zardeh Kuh
Fārsān
SHAHR-E KORD
Ardakān
Meybod
CHAHĀR MAHĀL va BAKHTIĀRI
Shushtar
Masjed Soleymān
Kārun
Shahrezā
Izeh
Borujen
YAZ
Susangerd
Taft
Kuh-e Bonkahar
Shir Kuh
KHUZESTĀN
Mehriz
Lordegān
AHVĀZ
Semirom
Rāmhormoz
Bahme'i
BOYER AHMAD va KOHGILUYEH
Ābādeh
Euphrates
Kārun
Abarku
Kohgiluyeh
Eqlid
Boyer Ahmad
Kuhha-ye Dinā
Shādegān
Dehdasht (Kohgiluyeh)
YĀSUJ
Basrah
Khorram Shahr
Ābādān
Bandar-e Māhshahr
Behbahān
Gāchsarān
Do Gonbadān
Mamasani
Ardakān
Kuhhā-ye Zāgros
Marvdasht
SHIRĀZ
Bandar-e Gonāveh
Kāzerun
FĀRS
Neyriz
Borazjān
Qara Agach
BANDAR-E BUSHEHR
BUSHEHR
Fasā
Mand
Firuz Ābād
Sur
Jahrom
Dozgah
Lār
N
0
200 km
CML Nov. 2000 & JT Dec 2001